# W. B. YEATS
# MAN & POET

# W. B. YEATS

## MAN AND POET

*by*

### A. NORMAN JEFFARES

*Professor of English, University of Stirling*

**ROUTLEDGE & KEGAN PAUL**
**LONDON AND HENLEY**

*First published in England 1949*
*by Routledge & Kegan Paul Ltd*
*39 Store Street*
*London WC1E 7DD and*
*Broadway House*
*Newtown Road*
*Henley-on-Thames*
*Oxon RG9 1EN*
*Second Edition 1962*
*Reprinted in 1966 and 1978*
*Printed in Great Britain by*
*Lowe & Brydone Printers Ltd*
*Thetford, Norfolk*

ISBN 0 7100 1607 7 (c)

To
## MY MOTHER

# CONTENTS

# ILLUSTRATIONS

*between pages 182 and 183*

# FOREWORD

Y EATS'S greatness is secure. He devoted his life to literature, and in a peculiarly personal way. He drew much of his material from his life; his emotions coloured all that he read; and almost all that he wrote was subjective. The man and the artist cannot be separated; his life and his writings are complementary and interwoven to an unusual degree. His life throws light on his works and his works reflect that life. Therefore, some knowledge of his life and background is necessary for the better understanding of his poetry.

Yeats has written freely and fully of his inmost thoughts and emotions. I have, in my attempt to illustrate the relationship of man and poet, made copious use of quotation from his published and unpublished works, in order that this great poet may reveal himself through his own words.

Mrs W. B. Yeats is the main source of information for any student of Yeats's work. She has preserved her husband's library and private papers intact; she has established the dating of many poems by reference to the original manuscripts and letters in her possession. She has not only allowed me access to her husband's library, unpublished diaries and documents, but also helped in the task of deciphering and interpreting their numerous obscurities; she has answered innumerable, often troublesome, questions; has made acute criticisms and given me every possible assistance in the preparation of this book, as well as allowing me to quote freely from the unpublished and published works of W. B. Yeats. I am extremely grateful to her for her help and never-failing kindness.

Madame Maud Gonne MacBride has discussed Yeats's character with me and given me information about his early poems and revolutionary activities, which I have very much appreciated.

Much assistance has been given to me by many others, to

whom I am deeply indebted: to Professor H. O. White, whose interest in and deep knowledge of Yeats's work has always been a great stimulus; to Dr D. A. Webb who instigated and encouraged this study; to Mr John Sparrow who lent me notes of his conversations with Yeats; to Mrs Francis Stuart (Íseult Gonne); and to Miss Lily Yeats who allowed me to copy many family documents and gave me information on life in the Pollexfen household in Sligo.

My thanks are also due to Professor David Nichol Smith, Professor D. E. W. Wormell, F.T.C.D., Mr John Bryson, Professor R. W. Zandvoort, Professor Mavrogordato, Mr Joseph Hone, Mr Austin Clarke, Dr N. Furlong, Professor E. R. Dodds, Dr Oliver Edwards, Mr Geoffrey Taylor, Dr James Starkey, Dr Maurice James Craig, Mrs Joseph O'Neill, Miss Isa MacNie, Mr R. L'E. Bryce, Mr E. G. Quin, F.T.C.D., Mr P. Casey, the late Dr Ella Webb, Mrs de Pauley, Mr R. B. D. French, Miss Beryl Young, Miss Olive Jackson, and Mr Slevin.

Messrs Macmillan have kindly given their permission to make quotations from Yeats's published work.

A. NORMAN JEFFARES

*Oxford*

# FOREWORD TO THE SECOND EDITION

THIS book was written at a time when Yeats's writings were
out of print. It therefore seemed useful to quote very freely
from both his published and unpublished work. But the book
was also written in order to present a view of the relationship
between Yeats's life and his work which might help the reader
to understand some poems better, to see the interrelationships
between work written at different periods of Yeats's life, and to
see something of how Yeats himself thought about his life and
his poetry.

Preparing this edition has made me realise how much considerations of space had forced me to omit from my original
work: but, since 1949, there have been several specialised
studies which deal with many of the topics which had to be
handled briefly here: Yeats's symbolism, his interest in the
occult, the sources of his visual imagery, his rôle in public life,
his thought and detailed criticism of his poetry. Despite the
publication of these other studies of Yeats (to which I have
added myself) some of the contents of this book are still un-
obtainable elsewhere and I believe that its attempt to keep the
reader's attention on the poet's writings rather than the critic's
has some value—for Yeats's own comments are illuminating,
and the conjunction between his prose and verse is rewarding
in the extreme as revealing some of the individualism of a great
poet.

Mrs Yeats has continued to give generous help and I am, as
ever, deeply sensible of her kindness and grateful for it. Professor Aitken, Professor M. Bryn Davies, Mr T. R. Henn, Professor George Brandon Saul and Professor H. O. White have all
assisted me in making various alterations and corrections and I
should like to record my indebtedness to them.

*Leeds, 1961*                                    A. NORMAN JEFFARES

# 1

# PRELUDE TO POETRY
## (Pre-1700—1885)

*Merchant and scholar who have left me blood*
*That has not passed through any huckster's loin.*

WILLIAM BUTLER YEATS was born on 13 June 1865, at 'Georgeville', a six-roomed semi-detached house in Sandymount, Dublin. Much of his unusual character can be explained by his heredity: his parents came from families of a completely different nature; and he was greatly affected by the personalities of the relatives who surrounded his childhood. The earliest known ancestor of the poet, Jervis Yeats,[1] who died in 1712, was a citizen of Dublin whose antecedents are obscure. A supposition that he may have come from Yorkshire is supported by the fact that in his will he bequeathed sums of money to two aunts, Sarah Barnes of Yorkshire, and Dorothy Westnage of Turbeck near Sheffield. He was a wholesale linen merchant, apparently of some substance, for he lived in the New Row, near to Thomas Street and to the river Poddle which now flows beneath the Dublin streets.[2] The New Row was built about the middle of the sixteenth century, and a century later it was the home of that William Molyneux[3] who founded the Dublin Philosophical Society and first wrote of the Dublin Merchants' desire for independence. The street was beginning to go down some time after the death of Jervis Yeats, for an inn was opened at its lower end in 1730;[4] and by 1770 'Allen's Court', a fine mansion originally built by John Allen, a factor for the Dutch in Elizabeth's reign and father of the first Lord Allen, Baron of Stillorgan, fell into the hands of sugar bakers and distillers.[5]

Benjamin, the son of Jervis, was apprenticed to the linen trade under his widowed mother's care, a training to fit him for his inheritance. In 1742 he married a Hannah Wichen or Warren[6] at St Catherine's Church, Dublin. Benjamin's son received his father's Christian name and must have prospered in his business, for he lived in William Street,[7] at that time the

I

residence of many well-to-do citizens. Thomas Rundle, of whom Pope wrote:

> Ev'n in a Bishop I can spy desert
> Secker is decent, Rundle has a heart[8]

lived there, as did Henry Brooke, author of *The Fool of Quality* and the father of Charlotte Brooke, whose *Reliques of Ancient Irish Poetry* are almost as important in the beginnings of Anglo-Irish literature as Molyneux's *Case of Ireland Stated*. The street must have been at the height of its fashion[9] in the seventies when Richard Wingfield, Viscount Powerscourt, erected his large and dignified town house in it. In 1773 Benjamin Yeats married Mary Butler,[10] the daughter of John Butler, chief clerk in the War Office at Dublin Castle for many years. This John Butler's grandfather, Edmond Butler, had married at St Werburgh's Church, Dublin, in 1696, a Mary Voisin of Huguenot[11] stock, whose grandfather had emigrated from Orleans to London. Both Benjamin Yeats and Mary Butler were residents of Dublin. It is therefore somewhat surprising to find that they were married at Tullamore from the house of a Tabuteau family.[12] Tullamore in those days must have been a troublesome journey from Dublin, and it would be tempting to surmise a runaway match were it not for a phrase in John Butler's will in which he left ten pounds to Mary Yeats 'to whom on her marriage I gave a portion'. A silver cup which remained in the family up to the poet's day served as a reminder of this wedding:

> It had upon it the Butler crest and had been already old at the date 1534, when the initials of some bride and bridegroom were engraved under the lip. All its history for generations was rolled up inside it upon a piece of paper yellow with age, until some caller took the paper to light his pipe.[13]

The Yeats family always set great store upon this marriage into the Butler family and regarded it as a proof of social distinction, using the surname as a family Christian name with great frequency.

From 1773, the year of his marriage, onwards Benjamin Yeats appears in the lists of merchants and traders given in Watson's *Gentleman's and Citizen's Almanack*, a Dublin directory. In 1783 his name is marked with an asterisk denoting that he was a wholesale merchant 'free of the six and ten per cent tax at the Custom-house, Dublin', a privilege generally extended to less than one-tenth of the merchants listed. His name appeared in subsequent numbers of Watson's *Almanack* up to and including 1795. The last year's entry omits the asterisk. The *Gentleman's Almanack* is not above the suspicion of an accidental omission of the mark, for Benjamin Yeats's name is given indifferently from year to year as 'Yeats' or 'Yeates'. Yet the phrase of his will, dated 1795, which speaks of 'the wreck of disappointments and the unforeseen misfortunes of this world' seems connected with a loss of the privilege.[14]

After her brothers had died Mary Yeats inherited some 700 acres of land at Thomastown, Co. Kildare, which remained with the Yeats family until the close of the nineteenth century. She had also obtained, as the daughter of a Castle Official, a pension of nine hundred pounds from the War Office, so that, despite the apparent wreck of Benjamin's fortunes, there was enough money for their son John, born in 1774, to enter Trinity College, Dublin.[15] His name was put on the College books at the age of eighteen in 1792, and he received his B.A. degree in 1797 after a distinguished career which included winning a Bishop Berkeley gold medal in Greek.[16] He took orders in the Church of Ireland and, like his father, maintained contact with the Castle officialdom through his marriage. This was with Jane Taylor, the sister of an hereditary Castle officer. Her father, William Taylor, was for forty years Chief Clerk at the Chief Secretary's Office in Dublin; he had a residence in Dublin Castle as well as a house at Churchtown, then well outside the city boundary.[17]

John Yeats was appointed to the living of Drumcliffe in County Sligo. Here he enjoyed a pleasant life with two curates to help him with his parochial duties; he hunted, fished, drank and read. He was popular amongst the Roman Catholics as well as the Anglo-Irish of the district, as a passage in the *County History of Sligo*, written by a Roman Catholic priest, reveals:

This person's name is still popular as that of a straightforward high-principled man: It is told of him, that, when he with Sir Robert Gore-Booth's agent Mr. Dodwell, and a Bailiff named Barber, went among Sir Robert's tenants asking them to send their children to the Milltown Protestant school, and was told by a man named James O'Hara that a child of his would never darken the door of that school-house, Mr. Yeates commended him for his spirit, and observed, that he was the honestest man they had come across that day.[18]

The Rector's first child, William Butler, was born in Dublin Castle in 1806, and he with his brother Thomas went to Dublin University after preliminary education with their father in Sligo. The elder brother entered college in 1828 and took his

B.A. in 1833;[19] the younger came up in 1831 and took the same degree in 1836, having been head of his year in mathematics all through his course. He returned to Sligo after finishing his studies and never left it again.[20] William Butler Yeats, however, followed his father's profession, after spending a time in College where his friends included Archer Butler, the famous Platonist, and Isaac Butt, with whom he edited the *Dublin University Magazine*.[21] The curacy which he took up in 1831 was that of Moira, County Down. His rector was said to have remarked of him 'I have hoped for a curate but they have sent me a jockey'. A later tale told of him splitting three pairs of riding breeches before getting into the saddle for a hunt.

The rector disapproved of this horsemanship and later came to dislike the new curate's preaching which had too much Evangelicism in it to please him. Later John Butler Yeats gave an amusing account of the quarrel:

> He was staying, as he often did, in the Rector's house, and it was Sunday morning. There was a rapid interchange of letters beginning at six in the morning and the argument was continued at breakfast, the ladies all on my father's side. Finally the Rector said he would preach himself that morning. As luck would have it, choosing at random among his stock of ready-made sermons, he took with him a sermon tainted with the abominable doctrine. My father described the smile that went round the Rector's pew.[22]

In 1835 he married Jane Grace Corbet, the granddaughter of a Registrar to the Lord Chancellor, and sister to the Governor of Penang. Her mother, Grace Armstrong, had a military tradition on both sides of her family.[23]

In 1839 the poet's father, John Butler Yeats, was born at Tullylish near Portadown where his father had been appointed rector shortly after his marriage.[24] A portrait of

> That red-headed rector in County Down
> A good man on a horse[24a]

still hangs on the vestry wall at Tullylish;[25] he was evangelical in his sympathies, but disliked the Presbyterianism of Northern Ireland, an idea that he handed on to his son. The rector lived a life not unlike his father's; he was a man of great personal charm and dignified manner; sociable, scholarly, and gentle. He began to undertake his son's education with:

> something in arithmetic, and I failed miserably as I would up to the present moment. Up to that moment I had been the pride of my father; not only was I his oldest son and the heir to the family property, but he was convinced I was exceedingly like his brother Tom, who in his course at Trinity College, Dublin, had never been beaten at mathematics. When therefore I failed in arithmetic the blow was too much for his fond hopes, and he gave

me a box on my ear. He had no sooner done so than he shook hands with me and hoped I was not offended and then glided out of the room, I was not offended but very much astounded.[26]

J. B. Yeats had all the loneliness and blessed solitude of an only child's life, for he was much older than his brothers:

Whether inside the house or out in the grounds I was always by myself, therefore I early learned to sustain myself by revery and dream. Years afterwards I suffered a good deal from the reproofs of my elders, for my habit of absentmindedness. Of course I was absentminded and am so still. In those childhood days I discovered the world of fantasy, and I still spend all my spare moments in that land of endearing enchantment. I think as a child I was perfectly happy; my father my friend and counsellor, my mother my conscience. My father theorized about things and that delighted me not because I had any mental conceit but because I delighted then as I still do in reasoning.[27]

Father and son were good companions and J. B. Yeats left a delightful vignette of the rector:

It was my father who made me the artist I am, and kindled the sort of ambition I have transmitted to my sons. My wife, once meeting an old man who in his youth had associated much with my father, judged it a good opportunity to ask about him, and whether he was a good preacher. The answer came promptly: 'Yes, good—but flighty—flighty.' I do think that romance, which is pleasant beauty unlike the austere beauty of the classical school, is born of sweet-tempered mien. My father was sweet-tempered and affectionate, also he constantly read Shelley, and, no less, Shelley's antidote, Charles Lamb. To be with him was to be caught up into a web of visionary hopefulness. Every night, when the whole house was quiet, and the servants gone to bed, he would sit for a while beside the kitchen fire and I would be with him. He never smoked during the day, and not for worlds would he have smoked in any part of the house except the kitchen and yet he considered himself a great smoker. He used a new clay pipe, and as he waved the smoke aside with his hand, he would talk of the men he had known—his fellow students—of Archer Butler, the Platonist, and of a man called Gray who was, I think, an astronomer, and of his friend Isaac Butt, that man of genius engulfed in law and politics. And he would talk of his youth and boyhood in the West of Ireland where he had fished and shot and hunted and had not a care, of how he would on the first day of the shooting climb to the top of a high mountain seven miles away and be there in the dark with his dogs and attendants, waiting for the dawn to break.[28]

This gentle clergyman had never been to school and regretted it. He was convinced that if he had not been taught by his father but had been efficiently flogged he would have risen to the highest eminences. He therefore sent his son until he was twelve to a 'very fashionable' school kept by a Miss Davenport at Liverpool;[29] and then began to talk 'with an enthusiasm that was infectious' of a Scottish schoolmaster who kept the Atholl Academy in the Isle of Man. The boy, who shared his father's ideas, went to his second school, his mind alive with pleasant anticipations; but the Scot 'brushed the sun out of my

sky'. The school of fifty or sixty boys was ruled by terror, for
the master knew no other method; yet the boys were individualistic and diverse types:

> It was a time when parents had little money and travelling expenses were
> heavy, so that holidays were scanty and far apart. For instance, we never
> went home at Christmas. The cheap railway had not yet supplanted the
> mail coach. Yet we lived haunted by the thought of our homes—it possessed
> us, it obsessed us, it was our food and drink with which we fed our imagina-
> tions and spiritually nourished ourselves. We would talk incessantly of our
> homes; and friendships, our only solace in that abode of sternness, were
> made up of similarities of taste and experience in the matter of homes.[30]

His own great friendship was with George Pollexfen, who came
from Sligo; and would have been especially attractive to
J. B. Y. because he lived in the places his own father had loved
as a boy and described so happily to his children. After leaving
school the youth entered Trinity College, Dublin, where he was
to follow the example of his father and grandfather and take
Orders in the Church of Ireland. J. B. Yeats, however, found
that he was not interested in religion: he read classics, metaphysics and logic; and decided not to enter the Church. After
winning a ten-pound prize in political economy he went for a
holiday to Sligo—to stay with his friend George Pollexfen, to
visit the region where his grandfather had been so popular,
where relatives were to be met, his father's brothers and sister
who had stayed in their birthplace, sinking slightly from a
worldly point of view, but enjoying life to the full.

It was an important visit, and some of the emotional undertones emerge in an autobiographical passage which describes
how the friends walked on the sandhills near Rosses Point:
George Pollexfen talkative, a Pollexfen way of demonstrating
great happiness; the other, impressed by the strange beauty of
the scene and the ceaseless murmur of the Atlantic on the rocks,
was moved by the tranquillity and companionship of his friend:
it must have seemed at once an adventure and a homecoming.[31]
At Sligo he also met George's eldest sister Susan, whom he
subsequently married, but not until after his father died and
left him the family income from the Kildare lands. The Rev.
W. B. Yeats had retired from his country rectory while his son
was at college and had come to live at Sandymount, a seaside
suburb south of Dublin looking out over the Bay towards
Howth. His brother-in-law, Robert Corbet,[32] had chosen
Sandymount as a place of retirement and lived in some state in
Sandymount Castle, where the Rector died quietly in 1862. In

September of the following year J. B. Yeats, then a student of law, married Susan Pollexfen at St John's Church, Sligo.

The Pollexfens were a strange family, and possessed an immense attraction for J. B. Yeats, who constantly speculated upon them, regarding them as the very stuff of poetry. The father of the founder of this Sligo branch of the family was an Anthony Pollexfen, keeper of the Forts at Berry Head, Torquay, who died in 1833 and was buried at Brixham,[33] Devon. His wife, Mary Stephens, who came from County Wexford, bore him a son, William, at Brixham in 1811. The boy ran away to sea 'through the hawse hole', eventually owning a fleet of merchant ships. In 1833 he arrived at Sligo, where a cousin of his, Elizabeth Pollexfen, a daughter of the Rev. Charles Pollexfen of Jersey, had survived the death of her husband William Middleton, who died of cholera in 1832. William Middleton had seen her in Jersey and brought her home to Sligo at the age of fifteen.[34] William Pollexfen married this cousin's daughter Elizabeth in 1835 and became a partner with her brother William in the family concern which had greatly prospered.[35] The Camphill mills at Colooney were leased to the firm of Middleton and Pollexfen; these turned out about three hundred tons of flour and two hundred and forty tons of meal each week. The author of the *County History* embarks on a panegyric over the Ballisodare property of the company:

If the Colooney mills are somewhat 'cabin'd cribb'd confin'd' in area though this facilitates supervision, and brings with it other advantages as well, those of Avena, Ballysadare, have 'ample room and verge enough', being built some on one side of the river, some on the other and all the buildings well apart. The bird's eye view from the top of Knockmildowney gives a good idea of the largeness and completeness of the concern bringing all the parts at once under the spectator—the long, and lofty, and spacious mills, three for dressing flour, one for grinding oats and maize, and one for crushing maize, or as it is more commonly called, Indian corn; the kilns and stores, and offices that serve for the working of these mills; the gas works that supply the gas with which all the buildings are lighted; the cottages of the millers and millwrights; the house of the superintendent; and commanding and overlooking all, Avena House, the residence of Mr Middleton.[36]

There were also the ships of the firm. The poet tells a story to illustrate his grandfather's strength and habit of never ordering anyone to do anything that he could not do himself, of how a captain of the fleet reported on arrival at Rosses Point that his ship had something the matter with its rudder and refused, with his crew, to examine the damage when ordered to do so.

William Pollexfen himself dived from the ship and emerged
with his skin badly torn but aware of the causes of the trouble.[37]
He was a silent solitary man, and his children inherited some of
his silence and detachment.  The poet's mother shared the low
spirits of her brother George, who later became a hypochondriac, while another member of the family had to be placed in
an asylum.

The attraction of the Pollexfens for J. B. Yeats must have
been in part due to their differences.  The Yeatses were a
family who talked easily, whose brains fed on ideas; since the
failure of their ancestor in business it seemed that they had
lost concern in their own worldly affairs; true, they lived well
and appreciated the good things of life; but they lacked an
interest in 'getting on'.  The Pollexfens were not so much
interested in the fluidity of ideas as in the solidarity of possessions; and yet J. B. Yeats envied them.  There was an affectionate interest in human personality in the Yeats family which
overlooked, yet belittled, trade; the well-to-do Pollexfens looked
down on the poverty of the Yeatses, and on the habit of the
Middletons of taking their friends from the cottages in their
neighbourhood.  The Middletons lacked the Pollexfen reserve
and all the sense of dignified order that underlay it.[38]  It is
possible that these differences were a basic element in the
character of the poet, who was born to John and Susan Yeats
on 13 June 1865; of whom his father said 'By marriage with a
Pollexfen I have given a tongue to the sea cliffs'.[39]

J. B. Yeats and his wife lived at 'Georgeville' for about a year
and a half; their son was wheeled in his pram in the grounds
of Robert Corbet's castle.  Meanwhile there were legal terms
to be kept, for J. B. Yeats was devil to Isaac Butt,[40] his father's
friend, who seemed to the young man to be a genius lost in
law and politics, whose poor muse could only visit him in
strange places:

in brothels and gaming houses she would meet her son, herself an exile; in
those days banished by the respectable poets and Bishops and all the old
stumbling bigotries of religious and social hatred.  Butt, who loved humanity
too much to hate any man, and knew too much of history to hate any
opinion—besides how can a man, with visions to follow, hate?  The career
of Butt is enough to prove the necessity of the Irish political movement.[41]

Terence de Vere White, Butt's biographer, has commented that
Butt may not have appeared in quite so romantic a light to men
who did not share Yeats's fineness of mind.  Yeats sympathised
with Butt's profound hopefulness and perhaps interpreted him

too much in the light of his own character when he wrote that 'the ordinary life of a legal practitioner isn't for a man of genius'[41a]—a sentence that would go far to explain his own decision to give up law and become an artist. He had always drawn well; his powers of imagination and of theorising demanded a freer air, a scope unrestricted by other men's laws. A shadow had fallen on Sandymount, for Robert Corbet's affairs had gone astray and he committed suicide. The Castle, which had been a place of happiness throughout J. B. Yeats's college days, lost all its attraction. Better to leave the shadows of its gothic turrets, the garden and its long pond where there was an island inhabited by tame eagles; better to begin a new career outside Dublin, a city more prone to depreciate than appreciate.

The young couple moved to 23 Fitzroy Road, Regent's Park, in 1867. One of the poet's first memories, which were, as so often happens, fragmentary and simultaneous, concerns this household. Looking out of a window he could see boys playing in the street, among them a boy in uniform, probably a telegraph messenger. When he asked a servant what that boy was, the servant stupidly told him that the boy was going to blow the town up, and he went to sleep in terror.[42] From 1867 to 1868 J. B. Yeats studied art at Heatherleigh's Art School in Newman Street.[43] There he met Samuel Butler and thought him, though the politest and most ceremonious of men, ready to sneer, in a manner the more palpable because so veiled. He would have seen more of Butler had he not been working so hard, for he valued a look of helpful kindness in a mocking face.[44] The hard work continued at the Academy School, where Yeats worked with Poynter. The family increased. Two boys, Robert, who died in 1873, and John Butler (Jack), were born at Fitzroy Road, as was Elizabeth (Lolly), the younger sister. Susan Mary (Lily) was born near Sligo when Mrs Yeats was visiting her parents. There were many visits—for J. B. Yeats was generous-minded and not good at husbanding his slender resources—so many, indeed, that the poet's memories of early childhood seemed to him to centre on Sligo and his grandparents.

It was not a happy childhood, and his father understood the reasons. He wrote from London to his wife, then at Merville, the Pollexfen house in Sligo, with the children:

I am very anxious about Willy, he is never out of my thoughts. I believe him to be intensely affectionate, but from shyness, sensitiveness and nervous-

ness, difficult to win and yet he is worth winning. I should of course like
to see him do what is right but he will only develop by kindness and affection and gentleness. Bobby is robust and hardy and does not mind rebuffs—
but Willy is sensitive intellectual and emotional, very easily rebuffed and
continually afraid of being rebuffed so that with him one has to use sensitiveness which is so rare at Merville.[45]

There was no reason for the unhappiness; some of it was due to
loneliness, some to fear of his grandfather William Pollexfen,[46]
a man always irritated by past and future, at peace only when
immersed in the present. His deep love for his wife compen-
sated him for a lonely childhood, but he was generally feared
for silence and fierceness. His silence kept his relatives from
enquiries about his past life. None of them knew how or where
he had got a scar from a whaling hook which marked his right
hand, or why he had won the freedom of a Spanish city, a fact
which emerged from the chance visit of a sailor, and was
admitted but not explained by the old man. The fierceness of
his blue-eyed, bearded grandfather impressed the boy as much
as his silence. A hatchet lay beside his bed in case of burglars
and once Willie saw him hunt men with a horse-whip. But
there were other factors which contributed to the unhappiness
—a general lack of understanding of children. When the Yeats
children went to meals at the long dining-room table they
always tried to sit on the same side as their grandfather, for if
they sat opposite him he was likely to notice them taking sugar,
which annoyed him. If he saw the sugar sifter lifted he would
roar at the offender—not meaning any unkindness but terrifying or at any rate humiliating the children.

There were the rare moments of amusement, almost worse
to endure than simple terror, for these had to be suppressed in
the presence of their elders—such moments as those provoked
when the children, sitting through some long meal at the end
of the long dining-table, could alone see the antics of the house-
maid, Kate McDermott, who was prancing on all fours outside
the door with lighted tapers in her hair. Screened from the
sober-minded Pollexfens by the open door she was doing her
best to amuse the children—and herself. The servants generally
spoke Irish among themselves and were all characters in their
own way. Scanlon the coachman, who shaved himself in the
reflection of a small fragment of the mirror in the stables, was
once abused by Lily Yeats for his 'dirty nasty, hairy face'; but
to her surprise did not resent the childish rudeness and told the
other servants with some pride what she had called him; in

return he always knew her as 'Miss Jack Jumper'. Watching
Scanlon shave was a daily amusement, terminated always with
his ritual phrase, 'Run off now, children, I'm going to strip'.
The children slept in a nursery above the large stable building,
joined to the house by a bridge, and at night they could hear
the chains of the animals rattling and clinking against the
mangers.

The Pollexfen uncles and aunts who came and went faded
from the poet's memory, except for some·harsh words that convinced him by 'a vividness out of proportion to their harshness' that they were habitually kind and considerate. Though
Yeats mainly remembered the pain of his childhood, there was
much in the Sligo life that was pleasant for him—the troubles
were in his own mind, caused by his nervous sensitivity. His
grandmother, who painted delicate water colours when her
busy Victorian housekeeping allowed her time, was kind in the
Middleton manner. She was

not forceful but strong—she was most unselfish, even-tempered, intuitive,
observant, progressive, and, I am sure, ambitious.

She had a delicate ivory complexion and must have looked a
charming figure in her black silk jacket and flowered silk sun-
bonnet when she collected 'the Healing Plant' from her garden
to make some special ointment, the secret of which died with her.

There were Middleton relatives to be visited, and it was from
them 'perhaps' that Willie first got an interest in country
stories, and the legends of fairies that were to be heard from
the pilots and tenants with whom the Middletons were friendly.
A Middleton cousin George, the son of the poet's great-uncle
William Middleton, lived at Ballisodare in the winter; he
possessed a piebald pony which sometimes remembered its past
circus life and turned in circles; in the summer he was a companion to visit at Rosses Point where Willie rowed with him
and was taken sailing. On one of these excursions a heavy sea
got up and a wave drenched him as he lay between mast and
bowsprit. At Rosses he was dressed in garments that did not
fit, given some whisky by a pilot to keep out the chill, and driven
home on an outside car from which he proclaimed loudly, to
his uncle's annoyance, that he was drunk—a touch of exhibition-
ism essential to his character which emerged only on rare occasions during his childhood.[47] Once he was told by an aunt that
he had struck his pony and reined it in at the same time to
show off as he passed through the town. This reproach caused

him some misery: for to the child it seemed a monstrous crime. His conscience was beginning to awaken. It was stimulated by someone talking to him of 'the voice of the conscience'. He heard no voice and 'had some wretched days' until he heard a whisper in his ear 'What a tease you are', assumed that this was the voice of his conscience and became happy once more.[48] It is unusual to find so striking a memory of the first operation of the conscience, even such a looked-for one. Thus Yeats:

> From that day the voice has come to me at moments of crisis, but it is a voice in my head that is sudden and startling. It does not tell me what to do, but often reproves me. It will say perhaps, 'That is unjust' of some thought; and once when I complained that a prayer had not been heard, it said 'You have been helped'.[48]

While honesty and scrupulousness generally result from this Protestant habit of consulting the conscience, there is a tendency towards introspection, and sometimes, a hidden unsureness; the outer preoccupation is with external things, a dogmatic façade concealing inner vacillation and condemnation. Where the Protestantism has drifted into indifference, as it did in the case of J. B. Yeats and his son, the condemnation is a realisation of futility:

> The unfinished man and his pain
> Brought face to face with his own clumsiness.[49]

A minor result of this preoccupation with conscience is the mental activity it generates. Much of the thought is unconscious, not to be defined by words, until conversation scintillates; a knife blade applied to the whirring grindstone of the mind. Willie Yeats found it hard to attend to anything less interesting than his own thoughts, and his uncles and aunts found him difficult to teach. Indeed they thought because they could not teach him to read that he was lacking. Several Irishmen of genius[50] have been similarly slow to begin reading and writing.

One Sunday the boy refused to go to church, and his father, who never went, said if he did not go to church he must learn to read instead. The lesson was stormy, for J. B. Yeats was impatient. The following Sunday Willie went to church; but his father persevered with the lessons on week days. Next came a dame school, where on his first day he was taught to sing high up in his head:

> Little drops of water
> Little grains of sand
> Make the mighty ocean
> And the pleasant land.

As he was tone deaf all his life it was perhaps as well that his
father wrote to the old woman to forbid further instruction in
singing.[51]   An early interest in rhythm was shown by his
appreciation of the stable-boy's reading Orange ballads to him
in the stable loft.  Later his father read him *The Lays of Ancient
Rome*, *Ivanhoe* and *The Lay of the Last Minstrel*, and he always
remembered them vividly.[52]  From the dame school he went,
with his sister Lily, to be taught spelling and grammar by an
old gentlewoman in a back street.  Once reading in one-
syllable words was left behind it was time to investigate the
'library' at Merville containing a few old novels which were
disregarded in favour of the many volumes of an eighteenth-
century encyclopaedia.

   In 1874 the Yeats family moved from Fitzroy Road to
14 Edith Villas, West Kensington.  Before settling there J. B. Y.
brought Willie with him to Burnham Beeches where he was
painting a pond.  The picture was begun in spring and continued through the year, changing with the seasons until it was
abandoned after the snow had been painted in upon its banks.
The artist was never satisfied, never able to think a picture
finished, and before this new move a Pollexfen aunt had
indirectly attacked his failure to become a popular or prosperous
painter by saying to Willie:

   You are going to London.  Here you are somebody.  There you will be
nobody.[53]

   Probably the most important fact emerging from Yeats's
account of his schooldays in *Autobiographies* was his awareness
in early life of his unusual personality.  This was a natural
result of his environment and his father's care.  There had been
differences all round him in Sligo.  He used to visit the Yeats
relatives and must have contrasted their stories of gentle behaviour and quiet humour (of John Yeats, the Rector of
Drumcliffe, always rattling his keys as he went into his kitchen
in case he should surprise someone doing wrong, of Mat Yeats,
the land agent, waiting up every night for a week to catch boys
stealing his apples, then giving them sixpence and telling them
not to do it again) with the adventurous Middleton legends of
smuggling ancestors, and with the undoubted fierceness of the
Pollexfens.  There was a contrast, too, between the freedom
with which his great-aunt Micky (Mary Yeats, a daughter of
the Rector of Drumcliffe) would expatiate upon the history of
the Yeats family, to the delight of the Sligo Yeatses, and the

Pollexfen reticence to enlarge upon such matters though there was a family tree which connected the Pollexfen family with the descendants of Sir Francis Drake. There were other differences, too: the Pollexfens, because of their descent, religion, education and traditions were orientated towards England; they felt superior to the superstitions of the Irish peasantry, yet were extremely critical of English ways of life:

They belonged to the small gentry, who, in the West, at any rate, love their native places without perhaps loving Ireland. They do not travel and are shut off from England by the whole breadth of Ireland with the result that they are forced to make their native town their world. [54]

All these contrasting elements in Sligo life became unalloyed happiness when the greater differences between English and Irish life began to be experienced. They were not noticed at once. After a very happy time at Burnham Beeches there was a year spent in London when J. B. Y. taught him lessons, and terrified him by descriptions of his 'moral degradation'; shouted at him, and often sent him with his sister to walk to the National Gallery with a penny each for buns. [55] Lily sometimes came with him to the Round Pond at Kensington Gardens. Hone tells how, when Willie's first model yacht 'The Rose' which he brought from Sligo was treated with a certain amount of contempt by the owners of larger vessels, his father ordered a model of 'The Sunbeam' from a shop in Holland Park Road. The name of his large yacht was changed to 'The Moonbeam' by Willie who gained great prestige at the Pond by his new possession. [56] The change to London was not relished. One day Willie and Lily had spoken together at the drinking fountain at Holland Park of their longing for Sligo and hatred of London. Willie longed for a sod of earth from a field he knew, for something of Sligo to grasp in his hand—a strange desire when the children had been brought up to despise emotional displays of any kind. This hatred of London was, so far, of the place rather than the people. Mrs Yeats spoke constantly of Sligo to her children, telling stories she had heard from the cottage folk in her childhood there, always assuming that her listeners agreed that Sligo was more beautiful than any other place. [57]

It was when Willie first went to school in England at about the age of ten that the difference of life and outlook impinged very forcibly upon him. He had to cope with two new aspects of living: companionship and enmity; both contributed to his sense of being an unusual person. He was sent to the Godolphin School at Hammersmith, a gothic building executed in yellow brick, a place for 'the sons of professional men who had failed or were at the outset of their career, where all pretended their parents were richer than they really were'. His Irish nationality began to assume some importance. After his first day's lesson the boys gathered round him to ask 'Who's your father?' 'What does he do?' 'How much money has he?' (the last a distressing question; he later told a boy who had seen his mother mending his clothes that she did this from pleasure, not, as was the case, through necessity). An insulting remark shocked him into his first attempt to fight anyone, and he was called names for being Irish. He tended to think 'the rough manners of a cheap school' typical of all England, and got many black eyes, had many occasions for grief and rage. An Irish master at the school would make him stand up and tell him that it was a scandal that he was so idle when all the world knew that any Irish boy was cleverer than a whole classroom of English boys—a description for which Yeats suffered when out of the classroom. His mental images were different. When reading of English victories at Cressy or Agincourt his English class-mates were conscious that such events formed part of their heritage. He was not, nor did he have any inherited pride in memories of Irish Catholic victories, such as Limerick, or the Yellow Ford, to counterbalance them. Being a somewhat timid boy his main defence was one of assuming that he was different from his fellows through superiority:

I have climbed to the top of a tree by the edge of a playing field and am looking at my school fellows and am as proud of myself as a March cock when it crows to its first sunrise. I am saying to myself 'If when I grow up, I am as clever among grown-up men as I am among these boys I shall be a famous man. I remind myself how they all think the same things and cover the school walls at election times with the opinions their fathers find in the newspapers. I remind myself that I am an artist's son and must take some work as the whole end of life and not think as the others do of becoming well off and living pleasantly.[58]

In disregarding the normal worldly ambitions he was under his father's influence; the latter's life was based on the premise that a gentleman was not interested in 'getting on'; life was full of more important and more interesting things than that. Yet Willie at times longed to be ordinary; his father's ideas and his own dreams were not enough to sustain him. In his early day-dreaming at Sligo he had envisaged dying a heroic death at

the head of a company of young men fighting the Fenians, an
idea started by hearing rumours of a Fenian rising; but, when
he was at the Godolphin School, Land League activities had
caused anti-Irish feeling; and he found himself afraid of the
other boys. There had been no doubt in his mind when he had
collected pieces of wood that might go towards the construction
of the dream vessel which would carry him on his glorious
campaign against the Fenians; but his lack of courage at school
depressed him. His best friend at school was an athletic boy,
Cyril Vesey, who shared his interest in moths and butterflies.
Vesey protected him and fought for him; and Willie followed
him, even in the fighting between the Godolphin pupils and
street boys or sometimes against the neighbouring charity
school. Vesey had taught his friend to box, refusing to fight
any more bullies for him and telling him to keep out of the way
of the other boys until he could defend himself. Eventually he
was permitted to approach the others and an opportunity at
once presented itself, for a boy threw mud at him shouting 'Mad
Irishman!' Yeats pummelled him, and, at an offer of peace,
knowing the other would ultimately beat him, shook hands. It
was his last fight with a school fellow.

When he first went to the Hammersmith Swimming Baths he
was afraid to enter the water until he had gone down the ladder
to his thighs, but a chance fall from a diving-board encouraged
him to dive from greater heights than the other boys. He had
other habits of delicate children endeavouring to prove themselves the equal of stronger contemporaries. He would pretend
not to be out of breath after swimming under water; he took
care never to appear out of breath or distressed after running in
a race. He had begun to run with his friend Vesey who was
training. In his last year at the school he won a silver cup for
running which gave him immense pleasure, for it seemed a sign
that he could compete with others in their own activities in
some small way.

When he first went to the Godolphin his father tried to stop
him reading boys' papers; his reason for this, that such publications were intended for the average person and restricted mental
growth, was an additional reminder that Willie was unusual.
After a time, however, his father decided he was over-anxious
about the boy's progress, and ceased to be angry if lessons were
not well learned. His reading was no longer supervised; boys'
papers received excited attention, and to add to the usual

schoolboys' habits, papers were bought to follow the career of some professional runner. Willie's general school work was described as 'very good' on a term report dated Christmas 1878. Latin was then his best subject. Another report describes his mathematics as 'very poor'. A time-table for lessons reveals his inability to spell in any orthodox fashion.[59] He was nearly at the lower end of his class, and made excuses through his timidity but was well treated by the masters.

The family had moved to 8 Woodstock Road, Bedford Park, in 1876. There was much romance in this adventurous region of winding streets and picturesquely unorthodox houses, in the peacock blue which pervaded the furniture of the house where there were dancing lessons, in the half-built houses which children always delight to explore. There were J. B. Y.'s friends, painters who were beginning to doubt the pre-Raphaelite doctrines, Nettleship, Page, Potter, Farrar and Wilson. Before Willie went to the Godolphin he had found a book given to his father by the author, a Dublin scientist, who described the sea-creatures found at Howth or dredged out of Dublin Bay. School had seemed likely to interrupt the reading of this book which was making him grow very wise. Apart from the time spent in going to and from school, in preparing lessons, in fighting, in making excursions to Richmond Park, Coomb Wood and Twyford Abbey with two other boys in search of beetles, butterflies and moths, Yeats thought himself 'a mine of information', yet somehow his rambles with these friends left him vaguely unsatisfied:

No matter how charming the place I knew that those other boys saw something that I did not see. I was a stranger there. There was something in their way of saying the names of places that made me feel this.[60]

Holidays in Sligo were eagerly anticipated: they added to the feeling of not belonging to any world but his own. He used to boast to the English boys about his voyages between the Clarence Basin, Liverpool, and Sligo Quay in the steamships *Sligo* and *Liverpool* owned by a company directed by William Pollexfen and William Middleton. There was romance in these journeys, especially the ones that brought him to Sligo, which he described in his only novel, *John Sherman*, and in his *Autobiographies*. Rathlin, the mist-covered Donegal cliffs, men from Tory Island 'coming alongside with lobsters, talking Irish, and, if it was night, blowing on a burning sod to attract attention', all brought him nearer to the place he loved. In Sligo

his activities were expanded. He began to climb the mountains, went sailing with local folk, listened to the tales of sailors
and fisher-boys, and rode the red pony to Rathbroughan to
play with the Land Agent's children at sailing toy boats in the
river there. His father gave him much advice and, aware of
the Pollexfens' self-confidence and efficiency, told him that he
must do everything the Pollexfens respected very well. He
criticised his son's riding, for Willie was not a dashing rider.
When he rode the red pony to a hunt it refused the first jump,
and he refused to let some country lads beat it. He found a gap,
and tried another ditch; later when the pony baulked at that
also he 'tied him to a tree and lay down among the ferns and
looked up into the sky'. It was not a successful day, for he met
the hunt on the way home and rode his pony amongst the
hounds to see why people avoided them; shouts from everyone
greeted this manœuvre. He shot at birds with an ancient
muzzle-loading pistol until someone shot a rabbit and he heard
it squeal. After that he would only kill fish. He fished for trout
with worms in the mountain streams, for pike at Castle Dargan,
the residence of a squireen married to a Middleton cousin.[61]

In 1880 the Land War had meant that rents from the portions of the Kildare lands not already mortgaged ceased to
arrive, and so the Yeats family returned to Ireland. They were
lent Balscadden Cottage at Howth, the headland that encloses
the north-eastern side of Dublin Bay. After a year they moved
to a small house called Island View which looked out over
Howth Harbour. J. B. Y. had a studio in Dublin; Mrs Yeats
was happy in the sights of a fishing village, in the setting out
and returning of the fleet of sailing-vessels. As in Sligo she took
pleasure in the conversation of fisher folk. Willie was sent at the
age of fifteen to the High School, Dublin, a secondary school
then recently established, which has provided several Provosts
and Fellows of Trinity College, Dublin, and still flourishes.
The headmaster was William Wilkins, an interesting minor
poet, whose brother George was also on the staff. The school
was unlike the Godolphin. The boys worked harder: games,
which had been encouraged in England, were regarded as
a hindrance to work. As this school was a day school there
was not much opportunity to meet his school fellows. As he
never worked unless the subject interested[62] him Willie found
the school difficult. His father's ideas on education were also
troublesome. J. B. Y. taught him Latin, but thought that he

should neglect his history and geography, for he would pick up all he needed in his general reading. Euclid seemed too easy and the idea that it trained the mind had been refuted and so his Latin lessons were well learned. He was told that he, who learned it in 'the terror that could alone check my wandering mind', was a disgrace to be so idle when so clever. His handwriting and spelling debarred him from ever winning a prize for an essay; and his opinions scandalised the staff— they represented what he had thought, or what his father had told him, or were memories of the conversation of his father's friends. Later the poet wrote of his father's theories:

> All he said, was, I now believe, right, but he should have taken me away from school. He would have taught me nothing but Greek and Latin, and I would now be an educated man, and would not have to look in useless longing at books that have been, through the poor mechanism of transla- tion, the builders of my soul, nor face authority with the timidity born of excuse and evasion.[63]

Boyhood was drawing to a close when Vesey spent a summer at Howth. The friendship was less satisfactory to Willie now; he became critical of his friend. Even their common interest in natural history was no longer a bond. Vesey collected moths and butterflies for the excitement of the pursuit, in a manner that seemed to Willie akin to the amassing of stamps, a hobby of Vesey's which had been disparaged by him in London. The growing gap between them was one of intelligence. J. B. Y. was an agnostic and his lack of belief had affected Willie earlier, for it made him think of the evidences of religion. He 'weighed the matter perpetually with great anxiety' for he did not think that he could live without religion. At the High School he caused some surprise by announcing that he was a follower of Darwin and Wallace, Huxley and Haeckel. His interests in natural history led him 'after much hesitation, trouble and bewilderment' to argument in refutation of Adam,[64] Noah, and the Seven Days. He planned to write a book about the yearly changes among the creatures of some hole in the rock at Howth, but he could not even argue with the more orthodox Vesey on such subjects. His interest in the scientists did not last long. It may not have been a conscious attempt to replace the authority of religion, though there was a period, after he had read Darwin and Huxley and believed as they did, when he had wanted, because an established au hority was on his side, to argue with everybody. The drift away from science (and later he came to hate Victorian science with a 'monkish hatred') was accompanied by the physical awakening of adolescence. He slept out at nights in a cave, difficult of access, with the excuse of catching moths; but later as his interests turned to literature the passage along the ledge to the cave called up visions of Manfred on his glacier. He had begun to play at being a sage, a magician or a poet.[65] Looking back on his collection of moths, butterflies and beetles, it seemed that he had learned very little for all the time and energy he had expended. A possible reason for his growing indifference to science is that he inherited his father's delightful, if occasionally irritating, habit of generalising arrestingly. A passage from the latter's autobiographical writing gives a charming picture of what growing up with the artist meant if we realise that the 'Irish boy' must be a member of a poor Anglo-Irish family, that he is in fact essentially a mixture of the experiences of J. B. Y. and his son:

> The typical Irish family is poor, ambitious, and intellectual, and all have the national habit, once indigenous in 'Merry England' of much conversation. In modern England they like a dull man, and so they like a dull boy. We like bright men and boys. When there is a dull boy we send him to England and put him into business where he may sink or swim; but a bright boy is a different story. Quickly he becomes the family confidant, learning all about the family necessities; with so much frank conversation it cannot be otherwise. He knows every detail in the school bills and what it will cost to put him through the University, and how that cost can be reduced by winning scholarships and prizes. As he grows older he watches like an expert the younger brothers coming on, and is eager to advise in his young wisdom as to their prospects. He studies constantly, perhaps overworks himself while his mother and sisters keep watch; and yet he is too serious, and they on their side are too anxious for compliments. It is indeed characteristic of the Irish mother that, unlike the flattering mothers of England, she loves too much to admire her children, with her intimate knowledge there goes a cautious judgment. The family habit of conversation into which he enters with the arrogance of his tender years gives him the chance of vitalizing his newly acquired knowledge. Father, Mother, brothers and sisters are all on his mind and the family fortunes are a responsibility. He is not dull-witted, as are those who go into business to exercise their will in plodding along some prescribed path; on the contrary, his intellect is in constant exercise. He is full of intellectual curiosity, so much curiosity keeping it alive and therein is unlike the English, the American boy. Indeed he experiences a constant temptation to spend in varied reading the time that should be given to restricted study. He is at once sceptical and credulous, but, provided his opinions are expressed gaily and frankly no one minds. With us intellect takes the place which in the English home is occupied by the business faculty. We love the valour of the free intellect; so that, the more audacious his opinion, the higher rise the family hopes. He and all his family approve of amusement—to do so is an Irish tradition unbroken from the days before St Patrick; but they have none.

They are too poor and too busy; or rather they have a great deal, but it is found in boyish friendships and in the bonds of the strongest family affection, inevitable because they are Irish and because they have hopes that make them dependent upon one another. The long family talks over the fire, the long talks between clever boys on country walks—these are not the least exciting amusements—even though they bear no resemblance to what is called 'sport'.[66]

It was no wonder that the poet looking back on his childhood was able to write:

At seventeen years old I was already an old fashioned brass cannon full of shot and nothing had kept me from going off but a doubt as to my capacity to shoot straight.[67]

# 2

## HIS FIRST BOOK OF POETRY
### (1885–1889)

*Words alone are certain good.*

W. B. YEATS

W HILE at the High School Willie appeared to some of his contemporaries to be uninterested in all about him, vacant in manner to the point of absent-mindedness,[1] 'a white blackbird among the others'.[2] Yet some of his school fellows, especially Charles Johnston and 'John Eglinton', realised his potential ability. In old age he wrote a poem published in the school magazine, *The Erasmian*, in which he remembered that:

> His chosen comrades thought at school
> He must grow a famous man:
> He thought the same and lived by rule
> All his twenties crammed with toil.[3]

At home his family considered it likely that he would become a writer, and the boy's growing interest in poetry was encouraged by his father. When Willie was fifteen or sixteen J. B. Y. had talked to him of Blake and Rossetti, given him their works to read, and told him of his own essentially pre-Raphaelite literary principles. The father read aloud his favourite passages from the poets and discussed them every morning in the train going to Dublin. They went together to York Street, to an eighteenth-century house turned tenement, in which Mr Yeats had a large room on the ground floor as his studio.[4] As York Street is near Harcourt Street, Willie breakfasted with him before going to school; the continued conversations on poetry with his father were one of the main factors in his education. J. B. Y., who disliked speculative poetry, generalisations and abstractions, chose always to read aloud the most dramatic moment of the play or poem. It was because his father considered dramatic poetry the superior of all other kinds that Willie wrote his first poetry in imitation of Spenser and of Shelley 'play after play'.[5]

22

The world he imagined in these poems was a retreat; his ideas of what a long poem should be were inspired by

a thicket between three roads, some distance from any of them, in the midst of Howth. . . . That thicket gave me my first thought of what a long poem should be; I thought of it as a region into which one should wander from the cares of life. The characters were to be no more real than the shadows that people the Howth thicket. Their mission was to lessen the solitude without destroying its peace.[6]

He began to invent fantastic and incoherent plots, one of which was inspired by one of his father's early designs:

A king's daughter loves a god seen in the luminous sky above her garden in childhood, and to be worthy of him and put away mortality, becomes without pity and commits crimes, and, at last, having made her way to the throne by murder, awaits his coming among her courtiers. One by one they become chilly and drop dead, for unseen by all but her, her god is in the hall. At last he is at the throne's foot, and she, her mind in the garden once more, dies babbling like a child.[7]

These plays often contained many lines that did not scan; Willie could not understand prosody. He read aloud his lines as he wrote them, and only discovered that they had no common music when he read them to someone else.[8]

Some of his youthful efforts were recited to Edward Dowden, the first holder of the Chair of English at Dublin University. He had been a college friend of J. B. Yeats, though the two men had developed widely varying attitudes to life. The artist thought the Professor had destroyed himself by turning from creative work—the poetry he had written earlier—to the critical studies which established his reputation as a sensitive and original scholar.[9] Dowden used to invite father and son to breakfast with him, and criticised Willie's poetry without damping the ardours of the youth. J. B. Y. wrote to him from Howth in 1884, asking for an MS. of Willie's and revealing how tentatively yet hopefully he regarded his son's efforts:

Of course I never dreamed of publishing the effort of a youth of eighteen. The only passage in it which seems to me finally to decide the question as to his poetic faculty is the dialogue between Time and the Queen.[10] There was evidence in it of some power (however rudimentary) of thinking—as if some day he might have something to tell. I tell him prose and verse are alike in one thing—the best is that to which went the hardest thoughts. This is also the secret of originality, also the secret of sincerity—so far I have his confidence—that he is a poet I have long believed—where he may rank is another matter. That his doubt may have a chance of resolving itself I favour his wish to be an artist—his bad metres arise very much from his composing in a loud voice, manipulating of course the quantities to his own taste.[11]

It was decided that Willie should attend the School of Art

in Kildare Street, Dublin. There had been discussion about
the prospects of his entering Trinity College in continuance of
the family tradition. This plan would have pleased J. B. Yeats,
but Willie's ability to pass the easy entrance examination was
doubtful, and the money for fees difficult to find. The School
of Art provided a means of staving off the problem of his
future; and the father developed a theory that every boy, no
matter what his goal in life, would be the better for a training
in art. Willie's work in the School of Art was not outstanding
and the instructors were not impressed by the manner in which
he exaggerated his father's unfashionable technique.

The influence of J. B. Y. upon Willie began to wane after
he left the High School.

The family moved house from Howth to 10 Ashfield Terrace,
off Harold's Cross Road, a suburban district within easy access
of the centre of Dublin. This change widened Willie's interest.
Although he still observed natural phenomena closely he had
begun to collect specimens of human nature instead of natural
history. Life at Howth had been ideal for natural history, but
the time, and often the money, required for travelling in and
out of Dublin had meant that there was little opportunity for
making friendships. Once in Rathgar these began to increase.
The house of his father's friend Edward Dowden was near and
he met there young writers, and heard most interesting conversation. His father had introduced him into the Contemporary Club which met in rooms in Trinity College, and here
through the Home Rule interests of Hubert Oldham (the
founder of the club) and his friends, he met some men of a
stronger nationalist feeling than he had previously encountered.
At the School of Art he met George Russell, who shared his
newly awakening interest in mysticism, and who had already
begun to see the strange visions which he endeavoured to
reproduce in his paintings. Russell was impressed by Yeats's
habit of writing continuously; they soon began to write plays
in friendly rivalry. He was a frequent visitor at the house in
Ashfield Terrace, and he and Willie sat in the kitchen long
after the family had gone to bed, reciting their verses to each
other and eating more supper cooked on the kitchen fire.[12]

Emergence from the shadow of his father's personality into
the scrutiny of these new acquaintances was difficult. Willie
needed some cover for his mixture of shyness and ambition.
He already possessed the ability to act a part. When he was

ten or twelve his father had taken him to see Irving play Hamlet:

for many years Hamlet was an image of heroic self-possession for the poses of childhood and youth to copy, a combatant of the battle within myself.[13]

While at the School of Art he sometimes adopted an artificial stride in memory of Hamlet, and used to gaze at his reflection in shop windows wishing that his red tie could be permanently blown out by the wind into a Byronic shape. The loose tie had been inspired by that of Oliver Sheppard the sculptor, at that time a senior student in the modelling class; both Russell and Yeats were envious and quickly blossomed forth into these demonstrations of their difference from the majority.[14] The tie was indeed the only finery that Willie could afford, and his high narrow trousers were popularly imagined at the School to have been his grandfather's. The gaunt youth added to the poetic trapping of the tie a habit of absentmindedness which sometimes puzzled the unitiated; yet he was sufficiently aware of the notice paid to his habits and appearance to be able to remember when writing of the time he lived in the Ashfield Terrace house that:

There seemed to be enemies everywhere. At one side there was a friendly architect but on the other some stupid stout woman and her family. I had a study with a window opposite some window of hers, and one night when I was writing I heard voices full of derision and saw the stout woman and her family standing in the window. I have a way of acting what I write and speaking it aloud without knowing what I am doing. Perhaps I was on my hands and knees, or looking down over the back of a chair talking into what I imagined an abyss. Another day a woman asked me to direct her on her way and while I was hesitating being so suddenly called out of my thought, a woman from some neighbouring street came by. She said I was a poet and my questioner turned away contemptuously. Upon the other hand, the policeman and tramway conductor thought my absence of mind sufficiently explained when our servant told them I was a poet. 'Oh well' said the policeman, who had been asking why I went indifferently through clean and muddy places, 'if it is only the poetry that is working in his head.'[15]

Yeats's first published poems appeared in *The Dublin University Review* (in March 1885), a newly founded literary and political magazine edited by Hubert Oldham.[16] The two poems, 'Song of the Fairies' and 'Voices', reflect the gentle dreaminess of their author. In the School of Art he had thought that only beautiful things should be painted, and that only ancient things were beautiful. He was not certain enough of his views to maintain them in argument or carry them out in his painting; but his verse was imbued with them. 'The Song of the Fairies' has three elements in it which recur in his early poetry: his love of natural beauty; his growing interest in the supernatural; and his desire for quietude.

Holidays in Sligo reflected his changed interests. He began to stay with his uncle George Pollexfen who had left Ballina to manage the affairs of the Middleton and Pollexfen firm, which were not so prosperous as formerly. A melancholy note is struck by the Rev. O'Rorke's comment, contrasting sadly with his previously quoted eulogy:

> Owing to the great contraction almost the stoppage of the business in recent years, there are scarce half a dozen men employed where there were formerly five or six score.[17]

William Middleton, who had been responsible for the commercial success of the firm, had died; the more spectacular William Pollexfen had retired and lived in Merville until 1886. It then seemed far too big a house with all his large family away, and he moved to a smaller residence, Rathedmond. He worked himself into rages over what he thought to be mismanagement of shipping in the harbour and began to superintend the making of his large tomb, which is still prominent in St John's Churchyard. Willie was no longer his grandfather's favourite; his place had been taken by his brother Jack, who lived permanently at Sligo, and had made many friends among the local boys. George's house, Thornhill (opposite Rathedmond), was a more congenial home for Willie, who retained his boyish fear of his grandfather. George, melancholy and tolerant, received many confidences from the young man. He approved of a plan to walk round Lough Gill which involved Willie's sleeping in Slish Wood, though unaware of the ambition behind the project.[18] J. B. Y. had read Thoreau's *Walden* to his son whose imagination was gripped by the idea of living like Thoreau in search of wisdom on Innisfree, a wooded island in Lough Gill opposite Slish Wood. Willie set off from Sligo in the evening and walked round the lake, sleeping out in Slish Wood and listening at dawn to the birds' cries which particularly interested him. On another occasion he asked his cousin Henry Middleton to take him out in his yacht at midnight to see which sea birds began to move before dawn. The cousin refused until provoked by his sister's telling him not to go, for he did not wish to be considered mad like Willie. The birds' cries were eventually described in *The Shadowy Waters*. The boy who was the crew of the yacht told wild tales to Yeats and his cousin. These stories, of a 'music hall at a neighbouring sea port and how the girls there gave themselves to men', and of some cottages fifty miles along the coast where there were girls and there would be 'a great welcome', impressed themselves on Yeats's mind[19] and his memory reproduced them in altered guise in old age when he was writing many poems linked with his memories:

Go your ways, O go your ways,
I choose another mark.
Girls down on the seashore
Who understand the dark;
Bawdy talk for the fishermen;
A dance for the fisher-lads;
When dark hangs upon the water
They turn down their beds.[20]

There were better raconteurs who appealed to him more— Paddy Flynn, 'a little bright-eyed old man, living in a leaky one roomed cottage of the village of Ballisodare',[21] and Mary Battle, his uncle's second-sighted servant.[22] Both Paddy Flynn and Mary Battle were believers in the supernatural and Yeats listened to them with eagerness. At Ballisodare there were unusual occurrences in the Middleton home, Avena House, which affected him strongly. A sound like someone throwing a handful of peas against the mirror under which a cousin was reading and a heavy thumping upon the wainscot in a different portion of the room were perplexing. Later in the same day steps were heard in the empty house by a servant, while at nightfall his cousin saw the ground under some trees all in a blaze of light:

I saw nothing, but presently we crossed the river and went along its edge where, they say, there was a village destroyed, I think in the wars of the seventeenth century, and near an old grave yard. Suddenly we all saw a light moving over the river where there is a great rush of water. It was like a very brilliant torch. A moment later the girl saw a man coming towards us who disappeared in the water. I kept asking myself if I could be deceived. Perhaps after all, though it seemed impossible, somebody was walking in the water with a torch. But we could see a small light low down on Knocknarea seven miles off, and it began to move upward over the mountain slope. I timed it on my watch and in five minutes it reached the summit, and I, who had so often climbed that mountain, knew that no human footstep was so speedy.[23]

These mysterious fires at Ballisodare seemed to repeat themselves at Rosses and Willie began to take a greater interest in fairy raths and the talk of old men and women. He told people

that anything that had ever been believed anywhere should be
believed rather than only things which could be proved:

> But I was already to deny or turn into a joke what was for all that my secret
> fanaticism.[24]

The unsureness of his character added to his gentleness, and
he lived in a fairy world of dreamy thought which his early
verse reflects:

> A man has a hope for heaven,
> But soulless a fairy dies,
> As a leaf that is old, and withered and cold
> When the wintry vapours rise.[25]

His observation of nature emerged through some slight disguise:

> So let us dance on the fringed waves
> And shout at the wisest owls
> In their downy caps, and startle the naps
> Of the dreaming water-fowls.[25]

The second poem 'Voices', later to appear with some superficial
alterations in his *Collected Poems* as 'The Cloak, the Boat and
the Shoes', was, like the first, part of a long Arcadian play *The
Island of Statues*. This was also published in *The Dublin University
Review*, following a reading to a large collection of interested
people in Trinity College, after which Professor Bury decided
favourably for its appearance. *The Island of Statues* is a romantic
poem which shows the influence of Spenser and Shelley, the
one for setting, the other for vocabulary. The whole tone of
the poem is melancholy, imbued with a sense of loneliness amid
a delicately weak beauty. The diction is consciously poetic:

> Maiden, come forth; the woods keep watch for thee;
> Within the drowsy blossom hangs the bee;
> 'Tis morn: thy sheep are wandering down the vale—
> 'Tis morn: like old men's eyes the stars are pale,
> And thro' the odorous air love dreams are winging—
> 'Tis morn, and from the dew drench'd wood I've fled
> To welcome thee, Naschina, with sweet singing.

Echoes of other poems are remembered, for instance the rhyme
of Wordsworth's 'The Daffodils':

> Or as day fills
> The brazen sky, so blaze the daffodils.

There is much repetition and personification and abundance of
'I trow' and 'I wis' incorporated for the sake of the rhyme.
There are some images which recur during later periods of

Yeats's poetry: sea shells, 'Sad sea shells where little echoes sit';[26] and the knight, who, to prove his love

> with lance in rest
> Will circle round the world upon a quest,
> Until afar appear the gleaming dragon scales:
> From morn the twain until the evening pales
> Will struggle.[27]

Fountains, perhaps ever since the one in Holland Park had reminded him of Sligo, were associated with solitude and loneliness, and in this poem, as in his later imagery, the idea of loneliness is stressed by the sense that perpetual understanding is achieved by the subject alone:

> And 'mong the stunted ash-trees' drooping rings,
> All flame-like gushing from the hollow stones,
> By day and night a lonely fountain sings,
> And there to its own heart for ever moans.[28]

The main impression left by *The Island of Statues* is cloying and uneven. The mournfulness of beauty specially attracted the poet, and penetrated the whole of the poem:

> For what is glad?
> For, look you, sad's the murmur of the bees,
> Yon wind goes sadly, and the grass and trees
> Reply like moaning of imprisoned elf:
> The whole world's sadly talking to itself.
> The waves in yonder lake where points my hand
> Beat out their lives lamenting o'er the sand.[28]

Two shorter poems, 'The Song of The Last Arcadian' and 'Miserrimus', also owe much to Shelley and the English romantic tradition. It has been suggested[29] that those lines in the former poem:

> Go gather by the humming sea
> Some twisted, echo-harbouring shell,
> And to its lips thy story tell[30]

were inspired by a passage in *Prometheus Unbound*:

> Give her that curved shell, which Prometheus old
> Made Asia's nuptial boon, breathing within it
> A voice to be accomplished. . . .[31]

The Spirit of the Hour, who considers the shell the fairest in the Ocean, believes its sound must be both sweet and strange, and is commanded by Prometheus to

> Outspeed the sun around the orbed world;
> And as thy chariot cleaves the kindling air,
> Thou breathe into the many folded shell,
> Loosening the mighty music, it shall be
> As thunder mingled with clear echoes.

In Yeats's two poems there is a typical alteration of the ideas. In 'Miserrimus' loneliness is stressed, that loneliness which his father had so often told him was the penalty paid for creative genius:

> Then he sang softly nigh the pearly rim;
> But the sad dweller by the sea ways lone
> Changed all he sang to inarticulate moan
> Among her wildering whirls, forgetting him.[32]

In 'The Song of the Last Arcadian' he is to tell his story to the lips of the shell:

> And they thy comforters will be
> Rewarding in melodious guile
> Thy fretful words a little while,
> Till they shall singing fade in ruth
> And die a pearly brotherhood;
> For words alone are certain good:
> Sing, then, for this is also sooth.[30]

These lines represent Yeats's own attitude to life at the time: words alone are certain good; deeds must not be worshipped, nor truth be hungered after. It was a state of poetic dreaming and escape from life:

> The sea swept on and cried her old cry still,
> Rolling along in dreams from hill to hill.
> He fled the persecution of her glory
> And in a far-off, gentle valley stopping
> Cried all his story to the dewdrops glistering.[32]

*Mosada* was the last long work he wrote for some time in blank verse (it was written, like *The Island of Statues*, in 1884). The setting is Spanish; he was still writing under the spell of a fervid imagination that drew from literary sources its romantic scenery and themes.[32a] There is a more dramatic approach to tragic feeling in this story of an inquisitor who discovered the identity of his beloved too late to save her. The poem appeared in *The Dublin University Review* in June 1886, and as it seemed to mark a great advance on his previous work his father had it reprinted by Sealy, Bryers and Walker, and issued by subscription. This was Willie's first book, and his father drew a portrait of him for a frontispiece. He was very proud of the work of his son, and presented a copy of the pamphlet to Gerard Manley Hopkins, among others.

This beginning of a long series of books approximately coincides with the end of J. B. Y.'s influence upon his ideas.

At the publication of *Mosada* Willie was writing poems of a different stamp, no longer following implicitly his father's belief in dramatic poetry. Some of these appeared in *The Dublin University Review* in October and December 1886— 'Miserrimus', 'From the Book of Kauri the Indian. Section V, On the Nature of God' and 'An Indian Song'. These poems reflected his new thoughts and interests.

He had begun to study psychical research and mysticism, and in doing so, as he tells us in *Autobiographies*,[33] broke away from his father's influence. J. B. Y. told him that his interest in religion would never be real. Though his father's scepticism had a great effect on him he still wished for some system of philosophy which would include his belief that the legends, personalities, and emotions handed down by poets and painters, philosophers and theologians were the nearest approach he knew to truth. One day he was visiting Dowden's house and heard A. P. Sinnett's *Esoteric Buddhism* discussed.[34] He read the book and passed it on to Charlie Johnston, who was reading beside him at the Kildare Street Library. Johnston, a son of the Orange Member of Parliament for South Belfast, was in his last year at the High School where the staff regarded him as a brilliant pupil. He intended to go to the South Seas as a missionary. The two had been reading Baron Reichenbach's book on Odic force, and had spent some time in the Museum in Kildare Street imagining they felt the Odic force flowing behind the larger crystals exhibited there. But the result of reading Sinnett's book was more striking. Johnston decided to give up his idea of becoming a missionary for he had become suddenly converted to Esoteric Buddhism. An article on this subject, written by him, appeared in *The Dublin University Review* in July 1885. This was a paper he had read to a new group known as the Dublin Hermetic Society. The Society was started, according to a note in the same issue of the magazine, to promote the study of Oriental Religions and Theosophy. At the first meeting 'Mr W. B. Yeats gave an address upon the objects of the society' which was named Hermetic because it was to deal with a philosophy which until recently had been kept secret or only revealed in symbolism. The group, of seven youths, rented a room at the top of a house in York Street.

Willie could not convert the others to the belief he had expressed at the first meeting that only the philosophy which exists in poetry is permanent. In a later essay on Shelley's

poetry he described how he went to a learned scholar (obviously
Dowden, who produced his life of Shelley in 1886) to ask about
the deep meanings of *Prometheus Unbound*. Despite the information given him that it was Godwin's *Political Justice* put into
rhyme, he was convinced that there was a system of belief
behind the poem which would make it a sacred book for his
fellow students.[35]

Charlie Johnston went to London to see Madame Blavatsky,
and returned to form the Dublin Theosophical Lodge. Yeats
did not become a member, though he had been instrumental in
starting the interests of the others on their way to theosophy.
Indeed his influence was deplored by many. George Russell's
parents disliked his sway over their son,[36] and the headmaster
of the High School had met Yeats in the street and asked him
to turn the thoughts of Johnston away from mysticism towards
his imminent examination. Yeats, alarmed, murmured about
the children of this world being wiser than the children of
light, and Mr Wilkins went off in disgust.[37] But it was Willie's
turn to be impressed by an outside influence. A Brahmin from
Bengal, Babu Mohini Chatterjee, had been invited to come on
a visit to Dublin to aid the foundation of the new Theosophical
Lodge; he stayed with the only member of the group who
had rooms of his own. Yeats, in those days seeking to be a
disciple with a pathetic insistence which revealed his lack of
self-confidence, adopted the quietist outlook of this philosopher,
a man of some repute among theosophists, of whom he wrote:

> He taught us by what seemed an invincible logic that those who die, in
> so far as they have imagined beauty or justice, are made part of that beauty
> or justice and move through the minds of living man, as Shelley believed;
> and that mind over-shadows mind even among the living, and by pathways
> that lie beyond the senses; and that he measured labour by his measure and
> put the hermit above all other labourers, because, being the most silent and
> the most hidden, he lived nearer to the Eternal Powers, and showed their
> mastery of the world. Alcibiades fled from Socrates lest he might do
> nothing but listen to him all life long, and I am certain that we, seeking as
> youth will for some unknown deed or thought, all dreamed that but to
> listen to this man who threw the enchantment of powers about silent and
> gentle things, and at last to think as he did, was the one thing worth doing
> and thinking and that all action and all words that lead to action were a
> little vulgar, a little trivial. Ah, how many years it has taken me to wake
> out of that dream.[38]

A note by the poet reveals how closely a poem, 'Kanva on
Himself', is related to the Brahmin's idea. The note reads like
a prose draft for the poem, which merely presents the Brahmin's
thoughts in verse:

Somebody asked him (Mohini Chatterjee) if we should pray, but even prayer was too full of hope, of desire, of life, to have any part in that acquiescence that was his beginning of wisdom, and he answered that one should say, before sleeping: 'I have lived many lives, I have been a slave and a prince. Many a beloved has sat upon my knees, and I have sat upon the knees of many a beloved. Everything that has been shall be again'. Beautiful words that I spoilt once by turning them into clumsy verse.

The lines Yeats wrote were these:

> Hast thou not sat of yore upon the knees
> Of myriads of beloveds, and on thine
> Have not a myriad swayed below strange trees
> In other lives? Hast thou not quaffed old wine
> By tables that were fallen into dust
> Ere yonder palm commenced his thousand years?[39]

He did not hesitate to use them again after an interval of thirty-nine years in another poem 'Mohini Chatterjee' which restates the theme of 'Kanva on Himself':

> That he might set at rest
> A boy's turbulent days
> Mohini Chatterjee
> Spoke these, or words like these.[40]

The publication of Willie's verses in *The Dublin University Review* gave him a certain prestige among the younger Dublin writers; while his own enthusiasm for poetry encouraged them in return. Katharine Tynan, to whom Hubert Oldham had introduced him in 1885, was greatly impressed by the beauty of his appearance, 'his dark face, its touch of vivid colouring, the night black hair, the eager dark eyes'. At the time he had a small beard, and was 'all dreams and gentleness'. She described how he

lived, breathed, ate, drank and slept poetry. . . . In those days we all bullied Willie Yeats, I myself not excepted. I believe it was because *we* did not want to live, breathe, drink, eat and sleep poetry; and he would have you do all these things if you allowed him. But then always I knew that he was that precious thing to the race and to the world, a genius. Driving Willie Yeats to and fro I used to say myself 'And did you once see Shelley plain?'[41]

He had begun to visit her home frequently. Her father was a dairy farmer living in a snug homestead, Whitehall, at Clondalkin in the south-west of County Dublin. He was a hospitable man, though it was his violent temper that Yeats later made the subject of an essay 'The Man of the Sheep' in *The Celtic Twilight*.[42] The early morning milk cart often brought visitors to the farm back to Dublin in the mornings if the weather had been too bad for them to walk back the previous night. Most of the travellers discreetly slipped from their conveyance on

entering the suburbs and arrived at their destinations in more
dignified fashion, but Willie generally remained happily beside
the driver till he had reached home. At Whitehall the farmer
had set aside a room for his poetess daughter as an elegant
study and there Willie, sometimes accompanied by his sister
Lily, would withdraw to talk of poetry while the other young
visitors, friends of other members of the Tynan family, rolled
up the parlour carpets and danced gaily, fortified by the
immense meals which were such a feature of the household.[43]
This dancing on Sundays was slightly objectionable to the
Yeats family and Willie had begun to notice that

> Irish Catholics among whom had been born so many political martyrs
> had not the good taste, the household courtesy and decency of the Protes-
> tant Ireland that I had known, yet Protestant Ireland seemed to think of
> nothing but getting on in the world.[44]

His father was mainly responsible for his dislike of the more
practical ambitions ascribed to Irish Protestants in general; he
had brought him up when at school 'never to think of the
future or of any practical result'.[45] Willie was now exploring
Irish Catholic society, and finding there a less critical acceptance of his indifference to worldly standards than prevailed
in the company of his father's friends.

J. B. Y. had initially imbued Willie with his own views on
the subject of Home Rule (they belonged to and used to attend
meetings of a Home Rule League) and had introduced him to
his friends in the Contemporary Club who were of similar
opinions, but Willie went further along the path of difference
between England and Ireland.[46] It was only natural that he,
steeped in Shelley, bubbling over with romance, should desire
larger achievements than his father thought possible.

He found in John O'Leary the more inspiring idealism and
positive patriotism that he sought, and turned from ideas of
Home Rule to the more absolute demands of nationalism.

O'Leary, whom he first met at the Contemporary Club, had
the air of sage and martyr that Willie's reading and imagination demanded of any leader. His personality was large and
interesting; and his appearance, bearded and venerable,
revealed a passionate nature, strengthened by a moral genius
the more real for having been tested in suffering. When a
medical student at Trinity College, O'Leary had been inspired
by the Young Ireland movement and had become a leader of
the Fenian movement which succeeded it. He was condemned

to twenty years' penal servitude, but had been set free after five years on condition that he did not return to Ireland for fifteen years. His exile was spent in Paris, and on his return he was highly respected by all parties in Dublin.

Though initially moved by the political sentiments which prompted the writings of Davis and other patriots he was intensely critical of their lack of literary taste. This was a common ground between him and Willie, to whom he lent the work of the nationalist poets, Davis, Callanan, Mangan and their fellows. It was to O'Leary that he owed his know- ledge of Irish patriotic literature. The old Fenian was presi- dent of a Young Ireland Society and Willie began to frequent its meetings. He had spoken at the Contemporary Club, not because he was greatly interested in politics, but from an ambition which he had formed of becoming self-possessed:

I spoke easily and I thought well until some one was rude and then I would become silent or exaggerate my opinion to absurdity, or hesitate and grow confused, or be carried away myself by some party passion.[47]

The debates in the Young Ireland Society were also attended 'more as a training for self-possession than from desire of speech'.[48] He spent hours going over his speeches afterwards and correcting his mistakes. The very inadequacy of his social poise seemed a challenge to attract him to public rather than private talents. At Howth he had begun 'to make blunders' when he paid calls; and as in the case of his early speeches, he made himself miserable by exaggerating the blunders to him- self afterwards. He then began to force himself to go to strange houses 'for schooling sake' because he felt at ease only with people he knew intimately.[49] On his first visit to O'Leary's house kept by his sister Ellen, a poetess, Willie found some middle-aged women playing cards. They suggested that he should take a hand and gave him some sherry which went to his head and he was 'impoverished for days by the loss of sixpence'.[50]

Another danger to be braved was argument with J. F. Taylor, a barrister of uncouth appearance but strong intellect, an orator, and a fellow disciple of O'Leary. Taylor disliked Yeats, probably from jealousy of his friendship with O'Leary, and because his Catholic orthodoxy disapproved of the other's interest in the supernatural. He appeared to Yeats as a tragic figure and several small anecdotes of him, preserved in *Auto-*

*biographies*, reveal how his personality loomed large to the youth. The only time Willie managed to refute him was when he trailed his coat at an evening party of O'Leary's by saying that five out of every six people had seen a ghost; Taylor took up the challenge and said he would ask everyone present. Willie arranged that the first two men he asked had both ghostly experiences to tell, and Taylor asked no more questions that night.

Willie's first experience of a spiritualistic séance took place some time in 1886. Katharine Tynan brought him to the house of a young man arrested for Fenianism but discharged through lack of evidence. Willie appeared to have psychic qualities, for his body began to twitch and he was thrown against the wall. The séance was resumed and the medium began walking round Willie making movements as if he were pushing something away. There seemed to be more force which compelled Willie to make movements which he had not willed. These became increasingly violent. He tried to pray but could not remember anything but the opening lines of *Paradise Lost* which he repeated aloud. The last thing Katharine Tynan saw was 'Willie Yeats banging his head on the table'.[51] He afterwards explained to her that the spirits present were evil, and at the time he was convinced that it was he who had banished them.[52] But for years he did not go near a séance; the strain had been too much for his nervous system.

The debates in the Young Ireland Society, O'Leary's conversation, and the patriotic books he read at the period, were the main reasons for his subsequent work. He had met a new style of speaking verse at the debates, for Taylor's method was public, whereas his father's was more subtle and private. He began to devour poetry that his father had never read to him, and to discuss it in the Young Ireland Society:

> We had no Gaelic but paid great honour to the Irish poets who wrote in English, and quoted them in our speeches. I could have told you at that time the dates of the birth and death, and quoted the chief poems of men whose names you have not heard, and perhaps of some whose names I have forgotten. I knew in my heart that the most of them wrote badly, and yet such romance clung about them, such a desire for Irish poetry was in all our minds, that I kept on saying, not only to others but to myself, that most of them wrote well, or all but well.[53]

He had read Victor Hugo's book on Shakespeare, and delighted in the abuse of critics and coteries which it contained, for he wanted to write like these Irish poets for a popular audience:

I thought that one must write without care, for that was of the coteries, but with a gusty energy that would put all straight if it came out of the right heart.[54]

John O'Leary's influence helped him to formulate his ideas, introduced him to the national elements in the verse which had been written up to Grattan's time, and gave him the example of a man without hope of success whose service was none the less devoted to a romantic ideal, a romantic concept of nationalism.

These new ideas on the need for a new type of Irish literature were a far cry from the quietism of Mohini Chatterjee, and his poems reflect the change. He veered from Indian subjects to Irish, from *The Dublin University Review* to *The Irish Monthly*[55] and *The Irish Fireside*, both Catholic and nationalist organs. His second-last contribution to *The Dublin University Review*, an article on 'The Poetry of the Sir Samuel Ferguson', published in November 1886, shows how he nailed his colours to the mast. He attacked the culture and outlook of Trinity College and the spirit of the Anglo-Irish ascendancy, from which stock he himself came, asserting that because Ferguson had something other than politics to write about he came nearer a true style and therefore was far nearer to perfection, that he had been neglected, while inferior poets received attention from the nationalists.

The effect of O'Leary upon the sensitive and receptive youth is shown by comment on how O'Leary had influenced his attitude to Ferguson:

One night about twelve years ago I was standing on the doorstep of a man who had spent several years in prison, and more in exile, for Fenianism, and at whose house I met from time to time most of the men and women who now make up what is called 'the Irish Literary Movement'. I had prolonged my 'Goodnight' to ask my host's opinion of Sir Samuel Ferguson, whose verse I was reading for the first time and with much enthusiasm. I was so accustomed to find Unionist hating Nationalist, and Nationalist hating Unionist, with the hatreds of Montague and Capulet, that his answer impressed itself on my memory with a distinctness which may seem inexplicable to those who live in more placid lands. 'Sir Samuel Ferguson' he replied, 'is, I understand, a Unionist, but he is a better patriot than I am; he has done more for Ireland than I have done or can ever hope to do.'[56]

In *The Irish Fireside* in March 1887 he published an article on Mangan, endeavouring to praise his work also. He realised the need for a style, un-English, and yet musical and colourful; a non-political tradition:

Then with a deliberateness that still surprises me, for in my heart of hearts I have never been quite certain that one should be more than an artist, that even patriotism is more than an impure desire in an artist, I set to work to find a style and things to write about that the ballad writers might be the better.[57]

Along with his intellectual belief that a new type of Irish literature was needed there was a personal emotion. He had been deeply moved by reading some badly written verses in a newspaper describing the shore of Ireland as seen by a returning, dying, emigrant. He discovered that the verses had been written by a man who died a few days after coming back to Ireland; and decided that he had been moved because the verses expressed the thoughts of a man at a passionate moment in life. He told his father that he thought personal utterance was needed in English literature once more. J. B. Y., full of his own enthusiasm for drama, replied that personal utterance was merely egotism.

Willie decided that from then on he would write out of his own emotions. There was an end to the largely derivative romantic plays, to the conventional themes he had been using. As he put it:

It is so many years before one can believe enough in what one feels even to know what the feeling is.[58]

What he did begin to write was concerned with himself in that it dealt with the scenery of Sligo which he loved, and with the fanciful folk-lore with which it was peopled. The resulting poetry, typified in 'The Stolen Child' which was published in *The Irish Monthly* of December 1886, possessed an airy delicacy and grace, an innocence, and the charm of unreality:

Where the wave of moonlight glosses
The dim grey sand with light,
Far off by furthest Rosses
We foot it all the night,
Weaving olden dances,
Mingling hands and mingling glances
Till the moon has taken flight;
To and fro we leap
And chase the frothy bubbles,
While the world is full of troubles
And is anxious in its sleep.
*Come away, O human child!*
*To the waters and the wild*
*With a faery, hand in hand,*
*For the world's more full of weeping than you can understand.*[59]

In 1887 J. B. Yeats decided to leave Ireland and settle in London once more. He had painted many fine portraits in Dublin of the leaders of the Bar, and of college figures; but he had charged such low prices that his genius had not been recognised. He was not a good business man, for, apart from his modesty, he was equally engrossed in painting chance comers for nothing if their heads interested him. He thought that he might be able to secure work as a black and white illustrator for the English magazines. The family moved to 58 Eardley Crescent, Earl's Court, in June, and Willie tried to make contacts with editors and publishers. Mrs Yeats had two strokes which affected her mind in the course of the summer; and the family prospects were generally depressing.

In September Willie had a poem published in England for the first time. The poem was 'The Madness of King Goll'; it appeared in *The Leisure Hour* illustrated by his father with a drawing of the poet as the king who, according to the legend, hid himself in a valley near Cork where all the madmen in Ireland would gather if they were free. The poem had the same melancholy of solitude, the same wistful romance as before:

> And toads, and every outlawed thing,
> With eyes of sadness rose to hear,
> From pools and rotting leaves, me sing
> The song of outlaws and their fear.
> My singing sang me fever-free.
> My singing fades, the strings are torn;
> I must away by wood and sea
> And lift an ulalo forlorn,
> And fling my laughter to the sun
> —For my remembering hour is done—
> In all his evening vapours rolled.[60]

In December Willie was in Dublin again, where he brought George Russell to visit Katharine Tynan.[61] He then went to Sligo for a short stay. The family had meanwhile moved back to Bedford Park, and were living in 3 Blenheim Road, 'a red-brick house with several mantelpieces designed by the brothers Adam, a balcony and a little garden shadowed by a great horse chestnut tree'.[62] The family finances were further embarrassed by the Ashbourne Act of this year (1888) which compelled them to sell the last remnant of the mortgaged land at Thomastown which had been brought into the family by Mary Butler.[63] Willie completed an anthology of the contemporary Irish poets for the Dublin publishing firm of Gill and Son. This anthology, entitled *Poems and Ballads of Young Ireland*, included four of his own poems, as well as those of Katharine Tynan and Douglas Hyde, who were consulted on

the selections.  The scanty sum he received for his work reinforced the lesson he was learning more thoroughly, that poetry
brought little financial return.  Willie was worried over the
fact that he was not helping to support the family in any way.
He considered continuing his study in art (he and his brother
had just painted a map of Sligo on the ceiling of his study) but
when he remembered his experiences at the Dublin School of
Art the prospect was not pleasant.  His health was not good.
A letter (dated 20 April 1889) to Katharine Tynan tells of his
having 'one of my collapses, having done over much walking
and reading.  I walk most of the way to the British Museum';[64]
and later the doctor ordered him to live 'more deliberately and
leisurely'.[65]

Then came work from the London publisher Walter Scott.
He was paid twelve pounds for a selection entitled *Stories from
Carleton*, and twenty pounds for *Fairy and Folk Tales of the Irish
Peasantry*.  This was not a high rate of pay although the publisher said .to the editor of the Camelot series of reprints,
Ernest Rhys, 'You must never again pay so much'.[66]  Yeats
spent more than three months on the preparation of each book.
He did the work at the British Museum, and remembered later
that he used often to put off consulting some books because he
found handling the heavy volumes of the catalogue a strain.
Yet he used to walk home to Bedford Park frequently in order
to save his pennies for afternoon coffee.  He inked his socks so
that the rents in his boots might not be visible, but was not
worried over this, for an ascetic attitude to life more than
justified the need to do so.  A sentence in a letter to Katharine
Tynan, dated June 1888, sums up his state of mind:

Ambitious, no—I am as easily pleased as a mouse in the wainscot, and
am only anxious to get along without being false to my literary notions of
what is good.[67]

George Russell found him some material for the book of fairy
stories in Dublin, and he included some of Douglas Hyde's
translations from modern Irish, as well as poems and articles
of his own on such subjects as Pookas, Banshees, Solitary
Fairies, and Witches.

All this labour was not without a very full reward in the non-
financial sense.  Despite the fact that no new poems were
published by Willie between September 1887 and November
1889 he did not lose from lack of practice, but gained through
his reading a vast new imagery drawn from Irish literature.

With John O'Leary's encouragement he had read in Dublin the poets of Irish outlook who wrote in English, and was in touch with the old sagas and their later developments. O'Leary further encouraged him by writing him postcards urging him to continue with his literary work, and arranged for him to send contributions to the *Boston Pilot* and the *Providence Journal* in the form of correspondence. His first letter to these Irish-American journals appeared in September 1888.

A minor employment which he undertook the same year was to visit Oxford, to copy a rare manuscript of Aesop in the Bodleian for Alfred Nutt (the following year he went there twice in order to copy an English translation of Franceso Colonna's *Hypneroto-machia Poliphili*).[68] He enjoyed these visits enormously and was affected by the beauty of the countryside. He went on a sixteen-mile walk to see the places mentioned in the *Scholar-Gypsy*. 'One understands English poetry more from seeing a place like this,' he wrote to Katharine Tynan. 'I wonder anybody does anything at Oxford but dream and remember, the place is so beautiful. One almost expects the people to sing instead of speaking. It is all—the colleges I mean—like an opera.'[69] He was able to jest at his lack of money amid rich life:

All the while I was there only one thing troubled my peace of mind,—the politeness of the man servant. It was perpetually 'Wine, sir? Coffee, sir? Anything, sir?' At every 'sir' I said to myself 'That means an extra shilling in his mind, at least'. When I was going I did not know what to give him but gave him five shillings. I tried a joke. My jokes had so far been all failures with him. It went explosively and I departed feeling I had given more than was expected.[70]

All the time he was thinking of his next poem, 'The Wanderings of Oisin', which he finished at the end of the summer when he was in Sligo. He wrote to Katharine Tynan to tell her that the work was nearly complete:

I have corrected the two first parts of 'Oisin'. The second part is much more coherent than I had hoped. You did not hear the second part. It is the most inspired but the least artistic of the three. The last has more art. Because I was in complete solitude—no one near me but old and reticent people [he was staying with his Pollexfen grandparents] when I wrote it. It was the greatest effort of all my things. When I had finished I brought it round to read to my uncle George Pollexfen and could hardly read, so collapsed was I. My voice quite broken. It really was a kind of vision. It beset me day and night. Not that I ever wrote more than a few lines in a day. But those few lines took me hours. And all the rest of the time I walked about the roads thinking of it. I wait impatiently the proof of it. With the other parts I am disappointed—they seem only shadows of what I saw. But the third must have got itself expressed—it kept me from my sleep too long. Yet the second part is more deep and poetic. It is not inspiration that exhausts one but Art. The first part I felt. I saw the second. Yet there perhaps too only shadows have got themselves on the paper. And I am like the people who dream some wonderful thing and get up in the middle of the night and write it and find next day only scribbling on the paper.[71]

He was completing 'Oisin' for a book of his own verse. John O'Leary had collected many subscribers to the venture, and it was published by Kegan Paul, Trench and Company early in 1889, under the title of *The Wanderings of Oisin and Other Poems*. The shorter poems varied in quality, being mainly those which he had published in various magazines in the previous four years. They showed a development from the earliest derivative verses, which seemed to mirror nature's details in the backwaters of the stream of English romantic writing, through the handling of quietist Theosophical themes, to localised events and folk-lore transformed into a wistful dreamland of the poet's own making. Examples of the last type were 'The Stolen Child'[72] and 'The Meditation of the Old Fisherman', founded upon some things said to Yeats by an old fisherman when out fishing in Sligo Bay.[73]

'The Wanderings of Oisin' breathed a freer air of inspiration. There was more scope in the Celtic legends than in minute local description seen through the eyes of earlier English poets. There was a sufficient hint of belief unlike the temporary break-up of religious conviction which distressed him. There was a mystic link between the ancient legends and the present folk-lore, and an escape into a larger world than the poet had imagined for himself in his earlier dreams.

His poem begins with Oisin's account to Saint Patrick of how, after the famous battle of Gabhra, Finn and those of the Fianna who survived were out hunting one morning by the shores of Loch Lein and there saw a beautiful lady riding on a white horse. She was Niamh, daughter of the king of Tir-nan-Oge the land of the Young, who had come to the land of men through her love for Oisin. She asks him to come away with her, and he, in love with her at first sight, is glad to do so, although it involves leaving his father Finn and his comrades of the Fianna. He mounts the white horse, and together the mortal and the fairy leave for the Land of the Young. They journey over the sea to the Island of the Living, and there they hunt and fish and love for a hundred years together. Then the staff of a dead warrior's lance is found in the sea by

Oisin, and he begins to remember the Fianna; Niamh understands and they depart on the magic horse.

In the second book the two lovers come to the Island of Victories. They find, at the top of a long flight of stairs, a maiden who is the prisoner of a demon. Oisin spends the next hundred years in struggles with his enemy, the demon; these struggles last a day and are followed by three days of feasting. At the end of the hundred years Oisin again remembers the Fianna and he and Niamh depart, this time for the Island of Forgetfulness.

In the third part the lovers sleep a troubled sleep amid the heroes of Ireland until Oisin is wakened by the fall of a starling; again remembrance of the Fianna comes upon him and he tells Niamh he must return to Ireland, to his companions. She warns him not to touch the ground with any part of his body; he promises and departs on the magic horse. He finds none of his old companions in Ireland, and turns again to the realms of his fairy bride.

But on the way he sees two men unable to lift a sack of sand, leans from his saddle and hurls the sack five yards with one hand. The saddle girths break, and as he falls upon the earth his years descend upon his body. In this pitiable state, though with unbroken spirit, he is brought to Patrick and he finally declares that he will dwell with the Fenians, whether in the flames of Hell, as Patrick affirms, or at their famous feasting.

The story was an old one;[74] it was known to Campion in 1571. The account which Yeats gives of his source tells how:

> The poem is founded upon the Middle Irish dialogues of Patrick and Oisin and a certain Gaelic poem of the last century. The events it describes are supposed to have taken place rather in the indefinite period made up of periods described by the folk tales, than in any particular century; it is like the later Fenian stories themselves, mixes much that is mediaeval with much that is ancient. The Gaelic poems do not make Oisin go to more than one island, but a story in *Silva Gadelica* describes paradise as an island to the North, an island to the West, an island to the South, and Adam's paradise in the East.

He did not know Gaelic so he relied on translations to give him the incidents of the story. He met the legend and its ramifications in many works during his compilation of *Fairy and Folk Tales of the Irish Peasantry* and his *Representative Irish Tales;* but he drew mainly from *The Transactions of the Ossianic Society* for his own poem. The first volume in this series is an account of the Battle of Gabhra, translated by Nicholas

O'Kearney; the third contains Standish O'Grady's translation
of 'The Lament of Oisin after the Fenians'; and in the fifth
there is John O'Daly's version of the 'Dialogues of Oisin and
Patrick'. The eighteenth-century poem to which Yeats alluded
has been identified as Michael Comyn's 'The Lay of Oisin in
the Land of Youth' which was translated by Brian O'Looney,
and is to be found in the fourth volume of the Ossianic Society's
*Transactions*.

This poem, translated by David Comyn, was issued by the
Gaelic Union Publications in 1880 and was therefore also avail-
able to Yeats. He departed fairly widely from the plot of this
version, which tells how Oisin and Niamh go only to the Land
of Virtues and Victories before they come to the Land of Youth.
A maiden in the Land of Virtues, held captive by the giant
whom Oisin beheads after three days' fighting, gives the hero
balsam after his struggles (in Yeats's version the distressed
maiden's fate is not told at all); after this Oisin and Niamh
depart for the Land of Young, where they marry and have in
the course of their three hundred years' sojourn three children,
Fionn, Oscar, and Plurnamban. Oisin then returns to Ireland,
and the poem ends with this device of the hero being exasperated by the puny strength of three hundred men trying to raise
a block of marble. Yeats took over much of the material of this
translation, often using descriptions almost as they were in the
original. His description of the Land of Youth, for example:

> We galloped over the glossy sea:
> I know not if days passed or hours,
> And Niamh sang continually
> Danaan songs, and their dewy showers
> Of pensive laughter, unhuman sound,
> Lulled weariness, and softly round
> My human sorrow her white arms wound.
> We galloped; now a hornless deer
> Passed by us, chased by a phantom hound
> All pearly white, save one red ear;
> And now a lady rode like the wind
> With an apple of gold in her tossing hand;
> And a beautiful young man followed behind
> With quenchless gaze and fluttering hair[75]

owes much to this passage of O'Looney's translation:

> We saw also, by our sides
> A hornless fawn leaping nimbly,
> And a red-eared white dog,
> Urging it boldly in the chase.
> We beheld also, without fiction
> A young maid on a brown steed,

> A golden apple in her right hand,
> And she going on top of the waves.
> We saw after her,
> A young rider on a white steed. . . .[76]

The source[77] which Yeats gives for the different paradises in his poem is *Silva Gadelica* but this was not published by Standish O'Grady until 1892 so that Yeats's note is mistaken, or else he had seen some unpublished version of the source which he lists. An American scholar, Russell K. Alspach, has used *Fairy and Folk Tales of the Irish Peasantry* and *Representative Irish Tales* to discover many other possible descriptions of paradises which Yeats might have used; they would have been fresh in his memory when he was writing 'Oisin'. In the first of these prose works Yeats described Tir-nan-Oge as triple, composed of the realms of the living, of victories, and of the underwater land. This account was probably inspired by O'Looney's translation. Other versions, however, appear in his two prose anthologies. These included accounts by Charles Henry Foote in *The Folk Lore Record*,[78] by Crofton Croker, who told of the underwater paradises in his *Fairy Legends and Traditions of the South of Ireland*,[79] and by Gerald Griffin, whose legend of Hy Brasil, the Isle of the Blest, was included in the first anthology by Yeats.[80]

There was a borrowing from Sir Samuel Ferguson's poem on Aideen's grave which concludes:

> A cup of bodkin pencill'd clay
> Holds Oscar; mighty heart and limb
> One handful now of ashes grey
> And she has died for him.[81]

This conclusion is echoed in Yeats's lines:

> We think on Oscar's pencilled urn,
> And on the heroes lying slain
> On Gabhra's raven-covered plain.[82]

The treatment of the Irish legends by Ferguson was very different to that of Yeats. Ferguson's somewhat scholarly approach possessed no sensuous appeal, focused attention on outlines rather than on detail, and gave few indications of being written out of his own experience. In all these things he was the opposite of Yeats: yet he was the nearer to the epic tradition of the Gaelic poetry. As Dowden put it, 'His verse at its best moves like the feet of well thewed warriors or queen-like women'.[83] Yeats was still under the influence of Shelley when he wrote 'Oisin' and his own dreaminess and sadness

tint the clarity of the originals into a cloudy beauty.[84] He
knew that something was lacking in his poetry, and confessed
to some depression in a letter written on 6 September 1888:

> I fear I have been somewhat inarticulate! I had indeed something I had
> to say. Don't know that I have said it. All seems confused, incoherent,
> inarticulate. Yet this I know, I am no idle poetaster. My life has been in
> my poems. To make them I have broken my life in a mortar as it were. I
> have brayed in it youth and fellowship peace and worldly hopes. I have
> seen others enjoying life while I stood alone with myself—commenting—
> commenting—a mere dead mirror on which things reflect themselves. I
> have buried my youth and raised over it a cairn—of clouds. Some day I
> shall be articulate perhaps.[85]

Although conscious of inarticulateness Yeats entered upon a
new type of poetry with 'Oisin', and he was aware of the fact.
He wrote to Katharine Tynan that when he had written 'The
Island of Statues' he had been living in an harmonious state:

> Never thinking out of my depth. Always harmonious, narrow, calm.
> Taking small interest in people but most ardently moved by the more
> minute kinds of natural beauty. . . . Since I have left 'The Island' I have
> been going about on shoreless seas. Nothing anywhere has any clear out-
> line. Everything is cloud and foam. 'Oisin' and 'The Seeker' are the only
> readable result. For the second part of 'Oisin' I have said several things
> to which I only have the key. The romance is for my readers. They must
> not even know there is a symbol anywhere. They will not find out. If they
> did it would spoil the art, yet the whole poem is full of symbols—if it be full
> of aught but clouds. The early poems I know to be quite coherent, and at
> no time are there clouds in my details, for I hate the soft modern manner.
> The clouds began about four years ago. I was finishing 'The Island'. They
> came and robbed Nachina of her shade. As you will see the rest is cloudless,
> narrow and calm.[86]

The symbolism of the poem is not the highly developed
symbolism which he was soon to achieve, but simple, more
important for his own love of secrecy than for any undertones
which it gave the poem. An example of its simplicity is given in
another letter to Katharine Tynan where he explains that man
is always seeking three incompatible things, 'infinite feeling,
infinite battle, infinite repose', hence the three islands in his
poem. The main light which the poem casts on Yeats's own
personality is that it reveals him in love with the idea of love.
In 'Oisin' the approach is made to the hero Oisin by the
heroine Niamh, who tells Finn, Oisin's father:

> I have not yet, war-weary king,
> Been spoken of with any man;
> Yet now I choose, for these four feet
> Ran through the foam and ran to this
> That I might have your son to kiss.[87]

There is, obviously, a great deal of Yeats to be discovered in Oisin's character. His words are poetic; Niamh describes them as

> Asian
> That are like coloured birds
> At evening in their rainless lands.[87]

He has not thought of making advances himself. He is still dreaming of the goddess who will come and inspire his love. In old age he realised this and called Niamh a 'manpicker'.[88] In a late poem he describes the whole of 'The Wanderings of Oisin' and it should be remarked that the essential symbolism of the poem is probably contained in three imperceptible things man is always seeking, which he again lists, altering 'feeling' to 'gaiety':

> What can I but enumerate old themes?
> First that sea-rider Oisin led by the nose
> Through three enchanted islands, allegorical dreams
> Vain gaiety, vain battle, vain repose,
> Themes of the embittered heart, or so it seems,
> That might adorn old songs or courtly shows;
> But what cared I that set him on to ride,
> I, starved for the bosom of his faery bride?[89]

# 3

# TECHNIQUE AND INSPIRATION
## (1889–1892)

*I was arrogant, indolent, excitable.*
W. B. YEATS

*When I first went to London*
*I was looking for a technique*
*I had the folk behind me*
*My food was there to seek*
*But without the subtlety London taught*
*I could not learn to speak.*
W. B. YEATS (*recorded by Vernon Watkins*)

AFTER the Yeats family had moved to London in 1887 a
great period of expansion began for Willie, especially in the
fields of personal relationships, with which this chapter is
largely concerned. The change from Howth to Dublin had
meant an opportunity for Willie to make new friendships
within an environment where his family's position and outlook
was known; the change to London from Dublin was a similar
opportunity for the acquisition of wider horizons, and an expansion in spheres where the Irish background of the family was
unknown.

In many ways Willie was less mature than his small beard
and moustache were meant to suggest.[1] At twenty-two he was
still adolescent. Although disappointed that he did not regain
the sense of romance he had known earlier in Bedford Park as a
schoolboy,[1a] he was in all things romantic, and in all things
pre-Raphaelite. What more natural than that he should find
his way to Kelmscott House in Hammersmith, the home of
William Morris?

He went there on Sunday evenings to hear the Socialist
lectures and was soon asked to join the little group who were
invited to stay to supper in the small formal room where on
one wall hung Rossetti's *Pomegranate* and on the other a beautiful
Persian carpet. He soon became a member of a French class,
begun for some Socialists who planned a visit to Paris. He
worked hard at this subject, became the favourite pupil of the
old French mistress, and was convinced that he would soon

48

know French. But the family environment could not be avoided, and prevented him, so he thought, from achieving a new and more poised personality. He had mentioned the class at home and his father asked him to get his sisters admitted to it. He made excuses, angered his father, and had unwillingly to arrange for his sisters to join him, for he could not explain even to himself why this would make it impossible for him to learn his lessons:

I had no longer the prowess, the exciting novelty of strange faces. I was but once more a figure in the comedy of domestic life and I was soon idle and careless.[2]

He had chosen, perhaps in imitation of William Morris, a pose of industry and carried the act so far that he learned his lessons for perfection's sake. But his sisters knew that he was not industrious, and by their mere kindly presence destroyed the image he was building up for himself. Indeed his sister Elizabeth wrote in her diary[3] for 18 January 1889:

Went to French. Willie's dramatic intense way of saying his French with his voice raised to telling distinctness and every pronunciation wrong as usual, seemed to amuse Mr Sparling (William Morris's son-in-law) more than ever, he simply doubled up when Willie commenced. Willie of course divided it up into any amount of full stops where there weren't any so Madame said, 'Mr Yeats, you don't read poetry like that, do you?' 'Yes he does, yes he does,' volunteered Mr Sparling and in truth it was rather like his natural way of reading.

Lily Yeats began to learn embroidery with May Morris, and annoyed Willie by not admiring Mrs Morris. Elizabeth's diary tells the story:

Lily was not back till tea time. Mrs Morris was there—*the beautiful Mrs Morris*—and she thinks her ugly—Willie is indignant.

Lily greatly impressed Morris by her stories, and became a frequent visitor at Hammersmith. After these visits she very often vexed Willie by describing life in the Morris household. She told of afternoon quarrels with the milkboy who rattled his can on the railings when Morris was sleeping, and of the parrot who followed him up and down the stairs when he was translating Homer aloud, imitating the murmur of the verses. She once said of Morris, 'He is always afraid that he is doing something wrong and he generally is'. Willie thought Morris his chief of men. When he had first met him some trick of manner had reminded him of his Pollexfen grandfather, and he had later admired his spontaneity and child-like joy. As a boy he had greatly liked *The Earthly Paradise* and *The Man who never Laughed again*,[4] while after the death of Morris the prose romances were

the only books he read slowly so as not to come to the end. For
many years his favourite description of happiness had been the
lines which his father had spoken to him to describe the life which
had once flourished in Robert Corbet's castle at Sandymount:

> Midways of a walled garden
> In the happy poplar land
> Did an ancient castle stand,
> With an old knight for a warden.
>
> Many scarlet bricks there were
> In its walls, and old grey stone;
> Over which red apples shone
> At the right time of the year.
>
> On the bricks the green moss grew,
> Yellow lichen on the stone,
> Over which red apples shone;
> Little war that castle knew.[5]

Willie, despite his admiration for Morris, became less Social-
istic in his ideas, and explained his attendance at the debates
by saying that he must learn to speak, that a man in Ireland
had to be able to speak as in olden times he had to carry a
sword. He disliked the young working-men revolutionaries,
one of whom told him, after he had preferred Parnell to Davitt
at somewhat excessive length, that he had talked more nonsense in one night than the workman had heard in the course
of a lifetime. His dislike included Bernard Shaw, whom he
met occasionally at Kelmscott House, and whose unruffled
logic he found unpalatable. He later rejoiced in the saying[5a]
that 'Mr Bernard Shaw has no enemies but is intensely disliked
by all his friends' and felt revenged 'upon a notorious hater of
romance' whose finer qualities he could not then appreciate.
He disliked the overstatement which was characteristic of the
meetings, and ceased attending them—after an outburst against
their attitude to religion for which Morris, the chairman, called
him to order. When this meeting was over Morris agreed with
him that there must be a change of heart and explained that
he had stopped Yeats speaking because he was not being
understood; but even though Yeats's ideas on the subject were
not fixed he did not return any more to Kelmscott House.

This habit of over-valuing moral zest made him tiresome. He
was constantly arguing, especially with his father, as we can
see from two entries in his sister Elizabeth's diary for 1888:

Sept. 9th. I can hear a murmur of talk from the dining room where Papa and Willie are arguing something or other. Sometimes they raise their voices so high that a stranger might fancy that they were both in a rage, not at all, it is only their way of arguing because they are natives of the Emerald Isle.
Sept. 18th. Papa and Willie had a hot argument on metaphysics.

Then there came a severe quarrel with his father on the subject of Ruskin's *Unto This Last*, which, combined with Willie's growing interest in mysticism and psychical research, maddened J. B. Y., a disciple of John Stuart Mill. [5b] Yeats's unpublished autobiography tells the story of the quarrel vividly:

One night a quarrel on Ruskin came to such a height that in putting me out of the room he broke the glass of a picture with the back of my head. Another night when we had been in argument over Ruskin or mysticism, I cannot remember which of them, he followed me upstairs to the room I shared with my brother. He squared up to me and wanted to box and when I said I could not fight my father replied 'I don't see why you should not'. My brother who had been in bed for some time started up in a violent passion because we had awakened him. My father fled without speaking, and my brother held me with: 'Mind, not a word till he apologises'. Though my father and I are very talkative a couple of days passed before I spoke or he apologised (I imagined that he feared for my sanity). (Everything had become abstract to me.)

Mysticism he sought at meetings of the Theosophists, where he was introduced by Charlie Johnston. He first met Madame Blavatsky in a house at Norwood where she had but three followers left, as the Society for Psychical Research had issued its report on some of her phenomena; but when he next saw her it was in Holland Park where her house was full of followers. [6] The 'pythoness of the movement' [7] gained his admiration, if not his belief. She seemed to him a great and passionate nature, full of a gaiety illogical and incalculable, out of touch with the commonplace formalism and abstract idealism of those who came to listen to her. Yeats found the Theosophists contemptuous of those who did not share their beliefs, and very conscious that they possessed the aim of improving mankind. He argued that much in life had in aim only itself, and what mainly interested him was the romantic figure of Madame Blavatsky and the air of mystery that her house possessed. He thought that wisdom could be found in the world only in some lonely mind communing with God; and it was possible that Madame Blavatsky could tell him of that Shelleyan sage who

in truth, by dreadful abstinence
And conquering penance of the mutinous flesh,
Deep contemplation and unwearied study,
In years outstretched beyond the date of man,

> May have attained to sovereignty and science
> Even those strong and secret things and thoughts
> Which others fear and know not.[8]

He got no proof of this idea from Madame Blavatsky. 'I have no theories about her,' he wrote to O'Leary, 'she is simply a note of interrogation.'[9] She gave him his best lesson in learning to speak. He had prepared a speech with care and read it out to the assembly. It was received in silence and he felt that none of it had been understood. Madame Blavatsky took his manuscript from him and told him 'to say his say' about it, which he then did with complete success.[10] If he found the Theosophists commonplace, they thought him troublesome.

He had been admitted to the Esoteric Section of the Society which met weekly to study tables of oriental mysticism:

Every organ of the body has its correspondence in the heavens and the seven principles which made the human soul and body correspond to the seven colours and the seven planets and the notes of the musical scale. We lived in perpetual discussion among the symbols of one of the seven principles which was the indigo extracted from the plant in some practical way. I got with some trouble a bottle of this indigo and got inner members to try experiments fixing their mind upon the bottle and letting it drift. They got impressions of mountainous country and then began to describe the different qualities according to the principles that I might expect from one article that I thought of then. I was always longing for evidence but ashamed to admit my longing, and having read in Sibley's *Astrology* if you burn a flower to ashes and then put the ashes under a bell glass in the moonlight the plaston of the flower would rear before you—and persuaded the members of the section who knew more about this and so could experiment. . . . Presently I was called before an official of the Section with great politeness and asked to resign. I was causing disturbance, causing disquiet in some way. I said 'By teaching an abstract system without experiment or evidence you are making your pupils dogmatic and you are taking this out of life. There is scarcely one of your pupils who does not need more than all else to enrich his soul, the common relation of life. They do not marry and nothing is so bad for them as asceticism.' He was a clever man who taught himself much mathematics and wrote a great deal of bad poetry and he admitted all I said but added Madame Blavatsky had told them that no more supernatural help would come to the movement after 1887 when some cycle or other ended. At whatever sacrifice of the individual they had to spread their philosophy through the world before that date. I resigned. I found afterwards that he had been used for action by a fanatical woman. Women do not keep their sanity in the presence of the abstract. Madame Blavatsky had as much of my admiration as William Morris.[11]

At the British Museum Yeats had often noticed a well-built man with a gaunt face and an air of resolution that made him appear a figure of romance.[12] He was Liddell Mathers, later to become, under the influence of the Celtic movement, MacGregor Mathers and finally MacGregor.

When introduced to him Yeats found that he was the author of *The Kabbala Unveiled*, and that he had an intense interest in magic. He had been copying manuscripts on magic in the British Museum and later continued this research on the Continent. He introduced Yeats to a Society of Christian Cabbalists, 'The Hermetic Students',[13] known to its members as the Order of the Golden Dawn. Mathers married Henri Bergson's sister and settled down at Forrest Hill, where he was the curator of a private museum. His house became in Yeats's imagination like that of Madame Blavatsky 'a romantic place'.

Mathers used symbols with more effect than the Theosophists and Yeats was impressed:

> He gave me a cardboard symbol and I closed my eyes. Sight came slowly, there was not that sudden miracle as if the darkness had been cut with a knife, for that miracle is mostly a woman's privilege, but there rose before me mental images that I could not control: a desert and black Titan raising himself up by his two hands from the middle of a heap of ancient ruins. Mathers explained that I had seen a being of the order of Salamanders because he had shown me their symbol, but it was not necessary even to show the symbol, it would have been sufficient that he imagined it.[14]

After meeting Madame Blavatsky and MacGregor Mathers he became interested in their symbolic systems, and the effect of these upon his writing was to make it more sensuous and vivid, as his mind drifted from image to image. He believed that with the images would come more profound states of the soul.[15]

His first step away from his father's intellectual leading-strings had been his interest in mysticism and psychical research. Since J. B. Y.'s agnosticism had initially perplexed Willie:

> My father's unbelief had set me thinking about the evidence of religion and I weighed the matter perpetually with great anxiety for I did not think that I could live without religion,[16]

and since it had driven him into the arms of Victorian Science for a short while in his efforts to find himself something in which he could believe, when the poet became a student of Theosophy and the Christian Cabbala he was in effect searching for a system of truth, a religion. As David Daiches has pointed out[17] he did not want to escape from orthodoxy but to find a substitute for it. In a classical age he would have joined in singing the praises of established authority: it was at once his tragedy and his gain that he was born in an age when he could not believe wholeheartedly; his personal tragedy, because

of his uneasy preoccupation with old age, death and the hereafter; his poetic gain because of the sharpened dualism of his
character, its dramatic alternations of quick enthusiasm for,
and subsequent, almost inevitable, mockery of some fantasy:

> I am one of those unhappy people for whom between Thought and
> Deed lies ever the terrible gulf of dreams. I sit down to write and go off
> into a brown study instead, at least if circumstances offer me the slightest
> excuse.[18]

When *The Wanderings of Oisin and Other Poems* was published
early in 1889 Yeats was fully launched on his poetic career. He
had begun to visit W. E. Henley at his home on the road to
Richmond, not far from Bedford Park, and admired him
greatly while not agreeing with any of his views. Henley, 'a
big burly man with a beard and a restless way of sitting and
moving, somewhat like William Morris in this',[18] disliked pre-
Raphaelitism, and wrote in *verse libre* description of an unim-
passioned nature; all of which was completely contrary to
Yeats's ideas. The Sunday visits to Henley led to more fruitful
results than those paid to Morris at Kelmscott House though
when Morris met the young poet by chance near Holborn
Viaduct he praised *The Wanderings of Oisin*. Yeats had given
a copy of the book to his daughter hoping that it would thus
reach the eye of the master. 'You write my sort of poetry', he
said, and promised to send his praise to *The Commonweal*, the
organ of the League. More might have been said about the
book had Morris not caught sight of a cast-iron lamp-post of a
new decorative style set up by the Corporation; this drew his
attention away from the subject and he turned to abuse of the
lamp-post, waving his umbrella and pouring forth an angry
tirade.[19] Henley began to publish Yeats's prose articles in *The
Scots Observer*. The first appeared in March 1889, and was a
by-product of the work which writing *Fairy and Folk Tales of the
Irish Peasantry* had involved. Three more articles on subjects
connected with folk-lore appeared during this year and for
several years to come his work was published in *The Scots
Observer* and its successor *The National Observer*.

Through his visits to Henley Yeats met other young men
with literary interests such as R. A. M. Stevenson, Barry Pain,
Charles Whibley and Kenneth Grahame, who, as yet unestab-
lished in reputation, accepted as their leader and confidant
this editor who was ready with praise of their work. He was

equally ready to rewrite their compositions. Yeats found himself a little ashamed of being rewritten; Henley often crossed out a line or a stanza in his lyrics and wrote in one of his own; but the poet took comfort in the belief that Kipling, then becoming very popular, had suffered the same indignity. The prose articles contained less that could be revised, being ghost stories and anecdotes unlikely to arouse the opposition of Henley's own ideas.

Oscar Wilde had written an approving review of *The Wanderings of Oisin* and Yeats met him at Henley's house shortly after it had appeared in print. He was greatly impressed by the conversational powers of Wilde, by the spontaneous and yet perfectly constructed sentences that passed from witticism to reverie without incongruity of any kind. He asked Yeats to eat his Christmas dinner with him believing him to be alone in London. The white dining-room of Wilde's home delighted Yeats, as did his pretty wife and children. He was still a poor man, not yet having written a successful play, and so Yeats did not see any of the insolence that later appeared. Instead, he envied, from a sense of his own sheepishness, the other's blend of scholar and man of the world.[19a] Wilde made him tell many long stories and compared his art to that of Homer; but he criticised him as well, casting a silent but damning eye upon an over-yellow pair of boots and telling him, when asked for information for some notes which Yeats was writing for *The Manchester Courier*, that writing literary gossip was no job for a gentleman. Yeats gave up the work, although it gave little trouble and was 'fairly profitable'. He would defend[19b] Wilde when his friends deprecated him: 'He is one of the eighteenth century duellists born in the wrong century'; or again he would compare him to Benvenuto Cellini, 'who because he found it impossible to equal Michael Angelo turned bravo out of the pride of his art'.[20]

Besides these friends and acquaintances whom Willie was meeting on his own, there were his father's friends, especially those in Bedford Park, who were kindly and encouraging, interested as they had to be in the son of the talkative and analytical painter. J. B. Yeats knew and admired York Powell, who held the Chair of History at Oxford, but lived in a house at Bedford Park at intervals; Todhunter, a Dublin doctor turned poet and playwright; Nettleship, the painter who had forsaken imaginative designs for the depiction of savage lions;

3

and Edwin Ellis, a painter pre-Raphaelite in outlook; the young
man found their conversations seldom ranged over those few
topics which he was always able to discuss with violent views.

York Powell, among other kindnesses—he had acted as
Willie's host when he was copying the manuscripts at Oxford—
offered to recommend him for the sub-editorship of a provincial
paper; but after long thought Willie told his father that
he could not accept the offer, even though it meant an immediate income, for the paper was strongly Unionist. He received
the characteristic reply, 'You have taken a great weight off
my mind'.[21] J. B. Y. brought him to dine with Nettleship, and
he talked too much for effect, this making his father, who hated
rhetoric and emphasis, extremely angry. Next day Willie
called to apologise but found that Nettleship had admired his
volubility.[22] He wrote some criticism of Nettleship's verse
which was accepted and then rejected by a magazine. An
earlier poem which had been included in *The Wanderings of
Oisin* was directly inspired by Nettleship's work, and itself
deserves the adjective 'melodramatic' which Yeats later applied
to the painter's lions in *Autobiographies*:[23]

> Yonder the sickle of the moon sails on,
> But here the Lioness licks her soft cub
> Tender and fearless on her funeral pyre;
> The Lion, the world's great solitary, bends
> Down low the head of his magnificence
> And roars, mad with the touch of the unknown,
> Not as he shakes the forest; but a cry
> Low, long and musical. A dewdrop hung
> Bright on a grass blade's underside, might hear,
> Nor tremble to its fall. The fire sweeps round
> Re-shining in his eyes. So ever moves
> The flaming circle of the outer Law,
> Nor heeds the old dim protest and the cry
> The orb of the most living heart
> Gives forth. He, the Eternal, works his will.[24]

Todhunter and Ellis had a more close connection with Yeats's
development. Ellis was particularly interested in Blake; he had
an abstract mind which delighted in symbolism.[25]

Soon after their first meeting he gave Yeats an explanation
of Blake's poems in which the four quarters of London represented Blake's Zoas. Yeats told Ellis of some attributions from
the Christian Cabbala, and they decided to work together on
an explanation of Blake's symbolism. This was in the spring
of 1889 (by December 1891 170 pages of the edition of Blake
were with the printer; Quaritch who eventually issued the

work in 1893 agreed to give the authors thirteen large paper copies each in payment[26]), and for some months they read and discussed the meaning of the Prophetic Books, before making a concordance of the mystical terms used by Blake. There was some copying to be done, often inaccurately, at the British Museum, and at Redhill, Surrey, where the Linnells lived. They were descendants of Blake's friend and patron, the artist John Linnell, and they allowed Ellis and Yeats to copy from the manuscripts in their possession, gave them port with their lunch, and finally presented Yeats with Blake's Dante engravings. Ellis was constantly 'upon the edge of trance', and in his conversation Yeats found much that was incomprehensible and exaggerated, much upon the subjects of religion and sex. The latter topic embarrassed Yeats:

My struggle with my senses made me dread the subject of sex and I always tried to change the subject when Ellis began any of his stories and reminiscences and I was often made uncomfortable by Mrs Ellis who, because I was very delicate, assumed that I was leading a dissipated life. Once when York Powell began to show some friends, among whom I was, characters of the night life of Paris by some famous French artist I left to take a walk up and down at the end of the room. Yet women filled me with curiosity and my mind seemed never to escape from the disturbances of my senses. I was a Romantic, my head full of the mysterious women of Rossetti, and those hesitating faces in the art of Burne Jones seemed always awaiting for some Alastor at the end of a long journey and I under the almost unendurable strain of my senses was convicted that I was without industry and without will. I saw my father painting from morning to night and day after day I had to work not as long as he but from hour to hour.[27]

The reference to Alastor is significant. He had spent his adolescence at Howth, and there in his day dreamings had imagined himself an Alastor, and

longed to share his melancholy, and maybe at last to disappear drifting in a boat along some slow-moving river between great trees. When I thought of women they were modelled on those in my favourite poets and loved in brief tragedy, or like the girl in *The Revolt of Islam*, accompanied their lovers through all manner of wild places, lawless women without homes and without children.[28]

At Howth he fell in love with a red-haired cousin, Laura Johnston. The sensitive and chivalrous nature of his love was accentuated:

I did not tell her I was in love, however, because she was engaged. She had chosen me for her confidant and I learned all about her quarrels with her lover. Several times he broke the engagement off, and she fell ill, and friends had to make peace. . . . I wrote her some bad poems and had more than one sleepless night through anger with her betrothed.[29]

This was a bad beginning for such a shy youth, whose first love was defeated from the start. He had accepted the engagement without question as a sufficient obstacle. Devotion without reward was the keynote of his love.

No more came of this friendship after the family moved from Howth. When they had settled in Ashfield Terrace Yeats's closest friends were George Russell and Katharine Tynan; both young men had been greatly impressed when she published *Louise de la Vallière*, a volume of verse, in 1885. Yeats's friendship with her had continued after the Yeats family went to London. His letters to her[30] over the next four or five years deal with common literary interests and friends—John O'Leary, Hubert Oldham, Father Russell, the editor of the *Irish Monthly*. These letters show us something of Yeats in London, occasionally rebelling against the hackwork he was undertaking, yet firmly resolved to do no work which might force him to make a compromise with his artistic conscience.

It was not until Yeats met Florence Farr that his sisters began to think that he was in love. She was according to Shaw

a young independent professional woman, who enjoyed, as such, an exceptional freedom of social intercourse in artistic circles in London. As she was clever, good natured, and very good looking, all her men friends fell in love with her. This had occurred so often that she had lost all patience with the hesitating preliminaries of her less practised adorers. Accordingly, when they clearly longed to kiss her, and she did not dislike them sufficiently to make their gratification too great a strain on her excessive good nature, she would seize the stammering suitor firmly by the wrists, bring him into her arms by a smart pull and saying 'Let's get it over' allow the startled gentleman to have his kiss, and then proceed to converse with him at her ease on subjects of more general interest.[31]

Thus Shaw, who was on 'her Leporello list which contained fourteen names in 1894'. But Yeats, who was not, thought that her stage life had given her a solitary perhaps unhappy personal life, and in a conversation with Mrs. Yeats, quoted in support of his belief a phrase of hers: 'When a man begins to make love to me I instantly see it as a stage performance.'[32] One remembers Hesketh Pearson's comment that in matters of love 'Shaw could act and did'. Yeats could act too; but then even his early day dreams had generally been of a defeatist nature. Shaw's had been equally unreal, but in his imaginings he had always been 'all-powerful and always victorious, supreme in war, irresistible in love'.[33]

Yeats dreamed of one great love:

All young men that I knew lived the life Edwin Ellis told me of but I had gathered from Shelley and the romantic poets an idea of perfect love. Perhaps I should never marry in church but I would love one woman all my life.[34]

When he imagined himself an Alastor at Howth his early
poetry was filled with minute details of natural beauty; and he
felt intensely the charm of his surroundings. Yet this was not
enough; his thoughts turned to beautiful women; and they
were modelled on the wild Shelleyan heroines. His was an
unusual character, and his ideal love was shaped by two of
the dominant traits which have been described before, his
sense of difference and his ability to suppress or accentuate
aspects of his personality; he idealised his love, yet it is easy to
see some of the reasons which led him to do so.

In love with love, he had a desire for an exciting and unusual
woman to love. Because he was different himself his love
should add to his distinction. She was to have some of the
qualities of those wild women, heroic and lawless. And because
he was still a boy there was an air of unreality about his ideas,
for he would sing his imagined mistress's charms with all the
tragedy and hopelessness of one of Morris's heroes, and all
would be for her approval, all in her service. She must have
beauty fit for a poet to sing. It was to be a great love. He knew
little of women and was shy, and like Oisin he had not realised
what his great love would be like when it came; unlike Oisin he
was aware that it might come. The tinder was dry, and he described the application of the spark in his unpublished autobiography:

I was twenty-three years old when the trouble of my life began. I heard
in a letter from Miss O'Leary, O'Leary's sister, of a most beautiful girl[35]
who had left the society of the Viceregal court for Dublin nationalism. In
after years I persuaded myself that I felt premonitory excitement at the first
reading of her name. Presently she drove up to our house in Bedford Park
in a hansom with an introduction from John O'Leary to my father.[35a] I had
never thought to see in a living woman so great beauty. It belonged to
famous pictures, to poetry, to some legendary past. A complexion like the
bloom of apples and yet face and body had the beauty of lineaments which
Blake calls the highest beauty because it changes least from youth to age,
and stature so great that she seemed of a divine race. Her movements
were works of grace and I understood at last why the poets of antiquity,
where we would but speak of face and form, sing, loving some lady, that
she seems like a goddess. I remember nothing of her speech that day except
that she vexed my father full always of Mill and humanitarianism, by her
praise of war, for she too was of the romantic movement; I found those
uncontrovertible Victorian reasons, that seemed to announce so prosperous
a future, a little grey. As I look backward it seems to me that she brought
into my life—and yet I saw only what lay upon the surface—the middle of
the tent, a sound as if of a Burmese gong, an overpowering tumult that had
yet many pleasant secondary notes. She asked me to dine with her that
evening in her rooms at Ebury Street, and I think that I dined with her all
but every day during her stay in London of I think perhaps nine days.
There was something so generous in her ways that it seemed natural that
she should give her hours in overflowing abundance. She had heard from

O'Leary of me. He praised me and it was natural that she should give and take without stint. She was surrounded by cages of unusual singing birds and she always travelled, it seemed, taking them even upon short journeys. They and she were now returning to Paris where their home was. I had seen upon her table *Tristan of Lyonesse* and she had read it with enthusiasm and she spoke to me of her wish for a play that she could act in Dublin. Somebody had suggested Todhunter's *Helen*, but he had refused. I told her of a story that I had found when I was preparing my *Fairy and Folk Tales of the Irish Peasantry*, and offered to write for her the play I have called *The Countess Kathleen*. When I told her I wished to become an Irish Victor Hugo was I wholly sincere, for, though a volume of bad verse translations from Hugo had been my companion in school, I had begun to simplify myself with great toil? I had seen on her table *Tristan of Lyonesse* and *Les Contemplations*, besides, it was natural to commend myself by a very public talent, for her beauty as I saw it in those days seemed incompatible with private intimate life. She like myself had received the political initiation of Davis with an added touch of hardness and heroism from John O'Leary. And when she spoke, William O'Brien was in gaol making a prolonged struggle against putting on prison clothes. She said 'There was a time when many sacrificed their lives for their country, but now they sacrifice their dignity'. But mixed with this feeling for what is permanent in human life there was something declamatory, but later in a bad sense perhaps even more unscrupulous. She spoke of desire of appraising facts for political power. . . . She spoke much of effectiveness, more winning of votes in the election. Her two and twenty years had taken some colour I thought from French Boulangist adventurers, journalists, arrivistes of whom she had already seen too much, and already had made some political journey to Russia in their interest. I was full of that thought of the *Anima Vagula* chapter 'Only the means justify the end'. She meant her ends to be unselfish but she thought almost any means justified in that service. As we were seeking different things she soon found the final consecration of her youth in memorable action for [indecipherable]; I after all was anxious to discover our common state of being. Perhaps even in politics it would be end enough to have lived and thought passionately and have like O'Leary a head like a Roman coin. I spoke much of my spiritual philosophy. How important it all seemed to me. How much would I have given so that she might think exactly right on all these great questions. And today all is faint to me beside a moment when she passed before a window dressed in white and re-arranged a spray of flowers in a vase. Twelve years after I put this impression into verse ('She pulled down the pale blossoms') I felt in the presence of a great generosity and courage and a mind without rest, and when she and all the singing birds had gone, my melancholy was not the mere melancholy of love. I had what I thought was a clairvoyant perception (of some immediate disaster) but was I can see now but an obvious deduction of an immediate waiting disaster. I was compiling for an American publisher selections from some Irish novelists and I can remember that all the tribulation of those heroes but reminds me of the dread. They too according to a fashion of writing of the early Victorians had been so often thrown without father or mother or guardian into a world of deception —and they too were incurably romantic. I was in love but had not spoken of love and never meant to speak of love and as the months passed I gained a mastery of myself again. What wife would she make, I thought, what share could she have in the life of a student?

The new play on which he began to work was to be completely different from those earlier attempts which were printed in *The Dublin University Review*. Apart from the initial stimulus given to the play by his meeting Maud Gonne, Yeats found an additional incentive in the performance of Todhunter's play *A Sicilian Idyll* at the small club-house at Bedford Park in 1890. He had urged the pastoral theme upon the author (whose neighbouring house contained specimens of J. B. Yeats's work) because it seemed to him that the theatre should keep within the general movements of literature. Such works as Shelley's *The Cenci* and Tennyson's *Becket* were oratorical and untrue to the poets' characteristics. For Yeats the main beauty of the performance had been the fine verse-speaking of Florence Farr, [36] and he thought that she would help him in the production of the verse plays he hoped to write. At any rate she was ready to discuss the project with him. Their friendship was very intimate. Yeats later told his wife that he could tell Florence Farr *everything*; [32] and the series of letters first published by the Cuala Press in 1941 shows what an influence she had upon the early plays, their writing and rewriting. After the production of Todhunter's play, his own dreams of such plays became less remote from reality. His work on *The Countess Kathleen* had begun by April 1889. At first he wrote out prose versions, but the creation of the play was a slow tedious process.

The effect of O'Leary's refined doctrines of nationalism upon Yeats's own development was profound. The poet had brought from Ireland a set of convictions which he was ready to publish whenever possible. In the articles which he wrote for *The Boston Pilot* and *The Providence Sunday Journal* the constant note is that 'there is no great literature without nationality, no great nationality without literature'. [37] He frequently quoted Allingham's delightful description of Ballyshannon:

> A wild West coast, a little town
> Where little folk go up and down,
> Tides flow and winds blow:
> Night and Tempest and the Sea,
> Human will and Human Fate:
> What is little, what is great?
> Howsoe'er the answer be,
> Let me sing of what I know. [38]

But Allingham did not win all his approval. From a nationalist point of view Allingham's lack of sympathy with the national life and history, and his refusal to take her people seriously, were to be criticised; and Yeats was eager to find any opinions which reinforced his own views. He seized on a letter written by one of Allingham's brothers which said that 'William Allingham's best work was Irish and that he would have written far more effectively in every sense had he remained in Ireland in touch with the people'.[39] Justin McCarthy's opinion that Irishmen left little impression on contemporary literature because they were absorbed into journalism and politics was used as a lever to reintroduce Yeats's opinion that cosmopolitanism was another hindrance to Irish progress in literature:

> We are not content to dig our own potato patch in peace. We peer over the wall at our neighbour's instead of making our own garden green and beautiful.[40]

As he was indulging in propaganda for a cause there is much repetition and use was made of examples and metaphors which his later and more critical judgment would have rejected. These articles are the work of a young and enthusiastic man. The poet in Yeats differed from the propagandist, however, and was attracted by the poetry of fairies and place names that were so familiar:

> Up the airy mountain
> Down the rushy glen,
> We daren't go a hunting
> For fear of little men;
> Wee folk, good folk,
> Trooping all together;
> Green jacket, red cap
> And white owl's feather.
>
> High on the hill top
> The old king sits;
> He is now so old and grey
> He's nigh lost his wits.
> With a bridge of white mist
> Columbkill he crosses
> On his stately journeys
> From Slieveleague to Rosses.

To understand these poems fully, he wrote, one needs to have been born and bred in one of those Irish Western towns:

> To remember how it was the centre of your world, how the mountains and the rivers and the roads became a portion of your life for ever; to have loved with a sense of possession even the roadside bushes where the roadside cottagers hung their clothes to dry. That sense of possession was the very centre of the matter. Elsewhere you are only a passer-by, for everything is owned by so many that it is owned by no one. Down there as you hummed over Allingham's *Fairies* and looked up at the mountain where they lived, it seemed to you that a portion of your life was the subject.[41]

Yeats saw nothing good in London, was unhappy there,[42] and constantly remembered that Ruskin had said to some friends of his father's that as he went to his work at the British Museum he saw the faces of the people becoming more corrupt daily. Yeats convinced himself for a while that he saw on the same journey with the same eyes as Ruskin. Old women's faces filled him with horror:

the fat blotched faces, rising above double chins, of women who have drunk too much beer and eaten much meat. In Dublin I had often seen old women walking with erect heads and gaunt bodies, talking to themselves with loud voices, mad with drink and poverty, but they were different, they belonged to romance. Da Vinci had drawn women who looked so, and so carried their bodies.[43]

After Willie had turned down York Powell's offer of a possible position on *The Manchester Courier* his father had suggested that he should write a story, partly in London and partly in Sligo. This resulted in *Dhoya*, a fantastic story of the heroic age in a Sligo setting; but his father had not meant this, and explained that a story about real people would be better.[44] *John Sherman* was then begun. This short tale had the simple plot of a first novel, its four main characters finding happiness in marriage. Virginia Woolf's early work *Night and Day* is a somewhat similar piece of early writing, with a plot which also involves a similarly neat, though more obviously chiasmic, transfer of lovers. Yeats's novel is refreshingly simple and pleasant to read, with an arrestingly jewelled precision of detail; his prose had not become ornate and luxuriant. The book's characters were drawn from life. John Sherman, the hero, was a sketch of Willie's cousin Henry Middleton, who later became a recluse. The difference between the Pollexfens and Yeats received due attention:

You Shermans are a deep people, much deeper than we Howards. We are like moths or butterflies or rather rapid rivulets, while you and yours are deep pools in the forest where the beasts go to drink. No! I have a better metaphor. Your mind and mine are two arrows. Yours has got no feathers, and mine has no metal on the point. I don't know which is most needed for right conduct.[45]

A letter which Yeats wrote to Katharine Tynan in December 1891 shows how aware he was that Allingham had influenced him:

I have an ambition to be taken as an Irish novelist, not as an English or cosmopolitan one, choosing Ireland as a background. I studied my characters in Ireland and described a typical Irish feeling in Sherman's devotion to Ballagh. A West of Ireland feeling, I might almost say like that of Allingham for Ballyshannon. It is West rather than National. Sherman belonged like Allingham to the small gentry who, in the West, at any rate, love their native places without perhaps loving Ireland. They do not travel and are shut off from England by the whole breadth of Ireland, with the result that they are forced to make their native town their world. I remember when we were children how intense our devotion was to all things in Sligo and I still see in my mother the old feeling.[46]

Yeats's homesickness for Ireland and, in particular, Sligo prompted his poem 'The Lake Isle of Innisfree'. Miss Lily Yeats remembers him composing the poem in his study at Bedford Park, then humming lines of it aloud and altering them slightly, to the delight of his family who liked the poem at once. It appeared in *The National Observer* in December 1890:

> I will arise and go now, and go to Innisfree,
> And a small cabin build there, of clay and wattles made:
> Nine bean-rows will I have there, a hive for the honey-bee,
> And live alone in the bee loud glade.
>
> And I shall have some peace there, for peace comes dropping slow,
> Dropping from the veils of morning to where the cricket sings;
> There midnight's all a glimmer, and noon a purple glow,
> And evening full of the linnet's wings.
>
> I will arise and go now, for always night and day
> I hear lake water lapping with low sounds by the shore;
> While I stand on the roadway, or on the pavements grey,
> I hear it in the deep heart's core.

This poem, probably still the best-known example of Yeats's work, owed its success to the proper fusion of universality and personal emotion which it contains. The universal appeal of the subject, the attraction of the hermit's life spent amid beautiful surroundings, has been experienced at some time or other by most persons.[47] The deeply personal element in the poem is stressed by a passage in *John Sherman* which was not published until 1891:

> Delayed by a crush in the Strand, he heard a faint trickling of water near by; it came from a shop window where a little water-jet balanced a wooden ball upon its point. The sound suggested a cataract with a long Gaelic name, that leaped crying into the gate of the winds at Ballagh. . . . He was set dreaming a whole day by walking down one Sunday morning to the borders of the Thames a few hundred yards from his house—and looking at the osier-covered Chiswick eyot. It made him remember an old day-dream of his. The source of the river that passed his garden at home was a certain wood-bordered and islanded lake, whither in childhood he had often gone blackberrying. At the further end was a little islet called Innisfree. Its rocky centre, covered with many bushes, rose some forty feet above the lake. Often when life and its difficulties had seemed to him like the lessons of some elder boy given to a younger by mistake, it had seemed good to dream of going away to that islet and building a wooden hut there and burning a few years out rowing to and fro fishing, or lying on the island slopes by day, and listening at night to the ripple of the water and the quivering of the bushes—full always of unknown creatures—and going out at morning to see the island's edge marked by the feet of birds.[47a]

His attitude to London was recorded in a letter to Katharine Tynan in which he wrote:

> London is always horrible to me. The fact that I can study some things I like here better than elsewhere is the only redeeming fact. The mere presence of more cultivated people is a gain, of course, but nothing in the world can make amends for the loss of green field and mountain slope, and for the tranquil hours of one's own countryside—where one gets tired and so into bad spirits it seems an especial misfortune to live here—it is like having so many years blotted out of life.[48]

When Yeats came to London he was provincial in his outlook, but this was an asset, for his provincialism did not seem that of the English town to the often parochially minded persons he met in London. His Irish background possessed a certain charm; and the strangeness of his interests, his vehemence, and his never-ending babble of conversational monologue added to the effect of his originality. The initial impression he made on Ernest Rhys, who later commissioned his *Fairy and Folk Tales of the Irish Peasantry*, gives some indication of his personality after he had arrived in London:

> The one figure that took my fancy was a very pale, exceedingly thin young man with a raven lock over his forehead, his face so narrow that there was hardly room in it for his luminous black eyes. . . . We left Morris's together when it was getting late and Yeats missed his train at Hammersmith station. But he did not mind that at all, and seemed to regard trains as things that came and went at random. He talked eagerly, continuously, in a soft Irish voice, quite content, late as it was, to walk on towards Chelsea with me . . . we stood talking till midnight under a lamp-post at the end of World's End passage and when we parted he was uncertain which way to go. A day or two later he turned up with a book of Irish Tales, Crofton Croker's I believe, and we supped sparely on cold bacon and cider. He ate as if by magic, the viands disappeared before I had taken a mouthful. He talked of Indian mysticism—of a wonderful seer called Mohini, and H.P.B. (Madame Blavatsky), or again of Irish folk like Paddy Flynn who had the secret of happiness, cooked mushrooms on a turf fire and smiled in his sleep under a hedge. In return he asked me to supper at his father's house in Bedford Park—the first genuine Irish house I had ever been to—all the inmates thoroughly in character, and his two sisters delightful. The father, John B. Yeats, was not only a rare portrait painter, but a vehement eloquent Irishman, hot on politics.[49]

Yeats later discussed with Rhys the need for the poets to know one another lest they become jealous at one another's success.[50] From this conversation came the Rhymers' Club, formed by the efforts of Yeats, Rhys, and T. W. Rolleston. It met in the Cheshire Cheese, and its members soon included Lionel Johnson, Ernest Dowson, Arthur Symons, Richard Le Gaillienne, Selvyn Image, Edwin Ellis, John Todhunter, John Davidson and Herbert Horne. The foundation of the

club in 1891 was a climax to Yeats's efforts to escape nostalgia
or loneliness. His ability to act a part was necessary for his
self-respect:

> I knew almost from the start that to overflow with reasons was to be not
> quite well-born; and when I could I hid them, as men hide a disagreeable
> ancestry; and there was no help for it seeing that my country was not born
> at all. Le Gallienne and Davidson, and even Symons, were provincial at
> their setting out, but their provincialism was curable, mine incurable.[51]

Among these poets there was an air of preparation, as yet they
were not established in reputation; and Yeats felt that the only
certain thing about them was that there were too many of
them.

The greatest change that came upon his poetry and did most
to bring him fame as a poet was his falling in love with Maud
Gonne. His love poetry was inspired by her and its wistful
strain can be understood the better for a knowledge of the
strange history of the poet's love. After their first meeting (of
which Madame MacBride has a different remembrance, for she
has told me personally that she first met Yeats at O'Leary's
house in Dublin, and that he helped her to carry home some
books, an account of which is also given in her autobiography
*A Servant of the Queen*[52]), Yeats had been greatly impressed by
her devotion to an ideal, though contrary to his own ideals;
the energy and self-confidence which she radiated from her
heroic beauty fitted her to be his heroine; though there were
aspects of her self-confidence verging on ruthlessness which
would have troubled him had he not been absorbed in the
mystery of her character, and decided that she was not at peace.
She always travelled with

> Cages full of birds, canaries, finches of all kinds, dogs, a parrot, and once
> a full grown hawk from Donegal. Once when I saw her to her railway
> carriage I noticed how the cages obstructed racks and cushions and
> wondered what her fellow-travellers would say, but the carriage remained
> empty.[53]

He would have been embarrassed by the discomfort caused to
the other travellers, and there were aspects of her character
like this which he disliked from the start, but suppressed. His
love was hopeless. At first he had decided never to speak of
it. He was penniless, and not likely to be otherwise for many
years. There was ample precedent for a poetic devotion; and,
besides, she was beyond his reach and understanding. His
youthfulness and idealism led him to think of her needs only.

Even if he had thought of his views he would never have spoken
of them:

> Sometimes the barrier between myself and other people filled me with
> terror, and the first and never finished version of *The Shadowy Waters* had
> this terror for their theme. I had to an extreme degree the shyness—I know
> no other word—that keeps a man from speaking his own thought.[54]

It did not occur to him to consider his full reactions to her; he
had more to do in considering her impressions of him. He
sought to serve her; and she found him a useful friend. Action
and results were what ultimately appealed to Maud Gonne;
though she too saw many of those visions which beset the mystics
of the nineties she was no dreamer.

Among the family friends in Dublin was the artist Miss Sarah
Purser, who had painted Maud Gonne's portrait in a manner
which displeased Yeats, for it seemed to him to imitate the
diary of Mary Bashkirtseff, 'the thoughts of a girl full of egotism, sensationalism and not very interesting talent'. Miss
Purser met him with the sentence 'So Maud Gonne was staying
in the South of France and her portrait was on sale', and went
on to tell him that she had lunched with Maud Gonne in Paris,
and there was a very tall Frenchman there and a doctor, who
had told her that 'They will both be dead in six months'.[54a]
But Yeats was not affected by such delicate warnings. A few
months later he was in Ireland, in the summer of 1891, and
heard that Maud Gonne was in Dublin. He called at the hotel
in Nassau Street where she stayed, and waited for her return:

> At the first sight of her as she came through the door her great height
> seeming to fill it I was overwhelmed with emotion and intoxication of pity.
> She did not seem to have any beauty, her face was wasted, the force of the
> tour showing, and there was no life in her manner. As our talk became
> intimate she hinted at some unhappiness, some disillusionment. The hard
> old resonance had gone, she had become gentle and indolent. I was in
> love once more and no longer wished to fight against it. I no longer
> thought what kind of a wife would this woman make, but of her need for
> protection and for peace.[55]

But the next day he left to spend some time with Charlie
Johnston in County Down. There he made fire balloons with
Johnston and his brother and then chased them over the
countryside; and bought ballads from a man of forty or fifty
years who claimed to be a survivor of Waterloo.[56] He seemed
to be not completely enslaved, but after a week there came a
letter from her touching a little on her sadness and telling of
a dream of some past life. He and she had been brother and

sister somewhere on the edge of the western desert and had
been sold into slavery together. He returned to Dublin at once
and that same evening asked her to marry him:

> I remember a curious thing. I had come into the room with the purpose
> in my mind and hardly looked at her or thought of her beauty but sat there
> holding her hand and speaking vehemently. She did not take away her
> hand for a while and I ceased to speak and presently as we sat in silence I
> knew my confidence had gone and an instant later she drew her hand away.
> No, she could not marry, there were reasons that she could never marry. . . .
> Her words were not of a conventional ring she asked for my friendship. We
> spent the next day upon the cliffs at Howth, we dined at a little cottage
> near the Baily lighthouse where her old nurse lived and I overheard the
> old nurse ask her if she were engaged to be married. At the day's end I
> found that I had spent ten shillings which seemed to me a very great sum. [57]

The day was responsible for the creation of one of his delicate
dreaming poems, 'The White Birds', published in *The National
Observer* in May 1892:

> I am haunted by numberless islands, and many a Danaan shore,
> Where Time would surely forget us, and Sorrow come near us no more;
> Soon far from the rose and the lily and fret of the flames would we be
> Were we only white birds, my beloved, buoyed out on the foam of the sea.

His note to the poem would be sufficient, 'I have read somewhere that the birds of faeryland are white as snow', yet the
limitless qualities he would have claimed for his symbolism can
be better understood by Madame MacBride's comment on the
poem. She told me that Yeats and she had gone walking on
the cliffs at Howth in the afternoon, and were resting when two
seagulls flew over their heads and out to sea. Maud Gonne
said that if she were to have the choice of being any bird she
would choose to be a seagull above all, a commonplace remark,
but 'in three days he sent me the poem', with its gentle theme:

> I would that we were, my beloved, white birds on the foam of the sea.

The importance of Howth was accentuated by the fact that
Maud Gonne had lived there as a child, and loved its natural
beauty, as she records in her autobiography:

> No place has ever seemed to me quite so lovely as Howth was then. Some-
> times the sea was as blue as Mama's turquoises, more strikingly blue even
> than the Mediterranean because so often grey mists made it invisible and
> mysterious. The little rock pools at the bottom of the high cliffs were very
> dear and full of wonder-life; sea anemones which open look like gorgeous
> flowers with blue and orange spots, and, if touched, close up into ugly
> brown lumps, tiny crabs, pink starfish, endless varieties of sea snails, white,
> green, striped and bright buttercup yellow. . . . The heather grew so high
> and strong there that we could make cubby houses and be entirely hidden
> and entirely warm and sheltered from the strong wind that blows over the

Head of Howth. After I was grown up I have often slept all night in that friendly heather. It is as springy as the finest spring mattress and, if one chooses the place well, so cosy and sheltered and quiet. From deep down in it one looks up at the stars in a wonderful security and falls asleep to wake up only with the call of the sea birds looking for their breakfasts.[58]

He saw her continuously, and read her the unfinished text of *The Countess Kathleen*[59] and noticed that she became moved at the passage 'The joy of losing joy and ceasing all resistance' as though she was hardened by a sense of responsibility to herself. He told her that after their meeting in London he had come to understand the tale of a woman selling her soul to buy bread for her starving people as a symbol of all souls who lose their pence or their fineness or any beauty of the spirit in political service, but chiefly of her soul that seemed to him so incapable of rest. Then there came a message from a secret society in France recalling her for some political action. She told him that she had come to regard its members as self-seeking adventurers but that she could not disobey this, the first difficult summons which the society had sent her. He went to Sligo to stay with George Pollexfen and to complete *The Countess Kathleen*.

A letter from France indicated that Maud Gonne was deeply affected by some personal grief. He went to Dublin to meet her at the Mailboat Pier, where she arrived in the same ship which brought Parnell's body. She was dressed in black, the prevailing Paris fashion, and always wore a black veil for travelling, but many people thought this a theatrical gesture of mourning for Parnell. Yeats learned a little of her sorrows. They were constantly together and again he thought that she must eventually love him; indeed he had a sense of cruelty as if of the hunter confident that he would take this beautiful creature captive. They went to London, and he saw her often at her sister's or her cousin's home. She had told him of the apparition of a woman in grey (whom she has described in *A Servant of the Queen*[60]) and he decided to attempt to make this woman appear at will for he thought it was an evil spirit threatening Maud Gonne's life, weakening her affection and creating a desire for power and excitement. If it were visible he thought that she would meet it with her intellect and then banish it, and he made a symbol to evoke it. It appeared, he wrote in a portion of the unpublished autobiography, 'as if palpably present'. It was, he thought, a spirit personality of hers seeking to be reunited to her.[61]

She seemed to have need of him, and to find consolation in his spiritual philosophy; her need seemed to be turning into love. He had brought her to meetings of the Hermetic Students, and she was initiated as a member, after some initial misgivings. Yeats brought her to a meeting of the Order which was held in a Masonic hall in Euston Road, and she was suspicious that the Order was connected with Freemasonry, which she considered one of the main supports of the British Empire. The hall, she was assured, had merely been borrowed for the occasion, and her suspicions were lulled. After she had passed four initiations and learnt some of the secret signs of the Order, she visited the house of Claude Lane, a prominent mason, and gave some of these signs in the course of conversation. Her host asked her to talk privately with him and expressed his surprise that a woman should know such masonic arcana. She resigned from Mather's Order at once, despite Yeats's attempts to persuade her to remain. She had thought that the members were 'an awful set' and dull; indeed she had been more impressed by Madame Blavatsky who did not forbid political activity, to whom Yeats had brought her before she had joined Mather's Order. All Yeats's talk of the magician Nicholas Flamel and his wife Pernella went for nothing.[62]

It is time to examine the effect which his love had upon his writing in some more detail.

After his proposal and her refusal in the summer of 1891, his position was unsatisfactory and full of strain. He was her close friend, and he had some hope in his own mind that his romantic devotion might have some reward. But he suffered much anxiety and torture on her account as well. He wrote an article in *United Ireland* for August 22nd entitled 'Clarence Mangan's Love Affair'. Mangan had come to know, between his twentieth and twenty-fifth years, a Miss Stacpoole who 'was a fascinating coquette, amused herself with his devotion, and then whistled him down the wind'. There is much understanding shown in Yeats's picture of Mangan's reaction. The date of the article supports the suggestion that this understanding may have been caused by his own unlucky experience:

When a man's love affair goes bankrupt, romance makers assure us, a little devil gets into the soles of his feet and drives him hither and hither, on into his heart and makes him seek out some exciting activity, but for Clarence Mangan there was nothing but scrivening—scrivening; he could only watch his labouring quill travelling over ream after ream of paper.

Yeats covered reams of paper himself, and he also sought out exciting activity. The contradiction of his love, hopeful devotion, more hopelessly involved, was evident as his friendship continued. Many years after he was to write:

My devotion might as well have been offered to an image in a milliner's shop, or to a statue in a museum, but romantic doctrine had reached its extreme development.[63]

He sought reasons for her unhappiness and began to attempt to persuade her that her political activities were swamping her more noble qualities. Presently he was to turn to political activity himself, partly to win her praise, partly for the sake of activity, partly because of his own ambitions. But in old age he understood more clearly and looked back on his writings:

> And then a counter truth filled out its play,
> The Countess Cathleen[63a] was the name I gave it;
> She, pity crazed, had given her soul away,
> But masterful Heaven had intervened to save it.
> I thought my dear must her own soul destroy,
> So did fanaticism and hate enslave it,
> And this brought forth a dream and soon enough
> This dream itself had all my thought and love.[64]

Maud Gonne had helped in the relief work among the peasants in Donegal who were overcome with famine. As a result of over-strain she was threatened with consumption and spent some time on the Continent recovering. Yeats was worried. He sent her 'A Dream of Death' when she was convalescing:

I was getting steadily better and was greatly amused when Willie Yeats sent me a poem, my epitaph he had written with much feeling:

> I dreamed that one had died in a strange place
> Near no accustomed hand;
> And they had nailed the boards above her face,
> The peasants of that land,
> And wondering, planted by her solitude
> A cypress and a yew.
> I came and wrote upon a cross of wood
> —Man had no more to do—
> 'She was more beautiful than thy first love
> This lady by the trees',
> And gazed upon the mournful stars above
> And heard the mournful breeze.[65]

This poem was published in December 1891. His play The Countess Kathleen was published in 1892, and with it were included 'Various Legends and Lyrics'. Initially the play had been intended to convince her of his ability to write as well for the limelight as the twilight. With her illness and her unhappi-

ness there must have been much revision to present her as in
danger of losing her soul by her passion for compassion. The
plot of the play is simple. Two agents of the devil come to
Ireland in time of famine, and take advantage of the starvation
of the peasants to offer to buy their souls for gold. The Countess
Kathleen, hearing of this, sacrifices her own goods to get money
that she may buy food for the people and so prevent them
selling their souls to the demons. The national aspect of the
play was obvious. Yeats wrote in his Preface:

> The chief poem is an attempt to mingle personal thought and feeling
> with the beliefs and customs of Christian Ireland; whereas the longest
> poems in my earlier book endeavoured to set forth the impress left on my
> imagination by the Pre-Christian cycle of legends. The Christian cycle
> being mainly concerned with contending moods and moral motives needed,
> I thought, a dramatic vehicle. The tumultuous and heroic Pagan cycles on
> the other hand, having to do with vast and shadowy activities and with the
> great impersonal emotions expressed itself naturally—or so I imagined—in
> epic and lyric measure. No epic method seemed sufficiently minute and
> subtle for the one, and no dramatic method elastic and all-containing for
> the other. Ireland having a huge body of tradition behind her in the depths
> of time will probably draw her deepest literary inspiration from this double
> fountain head if she ever, as is the hope of all her children, makes for herself
> a great distinctive poetic literature. She has already many roving songs and
> ballads which are quite her own. The 'Countess Cathleen' like the 'Wander-
> ings of Oisin' is an attempt to write a more ample method to feeling not
> less national, Celtic and distinctive.

The play gives us a picture of Yeats's own position *vis-à-vis*
his princess; he is symbolised as the bard Kevin, Maud Gonne
as Kathleen:

OONA: See you where Oisin and young Niam ride
    Wrapped in each other's arms, and where the Finians
    Follow their hounds along the fields of tapestry,
    How merry they lived once, yet men died then.
    I'll sing the ballad young bard Kevin sang
    By the great door, the light about his head,
    When he bid you cast off this cloud of care.

KATHLEEN: Sing how King Fergus in his brazen car
    Drove with a troop of dancers through the woods . . .
    A sad resolve awakes in me. I have heard
    A sound of wailing in unnumbered hovels,
    And I must go down, down, I know not where.
    Pray for the poor folk who are crazed with famine;
    Pray, you good neighbours.

This picture of Kathleen's resolve is due to Maud Gonne's
experiences in Donegal; she has recounted her reactions in
*A Servant of the Queen*.[66]
Yeats, it might be pointed out, had become interested in the

legend of Fergus, and included two lyrics on the theme of the
king who gave up his kingdom for poetry—'Who Goes With
Fergus?' and 'Fergus and the Druid' (published in *The National
Observer* in May 1892). Kevin, the bard, is a projection of
Yeats, and shows the effect of Maud Gonne's refusal to marry
him; life seemed at times futile without hope; and he offers his
soul to the demons:

KEVIN (*a young man who carries a harp with torn wires*):
    Here take my soul, for I am tired of it;
    I do not ask a price.

1ST MERCHANT (*reading*): A man of songs—
    Alone in the hushed passion of romance,
    His mind ran all on sheogues, and on tales
    Of Finian labours and the Red-branch kings,
    And he cared nothing for the life of man:
    But now all changes.

KEVIN: Aye, because her face,
    The face of Countess Kathleen dwells with me.
    The sadness of the world upon her brow—
    The crying of these strings grew burdensome,
    Therefore I tore them—see—now take my soul.

1ST MERCHANT: We cannot take your soul, for it is hers.

KEVIN: Ah, take it—take it. It nowise can help her,
    And therefore do I tire of it.

1ST MERCHANT: No—no——
    We may not touch it.

KEVIN: Is your power so small,
    Must I then bear it with me all my days?
    May scorn close deep about you.

1ST MERCHANT: Lead him hence. He troubles me. . . .

SHEMUS: He is called Kevin
    And has been crazy now these many days;
    But has no harm in him: his fits soon pass
    And one can go and lead home like a child.

Yeats again appears to speak in the person of Kevin when
Kathleen is on the point of selling her soul: he rushes forward,
snatches the parchment from her and says:

    You shall yet know the love of some great chief
    And children gathering round your knees. Leave you
    The peasants to the builder of the heavens.

He thought marriage would be a refuge for Maud from the
world which interested her. He could not foresee that she

would tell Lady Gregory at the close of a decade that she and
Willie were not the sort of people who should marry. He did
not understand people, and especially not Maud Gonne; yet
he thought he could alter her life and her character:

It was years before I could see into the mind that lay hidden under so
much beauty and so much energy.[67]

Before Kathleen dies there is a passage in the play which
connects Kevin more closely to Yeats, if we remember that
he had sent Maud a poem about his dream of her death:

I peered out through the window in the passage,
And saw bard Kevin wandering in the wood;
Sometimes he laid his head upon the ground.
They say he hears the sheogues down below
Nailing four boards. . . .
For love has made him crazy
And loneliness and famine dwell with him.

His admiration of the English poets (he described the opening
lyric of *The Countess Kathleen* as echoing the rhyme of Morris),
especially of the poets whom he met in the Rhymers' Club, led
him into obscurity in the poems which he included in *The
Countess Kathleen and Various Legends and Lyrics*, especially those
dealing with the rose. His own notes do not clear up the
symbolism of these poems very clearly; in the 1892 edition he
wrote by way of explanation that:

The rose is a favourite symbol with the Irish poets. It has given a name
to more than one poem, both Gaelic and English, and is used, not merely
in love poems, but in poems addressed to Ireland, as in De Vere's line 'The
little black rose shall be red at last' and in Mangan's 'Dark Rosaleen'. I
do not, of course, use it in this sense.

A note, dated 1925, is slightly more explicit:

I notice upon reading these poems for the first time for several years that
the quality symbolized as The Rose differs from Intellectual Beauty of
Shelley and of Spenser in that I have imagined it as suffering with man and
not as something pursued and seen from far.

A passage in *Autobiographies*, however, gives another explanation which contributes to the fuller understanding of the Rose
poems:

I had an unshakable conviction, arising how or whence I cannot tell,
that invisible gates would open as they opened for Blake, as they opened for
Swedenborg, as they opened for Boehme, and that this philosophy would
find its manuals of devotion in all imaginative literature and set before
Irishmen for special manual an Irish literature which, though made by
many minds, would seem the work of a single mind, and turn our places
of beauty or legendary association into holy symbols. I did not think this
philosophy would be altogether pagan, for it was plain that its symbols must
be selected from all those things that have moved men most during many,

mainly Christian, centuries. I thought for a time I could rhyme of love, calling it The Rose, because of the Rose's double meaning; of a fisherman who had 'never a crack' in his heart; of an old woman complaining of the idleness of the young, or of some cheerful fiddler, all those things that 'popular poets' write of, but that I must some day—on that day when the gates began to open—become difficult or obscure. With a rhythm that still echoed Morris I prayed to the Red Rose, to Intellectual Beauty:

> Come near, come near, come near,—Ah, leave me still
> A little space for the Rose-breath to fill,
> Lest I no more hear common things. . . .
> But seek alone to hear the strange things said
> By God to the bright hearts of those long dead,
> And learn to chant a tongue men do not know.[68]

Madame MacBride (Maud Gonne) has informed me that these Rose poems were also written to her. Yeats's statement that he symbolised love by the Rose is equivalent to saying that he was symbolising his love for her. The 'Rose of the World' proves this, as its first verse

> Who dreamed that beauty passes like a dream?
> For these red lips, with all their mournful pride,
> Mournful that no new wonder may betide,
> Troy passed away in one high funeral gleam,
> And Usna's children died[69]

makes use of the Helen symbol,[70] which is always used to describe Maud Gonne elsewhere. The Rose poems are then a mixture of intellectual beauty[71] and Maud's beauty. The earlier of the Rose poems were slightly over-esoteric; Yeats described English poetry as a terrible queen in whose service the stars rose and set,[72] while his own poem, 'The Rose of Peace', verges on this idea (put in the language of poetry which was at this time restricted by Yeats to the more beautiful or romantic aspects of his subjects) with its line:

> And white stars tell all your praises.[73]

'The Rose of Peace' was written under English influence, and 'To the Rose upon the Rood of Time' shows Yeats ready to return to Irish subjects lest he 'hear no more the common things that crave'.[74] The epilogue to the volume, *To Ireland in the Coming Time*, defends this obscurity as well as Yeats's patriotism, which, though difficult to follow, is to be thought none the less sincere and valuable by the fanatical Young Irelanders:

> Nor may I less be counted one
> With Davis, Mangan, Ferguson,
> Because, to him who ponders well,
> My rhymes more than their rhyming tell. . . .[75]

There were other love poems in the volume besides the Rose series and these were also written to Maud Gonne. These were 'When You are Old', 'The Pity of Love', 'The Sorrow of Love', 'A Dream of Death', 'Countess Kathleen', 'The White Birds', and 'The Two Trees'.[76] There is a division to be made between poems which draw upon the Celtic legends and those which owe their inspiration to localised memories of places. The Celtic subject-matter gave Yeats an opportunity to laud the dreamer over the man of action in 'Fergus and the Druid':

> A king is but a foolish labourer
> Who wastes his blood to be another's dream.[77]

Just as he later thought that his mystical order in Ireland must select its symbols from all sources, so he selected subject-matter which suited his poetic purpose. Again, he selected a West of Ireland legend as a source for 'The Death of Cuchullin', because it suited his purpose better than the bardic tradition.[78] Another localised poem is 'A Faery Song'[79] which is described in later editions as 'sung by the people of Faery over Diarmuid and Grania, in their bridal sleep under a Cromlech'. The 1892 edition described the poem as 'sung by the good people over Michael Dwyer and his bride, who had escaped into the mountains'. There is a note of direct and simple autobiography in 'The Man who Dreamed of Faeryland', especially in the lines:

> He wandered by the sands of Lissadell;
> His mind ran all on money cares and fears. . . .[80]

He used to return to Sligo in the summer months when his money was exhausted, as he could live with his relatives there.

The incidental poems are perhaps the most interesting in that they show how ready Yeats was to adopt an idea and use any scraps of conversation or incident for the making of a poem. At this stage of his development writing was a slow process, as he recorded in *Autobiographies*:

Metrical composition is always very difficult for me, nothing is done upon the first day, not one rhyme is in its place; and when at last the rhymes begin to come, the first rough draft of a six line stanza takes the whole day. At that time I had not formed a style and sometimes a six line stanza would take several days, and not seem finished even then; and I had not learned, as I have now, to put it all out of my head before night, and so the last night was generally sleepless, and the last day a day of nervous strain.[81]

Sometimes he wrote the poem almost directly from what he had heard. 'The Ballad of Father Gilligan', for example, is based on tradition of the people of Castleisland, County Kerry.[82] 'A Cradle Song', which was rewritten by Henley, is due to two lines remembered from Griffin's *Collegians*,[83] 'The Lamentation of the Old Pensioner', so drastically rewritten later, is 'little more than a translation into verse of the very words of an old Wicklow peasant'.[84] *The Celtic Twilight* gives a fuller account of the poem's source. Yeats's friend was George Russell:

A winter or two ago he spent much of the night walking up and down upon the mountain talking to an old peasant who, dumb to most men, poured out his cares for him. Both were unhappy: X because he had then first decided that art and poetry were not for him, and the old peasant because his life was ebbing out with no achievement remaining and no hope left him. Both how Celtic! How full of striving after a something never to be completely expressed in word or deed. The peasant was wandering in his mind with prolonged sorrow. Once he burst out with 'God possesses the heavens but he covets the earth' and once he lamented that his old neighbours were gone and that all had forgotten him: they used to draw a chair to the fire for him in every cabin, and now they said 'Who is that old fellow there?' 'The fret [Irish for doom] is over me', as he repeated, and then went on to talk once more of God and Heaven. More than once he said, waving his arm towards the mountain, 'Only myself knows what happened under the thorn tree forty years ago'; and as he said it the tears upon his face glistened in the moonlight. This old man always rises before me when I think of X. Both seek—one in wandering sentences, the other in symbolic pictures and subtle allegoric poetry—to express something that lies beyond the range of expression; and both, if X will forgive me, have within them the vast and vague extravagance that lies at the bottom of the Celtic heart. The peasant visionaries that are, the landlord duellists that were, and the whole hurly burly of legends—Cuchullin fighting the sea for two days until the waves pass over him and he dies, Caolte storming the palace of the Gods, Oisin seeking in vain for three hundred years, to appease his insatiable heart with all the pleasures of faeryland, these two mystics walking up and down upon the mountain uttering the central dream of their souls in no less dream-laden sentences, and this mind that finds X so interesting—all are a portion of that great Celtic phantasmagoria whose meaning no man has discovered nor any angel revealed.[85]

Put into verse this anecdote became:

> I had a chair at every hearth
> When no one turned to see,
> With 'Look at the old fellow there,
> And who may he be?'
> And therefore do I wander on,
> And the fret lies on me.
>
> The roadside trees keep murmuring
> Ah, wherefore murmur ye,
> As in the old days long gone by,
> Green oak and poplar tree?
> The well known faces are all gone
> And the fret lies on me.[86]

It is customary to quote 'The Sorrow of Love'[87] as an example
of Yeats's rewriting of these early poems, but 'The Lamentation
of the Old Pensioner' serves equally well, for Yeats's revised
version contains all the later realism and strength of his later
verse. The two versions are different poems, as are most of the
revised verses:

> Although I shelter from the rain
> Under a broken tree,
> My chair was nearest to the fire
> In every company
> That talked of love or politics,
> Ere Time transfigured me.
>
> Though lads are making pikes again
> For some conspiracy,
> And crazy rascals rage their fill
> At human tyranny;
> My contemplations are of Time
> That has transfigured me.
>
> There's not a woman turns her face
> Upon a broken tree,
> And yet the beauties that I loved
> Are in my memory;
> I spit into the face of Time
> That has transfigured me.[88]

Yeats also drew from varying literary models. There is a
vast difference between the somewhat crude ballads of 'Father
O'Hart', a story drawn from the pages of the local history of
Ballisodare and Kilvarnet,[89] and that of 'The Old Fox
Hunter' from an incident in Kickham's *Knocknagow*,[90] and the
delicate and sensitive love poem 'When You are Old' which
is founded upon Ronsard's sonnet to Hélène de Surgères:

> Quand vous serez bien vieille, au soir, à la chandelle,
> Assise auprès du feu, dévidant et filant,
> Direz, chantant mes vers, et vous esmerveillant. . . .

Forrest Reid very rightly decided that the greatest[91] advance
had been made in the love poems of *The Countess Kathleen*, a
natural result of Yeats's falling in love, and quoted 'When
You are Old' in illustration:

> When you are old and gray and full of sleep,
> And nodding by the fire, take down this book
> And slowly read, and dream of the soft look
> Your eyes had once, and of their shadows deep;
>
> How many loved your moments of glad grace,
> And loved your beauty with false love or true;
> But one man loved the pilgrim soul in you,
> And loved the sorrows of your changing face.

> And bending down beside the glowing bars,
> Murmur, a little sadly, how love fled
> And paced upon the mountains overhead
> And hid his face amid a crowd of stars.[92]

The dignity and gentleness of this poem are immensely moving, and it reveals the all-pervading nature of Yeats's love. The selflessness of his concern for his lady is shown in 'The Two Trees', a less direct poem, in which the beloved is asked to gaze in her own heart; but Maud

never indulged in self-analysis and often used to get impatient with Willie Yeats, who, like all writers, was terribly introspective and tried to make me so. 'I have no time to think of myself', I told him which was literally true, for unconsciously perhaps, I had redoubled work to avoid thought.[93]

He exhorted her to

> Gaze no more in the bitter glass
> The demons, with their subtle guile,
> Lift up before us when they pass,
> Or only gaze a little while . . .
>
> For all things turn to barrenness
> In the dim glass the demons hold,
> The glass of outer weariness,
> Made when God slept in times of old.[94]

'The Two Trees' is considerably more esoteric than the Rose poems,[95] and marks a transition in style between them and the love of *The Wind Among the Reeds* (1899) which is the ultimate refinement of Yeats's restricted expression of a love which only admitted the contemplation of an exalted beauty and an exalted sorrow.

It must not be supposed that Yeats's poetic path had been straight. Having apparently found a larger field and motives for his work in the use of Gaelic legends for subject-matter Yeats wrote 'The Wanderings of Oisin.' This long poem marked a distinct advance on anything that had gone before: its scope was far greater than any of the poems which he had included with it in 1889. We might expect his next volume to have contained a development of this new outlook; if his poetic path was one of steady progress there should have been a consolidation of the mental advance that had led him from a static plot to one of incidents, from local legends to mythology. Instead we find that there is almost the same division to be made among his next poems as there was in *The Wanderings of Oisin*, that between local and national. Again the difference marks a great advance in his conception of his poetic purpose. His local poetry in *The Countess Kathleen* is now on the level of the national purpose of Oisin; his national poetry has begun to be enriched with European qualities. The difference in his mental attitude can be seen in the motives underlying the creation of two poems, 'The Lake Isle of Innisfree' which has been discussed, and 'To the Rose upon the Rood of Time' with its conscious purpose:

> . . . I would before my time to go,
> Sing of old Eire and the ancient ways:
> Red Rose, proud Rose, sad Rose of all my days.

This changing in Yeats was a zigzag process. When he began writing he hurled himself away in pursuit of the shades of Spenser and Shelley; then veered in the opposite direction hunting after local legends, ballads, and fairies; became aware of more important and wider fields to be explored with 'The Wanderings of Oisin' and its few secret symbols; then hankered after Innisfree and Faeryland once more with deeper longing strengthened by his city-dwelling; again sought broader Irish themes with an increasing interest in European symbolism.

It is not necessary or correct to judge between the two extremes. It is not even very easy to attempt to do so. 'The Wanderings of Oisin' shows an advance in technique over the narrower poems of its volume; equally so 'The Lake Isle of Innisfree' deserves its popularity over the poems of sometimes larger vision which accompany it. The reason why one poem is successful, another not as strikingly so, is that Yeats was writing out of his emotions. 'The Wanderings of Oisin' and 'The Lake Isle of Innisfree' were written out of a different intellectual idea, and intellectual ideas can be compared; but each was written out of a similarly great emotional fervour, and no one, not even Yeats, could estimate the relative reality of emotion behind separate poems. This is why some of the love poems misfire, because the emotion was not a complete force. The emotion was being compelled into the matrix of the poem's form, but it was also being forced to conform to a romantic doctrine which could have been estimable had it been a thing of the intellect, but it was itself an emotion. Therefore what must be recognised is the parallel advance in technique and experience, a steady movement: the swinging of the pendulum was but marking the passing of time; and time is very necessary for a slow-maturing genius. If the progress is seen, then the variety and elusiveness of mind which were equally fervent at each extreme must be welcomed. Again, the ultimate achievement was the movement towards a greater unity of the man and the poet; the complex character of Yeats can only be understood by an examination of the many threads which made it.

# 4

# ANTICLIMAX
## (1891–1896)

*All things, apart from love and melancholy, were a study to us.*

W. B. YEATS

*Certainly I had gone a great distance from my first poems, from all
that I had copied from the folk art of Ireland . . . and yet why am I so
certain?*

W. B. YEATS

THE general explanation of the outburst of literary activity
which constituted the Anglo-Irish or Celtic literary revival, and
the support which this movement gained, is that there was a
reaction against politics after the fall of Parnell had created a
feeling of frustration in most Irish minds. Yeats had indeed
prophesied this contingency:

> A couple of years before the death of Parnell, I had wound up my
> introduction to those selections from the Irish novelists with the prophecy
> of an intellectual movement at the first lull in politics. I did not put it in
> that way, for I preferred to think that the sudden emotion that now came
> to me, the sudden certainty that Ireland was to be like soft wax for years
> to come, was a moment of supernatural insight. How could I tell, how can
> I tell even now?[1]

He preferred to think that there was a moment of insight.
He gave this conscious reason for the zest with which he entered
upon his crusade; yet there were other causes, for John
O'Leary's teaching and the patriotism of the Young Ireland
Society both played their part in preparing him for his role
in the literary movement; but Maud Gonne's fanaticism was
one of the main reasons for his approach to this self-appointed
task. In many of his later retrospective poems he saw in her
the inspiration of his work:

> O heart, be at peace, because
> Nor knave nor dolt can break
> What's not for their applause,
> Being for a woman's sake.[2]

The first step was to form a new Literary Society in London.[3]
He collected together the most energetic members of a Southwark Irish Society whose meetings he had attended with

Todhunter, and told them of his plans for a new movement. The tact and efficiency of T. W. Rolleston, who had also been invited to this informal meeting in Bedford Park, led to the foundation of the London Irish Literary Society. Shortly afterwards Yeats crossed to Dublin and there founded the National Literary Society.[3a] The leading figure in the Dublin Society was its President, John O'Leary. He aided Yeats in his criticisms of the 'Young Ireland' patriotism and its verse; but the opposition to this criticism was strong, for these songs and verses were written primarily from patriotic rather than literary motives. Yeats 'upon the other hand, being in the intemperance of my youth, denied, as publicly as possible, merit to all but a few ballads translated from Gaelic writers, or written out of a personal and generally tragic experience'.[4] He was not occupied with destructive tasks, however, for he toured many parts of Ireland, persuading Young Ireland Societies to add themselves to his new movement. The initial organisation went well. He planned a series of books to be published by Fisher Unwin, whose reader, Edward Garnett, was a friend of his. Before his selections could be decided upon Sir Charles Gavan Duffy, lately returned from Australia, in conjunction with one of the members of the London Irish Society, had offered their series to Fisher Unwin and had had it accepted. Yeats was furious at being forestalled and the affair grew complicated towards the end of 1892 as the inevitable political quarrel accompanied the literary problem as to what exactly should be published. Yeats represented the Parnellite faction, and disliked Sir Charles Gavan Duffy's wish to reprint old writings. Eventually after much dispute Hyde and Rolleston were chosen as editors of the series, which contained O'Grady's *Bog of Stars* and Hyde's *History of Gaelic Literature*. The inclusion of a rather dull unpublished work by Thomas Davis eventually killed interest in the venture.[5]

After the matter of the book publishing there came another difference, this time over a project which Yeats had put into operation, with the ultimate aim of establishing an audience for a travelling theatre. He had planned libraries of Irish literature for the country branches, and these were partially to be achieved from the proceeds of lectures given by Maud Gonne. The books were chosen for the country branches but appropriated for use in Dublin and the trouble came from half a dozen obscure young men, who having nothing to do attended every meeting and were able to overturn a project, that seemed my only bridge to other projects.[6]

O'Leary had warned him of the consequence of his behaviour some time before; he should not have lived on terms of intimacy with those whom he wished to influence but he had not been able to resist the charm of the listeners who always abound in Dublin, and

had sat talking in public bars, had talked late into the night at many men's houses, showing all my convictions to men that were but ready for one, and used conversation to explore and discover among men who looked for authority.[7]

All this activity had begun after he had met Maud Gonne on that morning on which Parnell's body was brought back to Ireland and had found her so unhappy and more ready than usual to listen to his convictions. He wrote a poem 'Mourn and then onward' which was published in *United Ireland*, a bad poem, and one which was written on a political event, contrary to his poetic principle of choosing only specialised subjects and the beautiful aspects of them. He thought he must set Maud Gonne to some new work, for he knew her energy would soon return. His account of the creation of the movement, interspersed with his concern for Maud, is recorded interestingly in his unpublished autobiography.

Mysticism, which fascinated him, was not enough to hold Maud's interest. He began to take a more active part in life himself. The influence of the Young Ireland Movement upon him had been that when he was first in London he had hoped to return to Ireland to found some similar organisation and movement; but he had gradually begun to think the idea absurd. Now, suddenly, he rushed into the vacuum caused by the death of Parnell with the aim of establishing societies and influencing newspapers. There was a division within him. The newer self, which found his ambitions for Ireland absurd, mocked his new efforts which his other self justified as being attempts to create a substitute for the critical press Ireland needed but could not support. He convicted himself of insincerity, of seeking a work which was undemoralising, especially for Maud, whose soul he thought distinguished and subtle, mainly on account of her beauty but also through an instinctive feeling that she might achieve peace if she lived among artists and writers.

It seemed to him that with the death of Parnell all romance had left Irish public life and that youthful national feeling would seek unpolitical channels for some years to come. He had occasionally lectured to a small society of Irish men and women in Southwark, but this society had ceased to meet as the women had taken to laughing at the lectures, which were always the' same. Yeats disliked flippancy on Irish subjects which seemed sacred. For instance, T. W. Rolleston, who had been appointed editor of *The Dublin University Review* at Yeats's suggestion, was first judged by his physical beauty which seemed akin to that of a Greek statue; but later he was considered 'an intimate enemy' and 'a hollow image' because he never seemed to Yeats to believe in the cause that he served faithfully. He was, in fact, the true founder of the Irish Literary Society. Though the first general idea was Yeats's, Rolleston understood how to run a society, resolutions and amendments being at that time unknown and terrifying territory to Yeats. When the two quarrelled over what should be done with the money collected for a library scheme, Yeats thought Rolleston's idea of spending the money on lectures restrictive. His own aims were more popular and it seemed to him that they could more easily be realised through a new society with a wider appeal. He had therefore gone to Dublin in a rage and sought out a butter merchant whose name he had got at Southwark, and the National Literary Society was planned on a butter tub. Yeats had acquired some knowledge of resolutions and amendments now, and had got his own way more easily. He had had John O'Leary elected President, and after he had resigned, Dr Douglas Hyde, followed by Dr Sigerson. He was pleased by the newspaper comment on the new enterprise and remembered long afterwards the contemporary saying that 'a new Ireland had been born, the Ireland of Davis'.

He seemed to himself for the only time in his life to be 'the popular personage, my name known to the crowd, and remembered in the affections of the wise'.

In his political activity the one indispensable figure was John O'Leary, whose personality towered above the other nationalists. O'Leary suggested that Yeats should take a lodging in the same house, and the young man often spent the day trying to persuade the old Fenian leader of the correctness of a resolution he wanted the Society to pass, or the desirability of some book he wished to have published. O'Leary had certain

formulae which were constantly repeated and Yeats, though
often agreeing with these, spent many days in argument upon
the correct method of applying them.

The other personalities of the movement were sufficiently
unusual to attract his attention. J. F. Taylor and he were
often at cross purposes; Yeats's quotation from Blake that 'it
is ordained that those who cannot defend the truth shall defend
an error that enthusiasm in life may not cease' put him in a
furious rage for he thought error could have no justification.
He was impassioned in his eloquence, and Yeats thought that
this was all he understood, that at times he even gave an
impression of insincerity. At first Taylor had terrified him;
later he noticed that though Taylor knew plays of Shakespeare by heart, and all the famous passages in Milton, he
knew nothing of poetry or painting:

> A gaunt ungainly man whose mind was perpetually occupied with an im-
> personal argument to which he brought vast histrionic erudition upon the
> justice of the native cause.[8]

Dr Sigerson, a friend of O'Leary's, was another patriot. At
first he impressed Yeats, for he spoke with a curious accent and
gave the impression of having played the part before ignorant
men of a great savant, a great foreign scientist. He fenced with
all of Yeats's arguments, avoiding their thrust, and after a
while Yeats found that Sigerson never revealed any convictions
of his own. He was kind and generous, as was Richard King,
a novelist who lived in a little cottage outside Dublin, whose
life Yeats troubled, for he persuaded him to write unpopular
truths. King was amazed that a man should be disliked for an
idea. Dr Douglas Hyde was another who, like Sigerson, did
not seem to Yeats to speak his real thoughts. He told Yeats,
who was on a brief visit to him in Connaught, that he was the
only man from Dublin who had ever stayed at his home because
he was afraid that 'they would draw me into their quarrels'.
It appeared to Yeats that he was diplomatising and evading
any prominent position among his fellows in order to escape
jealousy or distinction.

Professor Oldham was a member of the Society but took little
active part in it. He was often rude, yet himself sensitive to
adverse criticism. His morality amused Yeats:

> Another night he arrived to see the servant of a neighbouring house
> letting out a young man and had at once written and posted her a letter

of moral admonition. When he got up the next morning about noon he saw a cab at the neighbour's front door and the girl's box hoisted upon it. Unable to read she had carried the letter to her mistress.[8]

In *Autobiographies* he tells the story of Oldham providing necessary utensils for a hotel in the west of Ireland where some visiting French members of a political society had arrived. Oldham replied to the landlady's anger at this insult by saying 'I must consider the reputation of my country'. In later years it seemed to Yeats that this attitude, of considering the reputation of their country, led these patriots to excess, for they were driven to form opinions on matters beyond their experience. They were mainly opposed to Yeats and disregarded his theories on the importance of poetry as compared to political rhetoric.

He immersed himself in work. Activity and enthusiasm abounded. The National Literary Society formed committees and sub-committees, and one of these sub-committees resigned and became the Gaelic League:

We had dropped into the chemical solution the crystal that caused the whole mass to drop its crystals.

The history of the movement was published in book form a few months after the first meeting and on one visit to London Yeats dissuaded the Council from passing a circular which began:

Ireland despite the dramatic genius of our people has had no dramatist like Shakespeare, but a sub-committee of the Irish Literary Society has decided that the time has come . . .

He persuaded Maud Gonne, for whose sake he had entered upon this adventure, to take up the part he had planned for her, the formation of branches of the movement throughout Ireland. She was beautiful and eloquent, and he praised both her beauty and her eloquence in articles in *United Ireland*, and besides she had the necessary money to travel and could have a great influence upon the small country towns where life now seemed to Yeats so very dull. She was to become the fiery hand of the intellectual movement. He too for a time became a popular personality. He organised a literary scheme by which new books would be given to any group who could form a basic collection of books of Irish literature—the group having to arrange public lectures, half the proceeds of which would be given to the central society. The branches might form support for a travelling theatre, an idea of which was often in the poet's mind, for which he had thought of writing a play on the life and death of Robert Emmet.

His hope that this work would keep Maud out of dangerous activity was not realised. While he busied himself in work which was not congenial, for he was still shy and still hated crowds, and worked mainly through a desire to please her, she had found a more exciting task. After the fall of Parnell the cause of the tenants who had been evicted was no longer taken up by the political parties because political energy had gone into the disputes between Parnellites and anti-Parnellites. Irishmen who were in prison on charges of attempting to blow up public buildings were in bad health, and neither political party would take up their cause. Maud Gonne felt responsible for some of these men, and decided to lecture in France on their behalf as she thought that England's good name would be most vulnerable there. Her French contacts were good. M. Maynard placed *Le Figaro* at her disposal and her lectures, first delivered in Paris, then in the provinces, were a great success. This success moved Yeats, but he wondered if the few dynamiters released from prison or the few tenants restored to their holdings were sufficient gain for all her toil. He was dreaming of a general co-ordination of intellectual and political power; yet he thought her emotional oratory linked to something uncontrollable—something never to be co-ordinated. And his Dublin world did not see her powers as clearly as he did:

O'Leary saw but a beautiful woman seeking excitement and Miss Sarah Purser said, continuing her pictorial interpretation, 'Maud Gonne talks politics at Paris and Literature to you and at the Horse Show she could talk of a clinking brood mare'.[9] I always defended her, though I was full of disquiet—I said often 'None of you understand her force of character'. She came to Ireland again and again and often to the West where through her efforts all the tenants who had found some [combination] through her influence were restored to their houses and farms. When in Dublin we were always together and she collected books for our country branches and founded I think three of the seven branches which are all we ever attained to, but it was no longer possible for her to become that 'fiery hand'. Till some political project came into her head she was the woman I had come to love.

She lived as ever surrounded by dogs and birds and I became gradually aware of many charities—old women or old men past work were always seeking her out; and I began to notice a patience beyond my reach in handling birds or beasts. I could play with bird or beast half the day but I was not patient with its obstinacy. She seemed to understand every subtlety of my own art and especially all my spiritual philosophy and I was still full of William Blake and sometimes she would say I had saved her from despair.[10] We worked much with symbols.

. . . I heard much scandal about her but dismissed the grossest scandal at once and one persistent story I put away with the thought 'She would have told me if it were true'. It had come to seem as if the intimacy of our minds could not be greater and I explain the fact that marriage seemed to have slipped further away by my own immaturity and lack of achievement. One night when going to sleep I had seen suddenly a thimble, and a shapeless white mass that puzzled me. Next day on passing a tobacconist's I saw that it was a lump of meerschaum not yet made into a pipe. She was complete and I was not.

He came to hate her politics. One day when somebody had sent her a hawk from Donegal she gave up a political canvass to play with the bird to Yeats's great delight. The political candidate she was supporting was defeated. She was enraged, and told Yeats that but for him the man would have been returned. He could not think that the day they had spent was worth spoiling for the sake of another Irish member. There were so few days, and, besides, he felt that the movement he was beginning to organise would settle political problems in due time. They quarrelled, and the estrangement remained even after she had been to France and returned. He found that though she approved of his work she took the quarrels of the movement too lightly, as the mere disputes of friends. His emotions were harassed by jealousy:

Maud Gonne made me jealous by the strain upon my nerves by means of that perplexed wooing,

and, as a result, the quarrels of the movement became of great significance. The intellectual future of Ireland seemed at stake and Yeats found Sir Charles Gavan Duffy a troublesome opponent. His own desire was to make it an experience to be able to say with Walt Whitman 'I convince as a sleeping child convinces'. This was not a formidable aim, and he thought Ireland did not at all need to be formidable. His dreams of subordinating political to intellectual aims continued, but he had to fight a long battle with the secret hope of acquiring the forsaken leadership. He had constantly to oppose the publication of work which Gavan Duffy thought essential. There were fierce arguments. Dr Sigerson and J. F. Taylor sided with the older man, Taylor touched by the spectacle of an old man returning to take up the patriotic work of his youth afresh. Yeats, however, was too concerned with the future of Irish literature to be touched, and the more fiercely attacked, with John O'Leary's support, the patriotic verse of the Young Ireland Movement, in particular *The Spirit of a Nation*. For this he was accused of being under English influence, perhaps

of English-descended poets.  Committee meetings in Dublin
were so spirited, and passions ran so high, between Yeats and
Taylor, that ordinary business was laid aside for the while and
strangers came into the room with no one sufficiently disengaged
to turn them out:

> I took it all with the seriousness that amazes my more tolerant years
> believing as I did years before at the school debating society that I stood
> with Plato.  To Taylor, to Sigerson perhaps, I was but an over confident
> young man who had interrupted a charming compliment to an old states-
> man at the end of his career.

During these years of excitement, of preoccupation with love
and the literary revival, Yeats was publishing steadily.  In
1892, in addition to the *Countess Kathleen and Various Legends and
Lyrics*, he had compiled *Irish Fairy Tales*, illustrated by his
brother.  This little book included an appendix with a classification of Irish fairies into two groups, the sociable and the
solitary.  The edition of Blake undertaken in collaboration
with Edwin Ellis appeared in 1893 and was followed by a selection of Blake's poems edited by Yeats with an enthusiastic
introduction.  This year saw the appearance of *The Celtic
Twilight*, a collection of essays most of which had been published
previously in various periodicals.

The poems of *The Countess Kathleen* (except for the Rose
poems) and the essays of *The Celtic Twilight* mark the conclusion of a straightforward period of writing.  There is but the
beginning of mystery in these volumes, the mystery that culmi-
nated in the verse of *The Wind Among the Reeds* (1899) and in
the stories of *The Secret Rose* (1897).  Earlier writings were
included in *The Countess Kathleen*, such as 'The Ballad of Father
O'Hart', a poem founded upon a story told by the Rev. T. F.
O'Rorke in his parish history, a trivial ballad with a jingling
metre.[11]  'The Ballad of the Foxhunter' shows more skill except
for a somewhat staccato conclusion enforced by the rhyme
scheme:

> The blind hound with a mournful din
> Lifts slow his wintry head;
> The servants bear the body in;
> The hounds wail for the dead.[12]

But it is equally obvious, and represents Yeats's desire to
write of Irish subjects with a patriotic object, yet without
pandering to the political sentimentalism that had marred the
earlier Young Ireland writers who had admired the ballad form.

The other poems in the volume are written out of the same ambition, but with greater richness and deeper personal emotion. Yeats's own character was colouring 'The Lake Isle of Innisfree', 'Fergus and the Druid', 'The Death of Cuchullin', and 'When You are Old'; but not in an obtrusive manner. It is not necessary to know the sources of these poems to enjoy them; they are comprehensible and universal in appeal.

Likewise the essays in *The Celtic Twilight* are simple, sometimes almost naïve. They include descriptions of Drumcliffe and Rosses, of Æ and Katharine Tynan's father; all seen hesitatingly and through Yeats's own peculiar attitude. He found people constantly surprising, and some of his happiness in discovering unusual persons is transferred to these pages. His attitude is not argumentative; he offers these stories of fairies or of visionaries without the idea that they will be the subject of argument. It would have surprised him that anyone else might take a different view of a person, for he came gradually to understand personality. He thought that what he heard and saw would be heard and seen by all people. He often misjudged people and found more in them after he had known them a long time. His arguments seemed built upon ideas, not upon estimations of character, nor, obviously, upon the amount of credence which was to be placed in the fairy legends. There is a difference in his prose, a development, the beginning of a personal style in these essays. They are simple but not with the directness of his early propagandist writings to the American journals; they do not use commonplace metaphors and have a more polished style.

The curious thing is that his poetry began to differ from his propagandist ideals. In the latter he constantly urged upon Irishmen the return to native subjects. In England he heard men complain that the old themes of prose and verse had vanished and he fully realised where the doctrine of art for art's sake was leading English poetry. In *United Ireland* he wrote, on 15 October 1892:

In England amongst the best minds art and poetry are becoming every day more ends in themselves, and all life is made more and more but so much fuel to feed their fire. It is partly the influence of France that is bringing this about. In France a man may do anything he pleases, he may spend years in prison even, like Verlaine, and the more advanced of the young men will speak well of him if he have but loved his art sincerely, and they will worship his name as they worship Verlaine's life if he have but made beautiful things and added a little to the world's store of memorable experiences. The influence of France is every year more completely pervading English literary life. The influence of that school which calls itself, in the words of its leader, Verlaine, a school of the sunset or by the term which was flung at it 'as a reproach and caught up as a battle cry', Decadents, is now the dominating thing in many lives. Poetry is an end in itself; it has nothing to do with life, nothing to do with anything but the music of cadences, and beauty of phrase. This is the new doctrine of letters. To them [English imaginative writers] literature . . . had become a terrible queen in whose service the stars rose and set, and for whose pleasure life stumbles along in the darkness. . . . It is not possible to call a literature produced in this way the literature of energy and youth. Here in Ireland we are living in a young age, full of hopes and promises,—a young age which has only begun to make its literature.

His pleas increased in emphasis. Two months later he wrote a more outspoken article in the same paper:

Is there, then, no hope for the de-Anglicising of our people? Can we not build up a national tradition, a national literature, which shall be none the less Irish in spirit from being English in language? Can we not keep the continuity of the nation's life, not by trying what Dr. Hyde has practically pronounced impossible, but by translating or retelling in English which shall have an indefinable Irish quality of rhythm and style, all that is best of the ancient literature? Can we not write and persuade others to write histories and romances of the great Gaelic men of the past, from the son of Nessa to Owen Roe, until there has been made a golden bridge between the old and the new?

Yet his poems were becoming more complex, and in an un-Irish direction. The Rose poems in *The Countess Kathleen* were part of the other side of Yeats's character which was interested in Ireland as a means of creating better literature and art. The reasons for a dichotomy between propaganda and poems, and indeed between his subsequent prose for the Irish and the English audience, are to be sought in the vacillation of the poet's personality. His poetry and much of his attitude to life were strongly affected by the poets of the nineties whom he met in the Rhymers' Club.

From the first he had been attracted to Lionel Johnson, whose 'thought dominated the scene and gave the Club its character'.[13] It was a self-consciously literary gathering which met in The Cheshire Cheese in Fleet Street. After the members had supped downstairs in the old coffee-house boxes they adjourned to an upper smoking-room where long clays and churchwarden pipes were smoked, and the rhymers produced and read aloud their verses for the criticism of the Club.[14] Lionel Johnson impressed Yeats because he had poise, and was for some time a model of deportment:

A provincial, conscious of clumsiness and lack of self-possession, I still more envied Lionel Johnson who had met, as I believed, everybody of importance. If one spoke to him of some famous ecclesiastic or statesman he would say:

'I know him intimately', and quote some conversation that laid bare that man's soul. He was never a satirist, being too courteous, too just, for that distortion. One felt that these conversations had happened exactly as he said.[15]

Johnson wanted his fellow-members of the Club to believe that all the things in which he rejoiced, Greek and Latin, his religion with its appeals to the Fathers of the Church, and the art of courtesy, were all the achievement of intellect. No more could be discovered, only revealed by philosophy and religion.

Yeats always hankered after a scholarship which he knew he could never possess, and scholarship when combined with self-assurance was irresistible to him.[16] He envied Dowden, Wilde, and Johnson who combined the two gifts; but his own development had advanced enough for him to sweep Johnson into the Irish movement on the strength of that remote family connection, generally a grandmother, which every English family is wont to possess and produce quite proudly upon occasion. Yeats had a definite use for him, as for most of his allies. He had incurred some criticism from the Roman Catholic Church in Ireland, and as Johnson was a recent convert to that religion Yeats thought that his learned theology would be useful in forestalling any opposition to the new literary movement: 'his orthodoxy, too learned to question, had accepted all that we did, and most of our plans'.[17] Johnson, as an Englishman, and a mere poet, was not of great importance in the propagandist work of the literary revival. His manner had, however, its effect upon Yeats, for in 1893 when Katharine Tynan called on him for an interview for *The Sketch*, she found him changed. He had learnt to assume a dignity and courtliness of manner that gained in sincerity and strength with later years. He turned to a more artificial concept of what a poet should be.[17a] He could exclude much of his life from his poetry because of this ability to conform to a chosen pattern. The pattern was one of 'Pure' poetry:

I saw—now ashamed that I saw 'like a man of letters', now exasperated at the indifference of these poets to the fashion of their own river-bed—that Swinburne in one way, Browning in another, and Tennyson in a third, had filled their work with what I called 'impurities', curiosities about politics, about science, about history, about religion, and that we must create once more the pure work.[18]

The result was that when he wrote of love and called it the Rose he found that he 'was becoming unintelligible to the young men who had been in my thought'.[18a] But he did not simplify his work or return to comprehensible Irish subjects. Instead his complexity increased; his symbolism became more involved and began to dominate his poetry.

His own life was complicated. Though the English periodicals published his work, mainly reviews of the Irish writers, he found it difficult to make a living.[18b] The Rhymers, he thought, were unlike the Victorian poets because they were poor men and turned from every kind of money-making that prevented good art. They had felt the subconscious influence of Rossetti, but their gospel was that of Pater. Yeats was himself influenced by both men, but his instability was different from that of some of the poets of the nineties whom he later built into a legend. The unhappiness of his love affair was imposing a great strain on him.[19] He did not take to drink, or drugs, or harlots, as so many of his contemporaries thought it clever to do. He and Maud Gonne had achieved a community of mind, they understood each other's ideas, and he thought the achievement worth the cost of the frustration involved.

> Time drops in decay,
> Like a candle burnt out,
> And the mountains and woods
> Have their day, have their day;
> What one in the rout
> Of the fire-born moods
> Has fallen away?[20]

In February 1894 he made his first visit to Paris where Maud Gonne was living, but his love prospered no better. While there he visited Verlaine with Arthur Symons, for whom his respect was increasing. With Maud Gonne he went to see the performance of Count Villiers de l'Isle Adam's *Axel* which delighted him and exercised a great influence upon his symbolic poetry. Did it not exalt love and wisdom? And for his present state of mind where love promised no reward it was an additional merit that the play denies the fulfilment of a potentially great and noble love, for such seemed unattainable in any lasting form. He wrote an enthusiastic account of *Axel* for the April number of *The Bookman* and ever afterwards he returned to quote with pleasure some of the phrases which fascinated him, especially, 'As for living our servants will do that for us'. While in Paris he stayed with MacGregor Mathers and resumed his study of the Christian Cabbala.

After his visit he spent a few months in London, when he completed his work on *A Book of Irish Verse Selected from Modern*

*Writers* for Methuen and had the excitement of seeing his play *The Land of Heart's Desire* performed at the Avenue Theatre. This had been written on the suggestion of Florence Farr in order that her niece Dorothy Paget should act the part of a fairy child who tempts a young woman away from married life in a cottage to the faery host:

> Where nobody gets old and crafty and wise,
> Where nobody gets old and godly and grave,
> Where nobody gets old and bitter of tongue,
> And where kind tongues bring no captivity.[21]

It was a slight play but its appearance on the stage added greatly to Yeats's desire to write more verse plays and have them produced. He began to revise *The Countess Kathleen* in the light of the new experience he had gained from seeing the production of *The Land of Heart's Desire*.

This revision was carried out in Sligo where he had gone in the summer to stay with George Pollexfen. Lack of money compelled him to extend his visit for six months. In Sligo he lived a life of routine and yet of much interest.[21a] Walks after lunch and dinner, always to the same point, were a feature of George Pollexfen's leisurely existence. Yeats had managed to interest his puritanical uncle in the literary movement, and had found in him a readiness to practise astrology as well as to enquire into the strange practices his nephew had learned from MacGregor Mathers. George Pollexfen had a house at Rosses Point during the summer and it was there that he first became sensitive to the Cabbalistic symbols:

> There are some high sandhills and low cliffs, and I adopted the practice of walking by the seashore while he walked on cliff or sandhill; I without speaking would imagine the symbol, and he would notice what passed before his mind's eye and in a short time he would practically never fail of the appropriate vision.[22]

Others were involved in the experiments, and Yeats found that the symbols painted on the cards, rather than his conscious intention, produced the effect on the other person. If he told someone in error to gaze on the wrong symbol the vision suggested was that proper to the symbol, not his thought—but sometimes two visions appeared. He found that when two people had some sympathy the dream or reverie divided itself between them:

> We never began our work until George's old servant was in her bed; and yet, when we went upstairs to our beds, we constantly heard her crying out with nightmare, and in the morning we would find that her dream echoed our vision. One night, started by what symbol I forget, we had seen an

allegorical marriage of Heaven and Earth.  When Mary Battle brought in
the breakfast next morning I said 'Well, Mary, did you dream anything
last night?' and she replied (I am quoting from an old notebook) 'indeed
she had', and that it was 'a dream she would not have had twice in one
night'.  She had dreamed that her Bishop, the Catholic Bishop of Sligo,
had gone away and had married 'A very high up lady', 'and she was not
so young, either'.  She had thought in her dream 'Now all the clergy will
get married and it will be no use going to confession'.²³

These experiments troubled him.  He began to wonder whether
there was any certitude in anything, and found himself solitary
and inert.  Action-compelling arguments had lost all meaning,
and he began to trace ideas back to their sources.  He thought
that he might be able to discover a tradition of belief older than
the European Churches.  In pursuit of this hazy idea he began
to take a greater interest than before in the dreams and reveries
of the country people, especially those of Mary Battle.  George
Pollexfen fell ill as a result of being vaccinated, through fear (he
was a hypochondriac) of a supposed smallpox epidemic, and
was soon delirious and in some danger, with two doctors in
attendance.  At the height of the fever Yeats sat down by his
bed and asked him what he saw.  When told 'red dancing
figures' Yeats imagined the water symbol and his uncle said
almost at once that there was a river running through the
room, and a little later said that he could sleep:

  I told him what I had done and that, if the dancing figures came again,
he was to bid them to go in the name of the Archangel Gabriel.  Gabriel is
angel of the moon in the Cabbala and might, I considered, command the
waters at a pinch.  The Doctor found him much better and heard that I
had driven the delirium away and given him such a word of command
that when the red men came again in the middle of the night they looked
greatly startled and fled.  The Doctor came, questioned, and said 'Well,
I suppose it is a kind of hypnotism, but it is very strange, very strange'.
The delirium did not return.²⁴

The images which came to Yeats were incessant, and there
was no unity in them.  They were haphazard as his dreams
had been before.  Even before his visit to Sligo his dreams had
given him the raw materials for poetry.  That haunting and
strange poem 'The Cap and Bells', published in *The National
Observer* in March 1894, was but the record of a dream:

        'I have cap and bells' he pondered,
        'I will send them to her and die',
        And when the morning whitened
        He left them there when she went by.

        She laid them on her bosom
        Under a cloud of her hair,
        And her red lips sang them a love song
        Till stars grew out of the air.

She opened her door and her window,
And the heart and the soul came through,
To her right hand came the red one,
To her left hand came the blue.[25]

He described himself as lost on the path of the Chameleon, a region of which one of MacGregor Mathers's documents had warned him.

His literary friendships began to alter. Professor Dowden aroused his wrath by his antipathy to the young writers, and he found himself ill at ease as a visitor at Dowden's house after a violent quarrel between O'Grady and the Professor. A letter to Lionel Johnson dated 27 January (1895) from Thornhill, Sligo, reveals his irritation at the attitude taken by the scholars —Mahaffy agreed with Dowden:

Have you seen or heard of the controversy anent Dowden and his views in *The Daily Express?* Dowden at Sir Samuel Ferguson lectures the other day—one old lecture new by Miss Hickey—made an attack on the Irish literary movement—with such 'malice' and evident 'intent to injure' says O'Grady in a note to me today. The amiable Rolleston has complimented him on his tour and Rolleston replied and in the *Express* wrote a vigorous defence of Irish poetry; Dowden replied by sending to the Dublin papers an extract from the preface to a new book of his in which he says by implication that we go about raving of 'Brian Boru' and 'plastered with Shamrock'. Rolleston sent a rejoinder and then was followed by Larminie and myself and on Monday the *Express* will contain a letter of O'Grady's. I hear too that *The Times'* correspondent will give a little to the controversy in his own paper on Monday or Tuesday. Dowden thinks we praise every kind of Irish work 'whether good or bad', and Rolleston has alluded in reply to a 'scattering exposure of bad technique recently delivered in a lecture at the 'National Literary' (Your lecture). I have urged Methuen to publish my anthology at once as a shot in the battle, but don't know if he will or not. I wish some of the London men would write. How is the Society getting on? Has Nutt's lecture come off? Am busy with a revision of my poems for a collected edition and have rewritten *The Countess Kathleen*. . . .[26]

It was a time of revision, and selection too, for his *Poems* were published by Fisher Unwin in March 1895. In this volume he made a selection of the poems which he wished to preserve. He included the poems written before 1889 (*The Wanderings of Oisin*) in a section called 'Crossways' and those included in *The Countess Kathleen* of 1892 in a section called 'The Rose'. His groupings were never subsequently altered, though many of the poems appear in changed versions at later dates.

On his return to London J. B. Yeats urged him to call on Wilde to see if he could assist him in any way. Yeats went to William Wilde's house and brought letters of sympathy from some Dublin friends but did not see Wilde again. Johnson, not Wilde, represented tragedy for him. Their friendship was

waning. It was only in 1895 that Yeats began to think that
Johnson was drinking too much; but soon he found that if
Johnson visited him he sat silent until given something to drink,
while if Yeats visited him he felt he was aiding his weakness, for
Johnson drank excessively on these occasions. He also discovered that Johnson had never met the famous people whose
conversations formed the main stock of his reminiscences. He
never met anyone for he got up in the evening, and drank or
worked through the night. At first Yeats had accommodated
himself to Johnson's foibles and dicta, his moods and ideas, his
belief in the intellect as opposed to the emotions. But now these
began to pall. Johnson retold his fabricated anecdotes in the
same words every time, and he retold them often. This had
been a proof of his scholarly, accurate mind at first, but later
it had become tiresome. Yeats was more sure of himself and
no longer wished to fit into Johnson's ways. Besides he objected
to the drinking, and it was a shock to discover that Johnson
was not the romantic scholar he had imagined him to be.
Gradually Johnson slipped down, drinking himself to death.
He left the house in Charlotte Street where Yeats had been so
impressed by the brown corduroy curtains that kept the dust
from his large and fine library, and refused to put himself into
an institute, for he did not want to be cured.

It was only later that Yeats saw his tragedy entire, and after
1917 he wrote:

> Lionel Johnson comes the first to mind,
> That loved his learning better than mankind,
> Though courteous to the worst; much falling he
> Brooded upon sanctity
> Till all his Greek and Latin learning seemed
> A long blast upon the horn that brought
> A little nearer to his thought
> A measureless consummation that he dreamed.[27]

These lines echo Johnson's verses in 'Mystic and Cavalier'
which Yeats afterwards thought had been written in a moment
of foresight, as a prophetic herald of the hopelessness of 'The
Dark Angel'. Yeats's 'much falling', is, of course, an echo of
Johnson's first line:

> Go from me: I am one of those who fall.[28]

The lines which describe how Johnson's learning seemed a
prophetic blast upon a horn are probably a memory of
Johnson's

O rich and sounding voices of the air!
Interpreters and prophets of despair:
Priests of a fearful sacrament! I come
To make with you my home.

The friendship with Johnson was replaced by a closer companionship with Arthur Symons, who

took a hold upon my friendship that became very strong in later years.
At first I was repelled by Symons because with a superficial deduction I
suppose from the chapter in Marius 'Anima vagula'—Marius was I think
our contemporary classic, he saw nothing in literature but a source of impassioned philosophy.[29]

It is not possible to date with accuracy when Yeats left
Bedford Park for chambers in the Temple. These opened into
those of Symons by a little passage. Visitors were examined
through a window in the connecting passage, and a consultation held before they were admitted, as to whether

one or both should receive the visitor, whether his door or mine should be
opened, or whether both doors were to remain closed.[30]

Symons had a large effect upon Yeats's verse for he read him
selections from Verlaine and Mallarmé, and Yeats found encouragement and help in the ability of Symons to listen well;
his own thoughts clarified and became richer through the
other's sympathy.[31] Yeats was now almost thirty, and this
friendship was very welcome to him, for Symons was the first
man with whom he felt able to talk freely.[31a] When he had
been in London before he had disliked the place, but now, with
these rooms as a residence, he found a certain charm could be
discovered in some of the quiet empty places nearby. With
Symons there was the receptivity which he had previously only
been able to discover in women

on whom I would call towards five o'clock mainly to discuss my thoughts
that I could not bring to a man without meeting some competing thought,
but partly their tea and toast saved my pennies for the bus ride home; but
with women, apart from their intimate exchanges of thought, I was timid
and abashed.[32]

The Yeats family were a little worried over the possibility of
Willie's rebounding from the hopeless love of Maud Gonne now
that he was living away from Bedford Park. J. B. Yeats feared
that the charms of some chorus girl might affect the poet. His
new friend was a connoisseur of music halls, who would not
understand Yeats's ideal, an ideal passing away with his youth,

of romance—he described himself as 'an ascetic of passion'.
But Symons on their first journeys to Paris

> treated me with a now admiring, now mocking wonder, because being in
> love, and in no way lucky in that love, I had grown exceedingly puritanical
> so far as my immediate neighbourhood was concerned.[33]

The strain was temporarily slackened. His unpublished auto-
graphy tells the story:

> At a literary dinner I noticed opposite to me between two celebrated
> novelists a woman of great beauty. Her face had a perfectly Greek regularity
> though her skin was a little darker than a Greek would have been, and her
> hair was very dark. She was quietly dressed with what seemed to me very
> old lace over her breast and had the same sensitive look of destruction I had
> admired in Eva Gore Booth. She was it seemed alone of our age to suggest
> to me an incomparable distinction. I was not introduced to her. . . . We
> found that she was related to a member of the Rhymers' Club, had asked
> my name.
> On my return from France came the performance of my play and it had
> a measure of success perhaps from the kindness of the management of my
> friend Florence Farr for nearly seven weeks. Presently the member of the
> Rhymers' Club introduced me to the lady I had seen between the two
> famous novelists and a friendship I hope to keep till Death began. In this
> book I cannot give her her real name—Diana Vernon sounds pleasantly to
> my ears and will suit her as well as any other. When I went to see her she
> said 'So and so seemed decided to introduce us—after I saw your play I
> made up my mind to write to you if I could not meet you otherwise'. She
> had profound culture—a knowledge of French, English and Italian litera-
> ture and seemed always at leisure. Her nature was gentle and contempla-
> tive and she was content it seemed to have no more life than leisure to talk
> to her friends. Her husband whom I saw but once was much older and
> seemed a little heavy, a little [indecipherable]. As yet I did not know how
> utterly estranged they were. I told her of my love sorrow indeed it was my
> obsession never leaving me by day or night.
> I had received while in Sligo many letters from Diana Vernon kind letters
> that gave me sense of half-[indecipherable] excitement. I remember after
> one such letter asking some country women to throw the tea leaves for me
> and my disappointment of the vagueness of the oracle. I think Mary
> Battle, my uncle's second sighted servant was ill or away. She was to tell
> me later that my letters were unconscious love letters and I was taken by
> surprise at the description. I do not know how long after my return the
> conversation that was to decide so much in my life took place. I had found
> the Rhymer who had introduced me under the influence of drink—speaking
> urgently and with light movements and while we were speaking this recent
> memory came back. She spoke of her pagan life and in a way that made
> me believe she had many lovers and loathed her life. I thought of that
> young man so nearly related. Here is the same weakness I thought two
> souls so distinguished and contemplative that the common world seems
> empty. What is left but satiety or some satisfying affection or mere dissipa-
> tion. 'Folly a comforter' some Elizabethan has called it. Her beauty,
> dark and still, had the nobility of defeated things and how could it help but
> wring my heart? I took a fortnight to decide what I should do. I was poor
> and it would be a hard struggle if I asked her to come away and perhaps
> after all I would be adding my tragedy to hers for she might return to the
> evil life but after all if I could not get the woman I loved it would be a

comfort, even but for a little while, to devote myself to another. No doubt my excited senses had their share in this argument but it was an unconscious one. At the end of a fortnight I asked her to leave home with me. She became very joyous and a few days later praised me for what she called my beautiful tact in giving at the moment but a brother's kiss. Doubtless at the moment I was exalted above the senses and yet I do not think I knew any way of kissing for when on our first railway journey together—we were to spend the day in Kent—she gave me the long passionate kiss of love I was startled and a little shocked. Presently I told something of my thoughts during that fortnight and she was perplexed and ashamed that I should have had such imagination of her. Her wickedness had never gone further than her own mind—I would be her first lover. We decided that we should be friends till she could leave her home for mine but agreed to wait till her mother, a very old woman had died. We decided to consult a woman friend that we should be kept to the resolution—the sponsor of our adventure— and for a year met in railway carriages and at picture galleries and occasionally at her home. At Dulwich gallery she taught me to care for Wallace —she too was of Pater's school and at the National gallery the painters who pleased her best of all were [indecipherable]. I wrote her several poems all curiously alike in style—'The Shadowy Horses' and [indecipherable] and thought I was once more in love. I noticed that she was like the mild heroines of my plays. She seemed a part of myself. I noticed that she did not talk as well as when I first knew her, her mind seemed more burdened but she would give her movements an unforeseen youth, she seemed to have gone back to her twentieth year. For a short time—a few months I think I shared a flat with Arthur Symons in the Temple. Symons knew that I had such a friend and plan, but did not know her name. He indeed met my friend somewhere in society and asked if he might call and came back with her praises. At last she and her sponsor were to come to tea. I do not think that I had asked Symons for I went myself to buy the cake when I came in about three in the afternoon I found the door shut. I had left the key within and I went off in a great fuss to get a locksmith and found instead a man who climbed along the roof and in at an attic window. That night at twelve o'clock I said to Symons 'Did I ever tell you about Maud Gonne?' and till two o'clock or three o'clock in the morning I spoke of my love for her. Of all the men I have known he was the best listener—he could listen as a woman listens never meeting one's thought with a new thought but taking up what one said and changing it, giving it flesh and blood as it were. A couple of days leter I got a wild letter from Maud Gonne who was in Dublin 'Was I ill? had some accident happened?' I found the day I had had those guests and lost the key I walked into the room where she was sitting with friends. At first she thought I was really there but presently finding no one else saw me knew that it was my ghost she told me to return at twelve that night and I vanished. At twelve I had stood dressed in some outlandish costume at her bedside and taken her soul away, and we had wandered round the cliffs at Howth where we had been years before. I remembered the place very clearly 'it was very sad and all the sea gulls seemed asleep'. All the old love had returned and began to struggle with the new. Presently I was asked to call and see my friend's sponsor. She confirmed the idea of going away from home. There were many arguments that I cannot recall without perhaps, against my will, revealing Diana Vernon by name. My sponsor came to see me and I used the same argument and both people of the world advised us to live together without more ado.

Yeats then took his rooms at Woburn Buildings and furnished

them with inexpensive furniture which he could throw away
without regret later if he became prosperous. Diana Vernon
helped him to purchase all this furniture—there was one embarrassed conversation in some Tottenham Court Road shop
over the width of a bed, every inch increasing the expense.
The liaison began in the middle of Yeats's thirtieth year and
lasted for but a year that was interrupted briefly by a journey
of Diana Vernon to Italy and one of Yeats to Paris. He found
it hard to earn a living and was often preoccupied when she
came. He was troubled because Maud Gonne had written to
him that she was in London and would come and dine with
him, and he had not let her. At last one morning he wrote
letters instead of reading much love poetry as was his usual
custom. Diana Vernon found he did not answer her, and knew
there was someone else in his heart. It was the breaking
between them for many years, but the experience, with its
many days of happiness and its lasting sorrow that her love
could not be fully returned, was salutary to Yeats, and to him
it seemed that she saved his soul and inmost being.

As several comments have been made on the effect of physical
love upon Yeats's poetry it is interesting to find that there is
little of importance to be discovered in the poems which he
wrote to Diana Vernon. These are 'Michael Robartes bids his
beloved be at peace' and 'The Travail of Passion', both published in *The Savoy* in January 1896. These two poems are not
especially different from many others in *The Wind among the
Reeds*, and it is not likely that a critic would seize on them and
note any difference, without knowing that they were written
to Diana Vernon. Yet chronologically they usher in a certain
sensuality, and an awareness of physical nearness:

> . . . The Horses of Disaster plunge in the heavy clay:
> Beloved, let your eyes half close, and your heart beat
> Over my heart, and your hair fall over my breast,
> Drowning love's lonely hour in deep twilight of rest,
> And hiding their tossing manes and their tumultuous feet[34]

and

> We will bend down and loosen our hair over you,
> That it may drop faint perfume, and be heavy with dew,
> Lilies of death-pale hope, roses of passionate dream.[35]

The preoccupation with hair in many of the poems in this
volume has already been the subject of a comment.[36] There
are over twenty-three allusions to hair in *The Wind among the*

*Reeds* in descriptions of women, and these convey a sense of languorous abandonment.

Yeats's account has been followed, and there is room for comment which will indicate other aspects of this interlude. Such comment is perhaps best supplied by some sentences in a novel written by Yeats's friend Mrs Shakespear and published in 1896:

> It's such an old story. You fall in love with a girl's beautiful face—it's not the first time you've done it; you endow her with all sorts of qualities; you make her into an idol; and the whole thing only means that your aesthetic sense is gratified. That's a poor way of loving. . . .[37]
> 'The thing is so simple' said I with a bitterness I could not hide. 'You place beauty on a pedestal; her face is an index to her soul, you say: what happens if you find she does not possess the soul, which she never claimed to have, but which you insisted on crediting her with? You dethrone her with ignominy. The case of the other woman is hard: she has a face that does not attract you, so you deny her the soul that you forced on the other one.' . . .[38]

# 5

# THE END OF AESTHETICISM
### (1896–1899)

*It is curious how one's life falls into definite sections.*
*In 1897 a new scene was set, new actors appeared.*[1]

W. B. YEATS

THE year 1896 was a full one for Yeats. After he had settled into Woburn Buildings he asked Arthur Symons to come on a visit to Ireland with him while *The Savoy* was being published. The magazine was edited by Symons and published by Smithers, who had agreed to the condition stipulated by Symons before he took up the editorship that Beardsley should be the art editor of the magazine. This appointment was a gesture of annoyance and resentment at the treatment Beardsley had received at the hands of the Victorian readers of *The Yellow Book*, some of whom had demanded and obtained his dismissal from the art editorship of that magazine.[1a] When published, *The Savoy* appeared as yet another challenge to the conventions of the day. Yeats wrote in *Autobiographies*[1b] that if an excuse for the writings had been formulated it would have been that literature demanded the exploration of all that passed before the mind's eye merely because it passed there. Yeats's own attitude is revealed in his contention that, if a mythical critic was to point out that some of Yeats's generation wrote with an unscientific partiality for subjects long forbidden, it could be said that what has long been forbidden should be explored not only out of moral purpose but 'gaily, out of sheer mischief, or sheer delight in the play of the mind'. This quality of irresponsible mischief was to emerge with great *éclat* in the later Yeats, and explains many of his *obiter dicta* which are often taken a little over-seriously. But when making this hypothetical explanation, objection, and counter-claim he continued to admit that he later found a slight sentimental sensuality in some of his own early work, as well as in that of his contemporaries. What was daring then seems merely pathetic now.

At the time his association with the magazine perturbed his older friends for he had received letters from Rolleston and Æ expostulating with him and deploring the publication; further-more he was under no delusions as to the nature of the pub-lisher and in fact considered him scandalous.[1c] *The Savoy* enabled Yeats to raise his prices and gave him much space, as well as some notoriety, for it was the Beardsley drawing illustrat-ing one of his articles on Blake that caused the railway book-stalls to refuse to display the magazine.

Before the two friends left London for Sligo Yeats questioned Diana Vernon when she was in a state of semi-trance. She knew nothing of the mysticism of the period but was affected by Yeats's symbols.[1d] He was worried over his work. It seemed that he had lost his old emotions which were rooted in the countryside. His poems were becoming over-elaborate and slow-moving. He had written 'Rosa Alchemica' which was in its complexity a long way from the simplicity of the essays of *The Celtic Twilight*. This new work was not likely to help the revival of imaginative writing in Ireland. And he wondered if, after all his love of the Irish scenery, he was really to write an elaborate mysticism without any special birthplace. He got some sentences from Diana Vernon which were unintelligible to both of them:

He is to live near water and avoid woods which concentrate solar power.

Yeats, according to the doctrine of Mathers, translated solar as meaning elaborate, rich, and resembling the work of gold-smiths, while lunar meant all that was simple, traditional, and emotional.

After leaving Sligo the friends came to stay with Edward Martyn at Tulira Castle in Galway. Martyn was a friend of Symons's friend George Moore and the friendship was incongru-ous, for Martyn was a pious Roman Catholic, averse to women, and not likely to relish either Moore's jibes at the Church or his anecdotes. Yet the friendship flourished and Yeats was later to extract enough comedy and quaintness from it for his little play *The Cat and the Moon*.[2]

At Tulira Castle Yeats decided that he would invoke that lunar power which he believed was the chief source of his inspiration:

I evoked for nine evenings with no great result but on the ninth night as I was going to sleep I saw first a centaur and then a marvellous naked woman shooting an arrow at a star and the flesh tints of her body seemed to make all human flesh in the contrast seem unhealthy. Like the centaur, she moved amid brilliant light.[3] At breakfast Symons who know nothing of my vision read me a poem—the first he had written to a dream. He had been visited by a woman of great beauty, but clothed. 'O source of the songs of all poets' he called her or some like thing. In the house stayed Florimond de Basterot an old French count who had land on the sea shore. He had dreamed a couple of nights before—I was now too excited by my vision to keep it to myself—of Neptune so vividly that he got out of bed and locked his door. A dream so vivid might perhaps be solid enough to find a locked door an obstacle. A pious Catholic he was very serious. Martyn was really angry, for some of my invocations I admitted I had made in the waste room in the old tower of the castle where he lived and this waste room was over the chapel. I had not known that a room over a chapel must be left empty, and that an action such as mine might be considered to obstruct the passage of prayer. I was forbidden even to speak of my invocation, and I was sorry for I knew that I must have much in common with Martyn who spent hours after we had all gone to bed reading St. Chrysostom. My invocations were a form of prayer accompanied by an active desire for special result, a more conscious exercise perhaps of the human faculties. A few days afterwards a new friend Lady Gregory called and invited me to stay at Coole and even before I arrived began collecting for me stories of fairy belief. At moments I have believed or half believed— and we cannot judge the power of those shadows—that she came in reply to that evocation for are not the common people and their wisdom under the moon and her house is at the edge of a lake. But why those woods? I had evoked only the moon and water. I found at last what I had been seeking always, a life of order, and of labour, where all outward things were the image of an inward life. At my grandmother's I had learnt to love an elaborate house, a garden and trees, and those grey country houses, Lissadell, Hazelwood House and the far rarely seen Tower of Markree had always called to my mind a life set amid natural beauty and activities of servants and labourers, who seem themselves natural as birds and trees are natural. No house is a town, no solitary house even [two words indecipherable in MS.] to vegetables or to beast by seasonal activities has ever seemed to me but as 'the tent of the shepherd'. My grandmother's house was a new house, the sailing ship had foundered that was bringing my great-grandfather's possessions to Sligo, among them his sword and a clock so remarkable my grandfather would say there was 'only one other like it in the world' but here many generations, and no uncultured genera- tions, had left the images of their service in furniture, in statues, in pictures and in the outline of wood and of field. I think I was meant not for a master but for a servant and that it has been my unhappiness to see the analytical faculty dissolve all those things that meant our service, and so it is that all images of service are dear to me. Of Lady Gregory herself as yet I knew little. Women feared her I was told by old Mrs. Martyn. She was certainly kind and able, that I saw, but to what measure? She asked me when I had been but a few minutes in her library[4] where from those decades of the 18th century her husband's family have left works, fine editions of the classics bound in calf, books on tree planting and on agriculture, the favourite English books of four generations. She asked me if I could set her to some work for our intellectual movement. She sometimes bantered me by re- minding me that I could see nothing for her to do but read our books. My own memory of this is that I said 'If you get our books and watch what we are doing you will soon find your work'. While I was there and indeed upon a later visit I did little work—I was in poor health and she brought me much in the cottages of the people. I found afterwards that it was a dis- appointment to her that I had written nothing. Symons on his return to London found a story from William Sharp (or Fiona Macleod as we thought) called in his book I think 'The Archer'. Somebody sees in vision a woman shooting an arrow into the sky and then some other archer shooting at a fawn. The arrow pierces the fawn and with the transfixed heart clinging to it strikes into the tree. It seemed impossible that Sharp could have heard of my vision in time and that part of it was new. I went to see the Kabbalist Dr. Wynn Westcott and asked about the symbolism. He opened a drawer and showed me two drawings, one of a woman shooting at a star and one of a centaur. They were the symbolism of a Kabbalistic grade I had not yet attained to, a secret imagery. Then he showed me that what seemed a star was a little burning heart and he said this heart was Tiphareth the centre of the Kabbalistic tree, the Heart of Christ also. The archer woman and the centaur were the higher and the lower genius respectively of the path Samech which led from Chesed to Tiphereth, from Sun to Moon. I remembered that Christ was sometimes the mystic faun. Presently a soror of my order told me that her child had said 'O mother I have seen a woman shooting an arrow into the sky and I'm greatly afraid she has killed God'. Diana Vernon when I questioned her announced 'There were four that saw—the child will die—they will attain to a wisdom older than the serpent'. Did the child die? I do not know. I forgot its mother's name. Was the child that died a symbolic child? Iacchus perhaps and who were the three? The meaning of the serpent was plain enough though. I did not see it till some Kabbalist showed me. Samech is the straight path, that straight line which Seraphita calls the mark of man, the way of the intellectual will, and the Serpent is the Kabbalistic serpent-winding nature. Did the shadows accept me with that vision make with me as it were their painful bond. The Gods, Henry More says, throw their lines as we throw ours for the fish and they bait their lines with dreams and how can we help but leap at them. Certainly if it was no part of myself armed with supernatural knowledge, or what must seem so, that created a thought as it were in the midst of my daily thought so little did it resemble it or if it was I prefer to think the identity is no closer than between a man and his daemon. It was no mind no will that I knew that warned me in vain to leave this ceaseless wandering from myself.[5]

After a visit to the Aran Islands Yeats and Symons returned to Martyn's castle for a while. In 1896 Yeats again visited Paris, and his unhappiness was immense. His affair with Diana Vernon had been salutary at first, but now there was remorse because he could not return her love; his infatuation for Maud had returned in all its hopelessness:

I saw much now of Maud Gonne and my hope renewed again. If I could go to her and prove by putting my hand in the fire till I had burnt it badly would not that make her understand that devotion like mine should [not] be thrown away lightly. Often as I went to see her I had this thought in mind and I do not think that it was fear of pain that prevented me but fear of being mad. I wonder at moments if I was not really mad.[5]

Yeats stayed at the Hotel Corneille near the Luxembourg, and there met John Synge, who was living on the top floor of the hotel.[6] Synge was reading French literature, mainly Racine, with the idea of writing on French topics for the English papers, and Yeats urged him to study the more modern French writers. His account of their meeting suggests that he told Synge that Arthur Symons would always be the foremost critic and that Synge's knowledge of Irish (which he had studied with success at Trinity College) would be of use in the Irish literature movement. He suggested that Synge should go to Aran and find his material there. These suggestions were made, but at a later date. At first Yeats

liked him for his sincerity and his knowledge but did not discern his genius.

For the present Synge was introduced to Maud Gonne, and introduced as a member of a Young Ireland society which Yeats was helping to found in Paris with the idea of aiding Maud Gonne's work. Maud Gonne was giving this society a Fenian turn so Synge resigned and told Yeats that he thought that England would only do Ireland right when she thought herself to be safe, the only political sentence that Yeats ever heard from him.[7]

The object of the visit to Paris was to found an order of Celtic mysteries. MacGregor Mathers and George Pollexfen were interested and helpful, but the idea was Yeats's own. Maud Gonne was also sympathetic, and this might be a way of winning her:

> The wrong of unshapely things is a wrong too great to be told;
> I hunger to build them anew and sit on a green knoll apart,
> With the earth and the sky and the water, re-made, like a casket of gold
> For my dreams of your image that blossoms a rose in the deeps of my heart.[8]

On a visit to Dr Hyde I had seen the Castle Rock as it was called in Lough Key. . . .
There is a small island entirely covered and still [indecipherable] empty castle. The last man who lived there had been Dr Hyde's father who when a young man had lived there for a few weeks. All round it were the wooded and hilly shores—a place of great beauty. I believed that this castle could be hired for little money and I had long dreamed of a king, an Irish Eleusis or Samothrace. An obsession more constant than anything but my love itself was the need of mystical writing a retired system of evocation and meditation—to reunite the perception of the spirit, of the divine with natural beauty. I believed that instead of thinking of Judaea as holy we should [believe] our own land holy and most holy when most beautiful. Commerce and manufacture have made the world ugly. The death of pagan nature worship had robbed visible beauty of its inviolable sanctity and I was convinced that all lonely and lovely places were crowded with invisible beings and that it would be possible to communicate with them. I meant to interest young men and women in the worship which would unite the radical truths of Christianity with those of a more ancient world, and to use the Castle Rock for these occasional retirements from the world. For years to come I was in my thoughts as in much of my writing to seek alone to bring again imaginative life in the old sacred places. Slieve Knocknarea all that old reverence that hung above all conspicuous hills.

But I wished by writing and thought of the school I founded. . . . I believed
we were about to have a revelation. Maud Gonne entirely shared this idea
and I did not doubt that in carrying this out I should win her for myself.
Politics were merely a means of meeting her but this was a link so perfect
that would restore at once even in a quarrel the sense of intimacy.[8a]  At
every moment of leisure we obtained in visions long lists of various symbols
that corresponded to the cardinal points and all the old gods and heroes
took place gradually in the symbolic fabric that had for its centre the four
tales bringing the Tuatha de Danaan the sword the stone the pen and
the cauldron which related themselves in my mind to the Irish of the Tarot
cards.  George Pollexfen though already an old man shared my plans and
his slow and difficult clairvoyance added certain symbols. He and Maud
Gonne only met once—in politics he was an extreme unionist—but he and
she worked with another's symbols and I did much of the work in his
house.[9]

Later he saw his visits to Paris in the eighteen-nineties as
events separated from each other, without cause or consequence, apparently without any part in his life.  He could
never place the dates of these visits with any accuracy.[10]  In
his *Autobiographies* he merely gave incidents which occurred
there in a detached form, incidents which reveal the depression
underlying his life, and are not connected in the usual way in
which his prose flows onward.  He was on the verge of dissipation, taking hashish, and within the edge of that state where he
could easily have taken permanently to drink.  The effect of
the MacGregor Matherses upon his depressed introspective, un-
hinged state was not good.  He was brought further from
normality, involved in the unreal maze of magical speculation:

Then one morning I began telling myself a different story—which I do
not remember—but my arm suffered some other injury—was broken perhaps for I pictured myself as carrying it in a sling.  I had got up before
breakfast to get a newspaper and when I returned found the MacGregors
on the doorstep 'What has happened to your arm?' said Mrs MacGregor
'but it is all right; the woman said it was in a sling.'  For a moment my
concentration of thought had created a magical illusion.  These events
seem to have no very precise dates to me.  I made many visits to Paris and
I cannot be certain upon what visit certain events took place.  One morning
at breakfast MacGregor said to me 'I saw a man standing in an archway
last night and he wore a kilt with the Macleod and another tartan'.  In the
afternoon I began to shiver and then shivering at intervals went out for a
couple of hours and was associated in my mind with Wm. Sharp and Fiona
Macleod.  I told MacGregor to make himself clairvoyant, Sharp was in
mind.  'It is madness' he said 'but it is the madness of a god.'  We were
all under the shadow of Fiona Macleod the beautiful inspired woman living
in a remote island.  He then said 'It is my wife's business' and I went into
another room with him.  As I passed the door I said 'It is strange but my
mind was full of Sharp and Fiona Macleod till this moment but now it
seems quite empty'.  She said 'I have sent your soul away.'  I was fool
enough to write to Sharp and an unbelievable letter [came] from a seaside
hotel about the beautiful Fiona and himself.  He had been very ill, terrible
mental suffering and suddenly my soul had come to heal him and he had

found Fiona to tell her he was healed and I think that I had come as a great white bird. I learnt however from Mrs Sharp years afterwards that at the time he was certainly alone but mad. He had gone away to struggle alone with madness. MacGregor himself lived in a world of phantoms. He would describe himself as meeting perhaps in some crowded place a stranger whom he would distinguish from living man by a certain tension in his heart when strangers were his teachers I said 'How do you know you are not hallucinated?' He said 'The other night I followed one of those strangers down the passage (pointing to a narrow passage from his garden to the streets) and fell over the milk boy.' The boy said 'It is too bad to be fallen over by two of you.' The break up of his character that was soon to bring his expulsion from my order had begun. He was slowly demoralised by the Celtic Movement. As Sir Walter Scott he was taking to wearing highland costume though he had I believe never been in the highlands and his Scottish ancestor was [indecipherable] He called every young man 'lad' and drank much brandy which he spoke of always as whiskey is spoken of in Anglo-Scottish poetry. He wished to play some part in the manner of Rob Roy and dreamt of the restoration of the Stuarts to some highland kingdom. He was always expecting, as indeed were all the visionaries of his time, a universal war, and had made his wife learn ambulance work that they might together join some roving band. He showed me the wound of a sabre on his wrist and explained that he and his wife had been in some student riot hoping that general bloodshed had begun.[11]

Looking back on his old friends in the rich and beautiful poem 'All Souls' Night' which was written at Oxford in 1920 Yeats eventually gave his whole impressions of Mathers:

> And I call up MacGregor from the grave,
> For in my first hard springtime we were friends,
> Although of late estranged.
> I thought him half a lunatic, half knave,
> And told him so, but friendship never ends;
> And what if mind seems changed,
> And it seem changed with the mind,
> When thoughts rise up unbid
> On generous things that he did
> And I grow half contented to be blind!
>
> He had much industry at setting out,
> Much boisterous courage, before loneliness
> Had driven him crazed;
> For meditations upon unknown thought
> Make human intercourse grow less and less;
> They are neither paid nor praised.
> But he'd object to the host,
> The glass because my glass;
> A ghost-lover he was
> And may have grown more arrogant being a ghost.[12]

This obsession of Mathers with bloodshed may have influenced a poem which appeared in The Savoy in April 1896, entitled 'The Valley of the Black Pig':

> The dews drop slowly and dreams gather: unknown spears
> Suddenly hurtle before my dream-awakened eyes,

And then the clash of fallen horsemen and the cries
Of unknown perishing armies beat about my ears.
We who are labouring by the cromlech on the shore,
The grey cairn on the hill, when day sinks drowned in dew,
Being weary of the world's empires, bow down to you
Master of the still stars and of the flaming door.[13]

The poem is an example of Yeats's symbolic style as influenced
by his theorising on the methods and results of the French
symbolists and Blake, on whom he was writing critical articles
at the time. The grey cairn on the hill is a memory of Maeve's
Grave on Knocknarea, a mountain which seemed well worthy
to be a sacred place in his new mystical order; thus the personal
element in the poem was there to delight the author and hint
at more than the surface meaning, and perhaps connect the
reader with the mysteries of Celtic origin. The flaming dew is
taken from a phrase in Standish O'Grady's writings; thus the
literary element is continued in the poem with this echo.
Cuchulain met Fand in the flaming dew in 'The Secret Rose',
a poem published in *The Savoy* in September 1896. But the
note to the poem is more grandiloquent and vague in purport,
and typical of Yeats's explanations of the poetry written at this
time, a veil thrown over clarity with the hope that its edges
would swirl among the dust of past centuries:

All over Ireland there are prophecies of the coming rout of the enemies
of Ireland, in a certain Valley of the Black Pig, and these prophecies are,
no doubt, now, as they were in the Fenian days, a political force. . . .[14]

He went to anthropology in order to trace the legends:

If one reads Rhys' *Celtic Heathendom* by the light of Frazer's *Golden Bough*,
and puts together what one finds there about the boar that killed Diarmuid,
and other old Celtic boars and sows, one sees that the battle is mythological,
and that the Pig it is named from must be a type of cold and winter doing
battle with the summer, or of death battling with life.

This does not agree with the simpler and later note in *Autobiographies*[15] that the poem had been inspired by some talk of
Mathers. These notes which he wrote in the nineties do not
reveal all of the poems' meanings. Leaving some vagueness
meant that readers might read more into the poem, while they
had merely the beauty to appreciate if they had read the poem
without notes. The general tone of the poem, of weariness, is
of course a reflection of Yeats's own moods at the time. He
pleaded forgiveness for them later:

If this importunate heart trouble your peace
With words lighter than air,
Or hopes that in mere hoping flicker and cease;

> Crumple the rose in your hair;
> And cover your lips with odorous twilight and say,
> 'O Hearts of wind-blown flame!
> O Winds, older than changing of night and day,
> That murmuring and longing came
> From marble cities loud with tabors of old
> In dove-grey faery lands;
> From battle-banners, fold upon purple fold,
> Queens wrought with glimmering hands. . . .[16]

A new development took place in his poetry in 1896. He began to write poetry describing the passions of individuals called O'Sullivan Rua, Michael Robartes, Aedh and Mongan. They were described in Yeats's notes to *The Wind Among the Reeds* which appeared in 1899 and contained a selection of the poems written since the *The Countess Kathleen*:

> There are personages in 'The Secret Rose' but, with the exception of some of Hanrahan's and one of Aedh's poems, the poems are not of that book. I have used them in this book as principles of the mind rather than as actual personages. It is probable that only students of the magical tradition will understand me when I say that 'Michael Robartes' is fire reflected in water, and that Hanrahan is fire blown by the wind, and that Aedh, whose name is not merely the Irish form of Hugh, but the Irish for fire, is fire burning by itself. To put it in a different way Hanrahan is the simplicity of an imagination too changeable to gather permanent possessions, or the adoration of the Shepherd; and Michael Robartes is the pride of the imagination brooding upon the greatness of the possessions, or the adoration of Magi; while Aedh is the myrrh and frankincense that the imagination offers continually before all that it loves.[17]

Aedh is described as a God of death (in Standish O'Grady's *History of Ireland*) and any who hear his harp die, according to a note in the 1899 edition of *Poems*.[17a] Yeats did not particularly want these characters analysed too closely. They were merely shadowy projections of various aspects of his personality, with whom he played. They were real creations in one sense, for they came to mean more to him; they represented aspects of his nature that he could not fulfil. Michael Robartes was the mysterious magical figure who appeared in 'Rosa Alchemica', an essay included in *The Secret Rose* of 1897, and persuaded Yeats to become a member of the magical society which was attacked in a village riot. Later he represented the devil-may-care lover of women. In general Yeats was capable of holding conversations with these characters, as he wrote of them, as if they possessed distinct personalities. A friend of his described them simply and correctly as the imaginary beings that sensitive children create for themselves and endow with many human qualities.[18]

Yeats was to rationalise them into a theory in a few years, but in the nineties they were a release for aspects of himself that were not integrated. It is not possible to discover exactly what the significance of these figures is, but some points can be noticed. Aedh is generally the defeatist lover who sings of love with sadness because there is not much to be hoped for but devotion to his understanding mistress. The note of auto-biography is there always:

> Had I the heavens' embroidered cloths,
> Enwrought with golden and silver light,
> The blue and the dim and the dark cloths
> Of night and light and the half-light,
> I would spread the cloths under your feet;
> But I, being poor, have only my dreams;
> I have spread my dreams under your feet:
> Tread softly because you tread on my dreams.[19]

Aedh invokes the kindness of the elemental powers:

> Great Powers of falling wave and wind and windy fire,
> With your harmonious choir
> Encircle her I love and sing her into peace,
> That my old care may cease. . . .[20]

Evidence of his care for Maud's peace is obvious in all his thoughts recorded so openly in the unpublished autobiography, and in the poetry written long after the nineties. He was occasionally confronted with rumours about her, and wrote a poem on thinking of those who had spoken ill of his beloved:

> Half close your eyelids, loosen your hair,
> And dream about the great and their pride;
> They have spoken against you everywhere,
> But weigh this song with the great and their pride;
> I made it out of a mouthful of air,
> Their children's children shall say they have lied.[21]

The unhappiness of the disruption of his love affair with Diana Vernon added to by the barren passion for his beloved is sketched simply in a lament for the loss of love:

> Pale brows, still hands and dim hair,
> I had a beautiful friend
> And dreamed that the old despair
> Would end in love in the end:
> She looked in my heart one day
> And saw your image was there;
> She has gone weeping away.[22]

In different poems Aedh tells of the perfect beauty, of a valley full of lovers where the young man on seeing his love's beauty will find no other face fair until the valleys of the world have been withered away, and again of his wish that his beloved was dead so that she

> . . . would come hither, and bend your head,
> And I would lay my head on your breast;
> And you would murmur tender words,
> Forgiving me, because you were dead.[23]

In another delicate and sensitive poem he gives his lady certain rhymes:

> I bade my heart build these poor rhymes:
> It worked at them, day out, day in,
> Building a sorrowful loveliness
> Out of the battles of old times.[24]

These are poems of love which Aedh recites, and not many of them are derivative so much as wrung from a personal melancholy that touched all things. The one which has a more pretentious air, 'Aedh pleads with the elemental powers', especially in its first verse:

> The Powers whose name and shape no living creature knows
> Have pulled the Immortal Rose;
> And though the Seven Lights bowed in their dance and wept
> The Polar Dragon slept,
> His heavy rings uncoiled from glimmering deep to deep:
> When will he wake from sleep?[25]

is explained in a note as follows:

> The seven lights are the seven stars of the Great Bear and the Dragon is the constellation of the Dragon and these, in certain old mythologies encircle the tree of life, on which is here imagined the Rose of the Ideal Beauty growing before it was cast into the world.[26]

The state of mind in which such poems were written can be illustrated by a passage from *The Adoration of the Magi*, privately printed in 1897:

> Why it was only last night that I dreamed I saw a man with a red beard and red hair and dressed in red standing by my bedside. He held a rose in one hand and tore it in pieces with the other hand and the petals drifted about the room, and became beautiful people who began to dance slowly. When I woke I was all in a heat with terror.[27]

The Rose as a symbol shows the influence of Blake. In *The Countess Kathleen* there was a poem, 'The Rose of Peace', which echoed the simplicity of Blake with a final suggestion of his contrapuntal technique:

> And God would bid his warfare cease
> Saying all things were well;
> And softly make a rosy peace,
> A peace of Heaven and Hell.[23]

Of the poems in *The Wind among the Reeds* it has been noticed[29] that 'The Blessed',[30] published in *The Yellow Book* in April 1897, shares Blake's belief in the holiness of passion. Yeats pointed out that it symbolised the highest spiritual ideal. In 'The Secret Rose' this spiritual beauty was seen as part of Yeats's own belief that there would be a revelation[30a] due to the creation of Celtic mysteries (and a complete understanding between Yeats and Maud Gonne). Madame MacBride has told me that Yeats, as well as symbolising spiritual beauty by the Rose, intended at times to allude to her by the symbol. Thus in 'The Secret Rose' the blending of all these aspirations is built up with a wealth of imagery:

> Far-off, most secret, and inviolate Rose,
> Enfold in my hour of hours; where those
> Who sought thee in the Holy Sepulchre,
> Or in the wine-vat, dwell beyond the stir
> And tumult of defeated dreams; and deep
> Among pale eyelids, heavy with the sleep
> Men have named beauty.[31]

The poem continues with an exalted simplicity to list the persons who are enfolded in the Rose's leaves, who found wisdom and love in strange ways:

> I, too, await
> The hour of thy great wind of love and hate.
> When shall the stars be blown about the sky,
> Like the sparks blown out of a smithy, and die?
> Surely thine hour has come, thy great wind blows,
> Far-off, most secret, and inviolate Rose?

Had Yeats concerned himself with the proposed order of Celtic mysteries only he might have become enwrapped in this cloud of misty dreaminess. Instead he was launched into political life, which was the beginning of the end of his period of poetry for beauty's sake. Yeats was a member of the I.R.B., a secret organisation descending from the Fenian movement, into which he had been introduced by John O'Leary. He hoped that he could win this movement to his plans for a new movement of imagination in Ireland. Rolleston had asked him to aid this new political movement but shortly afterwards resigned from the organisation himself. Maud Gonne, sworn into the I.R.B. by Dr Mark Ryan, was immersed in political work (she told Yeats her correspondence at one time took up over eight hours a day) and shared her interest with Yeats.

Yeats found himself forming grandiose plans for the organisation and his own possible role in it. The situation interested him. Irish-American revolutionaries had split into two parties, one the Triangle, the other that of Devoy. Devoy had accused the Triangle of the murder of a certain Cronin. The Dublin Committee represented Devoy, and Yeats's own friends the supposed murderers. He thought that if he were elected President of the English Committee he would keep the movement from splitting up. There was to be a large collection for a monument to Wolfe Tone. It seemed possible to Yeats that after the laying of the stone all the Irish parties could be invited to subordinate themselves to his Council of the English Wolfe Tone Association which would then be, after careful re-election on a more permanent basis, the equivalent of an Irish Parliament for it would control the coming and going of the Irish members at Westminster and would have great strength.

His plan failed for he had courage only in his thoughts. He went to Dublin with Frank Hugh O'Donnell as a fellow-delegate but O'Donnell caused trouble there and O'Leary, the chairman of the meeting, suppressed Yeats's attempts to put things right. O'Donnell made his report afterwards, and though Yeats thought it untrue he did not protest, being easily overawed by a new personality and not yet realising how much trouble O'Donnell was to cause him.[32]

Yeats had been granted the use of a weekly column in a Dublin newspaper for the new movement, and mentioned this to O'Donnell. Within a few days, before Yeats had even brought the matter before his committee, a report of the activities of some unknown secret society appeared in the column. This had nothing to do with the new movement, and when Yeats went to visit O'Donnell, who was in hospital after a gas explosion in his flat, his conversation was given the following week as a report of 'Court Shannon', an imaginary branch of the imaginary secret society.

The unpublished autobiography contains many incidents of what was a time of turmoil for Yeats. The Jubilee Riots of 1897, in particular, troubled him. Maud Gonne had gone to decorate the graves of various Irish political martyrs and had been refused admission to some graveyard because it was Queen Victoria's Jubilee. That evening she spoke at a meeting and told the story, adding in a low voice 'must the graves of our dead go undecorated because Victoria has her Jubilee?' and the crowds went wild. Windows with Jubilee decorations began to be smashed, a crowd accompanied the Council on their way from a meeting in the City Hall to the National Club in Rutland Square where a magic lantern was to show statistics of the evictions, deaths and prosecutions during Victoria's reign. A coffin representing the British Empire formed part of the procession. Amongst all these crowds walked Maud Gonne, excited and joyous; Yeats knew that she would not interfere, her principle being that if a crowd commits some illegal action and one attempts to stop it, it is perhaps possible to succeed in checking it but at the cost of appearing to have done so to keep from danger oneself. At the National Club Yeats and she were given tea and he began in a whispered voice, for he had lost his voice during the earlier debate at the Council, a long talk upon a non-political Irish subject but was interrupted by a man in a state of great excitement who ran in shouting that it was awful outside, the police are battering the people. Maud Gonne got up to go out but Yeats prevented her. He refused to let her out until she explained what she meant to do. 'How do I know till I get out?' was her reply, and after he insisted on her staying in she told him he had made her do the only cowardly thing of her life. He offered to go out himself but his voice was still a whisper. Later that evening he went to the newspaper offices and took responsibility for his action in restraining her from going out. That evening, he remembered, more than two hundred people were taken to hospital.[33]

It is time to introduce the more pleasant subject of Yeats's great friendship with Lady Gregory. After the initial meeting in 1896 she had asked him to visit Coole the following summer, and this old house was to become almost a second home to him through many years of his life. It was set in the barren flat country to the south-east of Galway, a house approached, after a drive through fields, by way of a tunnel of trees, shady and mysterious. Before the house lay a field, wide and sloping, to the left a dignified stable yard with grey stone buildings, to the right walled gardens, and behind at a little distance, the swan-inhabited lake which Yeats was shortly to make so well known. There was one feature of the surroundings of the house which had significance; it marked the role Lady Gregory was to play:

The sun, nearing its evening disappearance behind the grey garden wall, the great row of sheltering beech, the distant Burren hills, shines with a special warmth, as it seems, on the colossal marble bust of Maecenas at the

end of the flower bordered gravel walk. Kiltartan tradition says this image
was carried across Europe on wagons drawn by oxen; but it is likely the
width of land between its birthplace and an Italian seaport is a truer measure
of its journey and I know not from what harbour in Ireland it was carried
to its resting place here.[33a]

In addition to this exterior scene of dignity and vastness the
interior of the house held a mellow charm, and the poet found
in its furnishing, the objects brought from the foreign countries
where the Gregories had served and travelled, the ordered and
cultured surroundings framing the life which came to mean so
much to him.[33b]

The library, in particular, afforded

delight in the mere appearance of these walls of leather and vellum,
mellowed by passing centuries, in the sudden illumination of golden
ornament and lettering as the sun sails towards the western hills.[33c]

Yeats in his desire to serve found that he could play courtier
to Lady Gregory as he played romantic lover, pre-Raphaelite
knight, to Maud Gonne. There was much for which he had
cause to be thankful to her. She was an interesting and intelligent woman, a Persse of Roxborough, who had also a capacity
for serving an ideal. She had become more Gregory than the
Gregories themselves, especially in her devotion to Coole, which
was to be preserved intact for her son Robert; but she was also
interested in Ireland, held Home Rule beliefs, and was ready
to join in the literary movement. She was kind and practical.
When Yeats made his first long visit in 1897 she saw how ill
he was:

I was never before so sad and miserable as in the year that followed my
first visit to Coole. In the second or during the first my nervous system
was worn out. The toil of dressing in the morning exhausted me and Lady
Gregory began to send me in cups of soup when I was called.[33]

The activity of politics had not taken his mind from his troubles,
the friendship with Maud Gonne was tantalising:

It was a time of great personal strain and sorrow—since my mistress had
left me no other woman had come into my life and for nearly seven years
none did. I was tortured with sexual desire and disappointed love. Often
as I walked in the woods at Coole it would have been a relief to have
screamed aloud.[33]

From this mood came poems of despair, perhaps accentuated
by his illness. There is more than a verbal echo (in the words
'sedge' and 'lake') of 'La Belle Dame Sans Merci' in this
poem:

> I wander by the edge
> Of this desolate lake
> Where wind cries in the sedge:
> *Until the axle break*
> *That keeps the stars in their round,*
> *And hands hurl in the deep*
> *The banners of East and West,*
> *And the girdle of light is unbound,*
> *Your breast will not lie by the breast*
> *Of your beloved in sleep.*[34]

The symbols which interested him, the tree of knowledge, the Celtic legendry, mingled with his sorrow. We must know that Mongan is a famous Celtic wizard who remembers his past lives, that the Country of the Young is the Celtic name for the land of the Gods and the happy dead, that the hazel is the Irish tree of life and knowledge, and probably the tree of the heavens, that the Crooked Plough and the Pilot Star are Celtic names for the Pilot Star before[35] we can derive fuller meanings from this poem 'Mongan thinks of his past greatness', which is also an expression of his own sadness:

> I have drunk ale from the Country of the Young
> And weep because I know all things now:
> I have been a hazel tree, and they hung
> The Pilot Star and the Crooked Plough
> Among my leaves in times out of mind:
> I became a rush that horses tread:
> I became a man, a hater of the wind,
> Knowing one, out of all things, alone, that his head
> May not lie on the breast nor his lips on the hair
> Of the woman that he loves, until he dies.
> O beast of the wilderness, bird of the air,
> Must I endure your amorous cries?[36]

Lady Gregory showed him a way out of his maze, from the thoughts that repeated themselves and from the multiformity of interests that occupied his mind. He was engaged upon a novel called *The Speckled Bird*, which he found increasingly difficult, although he was fascinated by the task.[37] The setting was contemporaneous, the personages occultists: his main character was to see all the visionary sects before his eyes, but could not achieve a philosophic unity any more than Yeats could an artistic. The remedy was simple, and in its simplicity lay the proper antidote to his trouble. Lady Gregory brought him gathering folk-lore[37a] from cottage to cottage, writing down what she heard herself, and knowing that the passive listening and the open-air walks would do his health good.[37b] He realised how much her watchfulness and care had meant to him and paid due tribute to her kindness in many of his writings; not only did she give a new and increasing interest in the country-side which was his first and lasting love; but she provided what was for him the perfect setting for creative work:[37c]

> When I was in good health again, I found myself indolent, partly perhaps because I was affrightened by that impossible novel, and asked her to send me to my work every day at eleven, and at some other hour to my letters, rating me with idleness if need be, and I doubt if I should have done much with my life but for her firmness and her care. After a time, though not very quickly, I recovered tolerable industry, though it has only been of late years that I have found it possible to face an hour's verse without a preliminary struggle and much putting off.[38]

In addition to the collection of Fairy belief there was an ease from tension in the fact that Yeats could enjoy Irish social life in an unworried atmosphere at Coole. In Dublin he had alienated many who might have been his friends by the bitter-ness of his propaganda, his attacks on Trinity College, and his anti-English attitude:

> I never met with, or but met to quarrel with, my father's old family acquaintance; or with acquaintance I myself might have found, and kept among the prosperous educated class, who had all the great appointments at University or Castle; and this I did by deliberate calculation. If I must attack so much that seemed so sacred to Irish nationalist opinion, I must, I knew, see to it that no man suspect me of doing it to flatter Unionist opinion.[39]

Baptism of the gutter was the only solution, when Unionists were *en masse* repelled by the fervency with which Nationalism expressed itself, and he

> thought many a time of the pleasant Dublin houses that would never ask me to dine; and the still pleasanter houses with trout-streams near at hand, that would never ask me upon a visit. I became absurdly sensitive, glancing about me in certain public places, the private view of our Academy, or the like, to discover imagined enemies; and even now, after twenty or thirty years, I feel at times that I have not recovered my natural manner.[40]

In his summers at Coole Lady Gregory invited congenial company for him, Douglas Hyde, Æ,[40a] William Sharp, and others who shared his interests and some of his ambitions.

At Coole he lived amid mystery for it seemed to him that the peasants possessed an ancient knowledge, a belief which Lady Gregory strengthened. 'That old man', she said of an old man who passed them in the woods, 'may have the mystery of the ages.'[41] He began to have visions and dreams full of wisdom and beauty; and it was at Coole that he experienced the first of those semi-trance thoughts which seemed part of a state between sleeping and waking:

It was during 1897 and 1898, when I was always just arriving from or just setting out to some political meeting, that the first dreams came. I was crossing a little stream near Inchy Wood and actually in the middle of a stride from bank to bank, when an emotion never experienced before swept down upon me. I said, 'That is what the devout Christian feels, that is how he surrenders his will to the will of God.' I felt an extreme surprise for my whole imagination was pre-occupied with the pagan mythology of Ireland, I was marking in red ink upon a large map every sacred mountain. The next morning I awoke near dawn, to hear a voice saying, 'The love of God is infinite for every human soul because every human soul is unique, no other can satisfy the same need in God'.[42]

He began to formulate his theories in praise of the extremes of society, the noble and the peasant. The note of distinction between these classes and the middle class begins to emerge in his work. The change was not a sudden one. In 1897 he was writing his most elaborate stories, 'The Tables of the Law' and 'The Adoration of the Magi', which reveal what his novel might have been like had he published it. In 1899 he published *The Wind Among the Reeds*, his most elaborate verse, his final poetry written for poetry's sake, for beauty's sake, and the swan song of his *fin de siècle* composition:

The more a poet notes in his verses of heterogeneous knowledge and irrelevant analysis, and purifies his mind with elaborate art, the more does the little ritual of his verse resemble the great ritual of nature, and become mysterious and inscrutable. He becomes, as all the great mystics have believed, a vessel of the creative power of God, and whether he be a great poet or a small poet, we can praise the poems, which but seem to be his with extremity of praise that we give his great ritual which is but copied from the same eternal model.[43]

Art for art's sake is not a doctrine that appeals to the balanced; art must be a part of life and concerned with all human activity. In excluding so much from his verse Yeats was concentrating on material that had to have an end. The verses in *The Wind Among the Reeds* have great beauty, but lack the honesty, even the bitter and brutal honesty, of much of his later work. That is why the newcomer to Yeats's poetry finds that the unreality of the earlier symbolism is less striking than the expression of the full man in the later work. The deliberate attempt to conceal the full meaning from the reader in the early symbolism, aggravated by the vague and often unsuitable notes, leaves an impression of spiritual weakness, a strange result when the poetry was written in a worship of spiritual beauty. Yeats had however to learn that spiritual beauty demanded more than a segregated attention to be conveyed through verse. One cannot love truly without knowledge and acceptance, and his

love was of a manufactured ideal, fabricated in the workshops
of his brain which had before them the blue-print of what a
poet's love should be. By imitation and concentration the love
had become a devotion, but all the elements which were
excluded from it were still at hand. The earlier readers of
Yeats knew only the early verse written for beauty's sake, and
so all the realistic writing seems to them a desecration, but to
those who survey the entirety of his work this writing of the
nineties seems to contain much of beauty, that is perfect in
technique, but too rarefied for life. There is something
exasperating about a man who is not true to himself, and the
close of Yeats's pre-Raphaelite period is out of keeping with
the path his life was beginning to take. Like his own description of Blake:

> He was a man crying out for a mythology, and trying to make one
> because he could not find one to his hand.[44]

In 1899 his essay 'The Autumn of the Body' is redolent of
the weariness his verse contained. Man had wooed the world
and won it with a weariness that would not end till the last
autumn when the stars shall be blown away like withered
leaves. His prose had become ornate and mannered, but its
beauty of phrase, like the beauty of his verse, cannot conceal
his uncertainty and his faint-hearted half-belief. He is less
interested in the message than in the way of saying it:

> The arts are, I believe, about to take upon their shoulders the burdens that
> have fallen from the shoulders of priests, and to lead us back upon our
> journey by filling our thoughts with the essences of things, and not with
> things. We are about to substitute once more the distillation of alchemy
> for the analyses of chemistry and for some other sciences; and certain of us
> are looking everywhere for the perfect alembic that no silver or golden
> drop may escape.[45]

Poetry was to be essences, separated from each other in little
and intense poems; a far step from the ideal of seeing life
steadily and seeing it whole. His lords in literature were still
Villiers de l'Isle Adam, and Maeterlinck, and Mallarmé. He
had gone far from his early beliefs that he should write popular
poetry; instead he was to write for a more select audience, but
with a renewed insistence on the importance of the Irish scene:

> We have a history fuller than any modern history of imaginative events;
> and legends which surpass, as I think, all legends but theirs in wild beauty,
> and in our land, as in theirs, there is no river or mountain that is not
> associated in the memory with some event or legend.[46]

Lady Gregory had been responsible for most of this return to earth, to the Galway plains where he discovered a people—

a community bound together by imaginative possessions, by stories and poems which have grown out of its own life, and by a past of great passions[47]

—and a house where tradition reigned and an orderly life where the cares of living did not interrupt his contemplation. He did not make these discoveries at once; his becoming a full man was accompanied by severe birth pangs.

# 6

## MAN OF ACTION
### (1899–1908)

*The world should thank me for not marrying you.*
MAUD GONNE MACBRIDE

*That had she done so who can say*
*What would have shaken from the sieve?*
*I might have thrown poor words away*
*And been content to live.*
W. B. YEATS

YEATS, as an artist, generally knew what result he wished to produce. His early work was written out of ideals, enthusiasms and convictions of whose nature he was fully aware. When he began to write he wished to describe outward things as vividly as he could, and he found pleasure in picturesque and declamatory books.[1] The intellectual purposes of his poetry of the early nineties, which utilised the material of the ancient Irish legends and the beauty of the Irish countryside, can be found in the essays which he wrote in the American journals, and in his subsequent propagandist work in the English and Irish papers and magazines. The self-conscious nature of the Irish intellectual movement was, of course, largely due to his vision and knowledge of what he wished to create.

When he turned from a desire to describe outward things, and began to seek spiritual and unemphatic books, his prose recorded the alteration of his interest. His early enthusiasm for Blake became caught up with a delight in the French symbolists. The effect of these beliefs became apparent in his verse; but while the verse can stand upon the merits of its own beauty, the beliefs themselves are the foundations of that beauty, and must, for the full understanding of the verse, be sought in his contemporary prose.

With the publication of *The Wind Among the Reeds* in 1899, Yeats had brought his early style to its fullest development. The thought upon which these poems were based is recorded in an essay of the same year, part of a controversy published in the Dublin *Daily Express*, in which, replying to John Eglinton's complaint that the poet 'looks too much away from himself and from his age, does not feel the facts of life enough, but seeks in art an escape from them', Yeats wrote:

> I believe that the renewal of belief which is the great movement of our time, will more and more liberate the arts from 'their age' and from life, and leave them more and more free to lose themselves in beauty, and to busy themselves like all the great poetry of the past and like religions of all times, with 'old faiths, myths and dreams', the accumulated beauty of the age. I believe that all men will more and more reject the opinion that 'poetry is a criticism of life' and be more and more convinced that it is a revelation of a hidden life, and that they may even come to think painting, poetry, and music the only means of conversing with eternity left to man on earth.[2]

This was the doctrine of art for art's sake carried as far as Yeats could support its burden. Man had wooed the earth and fallen weary. The arts were to lead men back to their true path by filling their thoughts with the essences of things and not with things themselves. Poetry was to become a search for disembodied ecstasy. Yet in 1906 Yeats wrote:

> I ask myself if my conception of my own art is altering;[2a] if there, too, I praise what I once derided. . . . I developed these principles [of aestheticism] to the rejection of all detailed description, that I might not steal the painter's business, and indeed I was always discovering some art or science that I might be rid of . . . yet those delighted senses when I had got from them all that I could, left me discontented. Impressions that needed so elaborate a record did not seem like the handiwork of those careless old writers one imagines squabbling over a mistress, or riding on a journey, or drinking round a tavern fire, brisk and active men.[3]

His new aims were summed up in the following sentence:

> We must ascend out of common interests, the thoughts of the newspapers, of the market place, of men of science, but only so far as we can carry the normal, passionate, reasoning self, the personality as a whole.[4]

He had cut away the props which supported his early work: he no longer relied on the elaborate mythology[4a] which he had created for himself out of the Romantic poets, the Celtic legends, folk-lore and a smattering of symbolism. His verse had changed and he had begun to write the poetry which was to make him leader of a new generation of poets, unique in the history of English literature as a poet who was able to change his style so completely, to write with increasing energy as he grew older.

What were the reasons for the change? There was, of course, a general sense that, with the passing of the century, an age, of poetry as well as of life, was over. Yeats was always aware of contemporary trends in literature and knew that the aesthetic period of the nineties had reached its end. 'Everybody', he wrote later, 'got down off their stilts.' Yet there was nothing similar to the rejoicing of Dryden:

> 'Tis well an old age is out
> And time to begin a new,[5]

for Yeats's changed attitude came into being in a peculiarly negative fashion, a particularly personal way. The rarefied atmosphere of his love poetry written to Maud Gonne could not last for ever. The sensuousness which had come with his first consummated love affair changed, when that brief relief ended, into a more critical attitude towards Maud Gonne. Describing his state of mind in 1897 he later wrote:

> I was involved in a miserable love affair, that had but for one brief interruption absorbed my thoughts for years past, and would for some years yet.[6]

He still saw Maud frequently; still admired her beauty. As President of the '98 Association he accompanied her on a tour of the Irish in England and Scotland, of which he left an eloquent memory:

> Her power over crowds was at its height, and some portion of the power came because she could still, even when pushing an abstract principle to what seemed to me an absurdity, keep her mind free, and so when men and women did her bidding they did it not only because she was beautiful but because that beauty suggested joy and freedom. Her beauty, backed by her great stature, could instantly affect an assembly, and not as often with our stage beauties because obvious and florid, for it was incredibly distinguished, and if—as must be that it might seem that assembly's very self, fused, unified, and solitary—her face, like the face of some Greek statue, showed little thought, her whole body seemed a master work of long labouring thought, as though a Scopas had measured and calculated, consorted with Egyptian sages, and mathematicians out of Babylon, that he might outface even Artemisia's sepulchral image with a living norm.[7]

While on the tour he was still in a hopeful frame of mind, writing to Lady Gregory from Manchester that Maud Gonne was 'very kind and friendly but whether more than that I cannot tell'. He visited Paris in 1899 and was rejected once more. Lady Gregory, enquiring from Maud in 1900 what her intentions were in regard to Yeats, was told that both she and Yeats had more important things than marriage to think about.[8] He had been in love with her since 1889 and it was small wonder that his appreciation became tempered, towards his thirty-fifth year, with a slightly more critical spirit. A hint of disillusion began to emerge in the poems of *In the Seven Woods* of 1903. In 'Never give all the Heart' he wondered whether his love would have been more successful if he had created a mysterious atmosphere about himself:

> Never give all the heart, for love
> Will hardly seem worth thinking of
> To passionate women if it seem
> Certain, and they never dream
> That it fades out from kiss to kiss . . .
> He that made this knows all the cost,
> For he gave all his heart and lost.[9]

The poem with its phrase 'all his heart' is reminiscent of Blake's 'Love's Secret':

> Never seek to tell thy love,
> Love that never told shall be;
> For the gentle mind does move
> Silently, invisibly.
>
> I told my love, I told my love,
> I told her all my heart,
> Trembling, cold, in ghastly fears.
> Ah! She did depart.[9a]

'The Arrow', a noble poem written in 1901, partially records the intensity of the first meeting twelve years before:

> I thought of your beauty, and this arrow
> Made out of a wild thought, is in my marrow.
> There's no man may look upon her, no man,
> As when newly grown to be a woman,
> Tall and noble but with face and bosom
> Delicate in colour as apple blossom.[10]

It derived from the symbolism of Blake's preface to *Milton*:

> Bring me my bow of burning gold:
> Bring me my arrows of desire;
> Bring me my spear: O clouds unfold;
> Bring me my chariot of fire.

This had been explained by Yeats and Ellis as follows:

He shall return again, aided by the bow, sexual symbolism, the arrow, desire, the spear, male potency, the chariot, joy.[11]

The autobiographical nature of the poem is revealed by this description in *Autobiographies* of how Maud had looked on the occasion:

Her complexion was luminous, like that of apple blossom through which the light falls, and I remember her standing that first day by a great heap of such blossoms in the window.[12]

A more personal, more real note enters his descriptions of

his love. In 'The Folly of Being Comforted' the strain of his hopeless passion vibrates through the poem in answer to the note of realism with which it opens:

> One that is ever kind said yesterday:
> 'Your well-belovèd's hair has threads of grey,
> And little shadows come about her eyes;
> Time can but make it easier to be wise
> Though now it seems impossible, and so
> All that you need is patience'. . . .[13]

'Adam's Curse' is an even more direct record of an actual happening in his life. The poem tells how the beloved, her friend and the poet had sat and talked of poetry one evening at the summer's end. The poet told of the difficulty of making verse; the friend murmured that it is also a toil for women to be beautiful; and the poet replied:

> I said, 'It's certain there is no fine thing
> Since Adam's fall but needs much labouring.
> There have been lovers who thought love should be
> So much compounded of high courtesy
> That they would sigh and quote with learned looks
> Precedents out of beautiful old books;
> Yet now it seems an idle trade enough.'
>
> We sat grown quiet at the name of love;
> We saw the last embers of daylight die,
> And in the trembling blue-green of the sky
> A moon, worn as if it had been a shell
> Washed by time's waters as they rose and fell
> About the stars and broke in days and years.
>
> I had a thought for no one's but your ears;
> That you were beautiful, and that I strove
> To love you in the old high way of love;
> That it had all seemed happy, and yet we'd grown
> As weary-hearted as that hollow moon.[14]

The story of the poem's inspiration is to be found in Madame MacBride's autobiography:

While we were still at dinner Willie Yeats arrived to see me and we all went into the drawing room for coffee. Kathleen [her sister, Mrs Pilcher] and I sat together on a big sofa amid piles of soft cushions. I was still in my dark clothes with the black veil I always wore when travelling instead of a hat, and we must have made a strange contrast. I saw Willie Yeats looking critically at me and he told Kathleen he liked her dress and that she was looking younger than ever. It was on that occasion Kathleen remarked that it was hard work being beautiful which Willie turned into his poem 'Adam's Curse'.

Next day when he called to take me out to pay my customary visit to the Lia Fail, he said: 'You don't take care of yourself as Kathleen does, so she looks younger than you; your face is worn and thin; but you will always be beautiful, more beautiful than anyone I have known. You can't help

that. Oh, Maud, why don't you marry me and give up this tragic struggle
and live a peaceful life? I could make such a beautiful life for you among
artists and writers who would understand you.'
   'Willie are you not tired of asking that question? How often have I told
you to thank the gods that I will not marry you. You would not be happy
with me.'
   'I am not happy without you.'
   'Oh yes, you are, because you make beautiful poetry out of what you call
your unhappiness and you are happy in that. Marriage would be such a
dull affair. Poets should never marry. The world should thank me for not
marrying you. I will tell you one thing, our friendship has meant a great
deal to me; it has helped me often when I needed help, needed it perhaps
more than you or anybody know, for I never talk or even think of these
things.'
   'Are you happy or unhappy?' he asked.
   'I have been happier and unhappier than most, but I don't think about
it. You and I are so different in this. It is a great thing to know one can
never suffer again as much as one has suffered; it gives one great calm and
great strength and makes one afraid of nothing. I am interested in the work
I have undertaken; that is my life and I live,—while so many people only
exist. Those are the people to be pitied; those who lead dull uneventful
lives; they might as well be dead in the ground. And now Willie, let us
talk of the Lia Fail.[14a] You know I hate talking of myself; I am not going
to let you make me.[15]

The last verse of the poem quoted above is explained by the
account of the second day's happenings when Yeats saw Maud
Gonne, unstained by travel, in town dress, and could again
write with all sincerity that she was beautiful. His striving after
love of the old romantic kind was difficult, but the problem
was how to reconcile this with the simple pleasure of taking
her to see the Lia Fail and talking quietly with her with great
understanding—and so the final conclusion is one of baffled
despair. The moon, recognised as the symbol of love when
first mentioned, has become 'hollow'.

   The change in Yeats's attitude was gradual, and it went
along with his renewed interest in the theatre as an art form.
In a sense this interest had never died. It had been formed
at an early age, and was stimulated by his father's belief that
the greatest poets had written for the public theatre. His first
poems, published in *The Dublin University Review*, had been
mainly cast in a dramatic mould.[15a] The early stages of
his friendship with Russell had stimulated his wish to write
plays. After he had left Dublin his interest had not flagged:
his contributions to *The Boston Pilot* and *The Providence Journal*
reveal his desire for a theatre in Ireland, at once nationalist
and free from the literary failings which marred the majority
of contemporary Irish writing, as well as from the vulgarity of

the commercial theatre. His sense of the importance of the theatre was strengthened by two events.

The first was his meeting Maud Gonne, when he had realised that she moved amid the drama of a colourful life which made his own shy reveries of study seem pallid by contrast. To impress her he had thought he must make himself appeal to that side of her nature which was at first so strange to him and which he did not fully understand. He had offered to write *The Countess Kathleen* for her since she wanted a play to act in Dublin. The second event had been his delight at the verse-speaking of Florence Farr. But there was very little likelihood of such a play as *The Countess Kathleen* being produced in the commercial theatres of England or Ireland of the time. The prevalent appetite was for musical comedy and melodrama; Ibsen's naturalism—much less Yeats's fantasy—would not be considered by the theatrical managers of the time. For a time his plans of having verse plays produced were in abeyance.

There was some interest in new forms of theatrical art. The Independent Theatre opened in London in 1891, and George Moore's play *The Strike at Arlingford* was produced there in 1893. In the following year, at the Avenue Theatre, there were performances of Shaw's *Arms and the Man*, and Yeats's *The Land of Heart's Desire*. After seeing this play on the stage Yeats began to revise *The Countess Kathleen* in the light of the new experience the performance had given him. His desire to write plays and have them produced increased. Early in 1898 when he visited Lady Gregory in London he was 'very full of play-writing'. Florence Farr seemed ready to help his plans of getting some small suburban theatre in which romantic dramas could be produced. He thought that there would be a reaction against Ibsen's realism, and that romance would have its turn. At the time he was writing *The Shadowy Waters* (1900) into which he had 'put a great deal of himself'. (The play was a beautiful pre-Raphaelite praise of beauty in which Forgael found himself through love of Dectora, the beautiful woman.[15b])

How Lady Gregory came to be associated with the project of an Irish theatre has been told with a flourish in Yeats's *Autobiographies*:

On the sea coast at Duras, a few miles from Coole, an old French count, Florimond de Basterot, lived for certain months in every year. Lady Gregory and I talked over my project of an Irish Theatre looking out upon the lawn of his house, watching a large flock of ducks that was always gathered for his arrival from Paris, and that would be a very small flock, if indeed it were a flock at all, when he set out for Rome in the Autumn. I told her that I had given up my project because it was impossible to get the few pounds necessary for a start in little halls, and she promised to collect or give the money necessary. That was her first great service to the Irish intellectual movement.[16]

Lady Gregory's account of the discussions in 1897 is taken from her book *Our Irish Theatre*:

Mr Edward Martyn came to see me, bringing with him Mr Yeats whom I did not know very well, though I cared for his work very much and had already, through his directions, been gathering folk lore. They had lunch with us, but it was a wet day and we could not go out. . . . We sat through the wet afternoon, and though I had never been at all interested in theatres, our talk turned on plays. Mr Martyn had written two, *The Heather Field* and *Maeve*. They had been offered to London managers, and now he thought of having them produced in Germany, where there seemed to be more room for new drama than in England. I said it was a pity we had no Irish theatre where such plays could be given. Mr Yeats said that had always been a dream of his, but he had of late thought it an impossible one, for it could not at first pay its way and there was no money to be found for such a thing in Ireland. We went on talking about it, and things seemed to grow possible as we talked, before the end of the afternoon we had made our plan. We said we would collect money, or rather ask to have a certain sum of money guaranteed. We would then take a Dublin theatre and give a performance of Mr Martyn's *Heather Field* and one of Mr Yeats's own plays *The Countess Kathleen*.[17]

As Yeats, Martyn, and Lady Gregory knew little of the technicalities of theatrical work Yeats suggested that George Moore would be a suitable ally on account of his new-found interest in the Irish literary movement[17a] and, more especially, from his knowledge of the Parisian and London stages. He was, moreover, highly critical of the conventional theatre, and so was well qualified to become one of the initial directors of the Irish Literary Theatre with Yeats and Martyn. Lady Gregory, an excellent organiser, gained widespread support in Ireland for the proposed theatre, the aims of which were stated in a letter asking for the support of guarantors. It was intended to perform Celtic and Irish plays in the spring of each year and to show that

Ireland is not the home of buffoonery and of easy sentiment, as it has been represented, but the home of an ancient feudalism.[18]

There was much publicity for the new venture. *Tableaux vivants* of *The Countess Cathleen* were given at the Viceregal Lodge, through the aid of Lady Betty Balfour. Yeats, owing to his political views, could not take part in this, but he welcomed it as propaganda for the theatre and suggested that Rolleston would be a help in the production of the tableaux.

The production of the actual plays presented difficulties.
The theatres in Dublin were too expensive to hire, and were
in any case booked for many months ahead. Theatrical performances, according to the law, could be given only at licensed
theatres. Yeats spent much of his time in London persuading
the Irish Members of Parliament to amend an Irish Local
Government Bill which was then before the House in order
that the Lord Lieutenant could grant a licence for an occasional
performance in any hall or building. The amendment was
carried, and the Antient Concert Rooms in Dublin were hired
for 8 and 9 May 1899.

The actors presented another problem. There were no local
actors to be found, and the rehearsals therefore took place
in London. Moore has described in *Ave* how he produced
Martyn's play and interfered with Florence Farr's ideas for
*The Countess Cathleen* by persuading an experienced actress and
her husband to attend to the rehearsals and production. Worse
troubles arose. While Martyn's play, on the theme of a dreaming Irish landlord driven mad by an over-interfering wife, did
not attract adverse opinion, Yeats's play provoked both religious and political condemnation. Lady Gregory was a staunch
Protestant, though on very good terms with the Catholic
peasantry at Coole, and Moore announced his conversion to
Protestantism during his stay at Dublin; but Martyn, who was
a strict Catholic, became anxious about the orthodoxy of *The
Countess Cathleen* and consulted an ecclesiastical authority, who
disapproved of it; Yeats and Lady Gregory, worried by the
possibility of Martyn resigning his directorship, immediately
consulted two other ecclesiastical authorities who gave their
approval of the play. Then Moore attacked Yeats for submit-
ting a work of art to the criticisms of theologians, and so irritated Martyn that he decided to resign. Whereupon Yeats
talked him round and all was well until a pamphlet entitled
*Souls for Gold* appeared. This was the work of Yeats's old
enemy, O'Donnell; it suggested that the selling of souls in his
play was a slight upon the morality of the people of Ireland
who would never sell so priceless a commodity. A controversy
arose in the public press: the play was condemned by Cardinal
Logue, who admitted that he had not read the text. Finally
the production took place—under police protection, and with
interruptions from a hostile section of the audience, which
reminded Moore of a 'cats' and dogs' home rolled into one'.

Thus Irish public opinion, so often ignorantly hostile to Irish plays, showed its dislike at the first performance of the Irish Theatre. Thirty-five years later[19] Yeats still remembered the sense of impending disaster which Florence Farr, in the part of Aleel, put into the words:

> . . . But now
> Two grey horned owls hooted above our heads.

Two English critics reviewed the plays very favourably; and Martyn was so pleased that he paid all the expenses of the venture.

O'Donnell's enmity towards Yeats and Maud Gonne continued after the affair of the pamphlet. So did Maud's interest in active and secret political designs. The proposals which Yeats made her in Paris in 1899, in London in 1900, in an attempt to win her from the hatred of politics to the spiritual quietude of his contemplative sedentary life among people who revered beauty, had had no effect. Her plots increased. Through her efforts an agent of the French Military Intelligence travelled to London to meet members of the I.R.B. who might be likely to give the French information. The Boer War roused much anti-British feeling among the Irish writers, and even J. B. Y. was moved to denounce the imperialist adventure. Maud Gonne's plotting went awry, and the events became intensely dramatic. She told Yeats of the difficulties. The French agent had arrived in London, met Dr Ryan, the leader of the I.R.B., and been entrusted to the care of O'Donnell. He was subsequently arrested. Another plan which Maud Gonne had offered to the Boer agent in Brussels of putting bombs in the coal of British troopships was considered dangerous politically but she was to be given two thousand pounds to aid revolutionary work in Ireland. After a short time this sum was collected by a supposed friend of hers, who was suspected to be O'Donnell, who was in funds, and had given a large donation to the Irish parliamentary party. Maud Gonne was depressed by this failure of her plan: when Yeats had spoken to Dillon of the affair the donation was returned to its source, but the credit of the Irish revolutionaries in France was seriously damaged, and all the effect of Maud Gonne's speeches and propaganda minimised. Then it was decided by some of the I.R.B. that O'Donnell should be murdered. Yeats and she spent a long time arguing with and eventually persuading the I.R.B. not to proceed to such extremes. After this they both

resigned from the I.R.B.[20] Her interests became less violent
and extremist, and she began to join in the *Sinn Fein* movement
led by Arthur Griffith, hoping that he and Yeats would
co-operate. But Yeats had had enough of the turmoil of
politics, merely aiding her to devise the rules for some new
Young Ireland societies which she was forming. Besides, other
interests were absorbing more of his time.

Another startling experience was the part he took in the rift
in the Order of the Golden Dawn. MacGregor Mathers had
greatly disturbed the members by his conduct and eventually
they ejected him, only to have to guard against his attacks
upon the rooms of the society. A letter to Lady Gregory, dated
1900, reveals the seriousness with which Yeats viewed the
situation:

> For a week I have been worried to death with meetings, law and watching
> to prevent a sudden attack on the rooms. For three nights I did not get
> more than $4\frac{1}{4}$ hours' sleep any night. The trouble is that my Cabalists
> are hopelessly unbusiness-like, and their minutes and the like are in com-
> plete confusion. I have had to take the whole responsibility for everything,
> and to decide on every step. I am hopeful of the result. Fortunately this
> wretched envoy has any number of false names and has signed the summons
> in one of them. He is also wanted for debt and a trade union representative
> is to attend court on Saturday. The envoy is, I believe, seeking vengeance
> for our refusal to initiate him. We did not admit him because we did not
> think that a mystical society was intended to be reformatory. I arraigned
> Mathers on Saturday last before a chapter of the Order. I was carefully
> polite and I am particularly pleased by the fact that in our correspondence
> and meetings not one word has been written or said, which forgot the past
> and the honour one owes to a fallen idol. Whatever happens the activities
> of the society will have nothing unworthy to pass down to posterity.

A new order was formed. Yeats's interest in secret societies was
maintained. In 1901 he wrote two short pamphlets, *Is the
Order of R.R. & A.C. to remain a Magical Order?* and *A Postscript*
to this essay, which were privately printed for the members of
the Order.

One of the troubles at the rehearsals of *The Countess Cathleen*
had been that Yeats had been explaining his theories on verse-
speaking to the players with the aid of Florence Farr, who
had been illustrating his method on the psaltery. This instrument was devised by Arnold Dolmetsch, after Yeats and
Russell had discovered that Martyn was able to play the tunes
to which they composed their poems, and Yeats had brought
the notation, as played on Martyn's organ, to Florence Farr,
who became interested in the experiment of matching verse-
speaking and music.[20a] A poem 'The Players ask for a Blessing

on the Psalteries and Themselves' which is included in *In the Seven Woods* bears witness to Yeats's enthusiasm for this new device to improve the rendering of rhythm and verbal euphony. He gave a lecture at the Cliffords' Inn Hall in June 1902 to demonstrate this new method on which Wilfrid Blunt commented in his Diary:

> As an entertainment it was excellent, as he had got three ladies who recited admirably to the accompaniment of the psaltery invented by Dolmetsch. . . . Yeats, however, was far from convincing me that the method was either new or good as a way of reading poetry, indeed it reduced the verse to the position it holds in an opera libretto. It was impossible to distinguish whether the words were sense or only sound and the whole effect depended on the reader.[21]

The strangeness of Yeats's connection with the verse-reading is that he was tone deaf. Arnold Dolmetsch, after listening for a whole evening to the poet reciting verse, and coming to the conclusion that Yeats did not recognise the inflection of his own voice, found that he had 'a short phrase of fairly indistinct tones' which he used in reciting any of his poems.[22] While Yeats recited his verse in this tuneless manner it is interesting to point out that he was conscious of tunes when composing poetry, and was inclined to look down on Æ who used only two tunes when making verses:

> Mr Russell found to his surprise that he did not make every poem to a different tune, and to the surprise of the musician that he did make them all to two quite definite tunes, which are, it seems, like very simple Arabic music. . . . I, on the other hand, did not often compose to a tune, though I sometimes did, yet always to notes that could be written down and played on my friend's organ, or turned into something like a Gregorian hymn if one sang them in the ordinary way. I varied more than Mr Russell, who never forgot his two tunes, one for long and one for short lines, and could not always speak a poem in the same way.[23]

His views on what the drama should be were stated in the occasional organ of the Irish Literary Theatre, *Beltaine*, later *Samhain*, which he edited. In 1900, while no play of his was produced by the Irish Literary Theatre, he helped Moore to rewrite Martyn's political satire *The Tale of a Town*, and drew much of Martyn's odium on his head. This play, when first written, did not reach the standard of *The Heather Field*. Moore hastened to explain to Yeats and Lady Gregory that though he had helped in the writing of *The Heather Field* Martyn would not take his advice on *The Tale of a Town*. Eventually Martyn handed over the play to Moore, who called in Yeats to help him with the political subject-matter. Yeats was invited to

Tulira Castle, and instead of sharing Moore's concern for the disconsolate Martyn sitting alone in the tower of the castle, merely said, 'We couldn't produce such a play as that'. *The Tale of a Town* became *The Bending of the Bough* and Moore appeared as its sole author:

> I am afraid Martyn suffered a great deal. He says I spoilt his play but that is an illusion. I recast the play, but not enough. I should have written a new play on the subject. Then Edward said he could not sign it and he refused to let it be played anonymously so I had to sign it.[24]

The following year Yeats and Moore finished *Diarmuid and Grania* at Coole, and after a troublesome amount of squabbling arrived at the compromise that Moore should attend to the play's construction, Yeats to its dialogue. At one stage in the partnership Yeats wanted to have the dialogue put into Irish and then retranslated into English with an Irish idiom. Moore declared that he could write it all in French much better and was begged to do so. The ludicrous elements of the situation are hinted at in Moore's later account of the collaboration where he describes one plan by which Lady Gregory would translate his French into English, a native Irish speaker would turn this English into Irish, and Lady Gregory would then translate this Irish text back into English. The Irish critics received the play without enthusiasm. Yeats remembered its success, and tells in *Dramatis Personae* how after the performance the crowd from the gallery wished to remove the horse from the shafts of the cab in which he and Maud Gonne were leaving the theatre for a supper party, and drag it to their destination. Moore's account to his brother is more explicit:

> They first of all enjoyed the play, and having enjoyed it they repented in sackcloth and ashes, and I really believe that the repentance was much greater than their enjoyment of the play. At the end of the week they all discovered that the irrelevancies of the legend (the folklore) which had collected round the essential story had been omitted. They also discovered that Grania was not as perfectly virtuous as an Irishwoman should be.[25]

Neither Yeats nor Moore wished to publish the play. They quarrelled more seriously than before over a story which was intended to provide a basis for further collaboration. Yeats offered the theme to Moore but then wished to withdraw because Moore was not a member of the newly formed Irish National Theatre. Moore threatened to write a novel on the theme and get an injunction if Yeats used the plot in a play. Yeats took the threat seriously and hastily published *Where There is Nothing* in order to save from a plagiarist a subject that seemed worth the keeping till a greater knowledge of the stage made an adequate treatment possible. [25a]

Moore, always troublesome because of his violent and tactless public and private pronouncements, was becoming discouraged in his efforts to support the Gaelic movement, and this quarrel disillusioned him more. Martyn too had different aims to those of Yeats: he preferred modern drama on social themes to Yeats's peasant and poetic subjects, and had already been alienated by the treatment of his play *A Tale of a Town*. By 1902 both Martyn and Moore had, as Yeats put it, 'dropped out of the movement'.

In 1902 the Irish Literary Theatre had been replaced by the Irish National Dramatic Society, of which Yeats was President. The importance of this new society was that it included Irish actors who were likely to portray the new Irish plays with more understanding than English players:

> Our first players came from England, but presently we began our real work with a company of Irish amateurs. Somebody had asked me at a lecture 'Where will you get your actors?' and I had said 'I will go into some crowded room, put the name of everybody in it on a different piece of paper, put all those pieces of paper into a hat and draw the first twelve'. I have often wondered at that prophecy, for though it was spoken probably to confound a questioner, it was very nearly fulfilled. [25b]

The new Irish actors had been trained in the Ormond Dramatic Society, which had been created by two brothers, Frank and William Fay, who were greatly interested in drama. They were themselves excellent actors: Frank, who only acted in his spare time, preferred verse plays; William, who had been a member of an obscure touring company, was an admirable comedian. They had persuaded George Russell to allow them to produce his *Deirdre*; when Yeats saw them rehearsing this he was so impressed that he gave them his play, *Cathleen ni Houlihan*.

The play represented the height of Yeats's nationalism and love. It was written for Maud Gonne, and was an imaginary presentation of Ireland's desire for freedom rising phoenix-like from the ashes of many unsuccessful rebellions. The plot may seem simple without a knowledge of its background. An old woman, Cathleen ni Houlihan, who symbolises Ireland, visits a cottage where a young man is about to make a good marriage. She talks of her wrongs and of those who have helped her and who will:

They that have red cheeks will have pale cheeks for my sake, and for all that, they will think they are well paid.[26]

She leaves the cottage, having affected the young man by her talk. There is a noise of cheering outside and the younger son enters the cottage shouting that the French are landing at Killala.[27] The elder son follows the old woman; asked if he had met an old woman on the way the younger answers:

I did not, but I saw a young girl, and she had the walk of a queen.

The effect of the symbolism depended on the audience's knowledge of a popular street ballad called the 'Shan Van Vocht' (Poor Old Woman) which preserved the tradition of French aid for Irish rebellions: but even without this knowledge audiences have been moved by the beauty and dramatic skill of the play's conclusion. The first production was made memorable by the acting of Maud Gonne in the title role. She made Cathleen seem a divine being, but by drawing on latent national emotions Yeats was handling explosive material, as Stephen Gwynn has explained:

The effect of *Cathleen ni Houlihan* on me was that I went home asking myself if such plays should be produced unless one was prepared for people to go out to shoot and be shot. Yeats was not alone responsible; no doubt but Lady Gregory[27a] had helped him to get the peasant speech so perfect; but above all Miss Gonne's impersonation had stirred the audience as I have never seen another audience stirred.[28]

In old age Yeats looked back to this play with somewhat the same feelings:

> All that I have said and done,
> Now that I am old and ill,
> Turns into a question till
> I lie awake night after night
> And never get the answers right.
> Did that play of mine send out
> Certain men the English shot?[29]

From this identification of Maud with the spirit of Ireland came her favourite poem, 'Red Hanrahan's Song about Ireland':

> The wind has bundled up the clouds high over Knocknarea,
> And thrown the thunder on the stones for all that Maeve can say;
> Angers that are like noisy clouds have set our hearts abeat;
> But we have all bent low and low and kissed the quiet feet
> Of Cathleen, the daughter of Houlihan.[30]

The theme was probably suggested by James Clarence Mangan's 'Kathleen Ny-Houlihan, a Jacobite relic translated from the Irish of William Heffernan, called William Dall, or blind William'.[31] Both poems use Cathleen's name in the last line of each verse with a refrain-like effect. Yeats used some of the thoughts in Mangan's poem which describe the bitter anguish of those who await their deliverer Kathleen; but he developed the invocation in Mangan's second last verse which calls upon

> Him who formed the mighty globe with all its thousand lands
> Girdling them with seas and mountains, rivers deep and strands

into the descriptions of actual scenery which he knew and loved, the brown thorn trees of Cummen strand, Knocknarea, and the yellow pool on Clooth-na-Bare. This poetry was written partially out of that early belief that Irish poetry should concentrate upon descriptions of Irish scenery so that Irishmen abroad would recognise the places and so be moved by the poems, partially too out of his early desire to

> create some new *Prometheus Unbound*; Patrick or Columbkil, Oisin or Fionn, in Prometheus' stead; and, instead of Caucasus, Cro-Patric or Ben Bulben. ... Have not all races their first unity from a polytheism that marries them to rock and hill?[32]

These were dreams associated with Maud Gonne with whom he had often discussed them. She has written that they both felt that the land of Ireland was powerfully alive and invisibly peopled, to her a land to be freed so that it could protect its children, to him 'the beauty of unattainable perfection' which all must worship.[33]

Then, in 1903, Maud married John MacBride. The news came to Yeats by telegram.[34] It was impossible to grasp its full meaning at once. He was deeply hurt, shocked and angry. Years later he could remember the emptiness the news brought:

> Some may have blamed you that you took away
> The verses that could move them on the day
> When, the ears being deafened, the sight of the eyes blind
> With lightning, you went from me, and I could find
> Nothing to make a song about but kings,
> Helmets, and swords, and half-forgotten things
> That were like memories of you.[35]

In the poems of *The Green Helmet* (1910) some of the other side of Yeats's love is revealed, though not very obviously—the disappointment which she had earlier caused by failing to understand or appreciate his love for her, as well as the baffled disgust which the marriage itself inspired. (It was a patriotic

wedding, but though John MacBride had fought against
England with the Boers it did not seem, even to his own family,
at all a suitable match.) Yeats later came to dislike the great
waste which love had made of his young life; but despite his
shattered feelings he continued to write poetry about Maud
Gonne, paying tribute to her great beauty and his own admiration of it. The words and rhythms which he uses in *The Green
Helmet* are cold and simple, but the comparisons to Helen are
very apt—'like Helen she is beyond praise or comment'[36]—
and it is enough to tell the story simply:

> Ah, that Time could touch a form
> That could show what Homer's age
> Bred to be a hero's wage.
> 'Were not all her life but storm,
> Would not painters paint a form
> Of such noble lines,' I said,
> 'Such a delicate high head,
> All that sternness amid charm,
> All that sweetness amid strength?'[37]

His genuinely romantic poetry had come to a stop. Once
she was married there was nothing to look forward to, even
with diminishing hope. The puzzle to him had been that, when
they went to see the Lia Fail, Maud had appeared to understand his plans, especially those for the Castle of the Heroes,[37a]
to be built of Irish stone and decorated with the four jewels of
the Tuatha de Danaan, with perhaps a statue of Ireland. The
Lia Fail corresponded with the Altar, and the other symbols
were the Cauldron of the Dagda, the Golden Spear of Victory
of Lugh, and the Sword of Light.[38]   It seemed impossible to him
that she could not marry him, knowing his love and his plans
for Ireland.   Her marriage carried conviction that all hope of
achieving the loveliness of his dreams was gone, and so there
is an air of finality about the love poetry written after 1903. It
is at once detached and poignant:

> And I that have not your faith, how shall I know
> That in the blinding light beyond the grave
> We'll find so good a thing as that we have lost?
> The hourly kindness, the day's common speech,
> The habitual content of each with each
> When neither soul or body has been crossed.[39]

In two years' time she sought a separation from MacBride
which was contested. When she appeared at the Abbey there
were hisses from some of MacBride's partisans and Yeats began
to hate the mob:

And how what her dreaming gave
Earned slander, ingratitude,
From self-same dolt and knave;
Aye, and worse wrong than these.[40]

Deeply sympathetic, he aided her in her new troubles, un-
selfishly proving his friendship for her. She had become a
Roman Catholic (this explains his reference to her faith in the
poem quoted above) and so there was no question of her obtaining a divorce or of Yeats marrying her. She gained her separation, and realised sadly that his ideas of serving Ireland had
changed since her marriage:

He hated crowds, I loved them. His generous desire to help and share
my work brought him into contact with crowds and with all sorts of people,
men from the country and men from the towns, working for Ireland's
freedom. I hardly realised then how important that contact was for him
and sometimes felt guilty at taking so much of his time from his literary
work. As we sat together through the long boredom of conventions and
committee meetings, where his dominating personality and practical grasp
of detail made him a powerful ally, it sometimes seemed like using a fine
Toledo blade instead of a loy in the spade work of political organisation,
but I remember Willie's astonished pleasure when, after a meeting, some
shy boy would come up and shake his hand because he had read his poems
and loved them; I know that contact was good for him. After my marriage
and during my long sojourn in France, he lost this contact and became more
unaware of the forces working for Ireland's freedom.[41]

The other side of the problem is revealed by a note in Yeats's
Diary for 22 January 1909 which reads:

To-day the thought came to me that P. I. A. L. (Maud Gonne) never
really understands my plans or notions or ideas. Then came the thought—
what matter?—how much of the best that I have done and still do is but
the attempt to explain myself to her? If she understood I should lack a
reason for writing and one can never have too many reasons for doing
what is so laborious.

There followed the poem 'Words':

I had this thought a while ago,
'My darling cannot understand
What I have done, or what would do
In this blind bitter land.'

And I grew weary of the sun
Until my thoughts cleared up again,
Remembering that the best I have done
Was done to make it plain;

That every year I have cried 'At length
My darling understands it all,
Because I have come into my strength,
And words obey my call.'[42]

He was too near his hurt perplexed feelings for many years
to be able to balance what he liked and disliked in her per-

sonality. His tone is resigned and regretful both. In an 'amo'
poem he moves quickly from her political schemes to a personal
dislike of the people for whom she worked, and excuses everything, as he had always done, by her beauty:

> Why should I blame her that she filled my days
> With misery, or that she would of late
> Have taught to ignorant men most violent ways,
> Or hurled the little streets upon the great,
> Had they but courage equal to desire?
> What could have made her peaceful with a mind
> That nobleness made simple as a fire,
> With beauty like a tightened bow, a kind
> That is not natural in an age like this,
> Being high and solitary and most stern?
> Why, what could she have done, being what she is?
> Was there another Troy for her to burn?[43]

The 'odi' of his passion appeared in the Diary:

> My dear is angry, that of late
> I cry all base blood down,
> As if she had not taught me hate
> By kisses to a clown.[44]

The poems of *The Green Helmet* which are not concerned with
the poet's love for Maud must be understood against the background of his life. They were written by a disillusioned but
by no means despairing Yeats. They are far from the languor
and resignation, the nostalgia and deliberate restriction of his
earlier poetry but they lack the full intellectual and rhetorical
content which was to give his succeeding poetry its peculiar
power. His ideals of love and patriotism were not yet replaced;
he was like a child who looks at its bricks before beginning to
integrate them in a new and real structure which will live not
merely in his imagination.[44a]

His contemporaries did not realise that the poetry of *The
Green Helmet* was transitional (indeed the appearance of his
*Collected Works* in 1908 had led to the Dublin gossip that he
had written himself out)[44b] and merely regarded *Responsibilities*,
the succeeding volume of poems published in 1914, as non-
poetical and a demonstration that Yeats had lost his inspiration.[45] C. L. Wrenn 'dismissed *Responsibilities* as a collection of
topical verses, the work of a tired man fighting for lost causes
and ideas', and Forrest Reid[46] thought *The Green Helmet* showed
'a marked falling off in both inspiration and expression'.[47]

*Responsibilities* has been described as the volume containing an
expression of doubt of the value of writing poetry alone, but it
is the poetry of *The Green Helmet* which reveals Yeats's psycho-

logical development at the transition stage of his poetic career. If the contents of this volume be compared with those of its predecessor *In the Seven Woods*, we can see how Yeats was extending the scope of his work. There are only two direct references to topical events in the earlier volume, a veiled and rude allusion to the coronation of Edward VII and Alexandra[48] and the prayer for a blessing on the players and their psalteries. *The Green Helmet*, on the other hand, reflects Yeats's views and beliefs on many subjects, refers directly to topical affairs and records more freely the poet's life. The poems are inspired by Yeats's feelings, rather than what he thought his feelings ought to be. Or, to put it another way, his ideas of what he thought his feelings ought to be had changed. He had been introduced to Nietzsche by John Quinn, the great Irish-American patron of the intellectual movement, and had found that Nietzsche divided the soul's main movements into the Dionysiac and Apollonian, transcending and creating forms respectively. He decided that his Dionysiac period was over, and that he must leave the methods of Mallarmé and Symons. He became dissatisfied with the beauty of his Celtic poetry and told H. W. Nevinson that Byron was the last *man* who made poetry; he wanted to combine the two sides of his character, the dreaming and the active.

*The Green Helmet* foreshadows what is to come. This flat negative writing forms the bare statement which Yeats whipped into vigour in *Responsibilities*. The rhetoric made from quarrels with others emerged in 'On hearing that the students of our new University have joined the agitation against immoral literature', and hints at the scornful bitterness to be inspired a few years later by the Lane controversy. That obsession with age, which stamps its way testily through the corridors of the middle poems, and finally roars for its rightful seat to be brought to the fireside of the *Last Poems*, is but climbing the steps to the hall door in 'The coming of wisdom with time':

> Though leaves are many, the root is one;
> Through all the lying days of my youth
> I swayed my leaves and flowers in the sun;
> Now I may wither into truth.[49]

His poems on Coole and the small poem on Lady Gregory's illness look forward to the poetry of praise which later attained such simplicity and dignity. Imitation, too, had its place in the volume, in 'At the Abbey Theatre' and 'A Drinking Song'.

The poet's satiric power[49a] is given a freer rein than before in 'To a poet [Æ] who would have me praise certain bad poets, imitators of his and mine', of which the Diary version runs

> You tell me that I often have given tongue
> To praise what other men have said or sung
> That it would get me friends if I praised these,
> But tell me, do the wolf dogs praise their fleas?

Yeats wrote to Russell of the latter's anthology of the work of these younger imitative poets, *New Songs*, that:

> Some of the poems I will probably underrate (though I am certain I could recognise a masterpiece come out of any temperament) because the dominant mood is one I have fought in myself and put down—This reign of shadows is full of false images of the spirit and of the body. I have come to feel towards it as O'Grady feels towards it and even as some of my stupidest critics feel.

He thought that he found no distinction between greatness and smallness among Æ's guests. There is an impassioned entry in his Diary of 1908–12, section 169:

> Went to Russell's Sunday night. Everybody either too tall or too short or crooked or lopsided. One woman had that terrible thing in a woman an excited voice and an interest without self-possession. There was a bad poet with a swollen neck. There was a man with the look of a wood-kern[?], who kept bringing the conversation back and back to Synge's wrong doing in having made a girl in the Playboy admire a man who had hamstrung 'mountain yeos'. He saw nothing else to object to but the one thing he declared that kept Englishmen from giving Home Rule was that they thought Ireland 'cruel' because of the hurt to animals during agrarian agitation. No such man should write a sentence to help them. There arose before my mind a vision of this man—he had been in India I think, arguing for years and years on this one subject with an endless procession of second rate men. At last I said 'When a country produces a man of genius he never is what it wants or believes it wants, he is always unlike the idea of itself. In the eighteenth century Scotland believed itself very religious and very moral and very gloomy and its national poet Burns came not to speak of these things but to speak of lust and drink and drunken gaiety. Ireland since the Young Irelanders has given itself up to apologetics. Every impression of life or impulse of imagination has been examined to see if it helped or hurt the glory of Ireland, or the political claim of Ireland. Gradually sincere impressions of life became impossible—all was artificial apologetics. There was no longer an impartial imagination delighting in things because they were naturally exciting. Synge was the rushing up of this buried fire, an explosion, a furious impartiality of an indifferent turbulent sorrow. Like Burns his work was to say all that people did not want to have said. He was able to do this because nature had made him incapable of a political thought.' The wood kern made no answer but did not understand me I daresay, but for the rest of the evening he kept saying over and over the same thing 'He objected to nothing but the passage about the mountain yeos'.

Later he added the comment that the poet with the swollen neck was an excellent poet; he had not known his work when he first met him. The next section of the Diary supplies a comment on his irritability at the time:

> Saw Lady Gregory yesterday. She said. 'I am very glad for you need a few days among normal and simple well-bred people.'

His work in *The Green Helmet* is varied; it contains poetry which is a mixture of business, dislike, thwarted love, humour, gossip, sensuality, dreams, introspection, snobbery and purposelessness. Mysticism and tangled urgency have not yet replaced the loss of Celtic imagery and delicate symbols of love. Yeats, as a man, is the link between the two styles of poetry. He had to dethrone the poetry which was in itself a purpose and champion the life of this world before his poetry and his life could be unified.

His energies were devoted to the theatre. Three of his plays were produced at the brief and successful appearance of the Irish National Dramatic Company in London in May 1903. These were *The Countess Cathleen*, *The Pot of Broth*, a comedy centring round the stone which a tramp sells to the farmer's wife, who believes that it will make broth, and gives him the chicken she is cooking for dinner in payment; and *The Hour Glass*, a morality play with a Fool, a Wise Man and an Angel, in which the Wise Man humbles himself to the Fool and receives salvation as a reward. Fay's performance as the Fool was excellent, and Digges, who took the part of the Wise Man, was coached by Yeats with great effect. The whole programme, which included Lady Gregory's *Twenty Five*, was received with enthusiasm by the London critics:

> To say the visit was a triumph is to use words mildly: actually Irish plays and Irish acting achieved fame in a night. [49b]

As an indirect result of this visit came support from Yeats's friend Miss Horniman, an English woman and a charitable fellow member of the Cabbalistic Society, who had admired the acting of the Irish players in London, and sympathised with the aims of the National Theatre as Yeats explained them. The idealism with which he stated his views can be seen in a passage from one of his essays in *Samhain*:

> We have to write or find plays that will make the theatre a place of intellectual excitement—a place where the mind goes to be liberated as it was liberated by the theatres of Greece and England and France at certain

great moments of their history, and as it is liberated in Scandinavia to-day. If we are to do this we must learn that beauty and truth are always justified of themselves. Truth and beauty judge and are above judgment. They justify and have no need of justification.

Since the production of *The Land of Heart's Desire* and *The Countess Cathleen* he had learned much of stage-craft, and the revisions of *The Countess Cathleen* indicate how ready he was to apply the lessons he had learned. He longed to give effect to new theories on the reform of play-writing, modes of speech and movement in acting, and scenery. He could write his own plays and influence others to write from the same motives.[49c] His theories on verse-speaking were amplified by Florence Farr's performances on the psaltery. His ideas on acting were partly due to the technique of the Fays who allowed but small movement and gesture, and that only to the actor who happened to be speaking. Scenery, he thought, should be simple; in this he was influenced by Gordon Craig. For all these aims to be realised a permanent theatre was necessary, and this was now built in Dublin at Miss Horniman's expense. An old theatre in the Mechanics' Institute was expanded by the addition of what had been the adjoining city morgue. Miss Horniman wrote to Yeats that she could only

afford to make a very little theatre, and it must be quite simple. You all must do the rest to make a powerful and prosperous theatre with a high artistic ideal.

There was delay in a patent being granted for the opening of the new theatre, as the application was opposed by the other Dublin theatres, but after an examination of witnesses the necessary permission was given to Lady Gregory. Meanwhile in November 1903 Yeats had gone on his first lecture tour to America, which John Quinn had arranged for him. This was a great success, and both his personality and his oratory made a deep impression on the many and varied audiences which he addressed. His political experiences in Ireland had taught him the value of tact, and he wrote an amusing account to Lady Gregory of a struggle with a woman reporter

who wanted to print, and probably will, a number of indiscreet remarks of mine. Here is an example. 'What do you think of Kipling?' 'I shall say nothing whatever about Kipling if you please. I will say nothing about any living poet. If he would have the goodness to die I would have plenty to say. Good heavens, have you written that down?' 'Yes, it is the one Irish remark you have made.' 'You will please rub it out again.' Thereon we had a struggle of ten minutes, and in spite of her promise I expect to see printed in large letters 'Yeats desires Kipling's death'. I have sent an urgent message demanding a proof. I had been painfully judicious for days, as the reporters had been Irish and asked about Ireland, but this woman asked about general literature and I was off my guard.

The Abbey Theatre opened in December 1904 with a programme of plays by Yeats, Synge and Lady Gregory. As producer-manager Yeats was constantly busy, advising the young actors, 'learning his instrument in those years of producing'. There was no opportunity, had there been the desire, for 'pure' poetry. Many of his friends, especially Maud Gonne and Arthur Symons, regretted his new preoccupation, and blamed Lady Gregory for it. His father, however, had different views, which he expressed in a letter to his daughter Lily:

> It seems that 'Arthur' hates Lady Gregory and moans at the mention of her. 'Well, Arthur, it was your fault.' 'Yes. I know it was I who brought him to Coole, and as soon as her terrible eye fell upon him I knew she would keep him, and he is now lost to lyrical poetry.' Probably Arthur Symons hates this theatre business like Æ who thinks the theatre only a peep show. On the whole I am very glad that Lady Gregory 'got' Willie. Arthur Symons never speaks of her except as the 'Strega' which is the Italian for witch. I don't regret her witchcraft, though it is not easy personally to like her. They are all so prejudiced that they think her plays are put into shape by Willie . . . which of course is nonsense. I for one won't turn against Lady Gregory. She is perfectly disinterested. She shows this disinterestedness. That is one of the reasons why she is so infernally haughty to lesser mortals—or whom she thinks lesser mortals.[49d]

'Lesser mortals' probably included Miss Horniman, who found that she was not *persona grata* in Dublin. She did not understand the flippancy of Dublin's talk, and she seemed to the nationalists a suspicious character when there were to be no cheap seats in her theatre. Madame MacBride is of the opinion that both Lady Gregory and Miss Horniman were in love with Yeats, and certainly in Miss Horniman's letters there is the suppressed sentimentality which would indicate this. Lady Gregory carried more weight in all Yeats's plans. She, with Synge, became Yeats's co-director in a limited company which replaced the National Theatre in 1905. The change was mainly due to Yeats, and caused some friction. The theatre had previously been run on a basis of communal discussion and Yeats thought that the system was too slack and haphazard.

How the 'theatre business' affected Yeats as a poet is recorded in his Diary for September 1909, an entry which demonstrates his method of drafting a poem in prose before he began to work out the ideas in verse:

> Subject. To complain of the fascination of what's difficult. It spoils spontaneity and pleasure, and wastes time. Repeat the line ending difficult

three times and rhyme on bolt, exalt, coalt [*sic*], jolt. One could use the thought that the winged and unbroken coalt must drag a cart of stones out of pride because it is difficult, and end by denouncing drama, accounts, public contests, and all that is merely difficult.

An entry in the Diary for March 1910 contains the final version with alternatives for the phrase 'Theatre business' written beneath—'On the day's letters' or 'On correspondence'. He adds 'Life is memory of what has never happened and hope for what will never happen' and there follow more versions of separate lines of the poem which runs:

> The fascination of what's difficult
> Has dried the sap out of my veins, and rent
> Spontaneous joy and natural content
> Out of my heart. There's something ails our colt
> That must, as if it had not holy blood
> Nor on Olympus leaped from cloud to cloud,
> Shiver under the lash, strain, sweat and jolt
> As though it dragged road metal. My curse on plays
> That have to be set up in fifty ways,
> On the day's war with every knave and dolt,
> Theatre business, management of men.
> I swear before the dawn comes round again
> I'll find the stable and pull out the bolt.[50]

The adjectives 'winged' and 'unbroken' in the draft of the poem make it completely certain that the colt was Pegasus. The image was more directly used by Yeats's friend Sturge Moore in conjectures concerning the invention of devils in *A Tale of a Tub*:

> Swift, as a rule, used his Pegasus for a cart horse since it was strong and he sorely importuned by the press of men and notions in need of condign punishment: but even when plodding in the ruts, its motion betrays the mettle in which it here revels.[51]

The similarity of the two friends' treatment of the idea extends even to the similarity of sound in 'mettle' and 'metal' which suggests that the thought was described verbally by one to the other. A likely source for a double borrowing might be Heine's *Atta Troll*:

> In the land of fable prances
> My beloved Pegasus.
> He's no useful, safely virtuous
> Cart horse of your citizen.[52]

Sturge Moore was one of Yeats's many new friends; another was Bridges, whom Yeats had first met in 1897, and who thought him a true poet and delightful company, but in 'great danger of fooling himself with Rosicrucianism and folk lore and erotical spiritualism'.[53] Constance Gore-Booth had taken

Yeats to a séance in London and he had found that the terror
inspired by his early experience did not return and that he
could resume his early interest in spiritualistic phenomena.
She had become his friend during the course of visits to Lissadell
in the winter of 1894, his first *entrée* into Irish county family
life, of which he possessed such gracious memories in later
years when he contrasted in his mind the promise of the sisters'
youth with what their lives became:

> Many a time I think to seek
> One or the other out and speak
> Of that old Georgian mansion, mix
> Pictures of the mind, recall
> That table and the talk of youth,
> Two girls in silk kimonos, both
> Beautiful, one a gazelle. [54]

Other friends included the artists Rothenstein, Ricketts and
Shannon, Pamela Coleman Smith and Althea Gyles. Mase-
field's company, [54a] though he was more an intimate of Jack
Yeats, was greatly enjoyed and the Poet Laureate has given a
detailed picture of the rooms in Woburn Buildings in *Some
Memories of W. B. Yeats*, published by the Cuala Press in 1940.
Yeats used the front room on the second floor as a sitting-room.
It was papered in brown and had originally brown curtains,
later replaced by Lady Gregory's gift of dark blue ones. His
pictures included Blake's first seven Dante engravings, 'The
Whirlwind of Loves', an engraving of Blake's head, and 'The
Ancient of Days', Beardsley's poster for the Florence Farr
production of *The Land of Heart's Desire*, a portrait of a woman
with a rose between her lips by Cecil French, and, ample
evidence of the artistic abilities of the Yeats family, one of
J. B. Y.'s impressions of his poet son, and an illustration of
Blake's, 'I thought love lived in the hot sunshine', Jack Yeats's
'Memory Harbour', an impression of Sligo which was reproduced in *Autobiographies*, and a pastel by the poet of the 'Lake
hills near Coole'. There was a Kelmscott Chaucer on a blue
lectern, enormous candles, a gong to summon Mrs. Old (the
wife of the carpenter who was Yeats's landlord) who looked
after the rooms. A settle, Lady Gregory's armchair, a table,
and bookshelves completed the room where Yeats held his
'Mondays'. [54b] When Masefield first visited Woburn Buildings
Yeats had a bad cold and had wanted to put off the visit but
had lost Masefield's address, so that Lady Gregory came later
and read, so as to save Yeats's throat.

Coole became, in a sense, his second home, and what Lady Gregory meant in his life was recorded in his Diary for February 1909:

This morning I got a letter telling me of Lady Gregory's illness. I did not recognise her son's writing at first and my mind wandered, I suppose because I am not well. I thought my mother was ill and that my sister was asking me to come at once: then I remembered my mother died years ago and that more than kin was at stake. She has been to me mother, friend, sister and brother. I cannot realise the world without her—she brought to my wavering thoughts steadfast nobility. All the day the thought of losing her is like a conflagration in the rafters. Friendship is all the house I have.

There follows more praise of Lady Gregory, some of which is published in *Estrangement*, and then comes the simple and dignified poem 'A Friend's Illness':

Sickness brought me this
Thought, in that scale of his:
Why should I be dismayed
Though flame had burned the whole
World, as it were a coal,
Now I have seen it weighed
Against a soul?[55]

The next section continues:

All Wednesday I heard Castiglione's phrase ringing in my memory 'Never be it spoken without tears, the Duchess is dead'—that slight phrase which coming as it did among the number of his dead had often moved me till my eyes dimmed; and I feel all his sorrow as though one saw the worth of life fade for ever.

If Yeats had come to grips with reality through a greater knowledge of Ireland, he had something with which to replace his old ideals. This was an increasing belief in aristocracy, a result of his friendship with Lady Gregory, which enabled him to appreciate the extremes of society more than before:

In spite of myself, my mind dwells more and more on ideas of class. Ireland has grown sterile because power has passed to men who lack the training which requires a certain amount of wealth to ensure continuity from generation to generation.[56]

Maud Gonne believed that after her wedding

His search for hidden knowledge had led him so far along strange paths that at times he almost forgot the object of the quest. He found himself among the comfortable and well-fed, who style themselves the 'upper classes', but whom Willie, shuddering at the words and discriminating even among them, called 'distinguished Persons'; and some undoubtedly deserved the title.[57]

This belief in the greatness of aristocracy began to flower upon that wreckage of his idealism which came both from the political

experiences into which his love had led him and from the disillusion of that love itself:

In our age it is impossible to create, as I had dreamed, an heroic and
passionate conception of life worthy of the study of men elsewhere and in
other lands, and to make this conception the dream of the Irish people. The
Irish people till they are better educated, must dream impermanent
dreams and if they do not find them they will be ruined by the Half-Sirs
with their squalid hates and envies. There was a time when I thought this
of a noble body for all eyes a soul for subtle understandings. . . . Instead
the people cry out for stones and weapons, pedantry and hysterics, rhetoric
and sentiment.[57a]

The part played by Coole in the creation of his new belief
in aristocracy was very important. 'Upon a house shaken by
the Land Agitation' was drafted in his Diary in a form almost
more attractive than the poem itself:

Subject for poem 'A Shaken House'. How should the world gain if this
house failed, even though a hundred little houses were the better for it, for
here power has gone forth, or lingered giving energy, precision; it gives to
a far people beneficent rule, and still under its roof loving intellect is
sweetened by old memories, of its descents from far off; how should the
world be better if the wren's nest flourish and the eagle's[58] house is
scattered?

There followed the final text of the poem and an explanation:

I wrote this poem on hearing the result of reduction of rent made by the
courts. One feels that when all must make their living they will live not
for life's sake but the work's and all be the poorer. My work is very near
to life itself and my father's very near to life itself but I am always feeling
a lack of life's own values behind my own thought. They should have been
there before the stream began, before it became necessary to let the work
create its values. This house has enriched my soul out of measure because
here life moves within restraint through gracious forms. Here there has
been no compelled labour, no poverty thwarted impulse.

Here he found peace, and quietude, and, above all an order
in life. His routine was gently imposed by Lady Gregory, and
he wrote to Florence Farr that Coole was always his place of
industry:

After breakfast Chaucer—garden for twenty minutes—Then work from
11 till 2, then lunch then I fish from 3 till 5, then I read and then work
again at lighter tasks till dinner—after dinner walk. To this I have added
sandow exercises daily.[58a]

His appearance had altered, and Wilfrid Blunt wrote of him
in 1909 as being plump, pink-cheeked and prosperous-looking
as any theatrical manager should be.[58b] Apart from the physical well-being which came with this regularised life there was

6

the beauty of Coole. He thought the lake the most beautiful place in the world, and the Galway plains were places of enchantment, where dwelt a people of imaginative possessions. These were the stories and poems of which Lady Gregory had shown the charm and emotional heritage.

What Maud Gonne had been unable to understand, Yeats's purpose in writing about

> kings,
> Helmets, and swords, and half-forgotten things,

was, however, fully understood by Lady Gregory and Synge. The work of these three directors of the Abbey was 'a deliberate attempt by three people to create an Irish literature by going back to the very sources of literature: myth, folk-lore and primitive speech'.[59] The common bond between their positive interests was cemented by a dislike of the middle classes:

> John Synge, I and Augusta Gregory, thought
> All that we did, all that we said or sang
> Must come from contact with the soil, from that
> Contact everything Antaeus-like grew strong.
> We three alone in modern times had brought
> Everything down to that sole test again,
> Dream of the noble and the beggar-man.[60]

The influence of Lady Gregory and Synge upon Yeats's plays is considerable. He drew from them the foils to his romantic figures, the Blind Man and the Fool,[60a] for instance, in *On Baile's Strand*. The peasant speech of these characters intensifies the depth of Cuchulain's passionate nature, and their presence on the stage reflects Yeats's interest in extremes, and in oppositions: the Wise Man and the Fool;[61] never the balanced man. His skill in drama increased. *On Baile's Strand* is a steady development to a crescendo of feeling, if not of dramatic action. Cuchulain, though the lover of many women, believes himself to be childless, and boasts that no pallid ghost or mockery of a man is left by him to drift in the corridors where he himself has laughed and sung. He is an heroic great man, drawn probably out of an admiration of Nietzsche's theories which were constantly in W. B.'s head at the time. His father wrote to him in 1906:

As you have dropped affection from the circle of your needs, have you also dropped love between man and woman? Is this the theory of the overman, if so, your demi-godship is after all but a doctrinaire demi-godship. Your words are idle—and you are far more human than you think. You would be a philosopher and are really a poet.[62]

Cuchulain would be the successful lover and rejoice in his childlessness, yet in his sleep he cried aloud poignantly and bitterly 'I have no son'. We think of a personal poem written ten years later:

> Pardon that for a barren passion's sake,
> Although I have come close on forty-nine,
> I have no child, I have nothing but a book
> Nothing but that to prove your blood and mine.[63]

He can describe Aoife, the Queen of Scotland, who is, though he knows it not, the mother of his son, in terms of the highest praise, remembering her pale cheeks and red-brown hair, her high laughing turbulent head, and he can praise her for a beauty unknown to any other queen or lover. He meets the son whom, as a champion come from Scotland, he must drive from the High King's land, does not recognise him, but for an unknown reason would have him as a friend. The High King forbids this, and Cuchulain turns on him; then, shocked at his own disloyalty, he fights and kills the young man. The Fool and Blind Man reveal the secret of his son's identity. There is all the impending doom of a Greek tragedy in this play, the same tragedy as of the passionate Ajax, the obtuse Agamemnon, or the self-deceiving Oedipus.

A question to be asked is whether Yeats was being true to the Irish legend in introducing the mystery of fate. The epic idea of fate did not trouble Homer or interest him as much as it did the almost theological tragedians of Greece. If we contrast Ferguson's scholarly version of the Deirdre legend with that of Yeats, we find that the Gaelic epic revolves in the former's adaptations more on human character than on any less easily understood sense of tragic fate. Ferguson used the ancient version of the legend given by Theophilus O'Flanagan,[64] by O'Curry[65] and by Keating.[66] He had no overhanging sadness throughout his more out of doors treatment; the tragedy is caused by Naisi's stupidity rather than blind fate:

NAISI:
> O dear-loved Deirdre, thy advice was good.
> I had been wiser, had I taken it,
> And all of us, I dread, had safer been.
> Yet thou dost not reproach me.

DEIRDRE:
> No reproach
> From lips of Deirdre shalt thou ever hear.
> All that my noble lord had done was right,
> Wise and magnanimous.[67]

The difference between the more scholarly, more Gaelic, more epic handling of the story by Ferguson and the more dramatic, sensuous and emotional approach of Yeats can be illustrated by their treatment of Deirdre's request for the burial of the dead heroes:

> Thanks, gentle Cormac, who hast won for me
> The boon to see these nobles buried.
> Give them an honourable sepulchre,
> And while ye dig their grave, let me begin
> My lamentable death song over them.
>
> (*Ferguson's version*)

> We lay the dead out, folding the hands,
> Closing the eyes, and stretching out the feet,
> And push a pillow underneath the head
> Till all's in order; and all this I'll do
> For Naisi, son of Usna.
>
> (*Yeats's version*)

In the elaboration we can see the effect of Lady Gregory's translations of heroic legends (though some of the detail in the passage quoted may remind the reader more of a peasant wake) which were based more on the later Fenian cycle than the Red Branch stories, and thus included more detail and sentimentality.[67a] Where O'Flanagan's source praised Deirdre as 'beautiful' MacPherson elaborated:

> Her hair sighs on Ocean's wind
> Her robe streams in dusky wreaths.
> She is like the fair spirit of heaven
> In the midst of his shadowy mist.[68]

In Lady Gregory's Kiltartan idiom Deirdre:

grew straight and clean like a rush on the bog, and she was comely beyond comparison of all the women of the world, and her movements were like the swan on the wave or as the deer on the hill.

Yeats's view of the heroine is seen through an even greater distance:

> There's nobody can say
> If she were human or of those begot
> By an invisible king of the air in a storm
> Of a king's daughter or anything at all
> Or who she was or why she was hidden then
> But that she had too much beauty for good luck.[69]

In the treating of the story of Deirdre he seized on what seemed to him the essential drama of the legend:

> One woman and two men; that is the quarrel
> That knows no mending,[69a]

and concentrated into one act the treachery and terror which kills Naisi, and the high lofty air of Deirdre which enables her to leave the stage with the fatal knife concealed beneath her dress. Suspense and suddenness of mood were fully achieved, and his imagination gave the full flavour of an essentially personal interpretation to the legend.

Neither Yeats's heroic legends nor Synge's strange plays based on an equally personal interpretation of peasant life appealed to the Abbey audience. The small theatre was unpopular, and for a time became a place of fierce contention. Yeats's struggle against Irish public opinion on behalf of Synge's work was both courageous and unselfish. Synge's early play *The Shadow of the Glen* had caused much annoyance to a section of public opinion which considered the plot a deliberate insult to the Irish peasantry. Despite this disapproval, often the uneasiness which came as the result of political tension and a national inferiority complex, no action was taken against the performance of the play.

Some years later, in 1907, a crisis arose over the first production of Synge's *The Playboy of the Western World*. On the first night some of the audience began to demonstrate, their modesty outraged by the use of the word 'shift'. Yeats has described the events in *The Arrow*:

> On the second performance of *The Playboy of the Western World* about forty men who sat in the middle of the pit succeeded in making the play entirely inaudible. Some of them brought tin trumpets, and the noise began immediately upon the rise of the curtain. For days articles in the papers called for the withdrawal of the play, but we played for the week we had announced; and before the week's end opinion had turned in our favour. There were, however, nightly disturbances and a good deal of rioting in the neighbouring streets. On the last night there were, I believe, five hundred police keeping order in the theatre and its neighbourhood. [70]

A public meeting was held in the Abbey to discuss *The Playboy*, and there Yeats fought the play's case against a hostile audience. Synge's reputation as a playwright largely depended upon Yeats's initial insistence on his merits.

This crisis was a blow to Yeats's plans for moulding a new cultural outlook in Ireland, and changed his attitude from doubt to certainty that there could be no appreciation of art or literature in 'this blind bitter land' twisted and strained by the hatreds of politics. He was deeply moved by the attack on Synge for he exalted him to a Homeric position, and so the attack on *The Playboy* became of more than political or religious significance. It was an attack upon the position of genius. He had written in his Diary of the sterility of Irish writing and thought as due to sexual abstinence and referred to this warping of repressed desire again in May 1910:

> When any part of human life has been left unexperienced there is a hunger for the experience in large numbers of men and if the expression is prevented artificially the hunger becomes morbid, and [then], if the educated do not beware, is born the ignorant will.

and in the essay which he wrote in memory of his friend in Normandy in the same year he showed the issue as he saw it:

> Some spontaneous dislike had been but natural, for genius like his can but slowly, amid what it has of harsh and strange, set forth the nobility of its beauty, and the depth of its compassion; but the frenzy that would have silenced his master work was, like most violent things, artificial, that defence of virtue by those who have but little, which is the pomp and gallantry of journalism and its right to govern the world.

After the trouble over *The Playboy*, Lady Gregory brought Yeats for a holiday to Italy, and this visit included Florence, Milan, Urbino, Ferrara, and Ravenna. The trip, apart from having a great compensatory value to Yeats—it was a further demonstration of the value of the aristocratic way of life— settled the relative influence possessed over the poet by Lady Gregory and Miss Horniman. Miss Horniman in 1906 had had her way in the curtailment of W. G. Fay's powers as stage manager, but afterwards agreed not to take a more active part in the direction of the theatre herself. Madame MacBride's comment on the situation was that Lady Gregory triumphed in 1907 for Miss Horniman brought back Italian plaques to decorate the Abbey but Lady Gregory carried off Willie to visit the Italian towns where they were made.

Yeats knew that the audience of the Abbey was not en-enthralled by the beauty of his verse.[70a] He did not, therefore, attempt to force his work on the theatre, as he had insisted on playing Synge's plays. Modesty and a realisation that the verse plays were not popular prevented him:

> When we are high and airy hundreds say
> That if we hold that flight they'll leave the place,
> While these same hundreds mock another day
> Because we have made our art of common things.[71]

Although he now disliked the 'cottage comedies' and the realism of the younger dramatists which the Abbey audience readily accepted Yeats paid great attention to the details of their production. His heartfelt concern for the theatre penetrated even to his dreams:

> Woke Monday morning having dreamed in early morning that I was in Dublin and wanted to go to England, but in a trireme. I proposed this to an assembly of people, members of the Abbey and some fashionable young men. . . . The project had to be given up and I surprised myself by doing this without regret but said: 'One has a thousand ideas and only one or two are carried out. Yet I am right. One cannot understand the Odyssey if one has not sailed in a trireme.' Was it all a symbol of the Abbey's lack of capital?[72]

This devotion to the theatre which was providing a home for the works of other writers whose plays Yeats did not like was an extraordinary example of unselfishness. In 1909 Bernard Shaw offered the Abbey his play, *The Shewing-up of Blanco Posnet*, which had been banned by the English censor. Yeats and Lady Gregory decided to accept the play and produce it in Horse Show week when there are many visitors. They could stage it in Dublin because the laws governing the Irish theatres had been made by the old Irish Government and therefore did not provide for the jurisdiction of the English censor in Ireland. The Lord Lieutenant, Lord Aberdeen, considered it his duty to withdraw the play, and pointed out that the play did not appear to him to conform to the conditions imposed by the Patent which had been granted to Lady Gregory. There ensued a long series of visits and letters between Yeats and Lady Gregory and the officials of the Castle, the details of which have been recorded by Lady Gregory in *Our Irish Theatre*. After much anxiety the directors decided to produce the play, which was already being rehearsed, and to risk losing the Patent[73] and the small capital which had been accumulated with such difficulty. The publicity gained for the theatre by this decision was immense: the play was not interfered with, and proved a success. Yeats, who had persuaded Shaw to give the Abbey the play, was again acting astutely in the ultimate interest of the theatre, for he disliked Shaw's work in general, and did not think highly of the play in question. He had always a strong dislike of censorship, fearing that the moral issues were liable to be overshadowed by political considerations. There was another crisis, this time with Miss Horniman, who thought a political use was made of the theatre when it remained open on the occasion of King Edward's death in 1910. She discontinued her subsidy. Yeats and Lady Gregory won their case when the matter was submitted to arbitration, but as their explanation was unacceptable to Miss Horniman they replaced the subsidy by means of a series of lectures to be held in London. By this time Yeats had resigned from his managership; the poet had proved himself a man of action.

# 7

# RESPONSIBILITIES

## (1908–1915)

*The poet finds and makes his mask in disappointment*
W. B. YEATS[1]

YEATS gradually evolved the doctrine that a man desires his opposite.[2] It is difficult to say precisely when he first formulated this thought. To a certain extent he had to wait for the full development of his own personality before he could formulate his theory of the anti-self. There was always a tension in Yeats from his childhood onwards, the creative antithetical tension of the opposite elements in his character:

> We make out of the quarrels with others rhetoric, but out of the quarrel with ourselves poetry.[3]

From his youth to the end of the nineties one aspect had been stressed, and the poet *par excellence* produced, a man who thought of beauty and how to express it; but the result of living to an exclusive formula of life for art's sake led to what might be described as an arrested development. The idealist and lover of what seemed the perfect land and lady did not maintain that suspension of criticism which an accepting love brings; but it was only after his thirtieth year that he had begun to find the edge of his enthusiasm blunted. The blows of Maud's marriage and the struggle over *The Playboy* brought him to a complete standstill. He realised the futility of his previous course more clearly; and he now swung in the opposite direction:

> All things can tempt me from this craft of verse:
> One time it was a woman's face, or worse—
> The seeming needs of my fool-driven land;
> Now nothing but comes readier to the hand
> Than this accustomed toil.[4]

In September 1909 he wrote in his Diary:

> Am I perhaps going against Nature in my constant attempt to fill my life with work? is my mind as rich as in idle days? Is not perhaps the poet's labour a mere reflection? If he seeks purity—the ridding of his life of all but poetry—will not inspiration come? Can one reach God by toil? He gives himself to the pure in heart. He asks nothing but attention.

He had met the idea of contraries in Blake and Boehme.[5] Hone suggests[6] that an early letter to Mrs Shakespear shows that the notion of contrary types of character was germinating in Yeats's brain before the turn of the century, for Yeats suggested that a character in one of her novels should be an actively athletic but passively artistic young man, and then went on to stress the contradiction between Morris's table manners and the tact of the characters in his romances. Hone also thinks that the many instances in the early poems where shadows are described are a contributory part of the beginning of the idea.[7] Yeats was greatly impressed by a painting by Æ which showed a man on a mountain shrinking from his shadow in the mist. There is, however, a poem of the early period which states the problem clearly.[7a] In 'Fergus and the Druid' the life of action is abandoned by Fergus, who seeks wisdom from the Druid, and would

> Be no more a king
> But learn the dreaming wisdom that is yours.[8]

An idea associated with the theory of the anti-self was that of the mask. An entry in the Diary of Stephen Daedalus reveals Joyce's insight. He describes in a sentence the Robartes that existed in Yeats's mind towards the end of the nineties:

> Michael Robartes remembers forgotten beauty and, when his arms wrap her round he presses in his arms the loveliness which has long faded from the world.[9]

When Yeats created[10] Robartes he was himself ill and disappointed in love. Robartes was strong, violent, romantic, and athletic, sun-tanned and weather-beaten, successful as lover and man of action. In 'Rosa Alchemica' Robartes is imagined as bringing Yeats to a magical society against his will and giving him transports of delight at the old mysterious beauty of its meeting. The romantic Robartes wore a mask:

> When we had started and Michael Robartes had fallen asleep, as he soon did, his sleeping face, in which there was no sign of all that had so shaken me and that now kept me so wakeful, was to my excited mind more like a mask than a face.[11]

In a later description of the hall where the meeting took place he wrote of the sleepers lying after the magical orgy, their upturned faces looking to his imagination like hollow masks. The masks had not yet attained their significance. It was as though Yeats was realising for the first time that a man's or a woman's exterior might not represent the inner being—it

was more than ten years after this that he wrote, with an
adolescent sensitivity:

> But when one shrinks from all business with a stranger and is unnatural
> with all who are intimate friends, because one underrates or overrates
> unknown people, one cannot adventure forth. The artist has grown more
> and more distinct, more and more a being in his own right as it were, but
> more and more loses grasp of the always more complete world. Some day
> setting out to find knowledge, like some pilgrim to the holy land he will
> become the most romantic of characters. He will play with masks.[12]

The masks began to interest him more and more as a subject.
In October 1909 he wrote in his Diary:

> I have been looking at some Venetian costumes of the sixteenth century
> as pictured in the mask.[12a] All fantastic bodily form hidden or disguised. . . .
> Life had become so leisured and courtly that men and women dressed with
> no thought of bodily activity. They no longer toiled much. One feels that
> if they still fought and hunted their imagination was not with these things.
> Does not the same thing happen to our passions when we grow contempla-
> tive and so liberate them from use. They also become fantastic and create
> the strange life of poets and artists.

The contradictions in his own life troubled him. An entry of
August 1910 reveals this:

> I see always this one thing, that in practical life . . . the Mask is more
> than face. I believe that I am speaking with more self-condemnation than
> self-defence when I say it. There are moments of life when one must say
> 'Such and such an act proves such and such a man to be a cad or fool' and
> not 'such and such a man has shown himself by this or that good action
> to be neither cad nor fool so why did he do this?' Then one must say 'Such
> and such a person could never have done such and such a thing' even
> though one's imagination suggests an endless array of circumstances in
> which anyone might be moved to do anything. Thus one must continually
> feel and believe what one's reason denies. I am so unfortunate that I can
> only conceive of this as a kind of playacting. I feel no emotion enough to
> act upon it, but faint lyrical emotion which only affects life indirectly. Then
> there is the difference that words are with me a means of investigation
> rather than a means of action. O Masters of life give me confidence in
> something even if it be my own reason. I can never believe in anything
> else now for I have accused the impulses of too many sins. I know that
> Reason is almost a blaspheming thing, a claim to infinity of being, while
> we are limited social creatures, truly artificial. Twenty, no a hundred
> times if I had acted upon impulse and against reason I should have created
> a fixed world of rights and wrongs. Yes, but I should have gone from my
> world. The passionate man must believe he obeys his reason. Reason is the
> stopping of the pendulum, a kind of death. Life is a perpetual injustice.

His thoughts on the mask were deepened by a personal crisis.
He felt that a friend with whom he was staying had been
insulted by Edmund Gösse and he wrote to Gosse to tell him
so. The letter, however, was removed from the postbag by
his hostess, who did not wish him to quarrel with Gosse on her
behalf. An apology from Gosse arrived shortly afterwards,

whereupon Yeats, informed that his earlier letter had not been posted, wrote to Gosse at once to tell him of this letter. Then he wrote a letter in his Diary addressed to his hostess's son, a friend of his. This letter was never delivered, never, in fact, emerged from the pages of the Diary, but it reveals the introspective conflict[12b] which so greatly troubled Yeats:

> All last week the moment my impulse told me that I should demand with indignation an apology from Gosse, my analysis said 'You think this from vanity. You want to do a passionate thing because it stirs your pride . . .' I would have explained it by saying that it is the world I have been brought up in—You have always lived among defined social relations and I only among defined ideas—but then my family seem to me to have more than enough of the usual impulses. . . . I have understood that I am trying to put myself right with myself even more than with you. I want you to understand that once one makes a thing subject to reason, as distinguished from impulse, one plays with it, even if it is a very serious thing. I am more ashamed because of the things I have played with in life than of any other thing. All my moral endeavour for years has been an attempt to recreate practical interest in myself. I can only conceive of it as a kind of acting.

After a week or so he began to apply his particular analysis to general life while denouncing generalisation at the same time:

> Why do I write all this? I suppose that I may learn at last to keep to my own in every situation in life. To discover and create in myself as I grow old that thing which is to life what style is to letters—moral radiance, a personal quality of universal meaning in action and in thought. I can see now how I lost myself. I must have been trying to recreate in myself the passions I wrote. Yes, but for me they must flow from reason itself. My talent would fade if I trafficked in general standards and yet Punchinello is ancient. They dug up a statue of him among the ruins of Rome. Is not all life the struggle of existence, naked, unarmed, timid, but immortal, against generalised thought, only the personal history in this is the reverse of the world's history. We see all arts and societies passing from experience to generalisation whereas the young begin with generalisation and end with experience, that is to say not what we call the 'results' which are generalisations but with its presence its energy. All good art is experience, all popular art generalisation.

Another passage, scrawled down when he was too tired to read or write, revealed his belief that he could change the constitution of the United Arts Club,[12c] where he sought most of his social life in Dublin, so that the club could become more vigorous. It would have been a victory over one who least understood the manhood of mere art; but he had thought the renunciation of the artist one of the things which in others are virtue and he did not go to find the man he would have had to persuade. From triumph his mood turned to introspection:

> Why have I these faculties which I cannot use. I know I have them and I know they are the chief temptation of life. It is easy to give up the

thought of wealth and domestic life even, but it is hard to give up those generalisations through which the will flings itself upon the world, those gleams of future victory, that are to one as though one cried aloud, all that makes one for the moment, of the race of the eagles. Did the first of us all hate the kindness that kept him from the oblivion of activity.

Then, some thirty-three sections later in the Diary, he had come to a provisional conclusion to these thoughts, which allowed him the escape of imagination:

I think all happiness in life depends on having the energy to assume the mask of some other self; that all joyous or creative life is a rebirth as something not oneself—something created in a moment and perpetually renewed; in playing a game like that of a child where one loses the infinite pain of self-realisation, a grotesque or solemn painted face put on that one may haste from the terrors of judgment. An imaginative saturnalia that one may forget reality. Perhaps all the sins and energies of the world are but the world's flight from the infinite blinding beam.

This thought found expression in 'The Grey Rock' where Aoife's hate and the sensual eyes of the gods are contrasted. She complains of her lover who threw away her gift of immortality. The terror of judgment is avoided:

> We should be dazed and terror-struck,
> If we but saw in dreams that room,
> Those wine drenched eyes . . .[13]

and, as Bronowski[14] has pointed out, Yeats avoids an end to the poem by escaping to his imaginative saturnalia:

> And she with Goban's wine adrip,
> No more remembering what had been,
> Stared at the Gods with laughing lip.[13]

The life which prompted these musings was crowded and barren between 1910 and 1916. Though Yeats had ceased to attend to the details of the Abbey management he still took a great interest in its well-being. After Miss Horniman had withdrawn her support he had lectured in London on the theatre's behalf. In 1911 he accompanied the players on the first part of their tour in America but left before the troubles of that visit—the angry reaction of Irish-American audiences to Synge's plays—had broken out. His loyalty to the theatre which had obviously ceased to be of great use to his own type of drama was striking. He warned Lady Gregory that the theatre would soon have to be handed over to the new dramatists; and in a poem, 'The New Faces', written in 1912 (but not published until 1928), there is a sense that the work which he had done with her aid was over:

> If you, that have grown old, were the first dead,
> Neither catalpa tree nor scented lime
> Should hear my living feet, nor would I tread
> Where we wrought that shall break the teeth of time.

There was also, however, a change in his own attitude, perhaps as a result of the preoccupation of the young Abbey
dramatists with realism; but this new approach was not likely
to appeal to the public at either of its extremes.  One development was represented by *The Player Queen*, on which he had
worked for many years, eventually publishing it in 1922:

> I began in, I think, 1907, a verse tragedy, but at that time the thought
> I have set forth in *Per Amica Silentia Lunae*[14a] was coming into my head, and
> I found examples of it everywhere.  I wasted the best working months of
> several years in an attempt to write a poetical play where every character
> became an example of the finding or not finding of what I have called the
> Antithetical Self; and because passion and not thought makes tragedy,
> what I made had neither simplicity nor life.  I knew precisely what was
> wrong and yet could neither escape from thought nor give up my play.
> At last it came into my head all of a sudden that I could get rid of the play
> if I turned it into a farce;—and never did I do anything so easily, for I
> think that I wrote the present play in about a month. . . .[14b]

The satirical mocking side of Yeats is shown in this play, and
its technique is realistic.  To understand how far he had
travelled from the idealism of *The Countess Cathleen* we must
consider how he treated the poets of the two plays.  In the early
work Aleel pleaded with the Countess to accept his love and
accepted her rejection with a certain humility.  The poet in
*The Player Queen*, on the other hand, enters the scene in a
drunken state, talking delightful nonsense.  He is unfaithful to
his actress wife, who exchanges places with a queen, and, in her
new role, dismisses the troupe of actors from her new kingdom.
This theme is drawn from Yeats's experience of the theatre and
from his interest in bizarre subjects; 'The Mask', a poem
incorporated in the play's structure, represents his own theories
on the mask in their lyric form.  The play also reveals a desire
to mock his earlier achievements and heroic themes.  In his
*Deirdre* Conchubar had cried:

> One woman and two men; that is the quarrel
> That knows no mending[15]

but in *The Player Queen* such struggles have altered.  Septimus
the poet is the cause of the quarrel between his wife and his
mistress which is resolved by no great tragedy such as that of
Deirdre, but by a tidy ending worthy of any of the Abbey's
comedies.

The other extreme was his positive interest in the *Noh* drama of Japan, to which Ezra Pound had introduced him. He found these plays an incentive to return to an early ideal of re-creating the Irish scenery he loved[15] by means of an art form:

> Perhaps some day a play in the form I am adapting for European purposes shall awake once more, whether in Gaelic or in English, under the slope of Slieve-na-man or Croagh Patrick, ancient memories.[16]

The new technique was simple, did away with the need for a theatre and allowed the incorporation of some idiosyncrasies. A Japanese traditional dancer, Mr Ito,[17] helped him to evolve the stylised movements, while Edmund Dulac designed the masks and costumes for *At the Hawk's Well*, the first of his new *Plays for Dancers*. This play was performed with success in March 1916 in Lady Cunard's London drawing-room. In the same year the Cuala Press, owned by Yeats's sister, published Fenollosa's Japanese plays, translated by Ezra Pound, with a long essay on the drama by Yeats. He thought that these plays which could be performed inexpensively and simply without a theatre would attain such a distance from reality that they could make credible 'strange events, elaborate words'. Lennox Robinson has pointed out that, when the second play, *The Only Jealousy of Emer*, was produced, Krop, Anthiel and Ninette de Valois collaborated with Yeats and the range of the drawing-room was passed, the mechanism of the western theatre again required.[18]

The place the Abbey had taken in the poet's life was partially replaced by a fuller social life,[18a] he became a welcome guest in many London houses. Besides staying at Coole he began to visit Maud Gonne MacBride who was living in retirement at Colville near Calvados in Normandy; and he also paid short visits to well-known English country houses, such as Taplow Court and Reigate Priory.[18b]

Visits which provided him with a subject for poetry were those he paid to Mabel Beardsley:

> Propped upon pillows, rouge on the pallor of her face.
> She would not have us sad because she is lying there,
> And when she meets our gaze her eyes are laughter-lit,
> Her speech a wicked tale that we may vie with her,
> Matching our broken-hearted wit against her wit,
> Thinking of saints and of Petronius Arbiter.[19]

He wrote to Lady Gregory from Woburn Buildings on 8 January 1913:

Strange that just after writing those lines of the Rhymers who 'unsuspecting faced their ends' I should be at the bedside of the dying sister of Beardsley, who was practically one of us. She has had a week of great pain but on Sunday was I think free from it. She was propped up on pillows with her cheeks I think a little rouged and looking very beautiful. Beside her an Xmas tree with little toys containing sweets, which she gave us. . . . I will keep the little toy she gave me and I dare say she knew that. On a table near were four dolls dressed like people out of her brother's drawings. Women with loose trousers and toys that looked like women. Ricketts had made them, modelling the faces and sewing the clothes. They must have taken him days. She had all her great lady airs and asked after my work and health as if they were the most important things in the world to her. 'A palmist told me' she said 'that when I was forty-two my life would take a turn for the better and now I shall spend my forty-second year in heaven' and then emphatically pretending we were incredulous. 'O Yes, I shall go to heaven. Papists do.' When I told her where Mrs Emery was she said 'How fine of her, but a girls' school!—why she knew how to make even me blush'. Then she began telling improper stories and inciting us (there were two men besides myself) to do the like. At moments she shook with laughter. . . . Just as I was going her mother came in and saw me to the door. As we were standing at it she said 'I do not think she wishes to live—how could she after such agony? She is all I have left now.' I lay awake most of the night with a poem in my head. I cannot overstate her strange charm—the pathetic gaiety—It was her brother but her brother was not I think lovable, only astonishing and intrepid. She has been ill since June last. . . .

Another letter to Lady Gregory, dated 11 February 1913, gives the background to the fifth section of the poem:

> And how should her heart fail her
> Or sickness break her will
> With her dead brother's valour
> For an example still.[19]

He wrote that Mabel Beardsley had said to him the previous Sunday:

'I wonder who will introduce me in heaven. It should be my brother but then they might not appreciate the introduction. They may not have very good taste.' She said of her brother 'He hated the people who denied the existence of evil and evil words, and so being young he filled his pictures with evil. He had a passion for reality.' She has the same passion and puts aside any attempt to suggest recovery and yet I have seen her in low spirits. . . . I always see her alone now. She keeps Sunday afternoons for me. I will send you the little series of poems when they are finished. One or two are I think very good. . . .

There was another part of the series which remained unpublished and this has a simple pleasant rhythm and rhyme:

> Although she has turned away
> The pretty waxen faces
> And hid their silk and laces
> For mass was said to-day
> She has not begun denying

Now that she is dying
The pleasures she loved well
The strong milk of her mother
The valour of her brother
Are in her body still
She will not die weeping
May God be with her sleeping.

His own rooms at Woburn Buildings received many interesting visitors,[19a] among them Rabindranath Tagore, for whose *Gitanjali* Yeats wrote an enthusiastic introduction[20] and who later thanked the poet for the 'intimate instruction' received at Woburn Buildings.[20a] His 'Mondays' were attractive gatherings. Douglas Goldring has sketched one in lively colours:

I shall never forget my surprise, when Ezra[20b] took me for the first time to one of Yeats's 'Mondays' at the way in which he dominated the room, distributed Yeats's cigarettes and Chianti, and laid down the law about poetry. Poor golden-bearded Sturge Moore, who sat in a corner with a large musical instrument by his side (on which he was never given a chance of performing) endeavoured to join the discussion on prosody, a subject on which he believed himself not entirely ignorant, but Ezra promptly reduced him to a glum silence. My own emotions on this particular evening, since I did not possess Ezra's transatlantic *brio*, were an equal blend of reverence and a desire to giggle. I was sitting next to Yeats on a settle when a young Indian woman[20c] in a *sari* came and squatted at his feet and asked him to sing 'Innisfree', saying she was certain he had composed it to an Irish air. Yeats was anxious to comply with this request, unfortunately, like so many poets, was completely unmusical, indeed almost tone-deaf. He compromised by a sort of dirge-like incantation, calculated to send any unhappy giggler into hysterics. I bore it as long as I could, but at last the back of the settle began to shake and I received the impact of one of the poet's nasty glances from behind his pince-nez. Mercifully I recovered but it was an awful experience.[21]

A letter to Lady Gregory dated 3 January 1913 shows Yeats's own attitude to Pound:

My digestion has got rather queer again—a result I think of sitting up late with Ezra and Sturge Moore and some light wine while the talk ran. However the criticism I have got from them has given me new life and I have made that Tara poem a new thing and am writing with a new confidence having got Milton off my back. Ezra is the best critic of the two. He is full of the middle ages and helps me to get back to the definite and the concrete away from modern abstractions. To talk over a poem with him is like getting you to put a sentence into dialect. All becomes clear and natural. Yet in his own work he is very uncertain, often very bad though very interesting sometimes. He spoils himself by too many experiments and has more sound principles than taste.

Mysticism still occupied a part of the poet's life. He re-read Swedenborg in 1913,[21a] and in 1912 he turned to a Rosicrucian theme with 'The Mountain Tomb' written at Colville. The last stanza shows a strength and simplicity of touch:

> In vain, in vain; the cataract still cries;
> The everlasting taper lights the gloom;
> All wisdom shut into his onyx eyes
> Our Father Rosicross sleeps in his tomb.[22]

An earlier essay of 1895[23] had dealt with the subject, Yeats then using the symbolism of the tomb to describe his own times—the imagination 'has been laid in a great tomb of criticism and had set over it inextinguishable magical lamps of wisdom and romance'. The subject had emerged in his mind; throughout his life he was constantly rediscovering ideas he had forgotten with the same thrill that had accompanied their first discovery.

Magic, according to Goldring, was not completely neglected at this period:

> In Yeats's flat I had seen unaccountable chalk marks in the form of a turkey's claw, and had been horrifyingly conscious of a 'nasty feeling' in a corner of the room near where the Tarot cards were kept and hadn't liked it a bit, 'if it's a question of spirits' I said 'I prefer mine out of a bottle'.[24]

But his main interest in the supernatural had turned to psychical research. With a new friend, the Hon. Everard Fielding, and Maud Gonne MacBride, he had gone to Mirabeau in June 1914 to investigate a miracle, about which he wrote an unpublished essay. Mrs Alfred Lyttelton and W. T. Horton,[25] for whose book of images Yeats had written an introduction in 1898, both gave him independent warnings of an evil counsellor; and his manuscript book before and during the period of the war has many references, generally cryptic, to mediums and séances.

In the war his sympathies lay with the allies, that is, as far as he was deeply roused by distress at the general turmoil and loss of life. He had exhausted his positive attitude to political events in Ireland, so he thought; he was too old to embark on a fresh crusade for his new aristocratic ideals, and besides he retained the old delight in imaginative art in a form which could not be passed on to the common herd:

> As a deep of the mind can only be approached through what is most human, most delicate, we should distrust bodily distance, mechanism, and loud noise.[26]

Public events outside Ireland found him interested, but only detached where his emotions were not deeply involved. Such a personal loss as Hugh Lane's death when a passenger on the *Lusitania* moved him, though he could afterwards complain that the political capital made out of the disaster by the English made them accessories after the fact.[27] His attitude was summed up in his reactions on being asked for a war poem; we must remember that most of his crusading had been done for what he thought would bring Ireland intellectual freedom, that the first world war was not totalitarian and could allow the elderly civilian his detachment. In such times the poet should be silent for

> We have no gift to set a statesman right;
> He has had enough of meddling who can please
> A young girl in the indolence of her youth,
> Or an old man upon a winter's night.[28]

The effect of this somewhat scattered life upon Yeats's poetry was revealed freely in the development of the new bare style he had found since he turned from the over-elaborate genre. The poems of *The Green Helmet* were a demonstration of how poetry had failed to make his life, but his life forms the poetry of *Responsibilities*, and there is in this volume the emergence of a new decoration which had been suggested in the poems which dealt with the glories of aristocratic life in *The Green Helmet*, 'At Galway Races', 'These are the Clouds', and 'Upon a House shaken by the Land Agitation'. The finest poems in the new volume are both political and private, and each category contains the germ of regenerated poetry within it. The Lane poems, while primarily expressing Yeats's immense disgust at the mob's treatment of a noble spirit, contain images of the new ideal of exalted service. Yeats was a born servant; his unsureness of himself found relief in serving either cause or person.[29]

The images drawn from Urbino's court are the compensatory glory, the flight of the eagle into the sun. Likewise, after he had reached a state of spiritual degradation in his sexual life, he reacted to an admiration of the purity of girlhood. The essence of all the writings, however, is a deep disappointment.

Stupidity, bigotry, and maliciousness were what seemed the qualities of the enemy in the Lane controversy, which occurred during 1912-13. Hugh Lane, Lady Gregory's nephew, had made a collection of modern French paintings which formed part of a Modern Art Gallery founded in Dublin in 1905. The paintings had become famous, and Lane thought that they should be given proper accommodation by the Dublin Corporation; he had a preference for a design made by Lutyens for a bridge gallery spanning the Liffey; but this design did not gain popular support:

When difficulties over that arose in Dublin, in a moment of pique he
sent them on loan to the London National Gallery, and in his will of 1913
bequeathed them to that Gallery. However, in 1915, he added a codicil in
his own hand revoking this bequest of thirty-nine pictures to his countrymen, on condition that within five years of his death they should provide a
suitable building for them. Lady Gregory was his sole trustee. Unfortunately, he went down with the *Lusitania* before getting a witness to that
codicil. None disputed its genuineness, yet—such meanness is almost
incredible—the rich National Gallery of England, taking legal advantage of
that omission, stuck to the booty. They were backed by the Government.[30]

Yeats took a prominent part in the controversy because he
regarded it as a struggle for the rightful position of genius and
culture in the community. Three public controversies had
stirred his imagination, those of Parnell, of *The Playboy*, and
of the Lane Gallery; he thought that they showed neither
religion nor politics could create minds wise and generous
enough to make a nation. He drifted before the storm of
controversy, riding the bitter waves of despair, and gathering
from his wrecked gear material for a storm anchor. Originally
he had sailed by a desire to shape Ireland by heroic standards;
now he had reduced this to the more practical objective of
'men of good will', and later he was to discard this in favour
of a belief in the purpose of great living which was the storm-
anchor by which he recreated himself as a poet. The storm's
violence shaped these Lane poems, first entitled *Poems
Written in Discouragement* and published in 1913.

The first poem of the series 'To a rich man who promises
a Bigger Subscription than his First to the Dublin Municipal
Gallery when the Amount collected proves that there is a
Popular Demand for the Pictures' was probably intended as
a reproof to Lord Ardilaun's argument that money should not
be given unless there was a demand.[31] Three Italian rulers are
drawn as examples of men who make a proper use of money
and power, live surrounded by beauty, use no popular standards to estimate it, and seek its continuance by extending
patronage to artists. The choice of the Italian courts was due
to his approval of Castiglione's *The Courtier*,[32] which Lady
Gregory had read to him in 1904,[33] and to his Italian journey
in 1907. The two sources, literary and visual, combine to
give the poem a convincing reality. What he praises is worth
experiencing, and vividly described with a telling economy of
detail. Later he wrote of

The green shadow of Ferrara wall[34]

a line showing his direct observation at work which suggests that the 'market place' and the 'onion-sellers' are also due to his gift of seizing on an unusual feature and giving it such authority that it seems the only thing worth attention. Thus the town of Ferrara is concentrated in his poem into the picture of the Duke and the onion-sellers, and so the contrast which he wanted to create is emphasised for his reader. The literary background to the poem comes from a note to *The Courtier* describing Duke Ercole's interest in Plautus.[35] Guido-baldo was the perfect model of the aristocratic lover of art. Yeats must have remembered the description of his interests in *The Courtier*.

Among his other praiseworthy deeds he built on the rugged site of Urbino a palace regarded by many as the most beautiful to be found in all Italy; and he so well furnished it that it seemed not a palace but a city in the form of a palace; and not merely with what is ordinarily used—such as silver vases, hangings of richest cloth-of-gold and silk, and other similar things—but for ornament he added countless antique statues in marble and bronze, pictures most choice, and musical instruments of every sort, nor would he admit anything there that was not very rare and excellent. Then at very great cost he collected a goodly number of most excellent and rare books in Greek, Latin and Hebrew, all of which he adorned with gold and silver, esteeming this to be the chiefest of his great palace.[36]

'Urbino's windy hill' was due mainly to memory and Yeats described in *Essays* how he had walked towards Urbino having crossed the Apennines from San Sepolcro, though in a passage in *The Bounty of Sweden* he

remembered a cry of Bembo's made years after. 'Would that I were a shepherd that I might look down daily upon Urbino.'[37]

The second poem of the series 'September 1913' is a more heated piece of writing. C. M. Bowra has said of it that the language and names recall political life and suggest that Yeats is talking politics.[38] The tone is truly rhetorical as we might expect from the association of memories which John O'Leary's nationalism would call up in Yeats, the loftiness of the old man's ideals, and the settings of his speeches where

sometimes he would say things that would have sounded well in some heroic Elizabethan play.[39]

Furthermore the initial impulse of the poem came from Yeats's own rhetoric, from a speech he made on 13 July 1913. He wrote to Lady Gregory from London:

I made a good speech on Monday. Lane was anxious about some vote coming on in Dublin that day, but I know nothing, of course, of what has happened. I spoke with him quite as much as the possible subscribers in mind. I described Ireland, if the present intellectual movement failed, as a little greasy huxtering nation groping for halfpence in a greasy till but did not add, except in thought, 'by the light of a holy candle'.

C. M. Bowra also remarks, in *The Heritage of Symbolism*, on the striking poetic effect of the use of the medical word 'Delirium' among the plain monosyllables. Why did Yeats use the word? His line:

All that delirium of the brave

is a summing-up of all the qualities and greatness of the wild geese and the political martyr heroes, Fitzgerald, Emmet and Tone, those figures who had seemed to carry on the ancient heroic Celtic tradition. In contrasting the old heroic outlook with the new he would naturally have remembered the phrases used in praise and belittlement of his old ideals of patriotic nobility. Swinburne in the introduction to his *William Blake* wrote rather contemptuously of Yeats's introduction to Blake (whom he sought to prove a fellow Celt)[40] and used the word delirious in connection with what he did not understand in Blake:

> Some Hibernian commentator on Blake, if I rightly remember a fact so insignificant, has somewhere said something to some such effect that I, when writing about some fitfully audacious and fancifully delirious deliverance of the poet he claimed as a countryman and trying to read into it some coherent and imaginative significance was innocent of any knowledge of Blake's meaning. It is possible, if the spiritual fact of his Hibernian heredity has been or can be established, that I was: for the excellent reason that, being a Celt, he now and then too probably had none worth the labour of deciphering—or at least worth the serious attention of any student belonging to a race in which reason and imagination are the possible preferable substitutes for fever and fancy.[41]

Yeats's attention was drawn to the phrase in a letter from his father:

> Have you seen this week's *Athenaeum*? Something is quoted from a preface by Swinburne to a book on Blake. It is a reference to you of a particularly insolent and contemptuous sort. . . . His criticism that the Celtic movement puts fever and fancy in the place of reason and imagination is I am afraid a true criticism—as true as to my mind it is obvious. It is not however specially Celtic—the Irish do it because they are primitive and kept so by a Church which in its Irish form at any rate exists on fever and fancy.[42]

That Yeats agreed with his father that their contemporary Ireland was such can be seen by an examination of the notes which he wrote to *Responsibilities*:

> Neither religion nor politics can of itself create minds with enough receptivity to become wise, or just and generous enough to make a nation. Our new middle class showed . . . how base at moments of excitement are minds without culture.[43]

It seems likely that he had stored Swinburne's phrase away and now used it proudly, remembering his old love for the 'fitfully audacious and fancifully delirious' heroes, contrasting their brave 'delirium' with the uncultured 'excitement' of his own time. He takes the word tossed in scorn by Swinburne and uses it in twofold fashion to exalt the old and belittle the new feverishness of Ireland.

'To a friend whose work has come to nothing'[44] was written to Lady Gregory, not, as she thought, to Hugh Lane.[45] It probably resulted from the note written on the back of a letter posted to Lady Gregory from London on 1 July 1913:

> Can you send me I.T. [*Irish Times*] with final decision of Corporation? It may move me to another poem.

This poem, and the next in the series, 'Paudeen', have a secret joy in the midst of their sorrow:

> Be secret and exult,
> Because of all things known
> That is most difficult.[44]

The expression of Yeats's anger is best seen in 'To a Shade'.[46] Lane's treatment is compared to that given to Parnell, the 'thin Shade' who is bidden to leave the town and return to the grave at Glasnevin:

> For they are at their old tricks yet.

Here the beauty of the town is sketched in lovingly:

> Where grey gulls flit about instead of men
> And the gaunt houses put on majesty

to make the inhabitants' behaviour the more unworthy. Yeats had a great dislike of William Martin Murphy, who controlled *The Irish Independent*, especially for the part he had taken against Parnell, a dislike that burst into rage when Murphy took part in the Lane controversy also:

> Your enemy, an old foul mouth, had set
> The pack on him.[47]

In May 1913 he drafted a poem in his manuscript book which was an imagining of ideal character, a man after his own heart:

> Who is this by the edge of the stream
> That walks in a good homespun coat
> And carries a fishing[rod] in his hand
> We singers have nothing of our own
> All our hopes, our loves, our dreams

> Are for the young, for those whom
> We stir into life. But [there is] one
> That I can see always though he is not yet born
> He walks by the edge of the stream
> In a good homespun coat
> And carries a fishing rod in his hand.

These lines formed the essential part of the poem, 'The Fisher-man',[48] but this poem opposes to the ideal man the reality which Yeats had found in Ireland and in the final poem, written in June 1914, he makes clear the contrast:

> Maybe a twelvemonth since
> Suddenly I began,
> In scorn of this audience,
> Imagining a man.

In the description of what he found his satire reaches a Swiftian savagery; all day he had looked in the face what he had hoped it would be to write for his own race, but this was what he discovered when he *contrasted* his hopes with the reality:[49]

> The living men that I hate,
> The dead man that I loved,
> The craven man in his seat,
> The insolent unreproved,
> And no knave brought to book
> Who has won a drunken cheer,
> The witty man and his joke
> Aimed at the commonest ear,
> The clever man who cries
> The catch-cries of the clown,
> The beating down of the wise
> And great Art beaten down.

Even the style is Swiftian in its simplicity, its listing of the abominable types of humanity, with its monosyllabic introduction to each line, its staccato verse, and then the slowing movement of the last lines with the essential word 'down' repeated as the final comment.

There was greater disillusion in Yeats's personal life. When he stayed in Normandy with Maud Gonne MacBride the memories of his ideal love kept recurring,[50] and were recorded as praise of the great beauty that was hers:

> Although crowds gathered once if she but showed her face,
> And even old men's eyes grew dim, this hand alone,
> Like some last courtier at a gypsy camping-place
> Babbling of fallen majesty, records what's gone.[51]

His reaction to the memories was recorded in that poignant poem 'The Cold Heaven':

Suddenly I saw the cold and rook-delighting heaven
That seemed as though ice burned and was but the more ice,
And thereupon imagination and heart were driven
So wild that every casual thought of that and this
Vanished, and left but memories, that should be out of season
With the hot blood of youth, of love crossed long ago;
And I took all the blame out of all sense and reason,
Until I cried and trembled and rocked to and fro
Riddled with light. [52]

Madame MacBride enquired the poem's meaning, and he told
her it was an attempt to describe the feelings aroused in him
by the cold and detachedly beautiful winter sky. He felt alone
and responsible in that loneliness for all the past mistakes that
tortured his peace of mind. It was a momentary intensity of
dream-like perception, where physical surroundings remained
fixed clear in the mind, to accentuate the years of thought and
reality that passed in review in an instantaneous and yet
eternal suspension of time.

In 'Friends' he had praised three women who had given
him joy in life: Diana Vernon, Lady Gregory, and Maud: [53]

How could I praise that one? . . .
Remembering what she had,
What eagle look still shows,
While up from my heart's root
So great a sweetness flows
I shake from head to foot [54]

but he had embarked, about 1910, upon a liaison with an un-
married woman which lasted for some years, and was dis-
rupted by a telegram sent by her to Coole. [55] Yeats wrongly
thought that the telegram, which announced pregnancy, also
wrongly, was an attempt to trap him into marriage, which,
owing to the lack of deep affection in the affair, would have
been unpleasant. His consternation was immense, and his
'love' poetry took on a sinister note of sordidness; the versions
of 'The Witch' in his Diary are disgusted and disgusting:

Toil and grow rich,
What's that but to lie
With some stale bitch
And after, drained dry,
To be brought
To the chamber where
Lies one long sought
With despair?

Out of this mood came 'Beggar to Beggar Cried' which also
reflects a sardonic reaction to Lady Gregory's treatment of this

new situation.  She decided that Yeats must marry lest some
similar upset occur to disturb his peace:

> 'Time to put off the world and go somewhere
> And find my health again in the sea air',
> *Beggar to beggar cried, being frenzy-struck,*
> 'And make my soul before my pate is bare'.
>
> 'And get a comfortable wife and house
> To rid me of the devil in my shoes',
> *Beggar to beggar cried, being frenzy-struck,*
> 'And the worse devil that is between my thighs'.[56]

A bitter note underlies the strangeness of some poems which
Yeats wrote at the time, notably 'The Three Beggars', 'The
Three Hermits', 'Running to Paradise' and 'The Hour before
Dawn'.  These are written in a style which seems Yeats's
imitation of Synge, aided perhaps by the influence of Ezra
Pound's vitality and mockery.  They are at once remote and
humorous poems, a strange combination.  In 'The Three
Beggars' Yeats derived a certain pleasure in placing his old
heroic figures into the new setting of beggars and coarseness;[57]
King Guare offers a thousand pounds to the beggar who can
sleep before the third day; but when he returns to shout 'Time's
up' the three were still fighting in the effort to keep the others
awake:

> 'Time's up', he cried, and all the three
> Fell down upon the dust and snored.

Two of 'The Three Hermits' are debating the hereafter, but

> While he'd rummaged rags and hair,
> Caught and cracked his flea, the third
> Giddy with his hundredth year,
> Sang unnoticed like a bird.[58]

This poem was written at Stone Cottage on 15 March 1913,
where he had settled for the autumn with Ezra Pound, who
had become an intimate friend, and spent the two following
winters with him there.  Pound read aloud to him when his
eyes were bad, and taught him to fence:

> I sometimes fence for half an hour at the day's end, and when I close my
> eyes upon the pillow I see a foil before me, the button to my face.[59]

His health was bad, and affected his spirits; in fact he became
aware that he was fifty:

> I thought no more was needed
> Youth to prolong
> Than dumb-bell and foil
> To keep the body young.
> *O who could have foretold*
> *That the heart grows old?*[60]

Pound's effect upon his poetry was to make it harsher and more outspoken.[61] For instance, 'The Scholars' was originally written, under Pound's influence, in 1915 in a harsher vein than the final version, toned down when Pound was not there to protest:

> There'll be their life to the world's end
> To wear the carpet with their shoes
> And earn respect; have no stranger friend;
> And only sin, when no one knows;
> Lord what would they say
> Should their Catullus walk that way?

The same note as that of 'The Three Beggars' runs through to 'Running to Paradise'[62] and, especially, 'The Hour before Dawn', which began in the manuscript version:

> A one-legged one-armed one-eyed man
> A bundle of rags upon a crutch
> Stumbled on windy Cruachan
> Cursing the wind . . .[63]

and continued with a fierce quarrel and an aspect of horror presented with a grimly smiling humour:

> And prayed and cursed and cursed and fled
> From Maeve and all that juggling plain,
> Nor gave God thanks till overhead
> The clouds were brightening with the dawn.

Echoes of Synge resound through the querulous strain of these lines:

> The beggar in a rage began
> Upon his hunkers in the hole,
> 'It's plain that you are no right man
> To mock at everything I love
> As if it were not worth the doing.
> I'd have a merry life enough
> If a good Easter wind were blowing,
> And though the winter wind is bad
> I should not be too down in the mouth
> For anything you said or did
> If but this wind were in the south'.

Louis MacNeice has suggested[64] a comparison with Synge's tramp in *The Shadow of the Glen*:

We'll be going now, I'm telling you, and the time you'll be feeling the cold, and the frost, the great rain and the sun again, and the south wind blowing in the glens, you'll not be sitting up in a wet ditch, the way you're after sitting in this place making yourself old with looking on each day and it passing you by. You'll be saying one time, 'It's a good evening, by the grace of God', and another time, 'It's a wild night, God help us; but it'll pass surely'.[65]

The effect of Synge penetrates another of the poems of *Responsibilities*, 'The Dolls', where

> A doll in the doll-maker's house
> Looks at the cradle and bawls:
> 'That is an insult to us'[66]

and the doll-maker's wife defends herself for bringing a child into the house when she knows that her husband has heard the dolls' complaint. The germ of the idea of bringing a doll into the house can be found in *The Aran Islands*:

> This old man talks usually in a mournful tone about his ill-health, and his death, which he feels to be approaching, yet he has occasional touches of humour that remind me of old Mourteen on the North Island. To-day a grotesque twopenny doll was lying on the floor near the old woman. He picked it up and examined it as if comparing it with her. Then he held it up: 'Is it you is after bringing that thing into the world,' he said, 'woman of the house?'[67]

The renunciation of the whole early Celtic twilight movement and its trappings was complete, and he made it quite clear that this was so in 'A Coat' which was more explicit in its manuscript version:

> I made my song a coat
> Covered with embroideries
> Out of old mythologies
> Dragons and gods and moons
> From heel to throat
> And gave it to my song
> And my song wore it;
> But the fools caught it,
> Wore it in the world's eyes
> As though they'd wrought it.
> Song, let them take it,
> For there's more enterprise
> In walking naked.[68]

As well as Lady Gregory's influence there was another factor to interest Yeats in the possibilities of settling down; his growing enthusiasm for heredity. A new constructive genre of poetry begins with his writings on his family of which he could write frankly in his new bare style, finding in the old personalities of the Pollexfens and the soldierly qualities of the Armstrongs, the social position of the Butlers and the intellect of the Yeats line ample material for building up a structure which demanded attention merely by its unusual nature. This interest in his family was to a certain extent negative in inception. The Prologue and Epilogue to *Responsibilities* were due to the stimulus of portions of Moore's *Ave*, which, when published in *The English Review*,[69] contained statements damaging to Yeats and Lady Gregory. Moore had described with some malice the speech made by Yeats after his return from America:

As soon as the applause died away Yeats who had lately returned to us from the States with a paunch, a huge stick and an immense fur overcoat, rose to speak. We were surprised at the change in his appearance, and could hardly believe our ears when, instead of talking to us as he used to do about the old stories come down from generation to generation, he began to thunder like Ben Tillett himself against the Middle Classes, stamping his feet, working himself into a great passion, and all because the middle classes did not dip their hands into their pockets and give Lane the money he wanted for his exhibition. It is impossible to imagine the hatred which came into his voice when he spoke the words 'the middle classes'. And we looked round asking each other with our eyes where on earth our Willie Yeats had picked up such extraordinary ideas. He could hardly have gathered in the United States the ridiculous idea that none but titled and carriage folk can appreciate pictures. And we asked ourselves why Willie Yeats should feel himself called upon to denounce the class to which he himself belonged essentially: one side excellent mercantile millers and ship-owners, and on the other a portrait painter of rare talent. With so admirable a parentage it did not seem to us necessary that a man should look back for an ancestry, and we had laughed at the story, thinking it as *ben trovato*, that on the occasion when Yeats was crooning over Æ's fire he had said that if he had his rights he would be Duke of Ormond and Æ had answered 'In any case, Willie, you are overlooking your father',—a detestable remark to make to a poet in search of an ancestry, and the addition, 'Yeats, we both belong to the lower middle classes', was in equally bad taste. Æ who is usually quick witted should have guessed that Yeats's belief in his lineal descent from the great Duke of Ormonde was part of his poetic equipment. . . . It did not occur to us till this last minute, but Æ knew that there were spoons in the Yeats family, bearing the Butler crest just as there are portraits in my family of Sir Thomas More, and he should have remembered that certain passages in *The Countess Cathleen* are clearly derivative from the spoons.[70]

The Diary records Yeats's reactions to all this:

George Moore in an outrageous article in *English Review* attacks Lady Gregory and myself. Lady Gregory has threatened a libel action and Moore has apologised and withdrawn a statement about her proselytising in early life. The statements about me are too indeterminate for any action though equally untrue.

He went to explain that he had not referred to the middle classes in the speech Moore described, but had appealed to the Irish aristocracy to support the Lane Gallery. Moore had turned this into an attack on the middle classes and confused it with another speech made at the National Literary Society where Yeats had used the word bourgeois in Ben Jonson's sense, 'cit', a word of artistic usage.

There was another purpose in the Prologue to *Responsibilities*, a desire to challenge Moore to talk of his own ancestors, as another entry in the Diary demonstrates:

That antithesis which I see in all artists between the artistic and the daily self was in his case too crude and simple and the daily part too powerful, and his ignorance, and ignorance often helps external vision, deprived him of all discipline. I have been told that the crudity common to all the Moores came from the mother's family—Mayo squireens probably half peasants in education and occupation—for his father was a man of education and old descent. His mother's blood seems to have affected him and his brother as the peasant strain has affected Edward Martyn. There has been a union of incompatibles and consequent sterility. In Martyn too one finds an intellect which should have given creative power but in Martyn the sterility is complete though unlike Moore he has self-possession and taste. He only fails in words. It is as though he had been put into the wrong lady. Both men are examples of the way Irish civilisation is held back by the lack of education of Irish women.

He had himself become interested in the question of his ancestors before the Moore attack. In his 1909 Diary he recorded that

> Duncan has been looking up my coat of arms for a book plate. I gave him the crest . . . a goat's head on a coronet. He found that a Mary Yeats of Lifford who died in 1673 had the following . . . [coat of arms] . . . Being a woman there was no crest but the English 'Yates' had the goat's head . . . Can my sister get back to 'Mary Yeates'? Mary is an old family name and we had relations not very far from Lifford in North Sligo.

By 1914 he had developed these tentative enquiries into the family history, aided largely by Lily Yeats's interest in the subject, for she had begun to collect the material which is now kept in a large book, press cuttings, letters, photographs, documents of all kinds. The ancestors described in the Prologue to *Responsibilities*:

> Old Dublin merchant 'free of the ten and four'
> Or trading out of Galway into Spain;
> Old country scholar, Robert Emmet's friend,
> A hundred-year-old memory to the poor;
> Merchant and scholar who have left me blood
> That has not passed through any huckster's loin,
> Soldiers that gave, whatever die was cast:
> A Butler or an Armstrong that withstood
> Beside the brackish waters of the Boyne
> James and his Irish when the Dutchman crossed;
> Old merchant skipper that leaped overboard
> After a ragged hat in Biscay Bay;
> You most of all, silent and fierce old man,
> Because the daily spectacle that stirred
> My fancy and set my boyish lips to say, [71]
> 'Only the wasteful virtues earn the sun' . . .

were dealt with in the section of his *Autobiographies* called 'Reveries' which he finished on Christmas Day 1914 and called, in a letter written to Lily Yeats four days later, 'some sort of an apologia for the Yeats family'. The poem itself was directly inspired by Moore's article and Yeats wrote to Lady Gregory that it was 'very carefully accurate'. Alas, it proved not to be.

The phrase 'free of the ten and four' was corrected in the notes to later editions; it was

> an error I cannot now correct without more rewriting than I have a mind for. Some merchant in Villon, I forget the reference, was 'free of the ten and four'. Irish merchants exempted by the Irish parliament were, unless my memory deceives me again—I cannot remember my authority—'free of the eight and six'.[72]

The ancestor was 'free of the six and ten'.[73] This was an unimportant slip, but it reveals how careless and undependable any of Yeats's references are. Lady Gregory's Diary for 17 June 1927 contains the perfect illustration of this:

> He says he sometimes gets a thought and ascribes it to another—he had been quoting from Gentile, 'the world is so incredible that we go about touching it with our hands to convince ourselves that it exists'. But now he has been looking for it in Gentile's book and can't find it.[74]

A minor change in the poem was the alteration from the original printed text's 'merchants'; only one of his ancestors seems to have had the privilege of the remission. Then the initial lines:

> Traders or soldiers who have left me blood
> That has not passed through any huckster's loin

were altered in the version quoted earlier to 'Merchant and scholar', perhaps because Yeats wished to make clear the difference between the old and the new middle classes. The contrast is indicated by the contrast of 'Merchant'—a better word for the purpose than 'Trader'—and 'huckster'. It is amusing to see how the word 'merchant' is affected by its companions; in 'At Galway Races' the poet shares the aristocratic life:

> Before the merchant and the clerk
> Breathed on the world with timid breath [75]

but in the later poem his merchant ancestor, accompanied by the scholar, is a person of worth. Perhaps the biggest blunder was the initial placing of the Butlers on the wrong side at the Battle of the Boyne:

> Old Butlers when you took to horse and stood
> Beside the brackish waters of the Boyne
> Till your bad master blenched and all was lost.

He added to the ritual of his ancestor-worship. In 1915 he wrote a poem 'In Memory of Alfred Pollexfen', a meditation upon the members of the family, including his uncle George who had died in 1910, and at whose funeral

> . . . Masons drove from miles away
> To scatter the Acacia spray
> Upon a melancholy man
> Who had ended where his breath began.[76]

In 1918 he wrote more fully of the uncle who had been a confidant and friend:

> And then I think of old George Pollexfen,
> In muscular youth well known to Mayo men
> For horsemanship at meets or at racecourses,
> That could have shown how pure-bred horses
> And solid men, for all their passion, live
> But as the outrageous stars incline
> By opposition, square and trine;
> Having grown sluggish and contemplative.[77]

Though he had found a new and plentiful subject for poetry he did not feel thankful to Moore. He hated him with the hatred that was only beginning to be allowed an entrance into his poetry. In his 1909 Diary he had scrawled:

> Moore once had visits from the Muse
> But fearing that she would refuse
> An ancient lecher, took to geese;
> He now gets novels at his ease.

Even his father's mild attitude and refusal to take umbrage at the insults to the family had no effect upon his rage; it seemed a public duty to repel the attack. John Butler Yeats had gone to New York in 1908, to stay till his death in 1922, always hopeful that he would paint a masterpiece, always sharing his lively and original ideas with his son in numerous letters which were sometimes not fully appreciated,[77a] perhaps because the old man's admiration was the more genuine for the touch of criticism it contained. When Yeats had seen his father in New York he was at the height of his rage at the article in *The English Review*. The concluding speech of *At the Hawk's Well* (written between 1912 and 1914), sums up his saddest thoughts:

> The man that I praise
> Cries out the empty well
> Lives all his days
> Where a hand on the bell
> Can call the milch-cows
> To the comfortable door of his house
> Who but an idiot would praise
> Dry stones in a well?

W. B. YEATS

*Reproduced from Richard Church's* Eight for Immortality *by permission of
Messrs. Macmillan and Co. Ltd.*

W. B. YEATS BY JOHN B. YEATS, R.H.A.

*Reproduced by permission of the Board of Governors and Guardians of the National Gallery of Ireland*

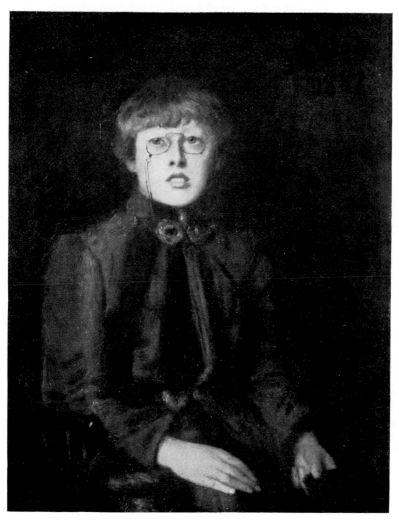

MRS. KATHERINE TYNAN HINKSON BY JOHN B. YEATS, R.H.A.
*From the portrait in the Municipal Gallery of Modern Art, Dublin*
*Reproduced by permission of the Dublin Corporation*

MAUD GONNE
*From the original in the possession of Madame MacBride*

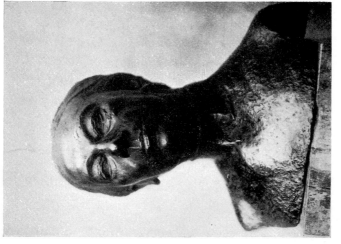

JOHN O'LEARY BY OLIVER SHEPPARD, R.H.A.      LADY GREGORY BY JACOB EPSTEIN

*From the busts in the Municipal Gallery of Modern Art, Dublin*
*Reproduced by permission of the Dublin Corporation*

J. M. SYNGE BY JOHN B. YEATS, R.H.A.
*From the original in the Municipal Gallery of Modern Art, Dublin*
*Reproduced by permission of the Dublin Corporation*

MRS. W. B. YEATS BY JOHN B. YEATS, R.H.A.
*From the original in the possession of Mrs. W. B. Yeats*

COOLE: A PASTEL BY W. B. YEATS

*Reproduced by permission of Mrs. W. B. Yeats and Messrs. Macmillan and Co. Ltd.*

> The man that I praise
> Cries out the leafless tree
> Has married and stays
> By an old hearth and he
> On nought has set store
> But children and dogs on the floor
> Who but an idiot would praise
> A withered tree?

The passionate feelings of 1913 and 1914 over, Yeats turned to writing lyrics in 1915 which possess a great dignity and a largeness of view, a return to the subject of his old love, seen without the misty veil of idealism, and without the cold light of anger and hate. These are among the great poems of his love and they have a delicate mixture of gentleness and excitement, the refinement of a troubled passion. The baser passions exhausted, he could once more see beauty:

> She might, so noble from head
> To great shapely knees
> The long flowing line,
> Have walked to the altar
> Through the holy images
> At Pallas Athene's side.[77b]

Even in 1912 he had written a poem to Maud's adopted daughter Iseult; but this had a touch of his general bitterness:

> Dance there upon the shore;
> What need have you to care
> For wind or water's roar?
> And tumble out your hair
> That the salt drops have wet;
> Being young you have not known
> The fool's triumph, nor yet
> Love lost as soon as won,
> Nor the best labourer dead
> And all the sheaves to bind.[78]

In 1914 he writes more compassionately in 'Two Years Later'[79] but is still thinking of Maud's mistake in marrying MacBride; the manuscript version of the poem is simpler and more explicit:

> Though you may be young and daring
> There is something to be learned.
> I could tell you how despairing
> The moth feels when it's burned,
> And I am old and you are young
> So we speak a different tongue
>
> O you will take what's offered
> Take the enemy for the friend
> Suffer as your mother suffered,
> Be as broken in the end.
> I could warn you but you are young,
> And I speak a barbarous tongue.

7

'Presences', written in November 1915, shows how his thoughts, on the person who had disgusted him, on, in contrast, Iseult's innocence, and on Maud, whose greatness of personality is being reassessed with his new praises, can call up vivid pictures of the women who seemed to climb up the creaking stair to his room and read

> All I had rhymed of that monstrous thing
> Returned and yet unrequited love.
> They stood in the door and stood between
> My great wood lectern and the fire
> Till I could hear their hearts beating:
> One is a harlot, and one a child
> That never looked upon man with desire,
> And one, it may be, a queen. . . .[80]

The other poems written to Maud at the time were also published in *The Wild Swans at Coole*,[81] the volume which followed five years after *Responsibilities*. 'Her Praise' is a memory of how

> Though she had young men's praise and old men's blame,
> Among the poor both old and young gave her praise.[82]

'The People'[83] on the other hand is a contrast between the ideal court of Urbino and Maud's love of the people, which never wavered even though she had been attacked when her luck was out. 'His Phoenix'[84] is a challenging attitude of bravado at first; he lists the various women who are beautiful and talented, but dismisses them all with the refrain:

> I knew a phoenix in my youth, so let them have their day

which attains a new tenderness in the last stanza and is a quieter conclusion to the last thought that no one else could ever be the same:

> . . . not the exact likeness, the simplicity of a child
> And that proud look as though she had gazed into the burning sun,
> And all the shapely body no tittle gone astray.
> I mourn for that most lonely thing; and yet God's will be done:
> I knew a phoenix in my youth, so let them have their day.

He is now sufficiently far from his youth to begin to record the passing of time's hand across Maud's features. It was with a shock that he had earlier heard someone else telling him that his well-beloved's hair had streaks of grey in it, but now he deals with the thought himself:

> There is grey in your hair.
> Young men no longer suddenly catch their breath
> When you are passing;

But maybe some old gaffer mutters a blessing
Because it was your prayer
Recovered him upon the bed of death . . .[85]

and, as before, he becomes deeply moved at the thoughts her image rouses in his mind:

Your beauty can but leave among us
Vague memories, nothing but memories.
A young man when the old men are done talking
Will say to an old man, 'Tell me of that lady
The poet stubborn with his passion sang us
When age might well have chilled his blood'.[85]

# 8

# THE MARRIED PHILOSOPHER
(1916–1919)

*For how should I forget the wisdom that you brought,*
*The comfort that you made?*

*I wished for a system of thought that would leave my imagina-*
*tion free to create as it chose and yet make all that it created, or*
*could create, part of the one history, and that the soul's.*

W. B. YEATS

THE Easter Rising of 1916 came as a surprise to Yeats. It was a matter for sorrow and anxiety. He wrote to Lady Gregory:

Cosgrave whom I saw a few months ago in connection with the Municipal Gallery project and found our best supporter, has got many years imprisonment and today I see that an old friend Henry Dixon—unless there are two of the same name—who began with me the whole work of the literary movement, has been shot in a barrack yard without trial of any kind. I have little doubt that there have been many miscarriages of justice. The wife of a Belgian Minister of War told me a few days ago that three British officers had told her that the command of the British Army in France should be made over to French generals, and that French generals have told her that they await with great anxiety the result of the coming German attack on the English lines because of the incompetence of the English Higher Command as a whole. Haig, however, they believed in. He was recommended by the French for the post. I see therefore no reason to believe that justice is being worked with precision in Dublin. I am trying to write a poem on the men executed 'terrible beauty has been born again'. If the English Conservative Party had made a declaration that they did not intend to rescind the Home Rule Bill there would have been no rebellion. I had no idea that any public event could so deeply move me and I am very despondent about the future. At the moment I feel that all the work of years has been overturned, all the freeing of Irish literature and criticism from politics. Maud Gonne reminds me that she saw the ruined houses about O'Connell Street, and the wounded and dying lying about the streets in the first few days of the war. I perfectly remember the vision and my making light of it and saying that if a true vision at all it could only have a symbolical meaning. This is the only letter I have had from her since she knew of Rebellion. I have sent her the papers every day. I do not yet know what she feels about her husband's death. Her letter was written before she heard of it. Her main thought seems to be 'Tragic dignity is restored to Ireland'. She had been told by two of the Irish party that 'Home Rule was betrayed'. She now thinks the sacrifice has made it safe. She is coming to London if she can get a passport, but I doubt her getting one. Indeed I shall be glad if she does not come yet—It is better for her to go on nursing the French wounded till the trials are over.[1]

The poem to which he alluded was 'Easter, 1916', dated 25 September 1916, in its final manuscript version. The poem was privately printed by Clement Shorter in the same year, but Yeats withheld it from general readers until 1920. The gibe made in 'September 1913'[2] (the similarity of the titles is noticeable) is withdrawn in 'Easter, 1916'.[3] Because Romantic Ireland was dead and gone he had sneered at those who fumbled in a greasy till; now, remembering this, he looked back and used the basic idea of the early image, put into a dignified guise, to describe how he had seen and undervalued the abilities of the revolutionary leaders

> Coming with vivid faces
> From counter or desk among grey
> Eighteenth-century houses[3]

but thought he had seen them as mere figures in a scene of motley :

> All changed, changed utterly:
> A terrible beauty is born. [3a]

Yeats knew the principal figures of the tragedy, and thought them theorists carried away by the belief that they must sacrifice themselves to a cause. He knew Constance Marcievicz in whose home he had stayed when she was still a Gore-Booth; knew Pearse the schoolmaster, and 'his helper and friend', Thomas MacDonagh, of whom he wrote in 1910:

A man with some literary faculty which will probably come to nothing through lack of culture and encouragement.[4]

Even MacBride, whom he had dreamed

> A drunken, vainglorious lout.
> He had done most bitter wrong
> To some who are near my heart[4]

became transformed utterly. He returned to his condemnation of hearts 'enchanted to stone', which leave life for the service of some abstraction.[3] From his study of Maud's character he had learned how

> Too long a sacrifice
> Can make a stone of the heart.[3]

'Easter, 1916' shares the general surprise at the Rising and when Yeats writes

> Was it needless death after all?[3]

he reflects his own continued reluctance to come to any conclusion on the subject. He could understand their dream:

> And what if excess of love
> Bewildered them till they died?[3]

The consequences of the execution of the leaders, that political
martyrdom which they had foreseen and for which they had
worked, changed popular disapproval of the Rising into the
spirit which praised the later triumphs of Sinn Fein. Yeats's
understanding of the inevitable result of the executions led to
his pointing out in 'Sixteen Dead Men' that logical discussion
was useless once passions had been raised by martyrdom:

> O But we talked at large before
> The sixteen men were shot,
> But who can talk of give and take
> What should be and what not
> While those dead men are loitering there
> To stir the boiling pot?
>
> You say that we should still the land
> Till Germany's overcome;
> But who is there to argue that
> Now Pearse is deaf and dumb?[5]

The touch of balladry in these lines is a recognition of the
popular reaction to the deaths of the leaders, whom he linked
with Lord Edward Fitzgerald and Wolfe Tone, because they
shared the idea that a spectacular sacrifice of blood must be
made for freedom's sake. The new heroes had not merely their
own sacrifice with which to appeal to Ireland's heart, but with
it went all the national passion symbolised in the deaths of
Fitzgerald and Tone.

In his own patriotic youth Yeats had thought of Ireland as
the Rose; but the difference between his ideals and those of
the new patriotism is shown in 'The Rose Tree' which he wrote
in 1917. In this poem Pearse tells Connolly that the Rose Tree
is withered. Connolly replies that it needs watering, to which
Pearse answers with the bitter political symbolism so unthink-
able in connection with Yeats's early literary imagery:

> 'But where can we draw water,'
> Said Pearse to Connolly,
> 'When all the wells are parched away?
> O plain as plain can be
> There's nothing but our own red blood
> Can make a right Rose Tree.'[6]

'On a Political Prisoner' dealt with Countess Marcievicz.
Yeats wrote in a letter[7] that he was

writing one on Con to avoid writing one on Maud. All of them are in
prison. . . .

The poem is a superb piece of technical achievement. The starting point, the symbol of the grey gull which came to the prisoner, is used to illustrate the change which had come upon the life of the Countess. The use of the adjective 'grey' suggests the monotony of the prison, yet the gull is in the poet's mind a means of returning to the contrast of her youth:

> When long ago I saw her ride
> Under Ben Bulben to the meet,
> The beauty of her countryside
> With all youth's lovely wildness stirred,
> She seemed to have grown clean and sweet
> Like any rock-bred sea-borne bird.[8]

The centre of the poem, its contrast of life which led to hatred and the prison, and the girl's carefree youth, is the more poignant for the poet's personal interest. The Gore-Booths were members of the local Sligo aristocracy when Yeats was a boy; but his family 'never more than small gentry' did not visit at Lissadell or the other 'big houses' of the district. There was a certain gulf between the county families and the traders, however wealthy, of the town.[9] Yeats's stay at Lissadell in the winter of 1894–5 was a pleasant introduction to the charm of Irish county society; and so there was the greatest disappointment for him now in seeing the girl who had represented for his youth the best elements of the countryside and the county *bonhomie*, becoming

> Blind and leader of the blind
> Drinking the foul ditch where they lie.[8]

She had deserted the role for which he had cast her in his mind's eye: she had become a member of the Dublin bohemian society which he disliked; and she had joined forces with the mob he hated. He attacked their rulers in 'The Leaders of the Crowd' written in 1918,[10] and reiterated his belief that they did not possess true wisdom. There was nothing left after his own enthusiasms and disillusionment but to understand and be moved by the tragedy.

His personal life was affected by the rebellion. His regard for Maud, whose husband, John MacBride, had been shot, was disturbed by messages which her daughter Iseult brought him in London. Her mother was ill and unhappy. He went again to Normandy; and yet again proposed to her. She refused his offer, and was disappointed that he did not share her enthusiasm for the events in Ireland where she longed to return. She was somewhat surprised to find him falling in love with Iseult. This was encouraged by Lady Gregory who had thought that he should not ask Maud to marry him as this would not only disturb him but do damage to the Abbey. Iseult, however, would be much more suitable, and Yeats, if married to her, would not be removed from Lady Gregory's influence.[11] He talked much to the girl, and she read him the young French Catholic poets; a dialogue from Jammes that moved them both to tears, some Claudel, and a volume of Peguy's *Mystère de la Charité de Jeanne d'Arc*.[12] He returned to London for the winter.

After spending the winter in London he went back to France in 1917. He was told by Maud that she had no objection to his proposing[13] to Iseult but that the young girl would probably not take him very seriously.[14] In fact, it was Iseult who had made the first proposal when she was fifteen, and had been refused because there was too much Mars in her horoscope.

In 1917 Yeats ignored her unsuitable horoscope and continually asked her to marry him; she, 'still mentally fifteen', enjoyed flirting with her mother's famous admirer throughout the summer. Eventually he managed to get passports for the family to enter the United Kingdom; and he accompanied them to London in September. The authorities did not allow Maud to proceed to Ireland. On the boat Yeats had delivered an ultimatum to Iseult: that she must make up her mind one way or the other, that he found the whole business an immense strain, and that if she would not marry him he had a friend who would be very suitable, a girl strikingly beautiful in a barbaric manner. He must receive her answer within a week at a certain A.B.C. in London.[11] Iseult refused him and he married Miss Hyde-Lees on 20th October.

Before 1917 the poems written to Iseult had all contrived to turn themselves into praise of her mother. She was still a child, a means of celebrating the glory of her mother's youth in 'To a Child Dancing in the Wind,'[15], 'Two Years Later'[16] and 'Presences'.[17] These poems contrast her youthful innocence with the past the poet knows. 'The Living Beauty' of 1915 also acts as a reminder of his own age:

> O Heart, we are old;
> The living beauty is for younger men:
> We cannot pay its tribute of wild tears.[18]

The next year he wrote to Lady Gregory that when Iseult had come to London she made him sad because he thought that if

his life had been normal he might have had a daughter of her
age, a sign that he was beginning to get old.[19] The question
of age mattered most when the poet discovered his love for the
young girl:

A strange thing surely that my Heart, when love had come unsought
Upon the Norman upland or in that poplar shade,
Should find no burden but itself and yet should be worn out.
It could not bear that burden and therefore it went mad.

The South wind brought it longing, and the East wind despair,
The West wind made it pitiful, and the North wind afraid.
It feared to give its love a hurt with all the tempest there;
It feared the hurt that she should give and therefore it went mad.

II

The Heart behind its rib laughed out. 'You have called me mad,' it said.
'Because I made you turn away and run from that young child;
How could she mate with fifty years that was so wildly bred?
Let the cage bird and the cage bird mate and the wild bird mate in the
wild.'

He wrote the first part of this poem, 'Owen Aherne and his
Dancers',[20] four days and the second part seven days after
he was married; it continues:

'You but imagine lies all day, O murderer,' I replied.
'And all those lies have but one end, poor wretches to betray,
I did not find in any cage the woman at my side.
O but her heart would break to learn my thoughts are far away.'

'Speak all your mind,' my Heart sang out, 'speak all your mind; who cares,
Now that your tongue cannot persuade the child till she mistake
Her childish gratitude for love and match your fifty years?
O let her choose a young man now and all for his wild sake.'

After their marriage Yeats and his wife stayed for a short
while at Ashdown Forest. It was obvious to Mrs Yeats that
her husband was extremely unhappy, and she decided that he
needed something to keep him from thinking of his personal
worries. She therefore decided to make an attempt at automatic
writing.

To her subsequent surprise and to her husband's eager
interest odd sentences were produced on a subject of which
she knew nothing. Yeats became convinced of the importance
of these revelations which they received by means of Mrs
Yeats's automatic script to which they devoted some hours
daily.[21] Thus was *A Vision* born. The poet ceased to worry
about Iseult, focused his attention on the interpretation of the

messages, and became more cheerful, writing to Lady Gregory after they had left Ashdown Forest for Woburn Buildings:

My wife is a perfect wife, kind wise and unselfish. I think you were such another young girl once. She has made my life serene and full of order.[22]

*A Vision* was published in 1925;[23] it represents the culmination of Yeats's attempts to find something in which he could believe. The fact that he could believe, even temporarily, in the strange system which he built up in *A Vision* is responsible for some of the positive strength of the poems he wrote after his marriage. It is essential for the interpretation of much of his later verse; for the system lurks behind many of those poems which are not acting directly as mouthpieces for his thought. It gives to all his work a cryptic, yet curiously concise, confidence.

Yeats's account of the creation of this incongruous collection of material, which contrives to reflect the poet's early interest in Theosophy, Magic, Swedenborg, and Boehme, Astrology and the fruits of his wide and varied reading, cannot be accepted. We might be suspicious at finding that the second edition of *A Vision*, published in 1937, contains a different account to the first, where Yeats played with the mythical figures of 'Owen Aherne' and 'Michael Robartes'. Owen Aherne is supposed to be the author of the Introduction to the first edition. He recounts how he met Robartes, lately returned from the Far East and searching for Yeats:

I felt a slight chill for we had both quarrelled with Mr Yeats on what I considered good grounds. Mr Yeats had given the name of Michael Robartes and that of Owen Aherne to fictitious characters and made those characters live through events that were a travesty of real events. 'Remember', I said, 'that he not only described your death but represented it as taking place amid associations which must, I should have thought, have been highly disagreeable to an honourable man.' 'I was fool enough to mind once', he said, 'but I soon found he had done me a service.' . . .[24]

Yeats's pleasure in making his characters real is indicated by a footnote in which he introduces himself into the triangle:

I think that Mr Aherne has remembered his own part in this conversation more accurately than that of his opponent. W. B. YEATS.

Robartes had found a strange book in his lodgings at Cracow:

One night I was thrown out of bed and when I lit my tallow candle found that the bed, which had fallen at one end, had been propped up by a joint stool and an old book bound in calf. In the morning I found that the book was called 'Speculum Angelorum et Hominorum'; had been written by Giraldus and printed at Cracow in 1594, a good many years before the celebrated Cracow publications and was of a very much earlier style both as to woodcut and type. It was very dilapidated and all the middle pages had been torn out; but at the end of the book were a number of curious allegorical pictures.[25]

He had also met an Arab tribe of Judwalis who, although they have lost their sacred book, attributed to Kusta ben Luka, a Christian philosopher at the court of Harun al Raschid, retain its doctrines which resemble those of Giraldus. Robartes finally meets Yeats and gives him the Giraldus document.

All this make-believe is acknowledged in *A Packet for Ezra Pound*, included in the second edition of *A Vision*:

I had invented an unnatural story of an Arabian traveller which I must amend and find a place for some day because I was fool enough to write half-a-dozen poems that are unintelligible without it.[26]

The 'unnatural story' had its lighter side. Yeats spent a long time trying to persuade Professor Louis Claude Purser to sanction 'Hominorum' as an irregular form of 'Hominum', without success.[27] The first edition contained many misprints and mistakes of various kinds, but, as regards the story of how the book came to be written, the second edition is not altogether satisfactory. The point to be made is that Yeats had invented the story of the Arabian traveller, and, more important, had been occupied with the subject-matter of *A Vision* before Mrs Yeats's automatic writing occurred. Before he was married he had written to his father that his thought was part of a religious system

more or less logically worked out. A system which will, I hope, interest you as a form of poetry. I find the setting of it all in order has helped my verse, has given me a new framework and new patterns. One goes on year after year getting the disorder of one's mind in order, and this is the real impulse to create.[28]

The 'system' on which he was occupied was the basis of *A Vision*, especially that connected with the various types of human personality. He had given expression to these philosophical thoughts in a series of essays called *Per Amica Silentia Lunae*, completed during the winter of 1916–17. With them he included 'Ego Dominus Tuus', the first MS of which is dated Oct. 1915, the second 5 December 1915. This poem is a dialogue between *Hic* and *Ille* and, as *Hic* defends the objective, *Ille* the subjective, there is some sense in a contemporary Dublin comment that *Hic* and *Willie* would be more correct. Yeats was at the time deeply interested in the clash of personalities within the one person, the self and the anti-self:

> I call to the mysterious one who yet
> Shall walk the wet sands by the edge of the stream
> And look most like me, being indeed my double,
> And prove of all imaginable things
> The most unlike, being my anti-self.[29]

When he went home after meeting others he used to go over all he had said with gloom and disappointment; but this mood generally passed when he was alone with his own thoughts:

All my thoughts have ease and joy, I am virtue and confidence. When I come to put in rhyme what I have found it will be a hard toil, but for a moment I believe I have found myself and not my anti-self.[30]

He found the like contrast in some of his friends, but the best example was to be found in Dante:

> I think he fashioned from his opposite
> An image that might have been a stony face
> Staring upon a Bedouin's horse-hair roof
> From doored and windowed cliff.[31]

Parts of the poem are explained by the prose essays of *Per Amica Silentia Lunae*. For example, these lines:

> We have lit upon the gentle, sensitive mind
> And lost the old nonchalance of the hand;
> Whether we have chosen chisel, pen or brush,
> We are but critics, or but half create,
> Timid, entangled, empty and abashed,
> Lacking the countenance of our friends[31]

are put more clearly in prose:

Some years ago I began to believe that our culture, with its doctrine of sincerity and self-realisation, made us gentle and passive, and that the Middle Ages and the Renaissance were right to found theirs upon the imitation of Christ or of some classic hero. St Francis and Caesar Borgia made themselves over-mastering, creative persons by turning from the mirror to meditation upon a mask.[32]

On the other hand, the slightly florid prose of such a passage as this:

Nor has any poet I have read of or heard or met with been a sentimentalist. The other self, the anti-self or the antithetical self, as one may choose to name it, comes but to those who are no longer deceived, whose passion is reality. The sentimentalists are practical men who believe in money, in position, in a marriage bell, and whose understanding of happiness is to be so busy whether at work or play, that all is forgotten but the momentary aim. They find their pleasure in a cup that is filled from Lethe's wharf, and for the awakening, for the vision, for the revelation of reality, tradition offers us a different word—ecstasy. . . .[33]

shows how tightly packed Yeats's verse was:

> . . . those that love the world serve it in action,
> Grow rich, popular and full of influence,
> And should they paint or write, still it is action:

The struggle of the fly in marmalade.
The rhetorician would deceive his neighbours,
The sentimentalist himself; while art
Is but a vision of reality.[31]

We can discover what lay behind the thoughts of the poem in many cases, the images that Yeats had in his own mind from which he generalised. For instance, *Ille*'s query:

What portion in the world can the artist have
Who has awakened from the common dream
But dissipation and despair?[31]

is based upon Yeats's observation:

Johnson and Dowson, friends of my youth, were dissipated men, the one a drunkard, the other a drunkard and mad about women, and yet they had the gravity of men who had found life out and were awakening from the dream.[33]

The labour of explaining these thoughts could not be left to verse alone. 'The Phases of the Moon', presumably written after *Per Amica Silentia Lunae*, contained the idea of the twenty-eight phases of the moon. This was probably suggested by a passage in Chaucer (whom Yeats had read carefully in 1910) rather than astrological or mystical sources, for shortly after his marriage he asked Mrs Yeats to type out the following passage:[34]

Til atte laste hym fil in remembraunce
That whiles he was at Orliens in Fraunce,
As yonge clerkes, that been lykerous
To reden artes that been curious,
Seken in every halke and every herne
Particular sciences for to lerne—
He hym remembred that, upon a day,
In Orliens in studie e book he say
Of magyk natureel . . .
Which book spak muchel of the operaciouns
Touchynge the eighte and twenty mansiouns
That longen to the moone, and swich folye
As in oure dayes is nat worthe a flye—
For hooly chirches feith is oure bileve
Ne suffreth noon illusioun us to greve.

Skeat's note on the passage which was added to the typescript may well have suggested the 'Judwalis' to Yeats:

The 28 'moonstations' of the Arabs are given in Ideler's Untersuchungen 'Uber die Bedeutung der Sternen Namen' p. 287. He gives the Arabic names, the stars that help to fix their positions etc. See also Mr Brae's edition of Chaucer's Astrolabe p. 89. For the influence of the moon in these mansions see 'Epitome Astrologiae' of Johannes Hispalensis Lib. I. Cap. 11, and Lib. IV. Cap. 18. Suffice it to say that there are twelve temperate mansions, 6 dry ones, and 10 moist ones. . . .

The meaning of the phases of the moon in the Yeatsian system could be provided only by a longer explanation than that of the poem so he wrote *The Discoveries of Michael Robartes* in the form of a dialogue about the *Speculum Angelorum et Hominorum* of Giraldus, but this was altered into the 1925 edition of *A Vision* in which Yeats wrote:

> I can now if I have the energy, find the simplicity I have sought in vain. I need no longer write poems like 'The Phases of the Moon' nor 'Ego Dominus Tuus'.[35]

There are two parts of *A Vision* which are of particular interest in connection with Yeats's poetry. One is the method by which he was able to categorise humanity under the various phases of the moon. The diagram included in *A Vision* makes this method clear. The First Phase is that of complete objectivity, and in Yeats's symbolism this is represented by the sun. Therefore there is no moon at this point (six o'clock on the circle of twenty-eight small circles) and the diagram shows a completely black circle to represent the absence of moon, or subjectivity. The Second Phase shows the first sliver of subjectivity emerging, and this increases till the Eighth Phase which possesses equal amounts of subjectivity and objectivity. The subjectivity begins to assume predominance from this Phase to the Twenty-second. The lower half of the circular diagram, that is, from Phase Twenty-two on the left through Phase One at the bottom to Phase Eight on the right, is basically objective, and its phases are called primary. Where the moon predominates Phases are Antithetical. Complete passivity occurs at Phase One, Unity of Being at Phase Fifteen. Yeats and his wife for many years used to categorise their friends according to the system; and it gave the poet confidence in his dealing with others to have this method of studying their character. In early youth he had been overprone to judge by exterior appearances but now, with self and anti-self, he erred in the other extreme of sometimes refusing to estimate persons upon their normal character. 'He simply did not', Mrs Yeats has said to me several times 'understand people'.

The second important part of the thought in *A Vision* is its method of dealing with history. Just as the phases of the moon were completed:

> When all the dough has been so kneaded up
> That it can take what form cook Nature fancy,
> The first thin crescent is wheeled round once more.

so the whole process of history is seen from a determinist view-point, and diagrammatically. These two points are illustrated by a note[36] which Yeats wrote in 1919, using the earlier make-believe setting:

Robartes copied out and gave to Aherne several mathematical diagrams from the 'Speculum'—squares and spheres, cones made up of revolving gyres intersecting each other at various angles, figures sometimes with great complexity. His explanation of these, obtained invariably from the followers of Kusta ben Luki is founded upon a single fundamental thought. The mind whether expressed in history or in the individual life has a precise movement which can be quickened or slackened but cannot be otherwise altered, and this movement can be expressed by a mathematical form. A plant or an animal has an order of development peculiar to it, a bamboo will not develop evenly like a willow nor a willow from joint to joint and both have branches that lessen and grow more light as they rise and no character-istic of the soil can alter these things. A poor soil may indeed check or stop the movement and rich prolong and quicken it. Mendel has shown that his sweet-peas bred long and short, white and pink varieties in certain mathematical proportions suggesting a mathematical law governing the transmission of parental characteristics. To the Judwalis as interpreted by Michael Robartes, all living minds have likewise a fundamental mathe-matical movement however adapted in plant or animal or man to particular circumstances and when you have found this movement and calculated its relation, you can foretell the entire future of that mind. A supreme religious act of their faith is to fix the attention on the mathematical form of this movement until the whole past and future of humanity or of an individual man shall be present to the intellect as if it were accomplished in a single movement. The intensity of the Beatific Vision when it comes depends upon the intensity of this realisation. It is possible in this way seeing that death itself is marked upon the mathematical figure which passes beyond it to follow the soul into the highest heaven and the deepest hell. This doctrine is they contend not fatalistic because the mathematical figure is an expression of the mind's desire and the more rapid the development of the figure the greater the freedom of the soul. The figure while the soul is in the body or suffering from the consequences of that life, is usually drawn as a double cone, the narrow end of each cone being in the centre of the broad end of the other. It has its origin from a straight line which repre-sents now time, now emotion, now subjective life and a plane at right angles to this line which represents, now space, now intellect, now objective life and it is marked out by two gyres which represent the conflict as it were of plane and line—two movements which circle above its centre because a movement outward on the plane is checked and in turn checks a movement outward upon the line; and the circling is always narrowing or spreading because one movement or other is always the stronger. In other words, the human soul is always moving outward into the objective, or inward into itself and this movement is double because the human soul has consciousness only because it is suspended between contraries, the greater the contrast the more intense the consciousness. The man in whom the movement inward is stronger than the movement outward the man who sees all reflected within himself, the subjective man reaches the narrow end of a gyre at death which is always they contend even when it seems the result of an accident, preceded by an intensification of the subjective life, and has a moment of realisation immediately after death a revelation which they describe as his being carried into the presence of all his kindred, a moment whose objectivity is exactly equal to the subjectivity of death. The objective man on the other hand, whose gyre moves outward receives at this moment the revelation not of himself seen from within for that is impossible to objective man but of himself as if he were somebody else. His figure also is true of history and the end of an age which always recedes, the revelation of the character of the next age is represented by the coming of one gyre to its place of greatest expansion and of the other to that of its greatest contraction; a religious dispensation ending when the gyres return to the same point they set out from generally 2000 years before, though dispensations are said for mathematical reasons to vary in length. At the present moment the life gyre is sweeping out unlike that before the birth of Christ which was narrowing and has almost reached its greatest expansion. The revelation which approaches will however, take its character from the contrary movement of the interior gyre. All our scientific democratic fact-accumulating heterogeneous civilisation belongs to the outward gyre and prepares not the continuance of itself but the revelation as in a lightning flash that will strike only in one place and will for a time be constantly repeated of the civilisation that must slowly take its place. This is too simple a statement for much detail is possible, there are certain points of stress on outer and inner gyre, a division of each now into ten, now into twenty-eight, stages or phases. However in the exposition of this detail so far as it affects their future, Robartes had little help from the Judwalis either because they cannot grasp the dates outside their experience or because certain studies seem to them unlucky. '"For a time the power," they have said to me', writes Robartes 'will be with us who are as like one another as the grains of sand but when the revelation comes it will not come to the poor but to the great and learned and establish again for 2000 years prince and vizier', nor do any among them doubt that it will come for their wise men have marked it upon the sand and it is because of these marks made generation after generation by the old for the young that they are named Judwalis, makers of measures or as we would say of diagrams.

The first aspect, the understanding and explanation of the individual by means of Phases, was accomplished partially in his poetry. Tentative as he thought 'The Phases of the Moon' to be, it is nevertheless a clear epitome of what he has to say about the first phases in *A Vision*:

> Twenty-and-eight the phases of the moon,
> The full and the moon's dark and all the crescents,
> Twenty-and-eight, and yet but six-and-twenty
> The cradles that a man must needs be rocked in:
> For there's no human life at the full or the dark.
> From the first crescent to the half, the dream
> But summons to adventure and the man
> Is always happy like a bird or a beast;
> But while the moon is rounding towards the full
> He follows whatever whim's most difficult
> Among whims not impossible, and though scarred,
> As with the cat-o-nine-tails of the mind,
> His body moulded from within his body
> Grows comelier. Eleven pass, and then
> Athena takes Achilles by the hair,
> Hector is in the dust, Nietzsche is born,

Because the heroes' crescent is the twelfth.
And yet, twice born, twice buried, grow he must,
Before the full moon, helpless as a worm.
The thirteenth moon but sets the soul at war
In its own being, and when that war's begun
There is no muscle in the arm; and after,
Under the frenzy of the fourteenth moon
The soul begins to tremble into stillness,
To die into the labyrinth of itself![37]

In *A Vision* Phase One[38] is described as complete plasticity when the body is completely absorbed in its supernatural element, Phase Fifteen[39] as complete beauty, when the moon is at its full. The 'bodies of fate', to give the Yeatsian terminology, of the Phases Two–Eight described simply in the poem as

From the first crescent to the half

are 'None except Monotony', 'Interest', 'Search', 'Natural Law', 'Humanity', 'Adventure that excites the individuality', 'The Beginning of strength'. After Phase Eight, according to the poem, man

. . . follows whatever whim's most difficult

while in *A Vision* the Phases become 'Enforced'. Phase Nine is 'Enforced Sensuality', Phase Ten 'Enforced Emotion', etc. What Nietzsche represents in the Twelfth Crescent is again revealed in *A Vision*:

The man of this phase is out of phase, is all a reaction, is driven from one self-conscious pose to another, is full of hesitation; or he is true to phase, a cup that remembers but its own fullness. It is therefore before all else the phase of the hero, of the man who overcomes himself, and so no longer needs, like Phase 10, the submission of others, or like Phase 11 conviction of others to prove his victory. . . . The man is pursued by a series of accidents, which, unless he meets them antithetically drive him into all sorts of temporary ambitions, opposed to his nature . . . and these ambitions he defends by some kind of superficial intellectual action, the pamphlet, the violent speech, the sword of the swashbuckler.[40]

When Yeats wrote

The thirteenth moon but sets the soul at war
In its own being

he was thinking of Baudelaire, Beardsley and Dowson, who represent the phase in *A Vision*, for it is the only one where a complete sensuality is possible, a preoccupation with the metaphors, symbols and images through which whatever is most morbid or strange is defined.[41] The next phase where

The soul begins to tremble into stillness

is represented by Keats, Giorgione and many beautiful
women.[42]

Many other poems contain this symbolism of the moon's
crescents. The 'girl at play' in 'The Double Vision of Michael
Robartes' is a being of the Fifteenth Phase; her

> Body perfection brought[43]

and this thought is elaborated in *A Vision* where the being of
the phase 'possesses the greatest possible beauty'. In 'The
Phases of the Moon'

> Hunchback and saint and fool are the last crescent

and another poem, 'The Saint and the Hunchback' of 1918,
deals with some aspects of these phases, but the Hunchback's
lines:

> Stand up and lift your hand and bless
> A man that finds great bitterness
> In thinking of his lost renown.
> A Roman Caesar is held down
> Under this hump.[44]

need the fuller explanation given in *A Vision*; where the
Hunchback is a man of the Twenty-sixth Phase,[45] the first for
which Yeats could find no examples from his own experience:

In the seemingly natural man, in Phase Twenty-six out of phase, there
is an attempt to substitute a new abstraction, a simulacrum of self-expression. Desiring emotion the man becomes the most completely solitary of
all possible men, for all emotional communication with his kind, that of a
common study, that of an interest in work done, that of a code accepted,
that of a belief shared, has passed; and without personality he is forced to
create its personal semblance. It is perhaps a slander of history that makes
us see Nero so, for he lacked the physical deformity which is, we are told,
first among this phase's inhibitions of personality. The deformity may be
of any kind, great or little, for it is but symbolised in the hump that thwarts
what seems the ambition of a Caesar or of an Achilles. He commits crimes,
not because he wants to, or like Phase Twenty-three out of phase, because
he can, but because he wants to feel certain that he can; and he is full of
malice because finding no impulse but in his own ambition, he is made
jealous by the impulses of others. He is all emphasis, and the greater that
emphasis the more does he display his sterility.

'The Double Vision of Michael Robartes' shows how Yeats's
imagination and his ability to enter through his dreaming
(whether day or night is immaterial) a condition of semi-
trance could produce a strangely weird unworldly effect in his
poetry. In this poem the determinism of his beliefs emerges
clearly; he has called up in his mind's eye a vision of the men

and spirits which are born when the old moon has gone and the new has not yet emerged—Phase One of *A Vision*:

> Under blank eyes and fingers never still
> The particular is pounded till it is man.
> When had I my own will?
> O not since life began.[43]

The first section of the poem is then a record of Yeats's impression of the age that will be ushered in, and reflects his new belief in an alternating series of historical cycles whose paths he symbolised by gyres.

It is not possible to trace the source of this idea with complete certainty.[46] In *A Vision*[47] Yeats gives his own sources as a story projected by Flaubert, to be called 'La Spirale', Swedenborg's ideas on gyration in his *Spiritual Diary* and in the *Principia*, Descartes's vortex,[47a] Blake's imagery in 'The Mental Traveller', and a passage in Heracleitus. Swedenborgian ideas on gyres[48] and the theory of vortices adopted by Descartes do not seem to have had a great influence upon the Yeatsian gyres. Boehme has several ideas[49] which Yeats took over in *A Vision*, notably that of the tinctures, and it seems very likely that he also based his ideas of the opposing gyres upon Boehme's semi-episodic view of the history of the universe, which was illustrated by opposing triangles.[50] In Boehme, as in *A Vision*, each era of history was overthrown by some catastrophic change.

What Yeats means by a gyre is explained in *A Vision*:

> A line is a symbol, of time, and expresses a movement, symbolising the emotional subjective mind, without extension in space; a plane, cutting the line at right angles, is spatial, the symbol of objectivity and intellect. A gyre is a combination of line and plane, and as one tendency or the other must always be stronger the gyre is always expanding or contracting. The gyre is drawn as a cone which represents sometimes the individual soul and its history, sometimes general life. For this two cones are substituted, since neither the soul of man or nature can be expressed without conflict.

These gyres are expanding, and narrowing, the apex of each coinciding with the base of the other:

> When, however, a narrowing and widening gyre reach their limit the one the utmost contraction, the other the utmost expansion, they change places, point to circle, circle to point, for this system conceives the world as catastrophic, and continue as before, one always narrowing, one always expanding, and yet bound for ever to one another.

There were other sources for the movement of gyration. In *A Vision* Yeats mentioned the description given by Irish countrymen of spirits departing from them in an ascending gyre; and in an early essay in *The Celtic Twilight* he recorded such a description given by an old Irish countrywoman of the same phenomenon:

> With that she gave a swirl round on her feet and raises up in the air and round and round she goes, and up and up, as if it was a winding stairs she went up, only far swifter. She went up and up, till she was no bigger than a bird up against the clouds, singing and singing the whole time the loveliest music I ever heard in my life from that day to this.[51]

Another source, not mentioned in Yeats's list, may be found in Dante. One of Yeats's best poems on the historical gyres, 'The Second Coming', begins:

> Turning and turning in the widening gyre
> The falcon cannot hear the falconer. . . .[52]

This is an image very reminiscent of the description of how Dante and Virgil reach the eighth circle of Hell seated on Geryon's back:

> But he whose succour then not first I proved,
> Soon as I mounted, in his arms aloft,
> Embracing, held me up; and thus he spake:
> 'Geryon, I now move thee: be thy wheeling gyres
> Of ample circuit, easy thy descent. . . .
> As falcon that hath long been on the wing
> But lure nor bird hath seen, while in despair
> The falconer cries, 'Ah me! thou stoop'st to earth',
> Wearied descends whence nimbly he arose
> In many an airy wheel and lighting sits
> At distance from his lord in angry mood.[53]

Yeats's falcon and Geryon travel in gyres. Yeats, according to Mrs Francis Stuart (Iseult Gonne, 'a girl that knew all Dante once'),[54] was extremely fond of the Dante illustrated by Doré which she owned. This edition contains a picture of Geryon[54a] emerging from the Abyss with his body shaped like the path of a gyre upon a cone. The shape of the monster is unusual and would have impressed Yeats by its peculiarity. When he thought of gyres in connection with a poem to be written on the historical cycles the shape assumed by Geryon might well have come into his mind, and from that to the image of Dante's falcon is a small step.

The succession of civilisations as Yeats envisaged it is shown in a passage of *A Vision*:

> Each age unwinds the threads another age had wound, and it amuses me to remember that before Phidias and his westward moving art, Persia fell, and that when full moon came round again, amid eastward moving thought, and brought Byzantine glory, Rome fell; and that at the outset of our westward moving Renaissance Byzantium fell; all things dying each other's life, living each other's death.[55]

When he turned to his own period he thought that his scientific fact-collecting age was nearing its conclusion. In 'The Double Vision of Michael Robartes' he pondered on the making of the new cycle:

> Constrained, arraigned, baffled, bent and unbent
> By these wire-jointed jaws and limbs,
> Themselves obedient
> Knowing not evil and good;
>
> Obedient to some hidden magical breath.
> They do not even feel, so abstract are they,
> So dead beyond our death,
> Triumph that we obey.[43]

*A Vision* uses the first of these stanzas as an illustration of the fact that there comes with the last gyre a desire to be ruled or rather, seeing that desire is all but dead, a complete adoration of force:

A decadence will descend, by perpetual moral improvement, upon a community which may seem like some woman of New York or Paris who has renounced her rouge pot to lose her figure and grow coarse of skin and dull of brain, feeding her calves and babies somewhere upon the edge of the wilderness. The decadence of the Graeco-Roman world with its violent soldiers and its mahogany dark young athletes was as great, but that suggested the bubbles of life turned into marbles, whereas what awaits us, being democratic and *primary*, may suggest bubbles in a frozen pond— mathematical Babylonian starlight. When the new era comes bringing its stream of irrational force it will, as did Christianity, find its philosophy already impressed upon the minority who have, true to phase, turned away at the last gyre from the *Physical Primary*. And it must wake into life, not Durer's, nor Blake's, nor Milton's human form divine—nor yet Nietzsche's superman nor Patmore's catholic, boasting 'a tongue that's dead'—the brood of the Sistine Chapel—but organic groups, *covens* of physical or intellectual kin melted out of the frozen mass. I imagine new races, as it were, seeking domination, a world resembling but for its immensity that of the Greek tribes—each with its own Daimon or ancestral hero—the brood of Leda, War and Love; history grown symbolic, the biography changed into a myth. Above all I imagine everywhere the opposites no mere alternation between nothing and something like the Christian brute and ascetic, but true opposites each living the other's death, dying the other's life.[56]

The grim picture was not fully drawn until 'The Second Coming' where the falconer is Christ, who began the era of history which has now almost reached its conclusion:

> In pity for man's darkening thought
> He walked that room and issued thence
> In Galilean turbulence.[52]

The falcon represents man, losing touch with Christianity. In Yeats's mind the era of Christianity began with the point of the cone, and the gyre thus begun had almost reached its fullest expansion.  That reached, there will be a revelation, a catastrophic happening, the change 'from circle to point', the new point being the apex of a history beginning its course in the opposite direction as the poem predicts in its macabre imagery:

> The darkness drops again; but now I know
> That twenty centuries of stony sleep
> Were vexed to nightmare by a rocking cradle,
> And what rough beast,[56a] its hour come round at last,
> Slouches towards Bethlehem to be born?[52]

the whole contrast between the horror of the new age and the old being suggested in the single word 'Bethlehem' opposed to the rough and slouching beast.

*A Vision* raises many questions in the reader's mind as to its importance, *per se*, the amount of belief which its author, if he was its author in the normal sense of the word, attached to its tenets, and for how long he held to those beliefs.  Whether the book is considered important in its own right or not is immaterial, though one might venture to prophesy that it will not be taken very seriously as a profound piece of thought. J. B. Y. wrote a sentence in a letter to his son that still seems to sum up this question:

> You would be a philosopher and are really a poet.[57]

Its main significance is the role it plays as Bible to Yeats's religion of poetry; to dismiss his accounts of visions and communications completely is too easy a method of treating the problem, as wrong as accepting all his own assertions on their face value.  The self-dramatisation which began in his childhood prompts us to a mischievous desire to pull at the surface skin of his poetry.  The passages already quoted from his unpublished autobiography, for instance, reveal the anxiety which lay behind the apparently devoted if defeatist love poetry of the nineties.  The apparent poise of the man of the world period is a façade as the 1909–10 Diaries demonstrate.[57a]  The desire to believe, however, seemed for a time after his marriage to have become allied to an actual belief.

Belief, for Yeats, was particularly difficult in some respects. The result of living in a dream-like state until the turn of the century produced in him a reluctance to come to decisions, which his practical life then remedied.  This is not to say that he had not convictions; he had, and they were so passionately held that they were fanatical. The nature of his character was thus, and therein lies the interest for us. In poetry his method of composition was unusual, and led to his believing, like Blake, that the dream world was more real than the external. His dreamy states of mind were often created by the chanting which accompanied the slow creation of poems, when he often repeated a phrase in a refrain that must have had an almost hypnotic effect. When thinking of a chorus of drums, for instance, he filled several pages of his manuscript book with the words 'barrum barrum barrum'.[57b] Madame MacBride described him as 'booming and buzzing like a bee' when in the course[58] of composition. This was a deliberate procedure:

If you suspend the critical faculty, I have discovered, either as the result of training, or, if you have the gift, by passing into a slight trance, images pass rapidly before you. If you can suspend also desire, and let them form at their own will, your absorption becomes more complete and they are more clear in colour, more precise in articulation, and you and they begin to move in what seems a powerful light. But the images pass before you linked by certain associations, and indeed in the first instance you have called them up by their association with traditional forms and sounds. You have discovered how, if you can but suspend will and intellect, to bring up from the 'subconscious' anything you already possess a fragment of. Those who follow the old rule keep their bodies still and their minds awake and clear, dreading especially any confusion between the images of the mind and the objects of sense; they seek to become, as it were, polished mirrors.[59]

Yeats had no gift for this clarity and quietude, because his mind was always off at a tangent:

And wisdom is a butterfly
And not a gloomy bird of prey.[60]

He had a different method of obtaining his imagery:

I had found that after evocation my sleep became at moments full of light and form, all that I had failed to find while awake; and I elaborated a symbolism of natural objects that I might give myself dreams during sleep, or rather visions, for they had none of the confusion of dreams, by laying upon my pillow or beside my bed certain flowers or leaves. Even to-day, after twenty years, the exaltations and the messages that came to me from bits of hawthorn or some other plant seem of all moments of my life the happiest and the wisest. After a time, perhaps because the novelty wearing off the symbol lost its power, or because my work at the Irish Theatre became too exciting, my sleep lost its responsiveness. I had fellow-scholars, and now it was I and now they who made some discovery. Before the mind's eye whether in sleep or in waking, came images that one was to discover presently in some book one had never read, and after looking in vain for explanation to the current theory of forgotten personal memory, I came to believe in a great memory passing on from generation to generation.[61]

The problem of *A Vision*'s composition is not aided by these habits of the poet. There is perhaps a clue in the sentence in *A Vision* saying that there was no longer any need to write poems like 'The Phases of the Moon' and 'Ego Dominus Tuus'. The difference between these poems and the work of *A Vision* (and the poems written in its symbolism) might be said to be Mrs Yeats's business. Through her automatic writing came the touch of authority that Yeats needed, and in the early twenties he thought little of talking of the mysterious agencies which gave his life the mixture of unorthodoxy and apparent order that he thought was an ideal state of living. It is possible considering how untidy his mind was, and how tidy that of Mrs Yeats is, that his thoughts may have, in passing through her mind, received order and precision.

His final account of the beginning of the book is given in *A Packet for Ezra Pound*, written in 1928:

> On the afternoon of October 24th, 1917, four days after my marriage, my wife surprised me by attempting automatic writing. What came in disjointed sentences, in almost illegible writing, was so exciting, sometimes so profound, that I persuaded her to give an hour or so day after day to the unknown writer, and after some half dozen such hours offered to spend what remained of life explaining and piecing together those scattered sentences. 'No' was the answer, 'we have come to give you metaphors for poetry.' The unknown writer took his theme at first from my just published 'Per Amica Silentia Lunae'. I had just made a distinction between the perfection that is from a man's combat with himself and that which is from a combat with circumstance, and upon this simple distinction he built up an elaborate classification of men according to their more or less complete expression of one type or the other. He supported his classification by a series of geometrical symbols and put these symbols in an order that answered the question in my essay as to whether some prophet could not prick upon the calendar the birth of a Napoleon or a Christ. A system of symbolism, strange to my wife and to myself, certainly awaited expression, and when I asked how long that would take I was told years. Sometimes when my mind strays back to those first days I remember that Browning's Paracelsus did not obtain the secret until he had written his spiritual history at the bidding of his Byzantine teacher, that before initiation Wilhelm Meister read his own history written by another, and I compare my 'Per Amica' to these histories.

After his marriage, partially because of his interest in the creation of *A Vision*, Yeats thought less of his age, and more of his wisdom. True, in such poems as 'Men Improve with the Years'[62] (July 1916) and 'The Living Beauty'[63] (1917) he was aware of wisdom, but it was thought of less in its own right than in comparison with the disadvantages of age. In the former poem he recorded the effect of Iseult's beauty:

I am worn out with dreams;
A weather-worn, marble triton
Among the streams;
And all day long I look
Upon this lady's beauty
As though I had found in a book
A pictured beauty,
Pleased to have filled the eyes
Or the discerning ears,
Delighted to be but wise,
For men improve with the years.[62]

He knew this was not an accurate record of his feelings and put down the doubt honestly:

And yet, and yet,
Is this my dream, or the truth?
O would that we had met
When I had my burning youth.[62]

His tragedy seemed to be that wisdom had come too late. He loved without wisdom in his youthful passion; now when he possesses the wisdom that would make his love successful, he is too old for passion.

Marriage changed this attitude. He thought that it was a means of experiencing love and wisdom together. 'Solomon and Sheba', a poem symbolising the pleasant relationship of the poet and his wife, written at Glendalough in 1918, illustrates this:

Said Solomon to Sheba,
And kissed her Arab eyes,
'There's not a man or woman
Born under the skies
Dare match in learning with us two,
And all day long we have found
There's not a thing but love can make
The world a narrow pound'.[64]

In 'Solomon and the Witch' (1918) there seemed an acceptance and contentment; he had forgotten his worries over the possibility that he had hurt both Maud and Iseult; and had found tranquillity:

Maybe the bride-bed brings despair
For each an imagined image brings
And finds a real image there.[65]

'An Image from a Past Life' (September 1919) might seem to imply that Yeats had still his imagined image in mind and that Mrs Yeats was disturbed by this when *He* hears:

that scream
From terrified, invisible beast or bird:
Image of poignant recollection

which *She* calls:

> An image of my heart that is smitten through
> Out of all likelihood, or reason,
> And when at last,
> Youth's bitterness being past,
> I had thought that all my days were cast
> Amid most lovely places; smitten as though
> It had not learned its lesson.

Also, when *She* describes the image which she sees:

> A sweetheart from another life floats there
> As though she had been forced to linger
> From vague distress
> Or arrogant loveliness,
> Merely to loosen out a tress
> Among the starry eddies of her hair
> Upon the paleness of a finger.[66]

the language reverts to the romantic and languorous ethos of the early love poetry written to Maud Gonne and, briefly, to Diana Vernon. Such words as 'loveliness', 'tress', 'starry eddies', 'paleness', and even the mention of hair[67] are typical of the earlier work, with only the adjective 'arrogant' to indicate how far Yeats had moved from such delicacy of expression. It might be tempting to assume that the image was not so much one of a past life as of a past love were it not for a note[68] by Yeats on the poem which explains what thoughts the poet wove out of the incident which prompted the poem:

Robartes writes to Aherne under the date May 12, 1917. 'I found among the Judwalis much biographical detail, probably legendary, about Kusta-ben-Luki. He saw occasionally during sleep a woman's form and later found in a Persian painting a form resembling, though not identical with the dream form which was he considered that of a woman loved in another life. Presently he met and loved a beautiful woman whose form also resembled without being identical with that of his dream. Later on he made a long journey to purchase the painting which was, he said, the better likeness and found on his return that his mistress had left him in a fit of jealousy.' In a dialogue and in letters, Robartes gives a classification and analysis of dreams which explains the survival of this story among the followers of Kusta-ben-Luki. They distinguish between the memory of concrete images and the abstract memory and affirm that no concrete dream image is ever from our memory. This is not only true they say of dreams, but of those visions seen between sleeping and waking. This doctrine at first found me incredulous for I thought it contradicted by my experience and by all I have read, not however a very great amount in books of psychology and of psycho-analysis. Did I not frequently dream of some friends or relation or that I was at school? I found, however, when I studied my dreams, as I was directed in a dialogue that the image seen was never really that of friend or relation or my own school. A substitution had taken place, often a very strange one though I forgot this if I did not notice it at once on waking. The name of some friend or the conception 'my Father' or 'at school' are a part of the abstract memory and therefore of the dream life, but the image of my Father or my friend or my old school being a part of the personal concrete memory appeared neither in sleep nor in visions between sleep and waking. I found sometimes that my father or my friend had been represented in sleep by a stool or a chair and I concluded that it was the entire absence of my personal memory that enabled me to accept such images without surprise. Was it not perhaps this very absence that constituted sleep? Would I perhaps awake if a single concrete image from my memory came before me? Even these images—stool, chair, etc., were never any particular stool, chair, etc., that I had known. Were those images, however, from the buried memory, had they floated up from the subconscious, had I seen them perhaps a long time ago, and forgotten having done so. Even if that were so, the exclusion of the conscious memory was a new, perhaps important truth; but Robartes denied their source even in the subconscious. But though I often see between sleep and waking elaborate landscapes, I have never seen one that seemed a possible representation of any place I have ever lived near from childhood up seems a corroboration. Robartes traces these substitute images to different sources. Those that come in sleep hours are (1) from the state immediately preceding our birth; (2) from the anima mundi—that is to say, from a general store house of images which have ceased to be a property of any personality or spirit. Those that come between sleeping and waking are, he says, re-shaped by what he calls the 'Automatic faculty' which can create pattern, balance, etc., from the others bound to us by certain emotional links through perhaps entire strangers and preserved in a kind of impersonal, often simply called the 'record' which takes much the same place in his system as the lower strata of the astral light does the disciples of Elephas Levi. This does not exhaust the contents of dreams for we have to account also for certain sentences, for certain ideas which are not concrete images and yet do not arise from our personal memory, but at the moment I have merely to account for certain images that affect passion or affection. Robartes writes to Aherne in a letter dated May 15, 1917: 'No lover, no husband, has ever met in dreams the true image of wife or mistress. She who has perhaps filled his whole life with joy or disquiet cannot enter there. Her image can fill every moment of his waking life but only its counterfeits will find that just in so far as they become concrete, sensuous, they are distinct individuals—never types but individuals. They are the forms of those whom he has loved in some past earthly life chosen from anima mundi by the subconscious will, and through them, for they are not always hollow shades, the dead cannot while . . . outface the living rival. They are the forms of the Over-Shadowers as they are called. All violent passion has to be expiated or atoned by one in life, by one in the state between life and life, because as the Judwalis believe there is always deceit or cruelty; but it is only in sleep that we can see these forms of those who as spirits influence our waking thought. Souls that are once linked by emotion till the last drop of that emotion is exhausted, desire, hate or what you will, never cease to affect one another remaining always as it were in contact. Those whose past passions are unatoned seldom love living man or woman, but only those loved long ago of whom the living man or woman is but a brief symbol unloved when some phase of some atonement is finished; but because in general the form does not pass into the memory, it is the moral being of the dead alone that is symbolised. Under certain circumstances which are precisely described the form indirectly and not necessarily from dreams enters the living memory for the subconscious will as Kusta-ben-Luki in the story selects among pictures or other ideal representations some form

that resembles what was once the physical body of the Over-Shadower and
this ideal form becomes to the living man an obsession continually perplexing and frustrating natural instinct.  It is therefore only after full atonement
or expiation, perhaps after many lives that a natural deep satisfying love
becomes possible, and this love in all subjective natures must precede the
Beatific vision.

The most important part of this note is the conclusion, which
shows how the sense of communion of mind between husband
and wife underlay the poem:

When I wrote 'An Image from a Past Life', I had merely begun my
study of the various papers upon the subject, but I do not think I misstated
Robartes' thought in permitting the woman and not the man to see the
'Over-Shadower' or ideal form, whichever it was.  No mind's contents are
necessarily shut off from another and in moments of excitement images
pass from one mind to the other with extraordinary ease, perhaps most
easily from that portion of the mind which for the time being is outside
consciousness.  I use the word 'pass' because it is familiar not because I
believe any movement in space to be necessary.  The second mind sees
what the first has already seen—that is all.

The interest for Yeats probably lay much more in the thought
transference than in pondering over the image of another love.
He and his wife had a more than sensual contact.  Another
poem illustrating this is 'Towards Break of Day' written in
January 1919:

Was it the double of my dream
The woman that by me lay
Dreamed, or did we halve a dream
Under the first cold gleam of day?[69]

He refers to this poem in *A Vision*, calling it an experience of
the kind which he described as follows:

When two people meditate upon the one theme, who have established a
supersensual link, they will invariably in my experience no matter how
many miles apart, see pass before the mind's eye complementary images,
images that complete one another.  One for instance may see a boat upon
a still sea full of tumultuous people, and the other a boat full of motionless
people upon a tumultuous sea.  Even when the link is momentary and superficial this takes place, and sometimes includes within its range a considerable
number of people.  One, for instance, will receive from a dream figure a
ripe apple, another an unripe; one a lighted and one an unlighted candle
and so on.  On the same night a mother will dream that her child is dead
or dying, the child that her mother is dead, while the father will wake in
the night with a sudden inexplicable anxiety for some material treasure.  I
put an experience of the kind into the poem that begins

Was it the double of my dream. . . .[70]

The happiness Yeats felt was at a certain simplicity in his
previously vacillating character, and this, even if it was only
a temporary sensation, seemed none the less delightful.  The

insistence upon the virtue of innocence in *A Vision* is echoed in
a poem 'Demon and Beast':

> Though I had long perned in the gyre,
> Between my hatred and desire
> I saw my freedom won,
> And all laugh in the sun.[71]

This was written when the Yeatses were staying at 73 St
Stephen's Green, Dublin, in the winter of 1918. From this
house Yeats went frequently to the National Art Gallery, where,
because of *A Vision*'s clarifying effect:

> The glittering eyes in a death's head
> Of old Luke Wadding's portrait said
> Welcome, and the Ormondes all
> Nodded upon the wall,
> And even Strafford smiled as though
> It made him happier to know
> I understood his plan.
> Now that the loud beast ran
> There was no portrait in the Gallery
> But beckoned to sweet company,
> For all men's thoughts grow clear
> Being dear as mine are dear.[71]

He was independent of the troubles Maud and Iseult could
cause his sensitivity while he remained friendly towards them.
In fact, when Maud, who had been imprisoned upon suspicion
in England (she had earlier defied the ban upon her proceeding
to Ireland and acquired 73 St Stephen's Green which she had
then lent to Yeats and his wife) and then, through Yeats's
efforts, removed to a sanatorium because of her health, again
eluded surveillance and arrived in Dublin in December, Yeats
refused to give her hospitality. Mrs Yeats was recovering
from an extremely severe attack of influenza, which had
developed into pneumonia and was, besides, expecting a child
in February, and W. B. thought that the possibility of police
searches or raids upon the house might cause a relapse. She
was not told of Maud's request to be taken in. There was a
violent quarrel between the old friends, but this soon died
down. Yeats and his wife, however, handed over the house to
Madame MacBride before Christmas.[72]

Iseult, whose future had been such an anxiety to Yeats when
he had returned to London from Normandy in 1917, had then
taken up a position there which he had obtained for her. In
this sense of protector he wrote in 'Two Songs of a Fool'
(1918)[73] that

> A speckled cat and a tame hare
> Eat at my hearthstone
> And sleep there;
> And both look up to me alone
> For learning and defence
> As I look up to Providence

where the 'speckled cat' was Mrs Yeats, the 'tame hare'
Iseult. In the preoccupation of his marriage, however, he had
forgotten about Iseult:

> I slept on my three-legged stool by the fire,
> The speckled cat slept on my knee;
> We never thought to enquire
> Where the brown hare might be,
> And whether the door were shut.
> Who knows how she drank the wind
> Stretched up on two legs from the mat,
> Before she had settled her mind
> To drum with her heel and leap?
> Had I but awakened from sleep
> And called her name, she had heard,
> It may be, and had not stirred,
> That now, it may be, has found
> The horn's sweet note and the tooth of the hound.

Iseult did become a source of anxiety to Yeats later, but this
time for her own sake, when she came to Dublin and began
to mix in its Bohemian circles; he admonished her in 'To a
Young Beauty' (1918):[74]

> Dear fellow-artist, why so free
> With every sort of company,
> With every Jack and Jill?
> Choose your companions from the best;
> Who draws a bucket with the rest
> Soon topples down the hill.

The thought that she might, with mirror for school, be passionate and yet not bountiful is repeated in 'Michael Robartes
and the Dancer' (1919) where, after the subject is introduced
by a description of Bordone's St George and the Dragon in
the National Gallery, Dublin, *He* tells how:

> That blest souls are not composite,
> And that all beautiful women may
> Live in uncomposite blessedness,
> And lead us to the like—if they
> Will banish every thought, unless
> The lineaments[74a] that please their view
> When the long looking-glass is full,
> Even from the foot-sole think it too.[75]

To which *She* replied, not unnaturally:

> They say such different things at school.

Yeats's first child was born on 26 February 1919, a girl, christened Anne Butler. In the summer Yeats wrote 'A Prayer for my Daughter',[76] showing that he had modified his views where his hopes for his daughter's life were concerned. The poem opens with excited reveries due to meditation upon the future as he had seen it in *A Vision*. The prayer for beauty which follows is restrained:

> May she be granted beauty and yet not
> Beauty to make a stranger's eye distraught.

He wishes that she may have courtesy, an aristocratic virtue to match the Butler name:

> Hearts are not had as a gift but hearts are earned
> By those that are not entirely beautiful.

And that she may avoid the failings of Maud:

> An intellectual hatred is the worst,
> So let her think opinions[77] are accursed.
> Have I not seen the loveliest woman born
> Out of the mouth of Plenty's horn,
> Because of her opinionated mind
> Barter that horn and every good
> By quiet natures understood
> For an old bellows full of angry wind?

He reflects on the wisdom and content which his marriage has brought:

> Yet many, that have played the fool
> For Beauty's very self, has charm made wise,
> And many a poor man that has roved,
> Loved and thought himself beloved,
> From a glad kindness cannot take his eyes.

# 9

# THE TOWER
## (1917–1928)

*And I, that count myself most prosperous,*
*Seeing that love and friendship are enough,*
*For an old neighbour's friendship chose the house*
*And decked and altered it for a girl's love,*
*And know whatever flourish and decline*
*These stones remain their monument and mine.*

W. B. YEATS[1]

*We are at our tower and I am writing poetry as I always do*
*here, and as always happens, no matter how I begin it becomes*
*love poetry before I am finished with it.*

W. B. YEATS[2]

WHEN Yeats wrote in disillusion that all life seemed a preparation for something that never happens, he did not foresee that the preparation of his own life would be rewarded so fully in the nineteen-twenties. His early activities in revolutionary politics, especially his membership of the I.R.B., led to his Senatorship in the Irish Free State; his early dabbling with mysticism, theology and magic had prepared him for writing *A Vision*. These new resumptions of old pursuits were positive, and, coming at an age when his disillusion might have been expected to kill all enthusiasm for aspects of life in which he had not found what he wanted, surprisingly they provided him with objects to which he could devote his energy and his capacity for service. They even brought him into fresh interests. Politics awakened his pride in the Anglo-Irish, in their history and characters; *A Vision* led him to history and philosophy.

His poetry, too, expanded in range. It had reblossomed in *The Wild Swans at Coole* and *Michael Robartes and the Dancer*, but the flowering came with *The Tower*. *The Tower* represented Yeats in all his moods and vacillations; it was the perfect and unique background for all aspects of his character and interests. The public aspects of his life gave him the directness he had often lacked, the sense of sharing in those public and literary heritages which he had earlier scorned. To a certain degree he became a member of a community, and, paradoxically enough, attempted to graft the old virtues of his own race on to the new experiment of the Free State. As a result of this his verse took on a new eloquence. His experience at the Abbey had given him a tautness of expression that added to the dramatic elements of his own character; his study of the eighteenth-century Anglo-Irish gave him rhetoric and clarity. The poetry of *The Tower* period is rich because of the fullness of Yeats's life, because his style was reaching maturity at the same time as his life. The poems of the twenties therefore deal with many of his interests: politics, philosophy, friendship and love; but they are all 'Tower' poems, the work of a personality and a public figure who is writing for an audience. He writes of what interests him: politics, philosophy and the rest, especially love, are seen as they affect his own life and imagination, not that of ordinary humanity. Yet he had come to share experiences common to all men; domesticity, and parenthood;[2a] he had also that experience of the responsibility of power common to so many great figures in English literature: Chaucer, Milton, Dryden, Swift.

The personal element, however, is always there in Yeats, and his account of his methods of creating poems, written in 1923 in *The Bounty of Sweden*, reveals this clearly:

Every now and then, when something has stirred my imagination, I begin talking to myself. I speak in my own person and dramatise myself very much as I have seen a mad old woman do upon the Dublin quays, and sometimes detect myself speaking and moving like an old man with fumbling steps. Occasionally, I write out what I have said in verse and generally, for no better reason, than because I remember that I have written no verse for a long time. I do not think of my soliloquies as having different literary qualities. They stir my interest by their appropriateness to the men I imagine myself to be or by their accurate description of some emotional circumstance, more than by any aesthetic value. When I begin to write I have no object but to find for them some natural speech, rhythm and syntax, and to set it out in some pattern, so seeming old that it may seem all men's speech, and though the labour is very great, I seemed to have used no faculty peculiar to myself, certainly no special gift. I print the poem and never hear of it again, until I find the book years after with a page dog-eared by some young man, or marked by some young girl with a violet, and when I have seen that I am slightly ashamed, as though somebody were to attribute to me a delicacy of feeling I should but do not possess. What came so easily at first and amidst so much drama, and was written so laboriously at the last cannot be counted among my possessions.

The story of *The Tower* is part of Yeats's life and reveals the essentially fresh qualities of his mind and outlook that were not satisfied merely to acquiesce in the achievement of an old

ambition. In the second edition of *The Celtic Twilight* (1902)
Yeats wrote an essay 'Dust hath closed Helen's eye' in which
he described Ballylee, a little group of houses in the neighbourhood of Coole, made famous in the West of Ireland because
Raftery, the Gaelic poet, had made a song about the peasant
beauty, Mary Hynes, who dwelt there. Yeats first heard the
song from an old woman who remembered both Raftery, then
almost blind, and Mary Hynes; he quoted the translation
which Lady Gregory made of the song:

> . . . What is the worth of greatness till you have the light
> Of the flowers of the branch that is by your side?
> There is no God to deny it or to try and hide it,
> She is the sun in the heavens who wounded my heart.
>
> There was no part of Ireland I did not travel,
> From the rivers to the tops of the mountains,
> To the edge of Lough Greine whose mouth is hidden,
> And I saw no beauty but was behind hers.
>
> Her face was shining, and her brows were shining too;
> Her face was like herself, her mouth pleasant and sweet.
> She is the pride, and I give her the branch,
> She is the shining flower of Ballylee. . . .[3]

## An old weaver there told Yeats that

Mary Hynes was the most beautiful thing ever made. My mother used
to tell me about her, for she'd be at every hurling, and wherever she was
she was dressed in white. As many as eleven men asked for her in marriage
in one day but she wouldn't have any of them. There was a lot of men
up beyond Kilbecanty one night sitting together drinking, and one of them
got up and set out to go to Ballylee and see her; but Cloon Bog was open
then and when he came to it he fell into the water and they found him
there in the morning.

Yeats's own observation picked out the similarities between
Mary and Maud, the theme of poet and lady for ever translated into his own experience:

She 'had seen too much of the world'; but these old men and women,
when they tell of her, blame another and not her, and though they can be
hard, they grow gentle as the old men of Troy grew gentle when Helen
passed by on the walls.

He echoed the idea in a poem written at Coole in September
1913, 'When Helen Lived':

> Yet we, had we walked within
> Those topless towers
> Where Helen walked with her boy,
> Had given but as the rest
> Of the men and women of Troy
> A word and a jest.[4]

Here the spirit is bitter, the use of the colloquial 'boy' setting
the tone; there followed the more noble poems written to Maud
in 1915; and by 1926 his poetry of her has still memories, but
memories which are less tortured and despairing. The two
themes are woven together now; memories of the story of Mary
Hynes and Maud, seen as Helen:

> Some few remembered still when I was young
> A peasant girl commended by a song,
> Who'd lived somewhere upon that rocky place,
> And praised the colour of her face,
> And had the greater joy in praising her,
> Remembering that, if walked she there,
> Farmers jostled at the fair
> So great a glory did the song confer.
>
> And certain men, being maddened by those rhymes,
> Or else by toasting her a score of times,
> Rose from the table and declared it right
> To test their fancy by their sight;
> But they mistook the brightness of the moon
> For the prosaic light of day—
> Music had driven their wits astray—
> And one was drowned in the great bog of Cloone.
>
> Strange, but the man who made the song was blind;
> Yet, now I have considered it, I find
> That nothing strange; the tragedy began
> With Homer that was a blind man,
> And Helen has all living hearts betrayed.[5]

Ballylee's romance lay not only in the story of Mary Hynes.
There was an

old square castle, Ballylee, inhabited by a farmer and his wife, and a cottage
where their daughter and their son-in-law live, and a little mill with an
old miller, and old ash-trees throwing green shadows upon a little river
and great stepping stones.[3]

Yeats often walked from Coole to visit the place where

Beauty has lived its life of sorrow

and, encouraged by Lady Gregory's son Robert, he began to
think, some years before his marriage, of acquiring the castle
as a residence. These day-dreams were first realised in two
poems written in 1915, 'Ego Dominus Tuus'[6] and 'The Phases
of the Moon',[7] where the tower provides the setting for a discussion of Yeats's theories of the anti-self and the phases of the
moon. The setting is chosen for its symbolic value. Yeats had
found in Milton,[8] in Shelley,[9] and in Count Villiers de l'Isle
Adam[10] towers used as symbols of the search for wisdom carried

on in solitude by the lonely student. These solitary figures were introverted; they sought to gain wisdom through an examination of their own thoughts and their personal reactions to what they read: Yeats himself was extremely self-centred[11] (though unselfish) and this explains some of the attraction of those Shelleyan heroes whose characters he attempted to assume in youth. In 1897 he wrote that

> In modern times we are agreed that we 'make our souls' out of some one of the great poets of ancient times, or out of Shelley, or—[12]

and by 1900 he was distinguishing between the symbolism of Shelley's towers and caves:

> I believe Shelley had more than a romantic scene in his mind when he made Prince Athanase follow his mysterious studies in a lighted tower above the sea, and when he made the old hermit watch over Laon in his sickness in a half-ruined tower, wherein the sea, here doubtless as to Cythna, 'the one mind', threw 'spangled sands' and 'rarest sea shells'. The tower, important in Maeterlinck, as in Shelley, is, like the sea, and rivers and caves with fountains, a very ancient symbol, and would perhaps, as years went by, have grown more important in his poetry. The contrast between it and the cave in *Laon and Cythna* suggests a contrast between the mind looking outward upon men and things and the mind looking inward upon itself, which may or may not have been in Shelley's mind, but certainly helps, with one knows not how many other dim meanings, to give the poem mystery and shadow. It is only by ancient symbols, by symbols that have numberless meanings beside the one or two the writer lays an emphasis upon, or the half-score he knows of, that any highly subjective art can escape from the barrenness and shallowness of a too conscious arrangement, into the abundance and depth of nature.[13]

He too saw the tower as a symbol of the pursuit of wisdom by the mind looking in upon itself:

> that shadow is the tower,
> And the light proves that he is reading still.
> He has found, after the manner of his kind,
> Mere images; chosen this place to live in
> Because, it may be, of the candle-light
> From the far tower where Milton's Platonist
> Sat late, or Shelley's visionary prince:
> The lonely light that Samuel Palmer engraved,
> An image of mysterious wisdom won by toil;
> And now he seeks in book or manuscript
> What he shall never find.[14]

All these day-dreams came nearer realisation when Yeats purchased the tower at Ballylee for thirty-five pounds in June 1917.[15] The Congested Districts Board were splitting up some of the Gregory estate into small holdings, and sold the castle cheaply, their chief land inspector having reported that its value as a residence was 'sentimental and therefore problematical'.[16] After marriage Yeats decided to spend some money putting the castle into order as a summer residence. He had brought his wife to Ireland in 1918. They stayed at Dublin and Glendalough, County Wicklow, where Yeats wrote several poems, one, 'Shepherd and Goatherd',[17] in memory of Lady Gregory's son who had lost his life on the Italian front. Thence they went to Sligo, and an incident there provided Yeats with the stimulus for a poem praising his wife's wisdom and kindness and excusing his saturnine mood:

> Although my wits have gone
> On a fantastic ride, my horse's flanks are spurred
> By childish memories of an old cross Pollexfen,
> And of a Middleton, whose name you never heard,
> And of a red-haired Yeats whose looks, although he died
> Before my time, seem like a vivid memory.
> You heard that labouring man who had served my people. He said
> Upon the open road, near to the Sligo quay—
> No, no, not said, but cried it out—'You have come again,
> And surely after twenty years it was time to come'.
> I am thinking of a child's vow sworn in vain
> Never to leave that valley his fathers called their home.[18]

In June they visited Coole and Lady Gregory lent them Ballinamantane House near Ballylee from which they supervised the alterations to the tower. There were two cottages built on to the massive stone building, one of which was in ruins; these were put in order, but the tower was a more difficult problem. It had four great rooms, one above the other, and the floors of these had long been decayed, as there was no roof on the building. The lower rooms were first made habitable, the ceilings alone keeping out the weather. In 1919 Yeats used the ground-floor room as a study; later the room above this was used for the purpose, while the second floor became the bedroom. Heavy elm furniture was made on the spot by local carpenters:

> No table or chair or stool not simple enough
> For shepherd lads in Galilee.[19]

The tower began to feature more in Yeats's poetry. In June 1918 he completed 'In memory of Major Robert Gregory':

> Now that we're almost settled in our house
> I'll name the friends that cannot sup with us
> Beside a fire of turf in th' ancient tower,
> And having talked to some late hour
> Climb up the narrow winding stair to bed:

> Discoverers of forgotten truth
> Or mere companions of my youth,
> All, all are in my thoughts to-night being dead. . . .
>
> I am accustomed to their lack of breath,
> But not that my dear friend's dear son,
> Our Sidney and our perfect man,
> Could share in that discourtesy of death.
>
> For all things the delighted eye now sees
> Were loved by him; the old storm-broken trees
> That cast their shadows upon road and bridge;
> The tower set on the stream's edge;
> The ford where drinking cattle make a stir
> Nightly, and startled by that sound
> The water hen must change her ground;
> He might have been your heartiest welcomer.[20]

The tower provided the setting for 'A Prayer for my Daughter' which was written at Ballylee the following year:

> Once more the storm is howling, and half-hid
> Under this cradle-hood and coverlid
> My child sleeps on. There is no obstacle
> But Gregory's wood and one bare hill
> Whereby the haystack and roof-levelling wind,
> Bred on the Atlantic, can be stayed.[21]

Yeats decided to spend the winter of 1919 in England. Ballylee was only possible in the summer. There was a danger from dampness if the stream which flowed round the castle were to flood, and provisions had to be brought several miles by Mrs Yeats. The tower suited the solitary mood of the poet but the gregarious side of his nature required company. The company which he had found in Dublin the previous winter had been obsessed with political unrest and excitement; he had given up his rooms in Woburn Buildings which had been lent to Douglas Goldring;[22] and he did not want to live in London again. As both he and Mrs Yeats liked Oxford (where they had lived for some months in the early part of 1918, in rooms in Broad Street) Mrs Yeats took a house, since demolished, in Broad Street opposite Balliol, and they moved in during October 1919.

'Nineteen Hundred and Nineteen',[23] written in that year, carries the depressed thought of the poems about the Lane controversy much further:

> We, who seven years ago
> Talked of honour and of truth,
> Shriek with pleasure if we show
> The weasel's twist, the weasel's tooth.

The difference is that he not only sees how bad matters are in
Ireland, but has no hope of their improvement.  The enormity
of the change is indicated by the introduction and conclusion of
the poem.  The first stanza describes some of the ingenious
lovely things of Athens, [24] stressing their beauty rather than
their disappearance.  Then he shows the hopes that had been
held, presumably not so much in the early idealistic period of
his literary work as in the time when, illusions shattered, he
hoped for a gradual improvement, and especially the growth
of public opinion in Ireland.  Then there was an impartial law,
and the great army seemed but a showy thing; now there is the
contrast—the 'Black and Tans':

> Now days are dragon-ridden, the nightmare
> Rides upon sleep: A drunken soldiery
> Can leave the mother murdered at her door,
> To crawl in her own blood, and go scot-free;
> The night can sweat with terror as before
> We pieced our thoughts into philosophy,
> And planned to bring the world under a rule,
> Who are but weasels fighting in a hole.

The turmoil and bloodshed of 1916 had been seen as part of a
single tragic event, but the thought of *A Vision* [25] sees the new
violence as the first signs of the coming of a new age, the end
of all that men treasure.  Yeats's answer to those who might
find his determinism unpalatable is the answer which satisfied
him:

> . . . all triumph would
> But break upon his ghostly solitude.

In other words, he understood what was happening (a fact that
of itself implied a certain detachment) in contemporary life.
The last stanza returns to the lovely things of Athens, to rein-
force the sense of change:

> That country round
> None dared admit, if such a thought were his,
> Incendiary or bigot could be found
> To burn that stump on the Acropolis,
> Or break in bits the famous ivories
> Or traffic in the grasshoppers and bees.

No one expected the burnings of houses in Ireland either; yet,
despite the sadness and gloom, there is a great richness in the
poem.  Verse stripped bare of its romantic cloak in *Responsibilities* is once more clothed with colour and sensuous appeal.
The new garments are worn with an air, the body of the poetry

stiffened with the truss of *A Vision*.[26] He no longer restricted, as in the twilight period, the use which he made of his reading. His reading had broadened in scope; in 1915 he writes:

> There is not a fool can call me friend
> And I may dine at journey's end
> With Landor and with Donne.[27]

This use of literary sources combined with personal experience succeeds because his life and the contemporary scene are interesting in their own right. The resultant mixture is bound together in a closely woven texture and the continuous pattern is the repetitive zigzag of Yeats's thought.

The whole of 'Nineteen Hundred and Nineteen' is a unity. The second section begins with a memory of Loie Fuller's dancers, who reintroduce the concept of the days being dragon-ridden:

> It seemed that a dragon of air
> Had fallen among dancers, had whirled them round
> Or hurried them off on its own furious path.

This leads the poet to the Platonic year, linked with the thought of *A Vision*,[28] and to the idea that the concepts of right and wrong are altering, that all men are dancers. The third section hesitates:

> Whether to play, or to ride
> Those winds that clamour of approaching night.

This conclusion of the third section, that earlier dreams were useless, is emphasised by the new conception of the swan symbol. Yeats believed that symbols could possess several and changing meanings, and his use of the swan illustrates this. When he wrote 'The Wild Swans at Coole' in 1916 he was 'very depressed',[29] and the swans symbolised the constancy which seemed less strong in his love for Maud. He remembers the love which had so troubled him in 1897 when he first came to Coole:

> The nineteenth autumn has come upon me
> Since first I made my count.[30]

But all is changed in 1916; Lady Gregory had shown him the way into the activity in which he lost the fierce passion of his hopeless love. He had been to France and been a 'little relieved' at Maud's refusal of his last offer of marriage, but the swans are still unwearied, and

> lover by lover
> They paddle in the cold
> Companionable streams or climb the air;

> Their hearts have not grown old;
> Passion or conquest, wander where they will,
> Attend upon them still.[30]

In 1919 the swan is solitary and not the Shelleyan symbol on which he had probably modelled 'The Wild Swans at Coole'. Alastor had also seen the swan rising and thought:

> Thou hast a home
> Beautiful bird! Thou voyagest to thine home
> Where thy sweet mate will twine her downy neck
> With thine and welcome thy return with eyes
> Bright in the lustre of their own fond joy.[31]

The swan is now seen by Yeats against the stormy background and becomes dramatic:

> That image can bring wildness, bring a rage
> To end all things, to end
> What my laborious life imagined, even
> The half-imagined, the half-written page.

Later in an equally dramatic poem 'Coole and Ballylee, 1931', 'The sudden thunder of the mounting swan' was 'a symbol of inspiration'.[31a] The phrase

> Those winds that clamour of approaching night

refers to the coming catastrophe which Yeats's system envisaged. What is meant by the swan riding these winds is the acceptance of the unpalatable facts:

> Man is in love and loves what vanishes
> What more is there to say?

Later he thought that the beginning of the Grecian cycle had been brought by the swan:

I imagine the annunciation that founded Greece as made to Leda, remembering that they showed in a Spartan temple, strung up to the roof as a holy relic, an unhatched egg of hers, and that from one of her eggs came love and from the other war.[32]

It had become the symbol of war. He wrote 'Leda and the Swan' for George Russell's *Irish Statesman* in 1923. Russell refused it,[33] telling him that 'his conservative readers would misunderstand the poem'. In the notes to the Cuala Press volume in which the poem appeared Yeats describes the thoughts which underlay the poem's initial stages:

After the individualistic, demagogic movements, founded by Hobbes and popularised by the Encyclopaedists and the French Revolution, we have a soil so exhausted that it cannot grow that crop again for centuries. Then I thought 'Nothing is now possible but some movement, or birth from above,

preceded by some violent annunciation'. My fancy began to play with
Leda and the Swan for metaphor, and I began this poem, but as I wrote,
bird and lady took such possession of the scene that all politics went
out of it. . . .[34]

The poem was founded upon Michelangelo's painting which
Yeats had seen in Venice and of which he had a large photographic coloured copy:

> A shudder in the loins engenders there
> The broken wall, the burning roof and tower
> And Agamemnon dead.
>                         Being so caught up,
> So mastered by the brute blood of the air,
> Did she put on his knowledge with his power
> Before the indifferent beak could let her drop.[35]

The transition from the third section to the fourth is easy.
Viewing the prospect of coming ruin, before which his early
enthusiasm seemed 'crack-pated', he turns to mockery. Here
the image of

> The weasel's twist, the weasel's tooth

is a mixture of experience and reading. He had seen weasels
fighting at Coole, and they had run across his path in the
woods.[36] He had read Landor's *Imaginary Conversations*, and as
he would have been especially interested in the Irish subjects
we can assume that to his own experience of weasels the
literary association of the conversation between Windham and
Sheridan on the question of Church Establishment in Ireland
was added:

Turn out the weasel against the rat, and at least while they are fighting,
neither of them can corrode the rafters or infest the larder.[37]

The situation is one which his divided personality can face
most easily by mockery, an old trait of his character which has
its revenge for the years in which its utterance was suppressed.
The fifth section, while based on this mocking element in
Yeats's personality, draws from literary sources for its enrich-
ment. Blake's lines:

> Mock on, mock on, Voltaire, Rousseau,
> Mock on, mock on; tis all in vain
> You throw the dust against the wind
> And the wind blows it back again[38]

which Yeats included in his edition of the poet, provide the
idea of repetition of mockery and the destructive force of the
wind. The latter is reminiscent of Mangan's fine poem 'Gone
in the Wind'[39] with refrain taken from Rückert:[40]

Vanish the glories and pomps of the world in the wind.
Solomon! Where is thy throne? It is gone in the wind.
Babylon! Where is thy might? It is gone in the wind.
Like the swift shadows of Noon, like the dreams of the Blind,

But the immediate and almost incessant reminder of the wind
was probably the actual Atlantic gales which blew in over Ballylee. In 'A Prayer for my Daughter', written in the same year,
he had progressed from a description of the tower's surroundings
with the gale battering in from the sea to the similar onslaught
of brutality which he envisaged sweeping over the world.

The wind forms the culmination of the poem in the sixth
section, linked to the third section by the use of the word
'labyrinth'.[40a] In the latter section the 'labyrinth of the wind'
is designedly reminiscent of the poet's own situation in the
former, where

> A man in his own secret meditation
> Is lost amid the labyrinth that he has made
> In art or politics.

The basis of the last section is the idea that, with the new
violence, spirits will come upon the wind, new and more violent
than those the country people see at certain times, and describe
as 'fallen angels' or 'ancient inhabitants of the country', riding
sometimes 'with flowers upon the heads of the horses'.[41] For
these new spirits Yeats remembers a poem by Arthur Symons,
'The Dance of the Daughters of Herodias',[42] where the
daughters dance:

> With their eternal white unfaltering feet,
> And always when they dance, for their delight,
> Always a man's head falls because of them.
> Yet they desire not death, they would not slay
> Body or soul, no, not to do them pleasure:
> They desire love and the desire of men
> And they are the eternal enemy—

They are unreal:

> Shapes on a mirror, perishable shapes,
> Fleeting, and without substance, or abode
> In a fixed place, or knowledge or ourselves.

Their meaning in Yeats's poem is perhaps made clearer by an
examination of Symons's lines describing their effect upon the
things men hold dear:

> The wisdom which is wiser than things known,
> The beauty which is fairer than things seen,
> Dreams which are nearer to eternity
> Than that most mortal tumult of the blood
> Which wars on itself in loving, droop and die.

With them Yeats placed characters in whom he was deeply interested, Dame Alice Kyteler and her incubus Robin Artisson. He had read the manuscript in the British Museum[43] which gives an account of the lady's dealings in magic; she was brought before an Inquisition held in Kilkenny in 1324 by Richard de Ledrede, Bishop of Ossory.[44] Yeats had begun to use proper names more freely in his verse from 1914 onwards. This added to the realism and the strength of his verse; the conclusion of this poem gains an exotic quality by the strangeness of the names of the witch and her demon. Yeats picked out the vivid items of her sacrifices with his unerring gift for selection of the striking and unusual image. Adjectives have come back into his verse, but they are not vague any more. The effect which he wants to gain is perfectly clear in his own mind; the words are chosen with the economy he had learned in disillusion: yet the result is both powerful and colourful; it evokes a direct response, in this case a slight shudder of horror at the grim doings of witchcraft and inquisition:

> But now wind drops, dust settles; thereupon
> There lurches past, his great eyes without thought
> Under the shadow of stupid straw-pale locks,
> That insolent fiend Robert Artisson
> To whom the love-lorn Lady Kyteler brought
> Bronzed peacock feathers, red combs of her cocks.

Shortly after moving into their Oxford house came an American lecture tour, which lasted until May 1920, its object being to earn money to provide for a roof for the tower. As work at Ballylee did not proceed at the speed anticipated Yeats and his wife settled in Oxford again on their return from America, after a brief spell in Ezra Pound's flat in London. In September Yeats was in Ireland. He spent a short time in Glenmalure in the cottage where Synge had written *The Shadow of the Glen*. Here he stayed with Madame MacBride, her son and their friend Cecil Salkeld, and wrote a poem on a picture painted by the latter,[45] which was entitled 'Suggested by a Picture of a Black Centaur' when it was first[46] published but later appeared as 'On a Picture of a Black Centaur by Edmund Dulac'.[47] Back in Oxford, after Dr Oliver Gogarty had removed his tonsils in Dublin, he wrote part of *The Trembling of the Veil*, a section of *Autobiographies* published privately in 1922 by Werner Laurie. He wrote his next poem out of memories of some of the friends of his youth. The setting of this poem 'All Souls' Night'[48] harmonises with the

strange personalities he commemorated; Horton, Florence
Farr, and MacGregor Mathers:

> Midnight has come, and the great Christ Church Bell
> And many a lesser bell sound through the room;
> And it is All Souls' Night,
> And two long glasses brimmed with muscatel
> Bubble upon the table. A ghost may come. . . .

In the winter he made a passionate speech in the Oxford
Union[49] against the terrorist policy of the British Government
in Ireland. He was kept informed of conditions in Ireland by
Lady Gregory and the information provided him with ample
material for denunciation.[50] From April to June the house in
Oxford was let, and the family lived at Michin's Cottage,
Shillingford. From there Yeats wrote to Mrs Shakespear on
9th April that he was searching out signs of the whirling gyres of
the historical cones in books such as Mrs Strong's *Apotheosis
and After-Life*. He was hoping by their study to see deeper into
what was to come. He was writing a series of poems, 'Thoughts
suggested by the present state of the world' (later entitled
'Nineteen Hundred and Nineteen') which he described as

not philosophical, but simple and passionate; a lamentation over lost peace
and lost hope. My own philosophy does not much brighten the prospect so
far as any future we shall live. . . .

A later poem, 'Meditations in Time of Civil War',[51] carries
the theme still further. The first section, written in 1921, was
in part inspired by Lady Ottoline Morrell's house and gardens
at Garsington where Yeats was a visitor:

> . . . where the peacock strays
> With delicate feet upon old terraces,
> Or else all Juno from an urn displays
> Before the indifferent garden deities.[52]

Yeats had the old houses of Ireland in his mind as well. The
overflowing abundance of life in these large estates of the
Anglo-Irish is compared to a fountain; but a better symbol
then occurs to him. The glory of the rich is like a sea-shell
flung out of streams. The germ of this idea may have been
suggested by the broken succession at Coole; the possessions
had become static, no longer moving on with increasing richness of life. In this case it seems derived from Shelley, in whose
poetry water is the symbol of existence[53] and where, in *The
Revolt of Islam*, the sea threw up shells and spangling sands
within the tower.[54] The symbol in 'Ancestral Houses' has

some of the meaning given it in the play *The Only Jealousy of Emer*[55] where the shell, an image of frail beauty, is cast upon the sands by a sudden storm. In each case Yeats ponders the violence which went to the making of the shell in the 'obscure dark'.

From June to September the Yeatses stayed in Cuttlebrook House at Thame. In August the poet's son Michael Butler Yeats was born:

> Bid a strong ghost stand at the head
> That my Michael may sleep sound,
> Nor cry, nor turn in the bed
> Till his morning meal come round;
> And may departing twilight keep
> All dread afar till morning's back,
> That his mother may not lack
> Her fill of sleep.[56]

In the autumn *Four Years*, the part of *Autobiographies* dealing with the years 1887–91, was published by the Cuala Press. Macmillan published the four *Noh* plays about the same time, and for a while Yeats thought of living in Cork, where there might be a possibility of establishing a theatre for the production of work which did not appeal to the Abbey audience.

The Treaty of December 1921 seemed to Yeats to confer effective freedom on Ireland, but he was somewhat pessimistic. He wrote to Mrs Shakespear[57] to say that he thought there might be civil war between the extremists and those who signed the treaty. In that case Ballylee would have to be abandoned, as well as his more recent plans to live in Dublin again. He felt that there might be bitterness for the children to inherit in Ireland, and that they might feel out of place in England.

These worries were settled by the purchase of a large Georgian house in Merrion Square, Dublin, in February. Yeats was disturbed by the bitterness of the partisans of the Treaty (which provided for the partition of Ulster and Dominion status for the South, the Irish Free State) and the extreme Republicans. He remained detached, feeling that both parties were responsible for the increasing hatred. He was well received upon his return. He was sent as a delegate from Sinn Fein to an Irish Race Congress held at Paris in May. He was given a Doctorate of Letters in Dublin University, a distinction welcome because it continued the family connection with Trinity (his brother Jack, the artist, has recently received an honorary degree from the University, and the poet's son Michael obtained a first-class Moderatorship in History in 1943, subsequently becoming Auditor of the College Historical Society). The Civil War broke out when Yeats was at Ballylee, somewhat cut off from the outside world. The railway bridges were blown up, the roads blocked with stones and trees. There were no newspapers, no reliable news:

> We are closed in, and the key is turned
> On our uncertainty; somewhere
> A man is killed, or a house burned,
> Yet no clear fact to be discerned.

He was possessed by a wish not to become unhappy or embittered; yet it was difficult to remain detached, especially when there was action and youth to envy.

The second, third, and fourth sections of the 'Meditations' are descriptions of the tower designed to afford a contrast with all that is going on outside:

One never knew what was happening on the other side of the hill or of the line of trees. Ford cars passed the house from time to time with coffins standing upon and between the seats, and sometimes at night we heard an explosion, and one day saw the smoke made by the burning of a great neighbouring house. Men must have lived so through many tumultuous centuries.[58]

He had brought Palmer's illustration to *Il Penseroso*[59] into being:

> Benighted travellers
> From markets and from fairs
> Have seen his midnight candle gleaming.

He possessed Sato's sword, given to him by a Japanese in Portland, Oregon, in 1920 (who had attended a lecture given there by Yeats), and this was a symbol of ancient art, a reminder of the tradition that passed from father to son. His thought turned to his own descendants and speculated on what might happen to them after his death:

> Life scarce can cast a fragrance on the wind,
> Scarce spread a glory to the morning beams,
> But the torn petals strew the garden plot;
> And there's but common greenness after that.

In the fifth section of the poem his contemplative life seems useless, measured against the active purpose and appeal of the soldier's life, a contrast accentuated by the previous descriptions of how his predecessor in the tower had been a man-at-arms who gathered a score of horse and spent his days in the

tumultuous place, and how he himself had found in the tower
a poetic symbol

> Befitting emblems of adversity—

His age was stressed by the youthfulness of the combatants who
came to Ballylee (the Republicans blew up the bridge leading
to the castle):

> An affable Irregular,
> A heavily-built Falstaffian man,
> Comes cracking jokes of civil war
> As though to die by gunshot were
> The finest play under the sun.

> A brown Lieutenant and his men,
> Half-dressed in national uniform,
> Stand at my door, and I complain
> Of the foul weather, hail and rain,
> A pear tree broken by the storm.

He envied them their purposefulness, their gregariousness and
their careless disregard for death, all the qualities he had wished
for his own life and had had to manufacture:

> I count those feathered balls of soot
> The moor-hen guides upon the stream,
> To silence the envy in my thought;
> And turn towards my chamber, caught
> In the cold snows of a dream.

There was a change from his mood in 1916; then, as now, he
had disliked revolution, but it had seemed to Sir William
Rothenstein, with whom he was staying when the 1916 Rising
broke out, that

he fretted somewhat that he had not been consulted, had been left in
ignorance of what was afoot.[60]

The change is a natural one. In 1916 he could see that the
leaders of the movements lacked any appreciation of the other
world of values in which he lived:

> How can they know
> Truth flourishes where the student's lamp has shone,
> And there alone, that have no solitude?
> So the crowd come they care not what may come.
> They have loud music, hope every day renewed
> And heartier loves; that lamp is from the tomb.[61]

Now his age leads him to a more openly expressed envy of their
youth and activity, and yet he is not so shocked by the events
taking place as before; he equates himself with the tower and

the lamp and the search for the wisdom of antiquity and finds
compensation in them:

> I turn away and shut the door, and on the stair
> Wonder how many times I could have proved my worth
> In something that all others understand or share;
> But O! ambitious heart, had such a proof drawn forth
> A company of friends, a conscience set at ease,
> It had but made us pine the more. The abstract joy,
> The half-read wisdom of daemonic images,
> Suffice the ageing man as once the growing boy.

His new self-confidence was increased by his appointment as
a Senator of the recently established Irish Free State. This
had been brought about by the activity of his friend Dr Oliver
Gogarty; ironically the appointment rested more upon his
having been a member of the I.R.B. than upon his work for
Irish literature. He joined in the work of creating the new
state with enthusiasm; and wrote to Mrs Shakespear that all
were like

coral insects with some design in our heads of the ultimate island. Meanwhile the country is full of arms and explosives ready for any violent hand
to use. Perhaps all our slow growing coral may be scattered but I think
not—not unless Europe takes to war again and starts new telepathic streams
of violence and cruelty.[62]

He joined the Kildare Street Club, the ultra-respectable strong-
hold of Irish (he would have called it in his nationalist days,
West-British) conservatism. He took an interest in the practical
matters discussed in the Senate, sharing in the ideas of those
members, mainly of the Protestant landlord and business
classes, who collected round his father's friend Andrew Jameson,
the distiller.[63] His main concern was the promotion of the
creative arts. He had plans for an Irish Academy of Letters
and he interested himself in a scheme for the better arrangement of the manuscripts of the Royal Irish Academy. In the
course of the year he wrote a poem on the mind-communication
between his wife and himself which he was later to discuss more
fully in *A Packet for Ezra Pound*. The poem 'The Gift of Harun
Al Raschid'[64] concludes with a passage showing his faith in
himself, his marriage and his art;[64a] this art, being based on
*A Vision*, is now free to deal with any subject that interests him:

> The voice has drawn
> A quality of wisdom from her love's
> Particular quality. The signs and shapes;
> All those abstractions that you fancied were
> From the great Treatise of Parmenides;

All, all those gyres and cubes and midnight things
Are but a new expression of her body
Drunk with the bitter sweetness of her youth.
And now my utmost mystery is out.
A woman's beauty is a storm-tossed banner;
Under it wisdom stands, and I alone—
Of all Arabia's lovers I alone—
Nor dazzled by the embroidery, nor lost
In the expression of its night dark folds,
Can hear the armed man speak.

At the close of this *annus mirabilis* Yeats was awarded the Nobel Prize. He and Mrs Yeats travelled to Stockholm in December for the presentation, and he was greatly taken by the ceremony of the Swedish Court and the Swedish Royal Family, the more so years afterwards when he was told that they said he had the manners of a courtier and that they had preferred him to other Nobel Prize winners.[65] The king seemed like an old country gentleman who can quote Horace and Catullus, and the Princess Margerita was a subtle beauty, with a still intensity suggesting, his highest praise of perfection reached after long struggles, 'that final consummate strength which rounds the spiral of a shell'.[65a] His attitude to his poetic powers is prompted by an examination of the medal which he received and

its charming decorative academic design, French in manner, a work of the nineties. It shows a young man listening to a muse, who stands young and beautiful with a great lyre in her hand, and I think as I examine it 'I was good looking once like that young man but my unpractised verse was full of infirmity, my Muse old as it were; and now I am old and rheumatic, and nothing to look at, but my Muse is young. I am even persuaded that she is like those Angels in Swedenborg's vision, and moves perpetually 'towards the day-spring of her youth'.[65b]

The Nobel award and the Senatorship crowned Yeats's progress as man and poet in search of fame. Their material rewards were also welcome,[66] and it was with thankfulness, even tinged as it is with a faint sadness, that he wrote in 1924:

Much did I rage when young
Being by the world oppressed,
But now with flattering tongue
It speeds the parting quest.[67]

This flourishing life is reflected fully in the 'Tower' poetry. By imprisoning his thought in a system he gained sanction for a belief that he knew and understood

. . . what is past, or passing, or to come.[68]

The freedom which he had sought fruitlessly from childhood onwards had apparently been captured at last. Life was exciting, but there was the bother of old age. The extremes of a varying attitude to life find still more outspoken expression in his verse. His remedy for age was a search for intellectual interests. Though this appeared new to him in 'The Tower':[67]

> It seems that I must bid the Muse go pack,
> Choose Plato and Plotinus for a friend
> Until imagination, ear and eye,
> Can be content with argument and deal
> In abstract things. . . .

it is but the old youthful desire to conquer bodily inclinations and live a lonely life of wisdom.[69] He was constantly rediscovering himself; this is the secret of the interest which all this poetry of the late periods holds for us. He had so many ways of expressing himself now, and his personality was now, after the many years of tension, so worth expressing. His personality is responsible for the momentary outbreak in the third section of the poem, in which, through forgetfulness[70] of his sources, he can:

> . . . declare my faith
> I mock Plotinus' thought
> And cry in Plato's teeth,
> Death and life were not
> Till man made up the whole,
> Made lock, stock and barrel
> Out of his bitter soul.

The antithetical aspects of his character can each inspire a poem that expresses him, hence the third and the first sections are closely linked, in spite of an apparent contradiction. The whole is a unity of complex thought. In the first section he declared that decrepit old age had been tied to him as a sort of battered kettle to a dog's tail, yet he had never had more

> Excited, passionate, fantastical
> Imagination, nor an ear and eye
> That more expected the impossible.

The thought was taken from Blake, probably echoed unconsciously, for Blake's thoughts, even his vocabulary, were an integral part of Yeats. He had quoted the passage in a letter to the *Boston Pilot* in 1889:

I have been very near the gates of Death, and have returned very weak, and an old man feeble and tottering, but not in spirits and life, not in the real man, the imagination which liveth for ever. In that I am stronger and stronger as this foolish body decays—[71]

In the second section he sends this vivid imagination forth, as if to prove its increasing strength. The result is a magnificent creation of what the atmosphere of the tower meant to him. When he had thought that it was the duty of a national poet to describe some particular place in Ireland[72] he had chosen the only place he knew which possessed romance and beauty for him. The poetry he wrote then of the places he visited:

> Where the wandering water gushes
> From the hills above Glen-Car,
> In pools among the rushes
> That scarce could bathe a star,
> We seek for slumbering trout
> And whispering in their ears
> Give them unquiet dreams;
> Leaning softly out
> From ferns that drop their tears
> Over the young streams[73]

was not definite, did not symbolise any mood more personal than a love of beauty and nature, and when it came to people the regions it did so with shadowy figures:

> Come away, O human child!
> To the waters and the wild
> With a faery, hand in hand,
> For the world's more full of weeping than you can understand.[73]

Therefore, though beautiful and haunting, it lacks the strength of the later 'Tower' poetry where the details are sketched in firmly:

> I pace upon the battlements and stare
> On the foundations of a house, or where
> Tree, like a sooty finger, starts from the earth

and the symbols repeated quite simply with a lack of unessential detail: the bridge,[74] the trees,[75] the wind[76], the cottages,[77] the water-hens,[78] the river,[79] the winding stair,[80] the stone chamber,[81] the light,[82] the battlement,[83] the tower's top.[84, 85] The meaning of the poetry is deeply personal, and the region peopled with unusual but intensely vivid people. The world is still full of weeping, but Yeats can understand it now. He has something to say: he concentrates into a stanza a story from Sir Jonah Barrington's *Sketches of his own Times* which Mrs Yeats had read to him, and follows it with the description, already quoted, of Mary Hynes and Raftery, the transition to Homer and Helen, and the memory of how he had himself created Hanrahan, a character who appeared in *The Secret*

*Rose* and *Stories of Red Hanrahan*. He broke off to remember a
bankrupt who had lived in the tower and its ghosts who played
dice, and then apostrophised them all, these persons associated
by legend and tradition with the immediate neighbourhood of
Thoor, Ballylee. He wondered if all the old men and women
who passed the place

> Whether in public or in secret rage
> As I do now against old age?

He turns to Hanrahan, first created as a wild romantic lover,
now an 'old lecher'; a figure representing aspects of his own
personality:

> Does the imagination dwell the most
> Upon a woman won or woman lost?
> If on the lost, admit you turned aside
> From a great labyrinth out of pride,
> Cowardice, some silly over-subtle thought
> Or anything called conscience once.

He uses the word 'labyrinth' frequently at this period. A word
or phrase such as 'mummy-wheat'[86] obsessed him for a time,
was forgotten, and then taken up later, often as if an entirely
new discovery. He did not avoid repetition of words, as it was
repetition of sound in his case, not the appearance of the finished
line which interested him. (His manuscripts are untidy, a form
of shorthand for the crooning over of his verse when it was being
composed.) Indeed he seems to have used repetition deliberately, getting from it highly original and unusual effects, not
merely of sound, but of meaning and emphasis.

In the third section these memories form the basis from
which the poet will make his soul. He returns to the image of
his youth used in the first section, that of climbing the mountain-
side to fish, but how altered it is from that early poem where
his vague shadowy faeries had whispered to the trout.[87] He
used the image in the first section thus:

> in boyhood when with rod and fly,
> Or the humbler worm, I climbed Ben Bulben's back
> And had the livelong summer day to spend.

Both in these lines and those of the third is an air of vigour
lacking in the early work. He alters the symbol in the third
section to that used in 'The Fisherman'[88] for the ideal man
who was simple 'as a man of action' and yet cultured:

> I leave both faith and pride
> To young upstanding men
> Climbing the mountain side,
> That under bursting dawn
> They may drop a fly.

The last stanza illustrates clearly how he must deal with the miseries of old age; bodily weakness and the death of friends and lovers:

> Now shall I make my soul,
> Compelling it to study
> In a learned school.

In September 1926 he began 'Sailing to Byzantium' in an intensified mood of envy of the young who are not too old for love, who think, in the first draft[89] of the poem, that he is:

> All that men know or think they know, being young,
> Cry that my tale is told, my story sung.

The early drafts of the poem are explicit and very near to Yeats's personal emotion. He decides to leave Ireland and the young 'at their gallantries' and travel to Byzantium, the city of unageing intellect. The artificial immortality which he will get there is to be free from sensual music; he prays to the sages of Byzantium:

> Consume my heart away; sick with desire
> And fastened to a dying animal
> It knows not what it is; and gather me
> Into the artifice of eternity.

His reading in the twenties was varied. He had spent some of the Nobel Prize money on reference books for his library: *The Encyclopaedia Britannica*, *The Encyclopaedia of Religion and Ethics*, the Cambridge Ancient, Mediaeval and Modern Histories, Gibbon's *Decline and Fall*, and Bryans' *Dictionary of Paintings*. In 1923 his letters to Mrs Shakespear comment on Mrs Strong's *Apotheosis and After-Life*, Binyon's *Blake*,[89a] and Joyce's *Ulysses*. Ossendowski's *Beasts, Men and Gods* was

> a strange vivid book with much superstitious incident, by a Russian traveller. I commend it here for it describes a half-German half-Russian Baron who tries to organise Russia under the rule of China to fight 'the depravity of Revolution' in the world. One reads it with delight but wonders if its incidents are not a little mysterious, heightened as in *Lavengro*.[90]

Most of 1924 had been occupied by the final work on the first edition of *A Vision*, but, this completed, he began to read philosophy. He annotated Croce's *Philosophy of Vico* in this year.

His health became troublesome and it was found that his blood pressure was too high, so in November he and Mrs Yeats went to Sicily, in February 1925 to Capri and then Rome, where he visited the Sistine Chapel and the Vatican galleries. In the autumn he lectured at Mürren and visited Milan. In the spring he had become interested in Gentile's work and his wife then summarised *La Riforma dell' Educazione* for him, while he later read *Teoria generale dello Spirito come Atto puro* in translation.

When he read philosophical works he related their terminology to that of *A Vision*. A letter written in April 1926 to Mrs Shakespear[91] illustrates this tendency:

The work of Whitehead's I have read is *Science and the Modern World* and I have ordered his *Concept of Nature* and another book of his. He thinks that nothing exists but 'organism' or minds—the 'cones' of my book—and that there is no such [sure?] thing as an object 'localised in space' except the minds—and that what we call physical objects of all kinds are 'aspects' or 'vistas' or other 'organisms'—in my book the 'Body of fate' of one's being is but the 'creative mind' of another. What we call an age is a limit of perception. We create each other's universe and are influenced by even the most remote organisms. It is as though we stood in the midst of space and saw upon all sides—above below right and left the rays of stars not those we supposed through a limit placed upon perception that some stars were at our elbow or even between our hands. He also uses the 'quantum theory' when speaking of minute organisms—molecules—in a way that suggests Anti—[thetical] or primary or rather if he applies it to the organism we can compare with ourselves it would become that theory. I partly delight in him because of something aristocratic in his mind. His packed logic, his difficult scornful lucidity seems to me the intellectual equivalent of my own imaginative richness of suggestion—certainly I am nothing if I have not these. (He is all 'spirit' whereas I am all 'passionate body') He is the opposite of Bertrand Russell who fills me with fury by his plebeian loquacity.

In May he brought two books to the tower, Baudelaire and MacKenna's translation of Plotinus. Plotinus was, he thought, 'a most ardent and wonderful person'.[92] MacKenna was delighted to hear of Yeats's interest:

Another little encouragement: Yeats, a friend tells me, came to London, glided into a bookshop and dreamily asked for the new Plotinus, began to read there and then, and read on and on till he's finished (he really has a colossal brain, you know), and now is preaching Plotinus to all his train of attendant Duchesses. He told my friend that he intended to give the winter in Dublin to Plotinus.[93]

This re-reading was responsible for the note added to the Cuala Press version of 'The Tower's' third section (dated 7 October 1925 on its manuscript), in which Yeats corrected his dismissal of Plato and Plotinus with a quotation from MacKenna's translation of the Fifth Ennead. He had forgotten when writing the poem that

> it is something in our own eyes that makes us see them as all transcendence. [94]

His letters to Sturge Moore and Mrs Shakespear continue to be concerned with philosophy. With the former he maintained a long correspondence, for Sturge Moore did not think that absolutes could be postulated. Letters to Mrs Shakespear were more general but the interest in philosophical reading is also revealed clearly in them, as in a portion of a letter written in July 1926:

> I am in better health than I was, and I do really believe that I owe it to Plotinus as much as to the Tower. By the by do get Spengler's *Decline and Fall of the West* and compare his general scheme with mine in *Dove and Swan*. While his first was going through the press in 1918 I was getting the outline and I think all the main diagrams of mine. There is exact correspondence in date after date. He was not translated till after my book was published. Had he been I could not have written. [95]

In September he was reading Croce's *Philosophy of the Practical* and writing verse:

> I read Croce and his like that I may at last make no concession to Darwinism—Croce because it is the opposite of his thought, in many ways clearer [clever?] and so find a position—ageless energy or perception. [96]

Bergson's *Creative Evolution* and *Matter and Memory* were read in the earlier part of 1927, followed by Wyndham Lewis's *Time and the Western Man* in November. In March of the same year he wrote to Mrs Shakespear:

> For some months I have been perplexed by certain strange philosophical judgments in the Times Literary Supplement. Somebody told me that they came from the papistical wife of the Editor but I now find that your friend Wyndham Lewis's effect upon a contributor or contributors has done the trick. I have been dipping into his essay in 'The Enemy' and find his proof that the popularity of Charlie Chaplin has been caused by the spread of Bergson's philosophy the most striking thought I have met this long time. But what will Ezra do? Will he pass by in silent dignity 'as we're told to do in childhood' or will he fill his pockets with all the necessary missiles and rush to the defence of Joyce, Picasso, Miss Stein and all the Gods. The Catholic Bulletin agrees with Lewis about Einstein's—it has mutual aesthetic 'booster[?]' He had protested against the pirating of 'Ulysses' in America. I shall never finish the essay. Englishmen are babes in philosophy and so faction-fighting to the labour of its unfamiliar thought. I have just finished a profound book by Angelo Crispi on 'Contemporary thought of Italy'. He attacks what Lewis attacks but is so obsessed by courtesy that he not only explains his opponents' thought more fully than his own, but expounds it with greater eloquence. I am slowly revising my Oedipus at Colonus and reading Plato. Lewis would fear the problem he discusses in the Theaetetus. . . . Lewis has some profound judgment—when he analyses public opinion or some definite work of art—and often a vivid phrase. [97]

His greater dislike was for the unaesthetic approach to life,
ultimately to the division of primary and secondary qualities,
that practical side of some English minds which enrages many
Irishmen:

> Locke sank into a swoon;
> The Garden died;
> God took the spinning jenny
> Out of his side.[98]

Towards contemporary British philosophy he was scornful; the
old bugbear of science still irritating him but not quite so
effectively:

> You have listened too much to B. Russell in his electioneering moods—the
> Plain Man has nothing to do with the matter. The Plain Man, even magni-
> fied into a man of science, would be very little content with your brother's
> last conception [of the world] as a bundle of the 'possibilities of sensation'
> (possibilities are immaterial, by the way, till they are transformed into
> something else). To your brother and B. Russell alike the sense data—the
> only reality—does not exist until it has been thought. You say 'idealism
> has to explain science'. But that has nothing to do with the matter (we
> are not compelled to write in the younger liberal reviews). Read Eding-
> ton's essay in 'Science, Religion and Reality.' He shows exactly why the
> discoveries of science can never affect reality. [99]

He found what he wanted in Berkeley and welcomed his
philosophy the more for his being Anglo-Irish. To a certain
extent the literary history of Ireland is reflected in Yeats's own
career. The Gaelic period, before the Norman conquest, with
all its strange beauty of legend and imagination; the Anglo-
Irish writings in English with the international outlook of
eighteenth- and nineteenth-century culture; then the Revival
blending the two strains, beginning with writings primarily
concerned with matters of Irish interest and then becoming
of more universal interest; all these have their parallels in
Yeats's life. He began his Celtic writings with a nationalist
point of view but left this extreme for a wider range, then,
when he returned to Dublin, began to attempt the fusion of
the Gaelic nationalist and Anglo-Irish elements in Ireland. He
now turned to the heritage he had scorned in his youth, the
clear-headed classical[100] Anglo-Irish tradition, its intellectual
freedom and its ability to speak its mind with an aristocratic
disregard for the mob. At school he had ignored the eighteenth
century because it was not romantic, then hated it because
romantic Irish literature was cried down by political opponents
bred in the eighteenth-century tradition:

More extreme in such things than Taylor and O'Leary who often seemed to live in the eighteenth century, to acknowledge its canons alone in literature and the arts, I turned from Goldsmith and from Burke because they had come to seem a part of the English system, from Swift because I acknowledged, being a romantic, no verse between Cowley and Smart's *Song to David*, no prose between Sir Thomas Browne and the *Conversations* of Landor.[101]

He had become, he wrote, like

that old woman in Balzac who after a rich marriage and association with the rich, made in old age the jokes of the concierge's lodge where she was born.[102]

These views were expressed in a speech to the Irish Literary Society on 30 November 1925:

In Gaelic literature we have something that the English speaking countries have never possessed—a great folk literature. We have in Burke and especially in Berkeley a philosophy on which it is possible to base the whole life of a nation. That too is something which England, great as she is in scientific thought and every kind of literature, has not I think. The modern Irish intellect was born more than two hundred years ago when Berkeley defined in three profound sentences the material philosophy of Newton, Locke and Hobbes, the philosophy of England in his day, and wrote after each sentence 'We Irish do not hold this view'. Feed the imagination upon that old folk life and the intellect upon Berkeley and the great modern idealist philosophy created by his influence, upon Burke who restored to political thought its sense of history, and Ireland is reborn, armed and wise.[103]

Unfortunately the need for reconciling Anglo-Irish and Nationalist was complicated by the religious differences which underlie Irish politics; and Yeats had not contributed to the reconciliation by the speech which he made in the Senate in June 1925, on the subject of divorce. The Free State Government was introducing measures to prohibit divorce, and in his speech Yeats regarded this measure as 'grossly oppressive' to the Protestant minority, who were as much part of Ireland as the majority, who had written most of its modern literature, and who had created the best of its political thought. It was a tactless speech. For instance, he introduced the private lives of the three public figures, Nelson, O'Connell, and Parnell, whose statues decorate Dublin's main street, of whom he wrote in 'The Three Monuments' with some bitterness after his speech:

> And all the popular statesmen say
> That purity built up the State
> And after kept it from decay;
> Admonish us to cling to that

> And let all base ambition be,
> For intellect would make us proud
> And pride bring in impurity:
> The three old rascals laugh aloud.[104]

One result of the speech was that Yeats was unlikely to be re-elected as a Senator in 1928 when his term of office would expire. He was slightly worried about this as the money was extremely useful, but the speech, like his desire to serve in the work of the Senate, was entirely sincere. Ireland, with its devotion to abstract principles, while possessing a love of private argument, lacks the ability to forget such outbursts.

His work in the Senate was interesting. He was Chairman of the Committee which sat at intervals from 1926 to 1928 to advise on a new coinage, eventually recommending the very beautiful designs of an Englishman, Percy Metcalfe. Yeats himself had favoured those of Carl Milles whose work he had admired when he went, with Mrs Yeats, to Stockholm to receive the Nobel Prize 1923. He was responsible for the designs of Charles Shannon being adopted for the robes of district justices in the Free State, but failed to get the same artist's designs for the robes of High and Supreme Court judges accepted by the Senate. Censorship was another subject which roused his feelings, and he spoke eloquently on the subject. One of his objects in founding the Irish Academy of Letters[105] was to give the opinion of Irish authors more weight on such subjects; some of his own views can be gathered from an article on Irish censorship which was published in *The Spectator* in 1928.[106] His antagonism to the restrictive censorship is shown more intimately in a letter to Mrs Shakespear, dated 13 March 1927:

> Which reminds me have you read O'Flaherty's *Informer* or his *Mr Gilhooley*. I think they are great novels and too full of abounding life to be terrible despite their subjects. They are full of that tragi-farce we have invented. I imagine that part of the desire for censorship here is the desire to keep them out. He joyously *imagines* when Moore *constructs*, and yet is more real than Moore.[107]

One of his main interests lay in education. He had seen the need for reform and radical change in 1909, but the new Ireland that had emerged from the 'troubles' had an even greater need:

> Teacher after teacher in Ireland has said to me that the young people are anarchic and violent and that we have to show them what the State is and what they owe to it. All over the world during the Great War, the

young people became anarchic and violent, but in Ireland it is worse than elsewhere for we have in a sense been at war for generations, and of late that war has taken the form of burning and destruction under the eyes of the children. They respect nothing, one teacher said to me, I cannot take them through Stephen's Green because they would pull up the plants. Go anywhere in Ireland and you will hear the same complaint. The children, everybody will tell you are intelligent and friendly, yet have so little sense of their duty to community and neighbour that if they meet an empty house in a lonely place they will smash all the windows. . . . The proper remedy is the teaching of religion.[108]

He had gained much of his knowledge of the Irish system from his friend Joseph O'Neill, who was secretary of the Department of Education, and with whom he discussed educational theory. He visited several schools in 1926, sometimes with a school-master friend. Of an expedition to Waterford to see a new school he wrote:

> I walk through the long school room questioning;
> A kind old nun in a white hood replies;
> The children learn to cipher and to sing,
> To study reading-books and history,
> To cut and sew, be neat in everything
> In the best modern way—the children's eyes
> In momentary wonder stare upon
> A sixty-year-old smiling public man.

The poem[109] became love poetry. He thought of Maud:

> I dream of a Ledaean body, bent
> Above a sinking fire, a tale that she
> Told of a harsh reproof, or trivial event
> That changed some childish day to tragedy—
> Told, and it seemed that our two natures blent
> Into a sphere from youthful sympathy,
> Or else, to alter Plato's parable,
> Into the yolk and white of the one shell.
>
> And thinking of that fit of grief or rage
> I look upon one child or t'other there
> And wonder if she stood so at that age—
> For even daughters of the swan can share
> Something of every paddler's heritage—
> And had that colour upon cheek or hair,
> And thereupon my heart is driven wild:
> She stands before me as a living child.

He remembered her present appearance, then his youth, and his present appearance—

> . . . enough of that
> Better to smile on all that smile, and show
> There is a comfortable kind of old scarecrow.

There followed the stanza with its bitter thought that no mother would think her son a compensation for the pang of birth if

she saw him sixty years old. The whole poem was, he wrote
to Mrs Shakespear, his last curse upon old age; it meant that
the greatest men are old scarecrows by the time their fame has
come. He then quoted the stanza which skilfully returns the
thought to the school scene with its lines upon the educators
of Greece:

> Plato thought nature but a spume that plays
> Upon a ghostly paradigm of things;
> Solider Aristotle played the taws
> Upon the bottom of a king of kings. . . .

His sense of form emerges in his choice of Plato and Aristotle,
because they serve to bind the thought of the poem closer.
In an early draft he had written:

> Caesar Augustus that made all the laws
> And the ordering of the century
> Plato that learned Geometry and was
> The foremost man at the soul's meaning . . .

and Aristotle was merely

> The first who had a place for everything[110]

but the idea of his birching Alexander is introduced so that
Yeats can use[110] examples of famous men who both suit his
mood of philosophy and the school theme of youth and age
which runs through the poem; the result has an epigrammatic
and closely packed meaning. The contrast between Alexander's
helpless youth and future greatness does not help Yeats's thesis
that all famous men have to wait for old age for their fame; he
conveniently left out the conquerors.

Love came constantly into his thoughts in 1926, one of his
great creative periods. A letter written in May to Mrs
Shakespear gives the underlying emotions which prompted
most of the poems written in that year:

My dear Olivia: We are at our tower and I am writing poetry as I always
do here, and as always happens, no matter how I begin, it becomes love
poetry before I am finished with it. I have lots of subjects in my head
including a play about Christ meeting the worshippers of Dionysos on the
mountain side—no doubt this will somehow become love poetry too. . . .
One feels at moments as if one could with a touch convey a vision—that
the mystic vision and sexual love use the same means, opposed yet parallel
existence (I cannot spell and there is no dictionary in the house). . . . My
moods fill me with surprise and some alarm. The other day I found at
Coole a reproduction of a drawing of two charming young persons in the
full stream of their Sapphoistic enthusiasm and it got into my dreams and
made a great racket there and yet I feel that spiritual things are very near

me. I think I shall be able to [deal?] with further remote parts of the system that are hardly touched on in *A Vision*. I suppose to grow old is to grow impersonal, to need nothing and to seek nothing in oneself—at least it may be thus.[111]

In July he wrote to her, in reply to her request for some love poems which he had written, that he had not sent them because they needed revision:

They are part of a series [in which] I have written the wild regrets for youth and love of an old man; and the poems you asked for are part of a series in which a woman speaks, first in youth and then in age.[112]

These poems were collected under the titles 'A Man Young and Old'[113] and 'A Woman Young and Old'.[114] The first series contains some memories of Yeats's own life. The first poem, 'First Love', is a memory of the effect of Maud's beauty upon him:

> She smiled and that transfigured me
> And left me but a lout

and the second, 'Human Dignity', is the effect which his heart's agony failed to produce upon her:

> Like the moon her kindness is,
> If kindness I may call
> What has no comprehension in 't,
> But is the same for all.

The fourth poem, 'The Death of the Hare', is a continuation of the thought in 'Two Songs of a Fool'[115] that in his married life he had neglected Iseult's happiness. Then he was afraid that the hare had run from his care, but now:

> . . . my heart is wrung
> By her distracted air
> And I remember wildness lost
> And after, swept from there,
> Am set down standing in the wood
> At the death of the hare.

This was probably his reaction to Iseult's marriage to Francis Stuart of which he wrote more bluntly in 1936, having known:

> . . . A girl that knew all Dante once
> Live to bear children to a dunce.[116]

The lines in 'The Secrets of the Old', the ninth poem:

> . . . none alive to-day
> Can know the stories that we know
> Or say the things we say

are perhaps the best answer to any attempt to extract the biographical basis from these poems. Their interest lies in the zest with which memories could be relived by the poet, and in the vivid language with which he could recapture their emotions, and express them with a bitter and brutal realism:

> The first of all the tribe lay there
> And did such pleasure take—
> She who had brought great Hector down
> And put all Troy to wreck—
> That she cried into this ear,
> 'Strike me if I shriek'.

The various poems of 'A Man Young and Old' when first published in *October Blast* were divided into two groups entitled 'The Young Countryman' and 'The Old Countryman', a fact which suggests that in them Yeats was drawing on the graphic speech which he had learned with Lady Gregory from the Galway peasants. There is a passage in a letter to Mrs Shakespear, written in May 1926, which also suggests (apart from the amusing picture it contains of Yeats's snobbery) that he was using their colourful style of speech:

An old beggar has just called—I knew him twenty years ago as [a] wandering piper but now he is paralysed and cannot play. He was lamenting the great houses burnt out or empty. 'The gentry have kept the shoes on my feet and the coat on my back and the shilling in my pocket. Never once in all these fourty and five years that I have been upon the road have I asked a penny of a farmer.' I gave him five shillings and he started off in the rain for the nearest town—I rather fancy to drink it. The last I gave to was at Coole and he opened the conversation by saying to Lady Gregory, 'My lady, you are in the winter of your age'. They are all full of contemplation and elaborate of speech and have their regular track.[117]

He took the phrase 'the winter of your age' into 'Among School Children' and wrote of the man 'with sixty or more winters' on his head. The full use of the country people's speech and anecdote was to come later with the Crazy Jane poems, founded on the talk of an old woman near Ballylee.

'A Woman Young and Old', the companion series, is, as Yeats wrote to Mrs Shakespear of one of its sections, 'not so innocent'. F. R. Higgins's dictum comes to mind:

There were, for him, only two commingling states of verse. One, simple, bucolic, or rabelaisian, the other, intellectual, exotic, or visionary. [118]

He mixed his strange lore with love in these poems, the only direct recording being the first poem 'Father and Child' made out of a saying of Anne Yeats about Fergus Fitzgerald. Most of the poems blend the ununderstandable, apparently inevitable, quality of love with its cruder physical elements:

> O but there is wisdom
> In what the sages said;
> But stretch that body for a while
> And lay down that head
> Till I have told the sages
> Where man is comforted.

In June he was back in Dublin, still working on 'A Woman Young and Old', and finding time for a characteristic letter:

We have been back here for some days—in perfect tranquillity, no children, no telephone, no callers—no companion but a large white dog with a face like the Prince Consort or a mid-Victorian statue—capable of error but not of sin. I write verse and read Hegel and the more I read I am but the more convinced that those invisible people knew all.[119]

The series of poems was completed in September and he then wrote 'Sailing to Byzantium' in order 'to recover my spirits'.[120] In the autumn he was in London, and, back in Dublin in October, he wrote to Mrs Shakespear that when he had gone to London he had just finished

a poem in which I appeal to the Saints in 'the holy fire' to send death or their ecstacy—In London I went to a medium called Cooper and . . . the medium gave me 'book test'—Third book from right bottom shelf study page 48 or 84—I have only this morning looked it up—the book was the complete Dante designs of Blake. It is not numbered by pages but by plates—Plate 84 is Dante entering the holy fire (Purgatorio Canto 27)—Plate 48 is 'the Serpent attacking Vanni Fucchi'—when I looked them up in Dante I found that as the serpent stung Vanni Fucchi is burnt to ashes and then is recreated from its ashes and this symbolises 'temporal fire'. The medium is the most stupid I know and certainly the knowledge wasn't in my head. After this and all that has gone before I must capitulate—if the dark mind lets me—Certainly we suck always at the eternal dugs. How well too it puts my own mood between spiritual excitement and the sexual torture the knowledge that these two are somehow inseparable! It is the eyes of the early Beatrice—she has not yet put on her divinity—that makes Dante risk the fire 'like a child that is offered an apple'.
Immediately afterwards there comes the Earthly Paradise and the Heavenly Beatrice. Yesterday as if my soul already foresaw to-day's discovery, I re-wrote a poor threadbare poem of my youth called 'The Dream of a Blessed Spirit' and named it 'The Countess Cathleen'. It . . . is almost a poem for school children.[121]

He had completed his version of Sophocles' *Oedipus Rex*, for which he used many translations, including the French version of Monsieur Paul Masqueray, and this was performed in the Abbey in December 1926. At the time he was working on 'A Man Young and Old' and another letter to Mrs Shakespear, written on 7 December, reveals his personal reactions to both subjects:

I think it likely that there will be yet another series upon the old man and his soul as he slowly comes to understand that the mountains are not solid that all he sees is a mathematical line drawn between Hope and

Memory. Whatever I do poetry will remain a torture. My version of
Oedipus comes on to-night. I think my shaping of the speech will prove
powerful on the stage though I have made it bare hard and natural like a
saga, I think it will be thought of—It will be well though not greatly acted—
it is all too new to our people. I am more anxious about the audience who
will have to sustain an hour and a half of tension. The actor who plays
Oedipus felt the strain so much at dress rehearsal that he could hardly act
in the last moments. A good audience will give him life, but how will
these Catholics take it? At rehearsal I had an overwhelming emotion, a
sense of the actual presence and terrible sacrament of the Gods but I have
got that always but never before so strongly from Greek Drama.[122]

The play was a success, and in March of 1927 he was at work
on his version of *Oedipus at Colonus*, using the same translations as before. He sent some of the choruses to Mrs Shakespear
with the remark that they made for cheerfulness; he was in
good spirits, active and with his health improved. At the
beginning of October he wrote a letter to say that Oedipus (at
Colonus) was haunted:

Two typed copies sent to the publisher have gone astray in the post and
that had held up publication for months—then a couple of weeks ago Mrs
P—— invited a woman to meet George[122a] who asked for the introduction
because at the first performance of the King (Oedipus Rex) a year ago
she had seen George she said first take me by the shoulders and then kiss
me—I said nothing of the sort had happened—but she insisted—then
George came into the room—upon which she said but that was not the
woman. Then there is a phantom dog. During 'Colonus' George and I
were infuriated by the loud barking of a dog apparently in the gallery—we
were surprised that nobody laughed. I went out after the play to find who
had brought the dog. Person after person had said they had heard no dog.
Then I heard two people who had heard it in a different place. It had
barked I heard in the middle of a performance of the King a week before—
Our one chorus appeals to Cerberus not to disturb Oedipus with its barking.
The Company think it is a dog that starved to death in the theatre when it
was closed for the summer. Poems seem to disturb the spirits—once with
Gogarty when I was reading out my *Calvary* and came to the description of
the [resurrection?] of Lazarus the door burst open as if by the blast of
wind where there could be no wind and the family ghost had a night of
great activity. From all which you will see that I am still of the opinion
that only two topics can be of the slightest interest to a serious and studious
mind—sex and the dead.[123]

Since July Yeats had been writing three poems, 'Death',
'Blood and the Moon', and 'A Dialogue of Self and Soul'.
The first two were begun at the time of the assassination of
Kevin O'Higgins, one of the Ministers of the Free State
Government, and a personal friend of Yeats. An undated
letter[124] told Mrs Shakespear how he and Mrs Yeats had
heard bursts of music and singing as they entered their house
the night before the murder and recognised these at the Mass

for the Dead.  In 'Death'[125] he exalts the pride which prompted
O'Higgins's actions; the Minister had said to his wife 'Nobody
can expect to live who has done what I have done', and Yeats
wrote:

> A great man in his pride
> Confronting murderous men
> Casts derision upon
> Supersession of breath;
> He knows death to the bone—
> Man has created death.[126]

'Blood and the Moon', begun under the intense feeling roused
by the murder—when he heard the news Yeats refused to eat
and spent the evening walking about the streets till nightfall—
is a glorification of the pride which he took in the Anglo-Irish
race who mastered the native Gaels, and towered above them
as the tower overshadowed the small storm-beaten cottages
beneath it.  He set the emblem up in mockery; the tower had
never been roofed according to the original plan by Lutyens,
there was instead a concrete roof and so the tower was

> Half dead at the top.

The meaning of this mockery becomes clearer as we read the
second section, which is a fuller glorification of the four great
Anglo-Irish figures who appealed to Yeats: Goldsmith, Swift,
Berkeley and Burke.  The assassination of O'Higgins had removed from the new Ireland one of the few men whom Yeats
saw as a successor to the old Anglo-Irish tradition:[127]

> . . . Although the Irish masses are vague and excitable because they have
> not yet been moulded and cast, we have as good blood as there is in Europe.
> Berkeley, Swift, Burke, Grattan, Parnell, Augusta Gregory, Synge, Kevin
> O'Higgins, are the true Irish people, and there is nothing too hard for such
> as these.[128]

Of the Ministers he wrote that

> They seemed men of skill and mother-wit, men who had survived hatred.
> But their minds knew no play that my mind could play at; I felt that I
> could never know them.  One of the most notable said he had long wanted
> to meet me.  We met, but my conversation shocked and embarrassed him.
> No, neither Gogarty nor I, with our habit of outrageous conversation, could
> get near those men.  Yet their descendants, if they grow rich enough for
> the travel and leisure that make a finished man, will constitute our ruling
> class, and date their origin from the Post Office as American families date
> theirs from the 'Mayflower'.[129]

The second section of the poem is a masterpiece of Yeats's skill
at evoking the essential qualities of what he likes; his appreciations are always fresh and penetrating:

Swift beating on his breast in sibylline frenzy blind
Because the heart in his blood-sodden breast had dragged him down
　　into mankind,
Goldsmith deliberately sipping at the honey-pot of his mind.

He understood these men; they were Irish in the sense that he
was Irish; and he claimed his kinship proudly:

I declare this tower is my symbol; I declare
This winding, gyring, spiring treadmill of a stair is my ancestral stair;
That Goldsmith and the Dean, Berkeley and Burke have travelled there.

They were to occupy his thought for many years, to appear
often in his writings; they seemed to possess the qualities which
he regarded as un-English and so he picked out the details that
interested him from this point of view:

Born in such community Berkeley with his belief in perception, that
abstract ideas are mere words, Swift with his love of perfect nature, of the
Houynhnms, his disbelief in Newton's system[129a] and every sort of machine,
Goldsmith and his delight in the particulars of common life that shocked
his contemporaries, Burke with his conviction that all states not grown
slowly like a forest tree are tyrannies, found in England an opposite that
stung their own thought into expression and made it lucid.[130]

His description of Berkeley, if philosophically unsound,[130a] is
still masterly:

And God-appointed Berkeley that proved all things a dream,
That this pragmatical, preposterous pig of a world, its farrow that so
　　solid seem,
Must vanish on the instant if the mind but change its theme.

The third section of the poem concludes with the allocation of
wisdom to the dead, power, like everything that has a stain of
blood, to the living:
　　　　　　　but no stain
　　　Can come upon the visage of the moon
　　　When it has looked in glory from a cloud.

In 'A Dialogue of Self and Soul'[131] he reaches the climax of
the 'Tower' period. His Soul summons him to the ascent in a
stanza that holds all the mystery of night:

Who can distinguish darkness from the soul?

This might seem to set the scene for a searching after wisdom.
We remember that, when he had envied the young soldiers,
he had turned away to the tower, then the symbol of wisdom;
that he had decided wisdom must be set against the regrets of
age for lost love and youth; and that he must finally wither into
truth. These were the aspects of one extreme of his character.
There was the happy period when he was Nobel Prize winner

and poet, Senator and man of action; and then it was that he seemed to combine all the unruly opposites. He told Sean O'Faolain, when speaking of *A Vision* which he was then preparing, that

> Some have kindled their philosophy like a lamp or candle in their own dark rooms, but I would go out into the world carrying mine like a lantern.[132]

But the reception of *A Vision* reminded him later of the stones he used to drop into a well as a child, the splash far off and very faint.[133] A period of balanced activity and contemplation did not last with Yeats. His confidence played the part of adding great intensity to each extreme. 'Sailing to Byzantium' and 'The Tower' were a fervent prayer for wisdom, an echo stronger than those early dreams of living alone in search of it, having overcome bodily desire. Now with yet increased confidence he embarks on the contrast of the two extremes in a contemporary setting. The Soul's summons to the tower's wisdom is contrasted with the Self's preoccupation with Sato's sword

> Emblematical of love and war.

The setting completed, and it may have been taken from Marvell's earlier dialogue of self and soul, he proceeded to the extreme of the Self's viewpoint. He was in a cheerful humour, writing to Mrs Shakespear in September that 'The Tower' (as published in the Cuala Press limited edition of *October Blast* the preceding June) had been a success:

> Curious but I have suddenly awakened out of despondency I found myself praying between sleeping and waking and then saw a 'key' and after that a long white walled road and from that though not particularly well have had all my cheerfulness back again. I have constantly noticed that change comes from some formula of words used quite lightly. I suppose the words are but the finger on the trigger and that the gun[133a] has been long loaded.[134]

In this mood he examined all his past life with a note of confidence and recklessness. With strength came sweetness, and he can look back on all his folly and say proudly that he would live it all again:

> I am content to follow to its source,
> Every event in action or in thought;
> Measure the lot; forgive myself the lot!
> When such as I cast out remorse
> So great a sweetness flows into the breast
> We must laugh and we must sing,
> We are blest by everything,
> Everything we look upon is blest.

In September he had been offered three hundred pounds for the use for six months of about sixteen pages of verse by an American, W. E. Rudge, who owned a private press in New York:

I had about half the amount. I agreed and undertook to write 150 lines in two months. I have already written 50 or 60 lines and he has already paid £150. I am giving him 'The Woman Young and Old', a poem called 'Blood and the Moon' (a Tower poem) which were written weeks ago; I am writing a new Tower poem 'Sword and Tower' which is a choice of rebirth rather than deliverance from birth. I make my Japanese sword and its silk covering my symbol of life.[135]

Despite illness[136] the proofs for the Macmillan edition of *The Tower* were corrected and he completed the poems for Mr. Rudge.[137] A letter of his stresses two elements of *The Tower*: its bitterness and its power. He might have added its fullness and maturity as well:

*The Tower* is a success, two thousand copies first month, much the largest sale I have ever had. I do nothing at present but potter over a new edition of *A Vision* which should be ready next year. When I get to back to Rapallo I hope to write verse again—but no more bitter passion I think. Re-reading the Tower I was astonished at its bitterness—and long to live out of Ireland that I may find some new vintage. Yet that bitterness gave that book its power and it is the best book I have written. Perhaps if I was in better health I should be content to be bitter.[138]

# 10 (i)

# VACILLATION
## (1927–1932)

*I—though heart might find relief*
*Did I become a Christian man and choose for my belief*
*What seems most welcome in the tomb—play a pre-destined part.*
*Homer is my example and his unchristened heart.*[1]

W. B. YEATS

*Though the great song return no more*
*There's keen delight in what we have:*
*The rattle of pebbles on the shore*
*Under the receding wave.*[2]

W. B. YEATS

*If this new work do not seem as good as the old to my friends*
*then I can take to some lesser task and live very contentedly—the*
*happiness of finding idleness a duty—no more opinions, no more*
*politics, no more practical tasks.*[3]

W. B. YEATS

YEATS spent the winter of 1927–8 in search of health. A cold caught in October had become worse and developed into congestion of the lungs, his first serious illness since childhood. The cure was warmth, and he travelled to Algeciras where he wrote a meditation on death in more sombre mood than 'A Dialogue of Self and Soul':

Greater glory in the sun,
An evening chill upon the air,
Bid imagination run
Much on the Great Questioner;
What he can question, what if questioned I
Can with a fitting confidence reply.[4]

From there he moved to Seville because it promised more sunshine. His lung began to bleed and, after a stay of ten days, Mrs Yeats thought that better treatment could be had at Cannes so they travelled there. He had two attacks of influenza, and his condition was serious. The main cause was overwork. He was told that he must not allow himself exciting thoughts; but he defied the ban. His detective novels were constantly laid aside for the less soporific subjects of Hegel and Wyndham Lewis's *Time and the Western Man*, sent to him by Sturge Moore.

He enjoyed the vigour of Lewis; he found in him a coherent root to his own hatred. Though he did not always hate what Lewis hated, he thought that he was always glad that Lewis did hate. He wrote to Mrs Shakespear:

Last night George read me extracts from Andre Maurois' *Disraeli* amongst them one about a Wyndham Lewis who was a Member of Parliament in 1840 or so and whose widow married Disraeli. Do find out if he was any relation to the artist—it seems unlikely there should be two Wyndham Lewises in London to-day and another two in our grandfathers' day if they are not connected together. A Member of Parliament was hardly eminent enough to have unrelated babies named after him—you will see from this that *Time and Western Man* still fills my imagination. I have a curiously personal feeling of gratitude—he has found an expression for my hatred—a hatred that through being half dumb has half poisoned me. I read the last chapters again and again. He reminds me of a Father of the Church, of Origen—the only one of them I have read or rather dipped into—he has some of the same virtues and thoughts—the same disordered energy. He will have an immense effect—but he is so clear the fools will think they understand him and hiss or bray what they never found. He should have remembered that even the least of the nine hierarchies chooses to remain invisible—afraid perhaps of those academy painters.[5]

Three days later he asked Mrs Shakespear to get him a translation of one of Proust's novels and a book called *The Idea of the Holy* 'by some German theologian'. He was recovering slowly.

At Cannes the 'communicators' again got in touch with him. They objected to his use of philosophy, but permitted him to read history and philosophy in conjunction with the system of *A Vision*. Later he praised these 'unknown instructors' in a poem reminiscent of Blake:

> What they undertook to do
> They brought to pass;
> All things hang like a drop of dew
> Upon a blade of grass.[6]

The 'instructors' or 'communicators' were a subject for *A Packet for Ezra Pound* which he began shortly after he moved from Cannes to Rapallo in the middle of February. He was advised to spend his winters out of Dublin and to avoid public life. He thought that it would be good to keep away from Dublin and thus avoid the bitterness and excitement that he found there; the fact that his term of office as a Senator would end in the summer of 1928 made it seem easier to withdraw from public life. Rapallo attracted him:

Mountains that shelter the bay from all but the south wind, bare brown branches of low vines and of tall trees blurring their outline as though with a soft mist; houses mirrored in an almost motionless sea; a verandahed gable a couple of miles away bringing to mind some Chinese painting.

Rapallo's thin line of broken mother-of-pearl along the water's edge. The little town described in the Ode on a Grecian Urn. In what better place could I, forbidden Dublin winters, and all excited crowded places, spend what winters yet remain?'

Plans were made: the children would go to school in Switzerland, thus escaping life among people with more money, as in London, or with less, as in Dublin; the Merrion Square house would be too large to keep up without the Senatorial salary, and some smaller place in Dublin would have to be found. Rooms at Rapallo were taken for the winter of 1929, in the Via Americhe, with balconies and a superb view. Yeats wrote to Lady Gregory that he longed to be settled there because his hopes were in his study; but in Dublin there was always much beside his study. During March he was working again in the mornings, but only on alternate days, as the effort left him tired. In April he was back in Dublin, and he wrote of his health amusingly to Mrs Shakespear:

> Two Dublin doctors have sat upon me; the Cannes man said 'lungs and nervous breakdown can be neglected, nothing matters but blood pressure' and gave me a white pill. The Monte Carlo man said 'Blood pressure and lungs can be neglected—nothing matters but nervous breakdown' and gave me a brown pill. The Dublin men say 'Blood pressure and nervous breakdown can be neglected, nothing matters but lungs' and have given me a black pill.[8]

In May the Merrion Square house was sold, and a flat taken in Fitzwilliam Square. In June the family stayed for a short time at Thoor, Ballylee, and in July they lived at Howth, the month in which Yeats made a brief and final speech in the Senate.

The winter of 1929 passed happily at Rapallo. There were conversations and arguments with Ezra Pound, and such friends of the latter as George Antheil, who stayed for a short time during which he wrote music for one of the *Plays for Dancers*, *Fighting the Waves*, and the German dramatist Gerhard Hauptmann, who lived in Rapallo and entertained lavishly. A letter to Mrs Shakespear reflects some of his benignity:

> To-night we dine with Ezra, the first dinner . . . meal since I got here— to meet Hauptmann who does not even know one word of English but is fine to look at—after the fashion of William Morris—I have turned from Browning, to me a dangerous influence, to Morris and read things in 'Defence of Guenevere' and some unfinished prose fragments with great wonder. I have come to find the world's last great poetical period is over.

> Though the great song returns no more
> There's keen delight in what we have
> A rattle of pebbles on the shore
> Under the receding wave.

The young do not feel like that. George does not nor Ezra, but men far off feel it—in Japan for instance.[9]

He experienced 'an intense feeling of vitality' and began to write poetry again after a year's silence. The poems were simple, and joyous, full of life and energy:

No matter how bad the weather I can make myself write verse—if I have it in my head—but little else. Now we are thawing I'm writing '12 Poems to Music'—have done three of them (and 2 other poems) not so much that they may be sung as that I may define their kindly emotion to myself. I want them to be all emotion and all impersonal. One of the three is my best lyric for some years I think. They are the opposite of my recent work and all praise of joyous life though in the best of them it is a dry bone on the shore that sings the praise.[9]

The first of these poems written after his illness was 'Mad as the Mist and Snow' which he described to John Sparrow as being 'perhaps a little mechanical'.[9a] He wrote to Lady Gregory that starting verse again after a long interval was very difficult.[10] Subjects, however, presented themselves. A dream, described in a letter to Mrs Shakespear, was made into a vigorous poem:

Last night I saw in a dream strange ragged excited people singing in a crowd. The most visible were a man and woman who were I think dancing. The man was swinging around his head a weight in the end of a rope or leather thong—I know that he did not know whether he would strike her dead or not and both had their eyes fixed on each other, and both sang their love for one-another. I suppose it was Blake's old thought [that] sexual love is founded on spiritual hate—I will probably find that I have written it in a poem in a few days—though my remembering the dream may prevent that by making my criticism work on it (at least there is evidence to that effect). . . .

> I found that ivory image there
> Dancing with her chosen youth,
> But when he wound her coal-black hair
> As though to strangle her, no scream
> Or bodily movement did I dare,
> Eyes under eyelid did so gleam;
> *Love is like the lion's tooth.*
>
> When she, and though some said she played
> I said that she had danced heart's truth,
> Drew a knife to strike him dead,
> I could but leave him to his fate;
> For no matter what is said
> They had all that had their hate;
> *Love is like the lion's tooth.*[11]

He questions in the last stanza whether the man or the woman died, or whether both died or seemed to die, and breaks off to praise the times when he cared not what happened to them so long as he had the limbs to try such a dance himself. When published this poem was entitled 'Crazy Jane grown old looks at the Dancers'. Initially it was called 'Cracked Mary and the Dancers'. Cracked Mary was an old peasant woman who lived at Gort, and Yeats changed the name in case some of her relatives should object to her somewhat outspoken comments on life as Yeats reproduced them. He explained her to Mrs Shakespear:

> Crazy Jane is more or less founded[11a] on an old woman who lives in a cottage near Gort. She loves her flower garden. She has just sent Lady Gregory some flowers in spite of the season and has amazing powers of acidulous speech—one of her queer performances is a description of how the meanness of a Gort shopkeeper's wife over the price of a glass of porter made her so despairing of the human race she got drunk. The incidents of the drunkenness are of an epic magnificence. She is the local satirist and a really terrible one.[12]

In this creative period in the spring of 1929 he wrote several 'Cracked Mary' poems—they appear in *Words for Music, Perhaps* as 'Crazy Jane and the Bishop', 'Crazy Jane Reproved', and 'Crazy Jane grown old looks at the Dancers'—as well as some of the other lyrics of that volume: 'Girl's Song', 'Those Dancing Days are Gone', 'Three Things', 'Lullaby', 'Mad as the Mist and Snow'. There were other poems, 'Mohini Chatterjee', 'The Nineteenth Century and After' and a re-written version of 'At Algeciras—a meditation upon death', all included in the Cuala Press *Words for Music, Perhaps* of 1932. He also wrote 'Cracked Mary's Vision', an unpublished poem, which dealt somewhat harshly with King George the Fifth; Hone suggests that it was probably provoked by the King's opening of the new wing of the Tate Gallery in which the Lane pictures were housed.[13]

The difficulty of writing of which he had written to Lady Gregory in January had disappeared in March when he wrote to Mrs Shakespear and enclosed 'Lullaby', telling her that he had done two or three other poems that seemed lucky, a thing that did not often happen:

> Yet I am full of doubt. I am writing more easily than I ever wrote and I am happy. Whereas I have always been unhappy when I wrote and worked with great difficulty. I feel like one of those Japanese who in the middle ages retired from the world at fifty or so—not like an Indian of that age to live in jungle but to devote himself 'to art and letters' which were considered sacred.[14]

The poem became 'perhaps' his favourite lyric of all that he had written. He was generally convinced after he had written any poem that it was one of the best things he had ever written: this fact often makes it difficult to discover which poems he is referring to in letters which do not give the titles or further details. In the case of 'Lullaby', however, he was consistent and praised the poem long after the first enthusiasm of writing it had passed away. It is a poem whose beauty is enhanced by an inversion of logical grammatical order typical of much of Yeats's verse, tuned, as F. R. Higgins has put it, 'slightly off the note':[15]

> Beloved may your sleep be sound
> That have found it where you fed;
> What were all the world's alarms
> To that great Paris when he found
> Sleep upon a golden bed
> That first dawn in Helen's arms?
>
> Sleep beloved such a sleep
> As did that wild Tristram know
> When, the potion's work being done,
> Stags could run and hares could leap,
> The beech-bough sway by the oak-bough
> And the world begin again.
>
> Beloved such a sleep as fell
> Upon Eurotas' grassy bank
> When the holy bird that there
> Accomplished his predestined will,
> From the limbs of Leda sank
> But not from her protecting care.[16]

A Packet for Ezra Pound was finished at Rapallo and published in June of the same year. It included the first account of how A Vision had come to be written through Mrs Yeats's psychic powers. Yeats had begun to rewrite A Vision, eradicating the numerous mistakes of the first edition, clarifying, enlarging, and using his new knowledge of metaphysics to make better distinctions in the work. In the summer he wrote from Fitzwilliam Square to Mrs Shakespear:

I am now full of virtue. I am still putting the philosophy in order but once that is done, and this summer must finish [it], I believe I shall have a poetic rebirth for as I write about my cones and gyres all kinds of images come before me. In a few days I go to Coole and escape charming Americans with introductory letters.[17]

In May Yeats spent a fortnight visiting friends in England, then returned to Fitzwilliam Square. The summer was not eventful: he visited Iseult Stuart at Laragh Castle, Glendalough,

in July, and then left for Coole. On September 7th he completed 'Coole Park, 1919' in praise and appreciation of all the

> dance-like glory that those walls begot.

In this poem he looked back on the men who had created the
drama of aristocratic life within Coole's walls:

> There Hyde before he had beaten into prose
> That noble blade the Muses buckled on,
> There one that ruffled in a manly pose
> For all his timid heart, there that slow man,
> That meditative man, John Synge, and those
> Impetuous men, Shaw Taylor and Hugh Lane,
> Found pride established in humility,
> A scene well set and excellent company.[18]

The manly pose which Yeats had affected on his early visits to
Coole had become genuine and his tribute to Lady Gregory's
strength of character is also manly:

> They came like swallows and like swallows went,
> And yet a woman's powerful character
> Could keep a swallow to its first intent;
> And half a dozen in formation there,
> That seemed to whirl upon a compass-point,
> Found certainty upon the dreaming air,
> The intellectual sweetness of those lines
> That cut through time or cross it withershins.

The tower was occupied by the Yeats family for the last time
in the summer of 1929. It was not entirely satisfactory as a
residence. Its situation was too remote from the nearest
country town, Gort, which was about four miles away. There
was no company in the neighbourhood except that of Lady
Gregory, and Coole was a little too far away for walking. The
presence of the river added dampness to the other minor dis-
comforts of the tower. There is a desolate and melancholy air
about it now: the cottages have fallen in; the garden has disappeared; and the tower is the home of numerous jackdaws.
Inside the tower everything is covered with grime, but the
rooms are protected by the concrete roof, and still house the
elm furniture made *in situ* by the local carpenters, which proved
too large to be removed down the winding stair.

In the autumn Yeats returned to Rapallo, after a brief stay
in London where he saw his old friend Mrs Shakespear:

> Speech after long silence; it is right,
> All other lovers being estranged or dead,
> Unfriendly lamplight hid under its shade,

> The curtains drawn upon unfriendly night,
> That we descant and yet again descant
> Upon the supreme theme of Art and Song:
> Bodily decrepitude is wisdom; young
> We loved each other and were ignorant.[19]

He wrote drafts of other poems and then became seriously ill. In London he had caught a cold at the performance of *The Apple Cart*, and his lung had begun bleeding again. The illness at Rapallo could not be diagnosed for some time, and he lay in a high fever on the point of death. The illness was eventually diagnosed by an Italian specialist as Malta fever, which, once Yeats was treated with injections (and given champagne as part of his diet), abated, leaving him weak and spending the best part of nine weeks in bed. Towards the end of March the doctor told him that another three months would be needed before he recovered his strength, but he moved to Portofino Vetta and was 'almost well again' after the first week of April had passed:

> I work at the new Version of *The Vision* every morning, then read Swift's Letters and only take to detective stories in the evening, and would be wholly well if my legs were stronger. Here I can slip in and out as I please, free from the stage fright I had at Rapallo whenever George brought me to the little Cafe by the sea. After all there may be something in climate which I have always denied. Here no mountains shut us in; I think three weeks should make me as well as ever.[20]

On 30 April he wrote in his Diary:

> Subject for a poem ... Describe Byzantium as it is in the system towards the end of the first Christian millennium. A walking mummy. Flames at the street corners where the soul is purified, birds of hammered gold singing in the golden trees, in the harbour, offering their backs to the wailing dead that they may carry them to paradise.[21]

The subject had been in his head for some time, and he 'warmed himself back into life'[22] with it and the poem 'Veronica's Napkin'. Byzantium in the system of *A Vision* was almost a paradise:[22a]

> I think that if I could be given a month of antiquity and leave to spend it where I chose, I would spend it in Byzantium a little before Justinian opened St. Sophia and closed the Academy of Plato. I think I would find in some little wine shop some philosophical worker in mosaic who could answer all my questions, the supernatural descending nearer him than Plotinus even, for the pride of his delicate skill would make what was an instrument of power to Princes and Clerics and a murderous madness in the mob, show as a lovely flexible presence like that of a perfect human body. I think that in early Byzantium, and maybe never before or since in recorded history, religious, aesthetic and practical life were one, and that architects and artificers—though not, it may be, poets, for language had

been the instrument of controversy and must have grown abstract—spoke
to the multitude and the few alike. The painter and the mosaic worker,
the worker in gold and silver, the illuminator of Sacred Books were almost
impersonal, almost perhaps without the consciousness of individual design,
absorbed in their subject matter and that the vision of a whole people.[23]

He set the scene for his poem with a masterly touch:

> The unpurged images of day recede;
> The Emperor's drunken soldiery are abed;
> Night resonance recedes, night walkers' song
> After great cathedral gong;
> A starlit or a moonlit dome disdains
> All that man is,
> All mere complexities,
> The fury and the mire of human veins.[24]

The material was drawn from his knowledge of several
books[25]—*The Age of Justinian and Theodora* by W. G. Holmes,
*Byzantine Art and Archaeology* by O. M. Dalton, and *Apotheosis
and After-life* by Mrs Strong. The fourth line, 'after great
cathedral gong', for instance, came from a description in the
first work of the boom of the great *semantron*, a sonorous board
suspended in the porch of each church and beaten by deacons
with mallets, for opposite this Yeats pencilled in the margin the
word 'gong' which he used to conclude the poem:

> Those images that yet
> Fresh images beget,
> That dolphin-torn, that gong-tormented sea.

He had developed the early Byzantine poem which sketched
in the elements of the Byzantine scene which appealed to him.
Some of the pictorial elegance of the 1926 drafts for 'Sailing
to Byzantium' is recaptured in the later poem, as for instance
in the unpublished lines:

> I therefore travel towards Byzantium
> Among these sunbrown pleasant mariners
> Another dozen days and we shall come
> Under the jetty and the marble stair. . . .
> But now these pleasant dark-skinned mariners
> Carry me towards that great Byzantium
> Where all is ancient, singing at the oars
> That I may look in the great church's dome
> On gold-embedded saints and emperors
> After the mirroring waters and the foam
> Where the dark drowsy fins a moment rise
> Of fish that carry souls to paradise.

The eternal and artificial bird of the early poem which was
implicitly contrasted with the singing birds of Ireland is now
directly contrasted with ordinary birds, and its setting, in the
early poem 'a golden bough', is now enhanced by the adjective

which gives the whole picture of the town its starlit or moonlit
luminosity:

> Miracle, bird or golden handiwork,
> More miracle than bird or handiwork,
> Planted on the star-lit golden bough,
> Can like the cocks of Hades crow,
> Or, by the moon embittered, scorn aloud
> In glory of changeless metal
> Common bird or petal
> And all complexities of mire or blood.

Another piece of detail taken from *The Age of Justinian and
Theodora*, in which Yeats marked the passage describing the
Forum of Constantine, known as 'The Pavement' from its
finished marble floor, is the use of the spirits seen on the
Emperor's Pavement:

> Astraddle on the dolphin's mire and blood

a description due to Mrs Strong's account of the symbolic
meaning of dolphins in the art of the ancient world; they were
emblems of the soul or its transit.

There is a subtle difference of attitude in the writing of the
two poems. The first escapes from the sensual music[25a] of
Ireland and the gallantries of youth, from

> Whatever is begotten, born, and dies.

It was written to recover his spirits, and is Byzantium approached from afar. The second poem also scorns

> The fury and the mire of human veins.

It too was written in the emergence from a fit of depression in
an attempt to find a theme to befit his years; but it is Byzantium
seen from within. Arrival at the state of eternity was not so
instantaneous as the prayers to the mosaic saints had suggested
in 'Sailing to Byzantium'; in 'Byzantium' there is purgation
by mysterious fire, 'flames at the street corners where the soul
is purified':

> Flames that no faggot feeds, nor steel has lit,
> Nor storm disturbs, flames begotten of flame,
> Where blood-begotten spirits come
> And all complexities of fury leave. . . .

Yeats had been near death in the fiery heat of Maltese fever;
and he makes the birds (in the draft of the poem) offer their

backs to the wailing dead that they may carry them to Paradise. Both poems are an attempt to praise eternity as a means of forgetting regrets for youth and vigour; but the later poem has been written out of an experience further from life and nearer to death.

Until June he remained at Rapallo, reading Swift's letters and his political essays and contrasting them with F. S. Oliver's *The Endless Adventure*. Oliver saw history as a reasoned conflict of mechanical interests intelligible to all; but this confirmed Yeats's view that history was a human drama

keeping the classical unities by the clear division of its epochs, turning one way or the other because this man hates or that man loves. . . . Yet the drama has its plot, and this plot ordained character and passions and exists for their sake.[26]

He began to read history after he had the dates and diagrams which form the basis of the chapter on the 'Great Year'; but it was not a very deep study which he made. He read to find what he wanted and, once he had found or selected it, tended to forget where it had originated:

Sometimes I did indeed stray from them (the obvious authorities), and sometimes the more vivid the fact the less do I remember my authority. Where did I pick up that story of the Byzantine bishop and the singer of Antioch, where learn that to anoint your body with the fat of a lion ensured the favour of a king?[27]

Swift was in his thoughts continually, his *saeva indignatio* appealed to him, and he worked hard to get his translation of Swift's epitaph exactly right. He wanted to discover the originals of his own thought:

I seek more than idioms, for thoughts become more vivid when I find they were thought out in historical circumstances which affect those in which I live, or, which is perhaps the same thing, were thought by men my ancestors may have known. Some of my ancestors may have seen Swift, and probably my Huguenot grandmother who asked burial near Bishop King, spoke both to Swift and Berkeley. I have before me an ideal expression in which all that I have, clay and spirits, assist; it is as though I most approximate towards that expression when I carry with me the greatest possible amount of hereditary thought and feeling, even national and family hatred and pride.[28]

When he returned to Ireland after the middle of June Gogarty wrote to him to say that Augustus John would like to do a serious portrait, and Yeats agreed to this. At Renvyle, Connemara, he stood in front of his mirror noting lines about his mouth in which he saw

the marks of recent illness, marks of time, growing irresolution, perhaps
some faults that I have long dreaded; but then my character is so little myself
that all my life it has thwarted me.  It has affected my poems, my true self,
no more than the character of a dancer affects the movement of the dance.
When I was painted by John years ago and saw for the first time the portrait
(or rather the etching taken from it) now in a Birmingham gallery, I
shuddered.  Always particular about my clothes, never dissipated, never
unshaved except during illness, I saw myself there an unshaven, drunken
bar-tender, and then I began to feel John had found something that he
liked in me, something closer than character, and by that very transforma-
tion made it visible.  He had found Anglo-Irish solitude, a solitude I have
made for myself, an outlawed solitude.[29]

He steeped himself in the Anglo-Irish writers.  Swift haunted
him; he was always 'just round the corner'[29a] and he read him

for months together Burke and Berkeley less often but always with excitement, and Goldsmith lures and waits.  I collect materials for my thought
and work, for some identification of my beliefs with the nation itself, I seek
an image of the modern mind's discovery of itself, of its own permanent
form, in that one Irish century that escaped from darkness and confusion.
I would that our fifteenth, sixteenth, or even our seventeenth century had
been the clear mirror, but fate decided against us.[30]

When he went to Coole after Renvyle he wrote *The Words
Upon the Window-Pane* on the theme of Swift and the mystery
of Stella and Vanessa.  The setting of the play, a spiritualist
séance, which takes place in an old eighteenth-century house
associated with Swift and Stella, reveals how realistically Yeats
could write, and how skilfully he created contemporary character.  The characters are middle-class Dubliners with the addition of a Cambridge student who is writing a thesis on Swift
and Stella: they explain the procedure of the séance and the
difficulties which there have been, the presence of a supposed
evil spirit at the previous séance and the history of Swift, Stella
and Vanessa is sketched in sufficiently for the ensuing voices
of Swift and Vanessa to be understood by the audience.  The
device of making the medium act the parts of medium, control,
Swift and Vanessa is intensely dramatic; there are two plays
skilfully blended together, the tension of the séance and the
tension of Swift.  There is skill in all the play's construction,
the initial explanations are effective and come naturally in the
dialogue, and there is a break in the tension which brings the
play back to the ordinary room and sitters which accentuates
the increase in intensity of the latter portion of the play.  The
final incident is impressive and even terrifying.  The Cambridge student returns to question the medium, who knows
nothing of Swift or Stella, and, when he has gone again, begins

to prepare herself some tea only to break off into Swift's voice
again with its final:

> Perish the day on which I was born!

While at Coole Yeats was pondering more deeply on the
nature of Swift's thought. Swift was more important to modern
thought than Vico:

> Swift seemed to shape his narrative upon some clairvoyant vision of his
> own life, for he saw civilisation pass from comparative happiness and youth-
> ful vigour to an old age of violence and self-contempt, whereas Vico saw it
> begin in penury like himself and end as he would end in a long inactive
> peace. But there was a greater difference; Swift, a practical politician in
> everything he wrote, ascribed its rise and fall to virtues and vices all could
> understand, whereas the philosophical Vico ascribed them to 'the rhythm
> of the elemental forms of the mind'.[31]

Swift saw civilisations 'exploding' and he took the idea from
Polybius that every civilisation carries with it from the beginning what shall bring it to an end; Vico, he thought, created
the thought of modern Italy, influenced Croce and Gentile, and
all these philosophies were important for the future:

> These thoughts in the next few generations, as elaborated by Oswald
> Spengler, who has followed Vico without essential change, by Flinders
> Petrie, by the German traveller Frobenius, by Henry Adams, and perhaps
> by my friend Gerald Heard, may affect the masses. They have already
> deepened our sense of tragedy and somewhat checked the naiver among
> those creeds and parties who push their way to power by flattering our
> moral hopes. Pascal thought there was evidence of God, but that if a man
> kept his mind in suspense about it he could not live a rich and active life,
> and I suggest to the Cellars and Garrets that though history is too short
> to change either the idea of progress or the eternal circuit into scientific
> fact, the eternal circuit may best suit our preoccupation with the soul's
> salvation, our individualism, our solitude. Besides we love antiquity, and
> that other idea—progress—the sole religious myth of modern man, is only
> two hundred years old.[32]

He had heard[33] that Dublin was full of little clubs of Catholics or Marxists or even both, and the essay which he wrote as
a commentary on *The Words on the Window-Pane* and published
in *The Dublin Magazine*[34] was directed to them. He hoped that
his ideas on the relationship of individual and state might
appeal to them. These ideas were drawn from Swift and the
other Anglo-Irish writers. In *A Discourse of the Contests and
Dissentions of the Nobles and Commons at Athens and Rome*, an essay
which seemed to Yeats to have led up to Burke so clearly that
one could claim that Anglo-Ireland recreated conservative
thought as much in one as in the other, he had found that the

saying *vox populi*, *vox dei* was to be understood of the universal
bent and current of a people, not the bare majority of a few
representatives. The *vox populi* seemed to Yeats to emerge in
the *Drapier's Letters*, and the right for it to be expressed by men
who had won general consent: Swift had enforced his moral
by proving that the war of the many on the few had destroyed
Greece and Rome; and all states must depend upon a right
balance between the One, the Few and the Many.[35]

In November 1930 Yeats went to England, and visited Lady
Ottoline Morrell and John Masefield, at whose house five girls
recited a long programme of his lyrics after Masefield had made
an appreciative speech about Yeats's work, it being the thirtieth
anniversary of their meeting. He decided to stay in Ireland
and rented a furnished house on Killiney Hill, south of Dublin,
for the winter, so that he would be within reach of Lady
Gregory, whose powers were beginning to fail. In September
he had dreamed of a large house, a mixture of Sandymount
Castle and Coole, of which he used to dream several times a
year:

This time all the house was castellated and about to pass into other
hands, its pictures auctioned. I remember looking at a picture and thinking that it would now lose its value, for its value was that it had been put
there by some past member of the family. Coole as a Gregory house is
near its end, it will be before long an office and residence for foresters, a
little cheap furniture in the great rooms a few religious oleographs its only
pictures, and yet when in my dreams I had some such thought I stood in a
Gothic door which I now recognise as the door at Sandymount. . . .[36]

At Coole in the autumn of 1930 he had been reading
Berkeley, and altered the philosopher into what he wanted
him to be:

That philanthropic serene Bishop, that pasteboard man, never wrote the
*Commonplace Book*. Attracted beyond expression by Berkeley's thought I
have been repelled by the man as we have received him from tradition.[37]

He tried to recreate his own attitude to life in Berkeley and
described him as wearing the mask of benevolence in order to
hide his childlike, naïve and mischievous curiosity. Berkeley
knew nothing of men and women and loved discourse for its
own sake; the Diary goes even further:

What did he really say in those three sermons to undergraduates, that
got him into such a political mess—not quite I think what he says in that
irrational essay on *Passive Obedience* written to save his face. Was the
Bermuda project more than a justification for curiosity and discourse? was
not that curiosity already half satisfied when he drew the plans of his
learned city—a steeple in the centre and markets in the corners? . . . Berkeley

the Bishop was a humbug.  His wife, that charming daughter who played
the viol, Queen Caroline, Ministers of State, imposed it upon him; but he
was meant for a Greek tub or an Indian palm tree.  Only once in his life
was he free, still an undergraduate, he filled the *Commonplace Book* with
snorts of defiance.  Descartes, Locke and Newton took away the world and
gave us its excrement instead.  Berkeley restored the world.[38]

He had written earlier in his Diary that Berkeley thought that
by showing that the primary qualities, abstractions, did not
exist he could create a philosophy so concrete that the common
people could understand it.  Yeats's own wish was for a literature founded upon the three things that Kant thought must be
postulated in order to make life livable: Freedom, God, and
Immortality.  He thought that the fading of these three before
Bacon, Newton, and Locke[38a] had made literature decadent:
and that the state which was not founded upon preparation
for these three convictions would be a prison house.

In January 1931 he wrote 'The Seven Sages' in which he
praised 'four great minds that hated Whiggery' and disregarded
Burke's whig outlook in a fine piece of vigorous writing:

> Whether they knew it or not,
> Goldsmith and Burke, Swift and the Bishop of Cloyne
> All hated Whiggery; but what is Whiggery?
> A levelling, rancorous, rational sort of mind
> That never looked out of the eye of a saint
> Or out of drunkard's eye. . . .
>
> They walked the roads
> Mimicking what they heard, as children mimic;
> They understood that wisdom comes of beggary.[39]

All these thoughts were in his head when he went to Oxford
in May to receive an honorary degree of Doctor of Letters.
There for two hours he talked to John Sparrow whose recollections of the conversation give a glimpse of the range and
dynamic quality of Yeats's conversational powers and his views
on various subjects.[40]  To place Yeats fully in the correct
setting for conversation his appearance must be imagined.  He
was always beautifully dressed, generally in quiet corn or brown
tweeds, with bright blue or dark green shirts, always with
matching handkerchief.  He had an air of quiet elegance, his
long white-blue hair crowning a face often sunburnt and always
carefully shaved, his movements graceful and dignified, especially his salute, a slow raising of the hand as if in blessing, 'a
compromise between that of Mussolini and the Pope'.  At
Oxford he told John Sparrow that

he had just read a book on Lenin by Prince Mirski and thought it amusing and charmingly naive. He selected a quotation from Marx [?] to the effect that the greatness of a man depends upon the greatness of the social movement which he embodies. 'That saying will be very useful to me, I think.' He quoted the passage in which he had already used it, a passage aimed against Catholics and Marxists. He spoke of his hatred of the Marxian interpretation of and criticism of the history of literature; he, on the contrary, was interested in personality and the flowering of the spirit. He must attempt to get into the framework of the man he was studying: 'If he believed the world was flat, I must see everything from the viewpoint of a flat world.' The *Drapier Letters* were no more important than many trifling incidents in Swift's life. Swift learned Irish nationalism in politics, Berkeley at the University. He talked of his interest in Berkeley and the *Commonplace Books* especially the passage where he thought Berkeley distinguished Irish thought from that of other nations, an event as important as the Battle of the Boyne. He was trying to inspire the youth of Ireland with the national ideals to be found in Berkeley and Swift. His attitude to poetry, he explained, was quite unlike that of his brother Jack to art. His brother said he painted merely to amuse himself and that the public chose to pay him for the work. W. B. was entirely against this in his attitude to poetry: 'You must always remember your audience; it is always there and you cannot write without it.' He had compared it to the congregation of a church and had said to a friend that he could understand why a Catholic went to mass, but not why a Protestant went to church: 'My friend said that I had forgotten the liturgy, the congregation. I saw at once that he was right.' The upholders of free verse claimed in defence of their writing that the form was accommodated to the matter without restriction. This was the opposite of his theory, the essence of poetry was for him putting the personal into a static form, which he compared to the metaphysical antinomy of the individual and the infinite, the many and the one. The form could, of course, be changed and adapted. He was a traditionalist, and gave as an example of what he meant Byron's 'so we'll go no more a roving' where personal feelings are hitched not only on to traditional words and metre, but on to an old quotation, by which much more melancholy is created. He could not accept the new realism, that the seen can exist independently of seeing. Berkeley was again appealed to, and he carried an Everyman Berkeley in his pocket. The finest description of sexual intercourse ever written was in Dryden's translation of Lucretius, and it was justified; it was introduced to illustrate the difficulty of two becoming a unity: 'The tragedy of sexual intercourse is the perpetual virginity of the soul.' Sexual intercourse is an attempt to solve the eternal antinomy, doomed to failure because it takes place only on one side of the gulf. The gulf is that which separates the one and the many, or if you like, God and man. Philosophers have tried to deny the antinomy and to give a complete account of existence, either as a unity (as in the case of Spinoza and Hegel) or as a plurality (as in the case of Leibnitz) but the antinomy is there and can be represented only by a myth. He quoted a story of Hafiz, of a man who knocked on the door of his beloved, 'Let me in' and was told to go away; he knocked again and was again sent away; he knocked a third time and was asked 'Who are you?' 'I am thyself' 'Enter'. The whole of life, the world itself arises out of the opposition of these two. He thought it necessary to have a myth; 'No one can live without a myth'. The myth cannot be proved, but we test it in every day experience. The antinomy was illustrated in his early verse by a poem about a blind man and a fool. There was a similar Indian parable which represented man by a blind man carrying a lame man. It is the same contrast as Kant's—concepts without perception are empty, perception without concepts is blind: 'But that contrast may not have been present to my mind—I had no metaphysics then, though plenty of mysticism.' The difference between his early and his late poetry was that when he wrote his later he had a philosophy. He did not write philosophical poetry: 'I do not write about ideas; I try to write about my emotions. But my philosophy prevents me from writing much that I might otherwise write about.' He said that he sometimes thought that decent things even happiness itself were becoming more expensive: 'When I was a boy, people of our class, people of what Swift called "a middling condition" sent their children to a day school. Now, to get the same education they must send them to a boarding school, and so it is in all things and all up the scale.' He disliked 'reactiveness': 'The acceptance of tradition is the tragedy of life. To accept it is a life long discipline.' But he did not praise mere acceptiveness. Wherever there is thought there is opposition. You cannot think *in vacuo*: 'Wherever I have met a man with great gifts who has been a failure I have said "That man has learned in his youth to be reactive".' It was, he said, a danger to which clever people were particularly exposed, especially in youth, and especially those brought up in a provincial society. Reactiveness ruined Pound, who hated success. . . . Shall we ever have a traditional philosophy? It is open to a man to deny the existence of God and the immortality of the soul and to remain traditional, to take in account the feeling of the common man: 'He may believe that the soul dies with the body—it is when he says he doesn't care that I disbelieve him.' He complained of Bradley and most philosophers because they reacted against the common man, because so donnish[ly] philosophical, ashamed of common experience. He complained of Bradley's passage about immortality: 'In one of my philosophical writings I have said that Mr Bradley believes that it is possible to stand by the deathbed of mother or of sweetheart or of wife and not wish for some immortality. He's a liar.' McTaggart he admired as much as any English philosopher, but deplored the fault he shared with Moore and most English philosophers that they must make jokes and concessions to the popular readers. . . . He complained that Valéry in some verses pretended to be satisfied with the prospects of the soul's mortality. He did not believe anyone was. Also he disliked in the same poem (which, on the whole, he admired greatly) a pre-occupation with flux—Bergsonian, he supposed. He contrasted the white ardour of Gentile . . . 'Damn Bertrand Russell. He's a proletarian. He has a wicked and a vulgar spirit. I suppose if you had so many ancestors at that date [Hume's] in the peerage you can't help your behaviour being that of the public house.' It was his spirit that he chiefly complained of.

These views were constant, and they are echoed in his prose and verse and letters of the period. His interest in Berkeley was further stimulated by the visit of Dr Mario M. Rossi to Ireland. He wrote to Mrs Shakespear:

When I got to Dublin Berkeley and an Italian philosopher who came to work on Hone's book absorbed my vitality. . . . I finished my own work on Berkeley 2 or 3 weeks ago and since then I have been writing poetry. . . . I am reading 'The Savage Messiah', a most moving book but one wonders how much is from Miss Breska's Diary—if she was not after all a great novelist. The letters where he speaks of art and literature are Ezra articulate. It is the generation of Bergson. I am full of admiration [and] respect,

but I hate the Jewish element in Bergson, this deification of the moment . . .
this for minds less hard and masculine [MS. almost illegible] turned the
world into fruit salad . . . and thus I saw that later philosophy has in general
agreed with your dislike of Berkeley's deism. You asked for some books of
Croce's but may have meant *The Mind as Pure Act* by Gentile for that founds
itself on Berkeley. It is a dry difficult beautiful book. Croce's *Aesthetics* is
much easier and perhaps a better preparation for philosophy.[41]

His ideas on the immortality of the soul were put in the
preface to *Resurrection*, a play on a Christian theme which he
had drafted in 1925 and read to a small audience in his Merrion
Square house, and on which he had worked at intervals later.
'Two Songs for a Play' were included in *The Tower*, and he
was working on other lyrics for the play in 1929. He quoted
the verse of Magnus Annus in the first song to John Sparrow
as an illustration of his own myth: the verses state his belief that
Christianity brought a radical violence into the world and
ushered in a new historical period. In *A Vision* Yeats reveals
that when he writes of Magnus Annus he is thinking of Virgil's
Fourth Eclogue and its virgin, for he quotes:

The latest age of Cumean song is at hand; the cycles in their vast array
begin anew; Virgin Astrea comes, the reign of Saturn comes, the generation
of mankind descends. . . . Apollo now is king and in your consulship, in
yours, Pollio, the age of glory shall commence and the mighty months
begin to run their course. . . .[42]

The poem's first stanza introduces another idea:

> I saw a staring virgin stand
> Where holy Dionysus died,
> And tear the heart out of his side,
> And lay the heart upon her hand
> And bear that beating heart away;
> And then did all the Muses sing
> Of Magnus Annus at the spring,
> As though God's death were but a play[43]

the source of which Yeats gives in the introduction to the play:

What if there is always something that lies outside knowledge, outside
order? . . . What if the irrational return? What if the circle begin again?
Years ago I read Sir William Crookes' *Studies in Psychical Research*. After
examining every possibility of fraud he touched a materialised form and
found the heart beating. I felt, though my intellect rejected what I read,
the terror of the supernatural described by Job. Just before the war a
much respected man of science entering a room in his own house found
there two girl visitors—I have questioned all three—one lying asleep on the
table, the other sitting on the end of the table screaming, the table floating
in the air, and 'immediately vomited'. I took from the beating heart, from
my momentary terror, from the shock of a man of science, the central situation of my play: the young man touching the heart of the phantom and
screaming. It has seemed to me of late that the sense of spiritual reality
comes whether to the individual or to crowds from violent shock, and that
idea has the support of tradition.[44]

The second stanza seems to draw further material from Virgil's Eclogue for its picture of the future ages of mankind. Virgil mentions a second Troy, a second Argo:

Yet shall some traces of olden sin linger behind, to call men to sail the sea in ships, to enclose towns with walls, and to cleave the earth with furrows. A second Tiphys shall then arise, and a second Argo to carry heroes; a second warfare, too, shall come about, and again a great Achilles be sent to Troy.[45]

The idea of the new Argo appealed to Yeats and he used the image several times; but its source may not be Virgil so much as Shelley's *Hellas*:

The world's great age begins anew,
The golden years return,
The earth doth like a snake renew
Her winter weeds outworn:
Heaven smiles, and faiths and empires gleam
Like wrecks of a dissolving stream. . . .

A loftier Argo cleaves the main,
Fraught with a later prize;
Another Orpheus sings again,
And loves, and weeps, and dies;
A new Ulysses leaves once more
Calypso for his native shore.

Oh! write no more the tale of Troy,
If earth Death's scroll must be. . . .[46]

The preface to the play, completed in 1931, repeats his views on the question of the rebirth of the soul. All ancient nations he wrote, believed in it and

In our time Schopenhauer believed it, and McTaggart thinks Hegel did, though lack of interest in the individual Soul kept him silent. It is the foundation of McTaggart's own philosophical system. Cardinal Mercier saw no evidence for it, but did not think it heretical; and its rejection compelled the sincere and noble Von Hügel to say that children dead too young to have earned Heaven suffered no wrong, having never heard of a better place than limbo.[47]

The summer and autumn of 1931 were another productive period for verse. In June Yeats wrote 'Tom the Lunatic' with its proud vigorous declaration:

Whatever stands in field or flood
Bird, beast, fish or man,
Mare or stallion, cock or hen,
Stands in God's unchanging eye
In all the vigour of its blood;
In that faith I live or die.[48]

'Tom at Cruachan', a brief poem on time and eternity, followed in July, with a Crazy Jane poem, 'Crazy Jane on

God'. In August he wrote his 'Remorse for Intemperate Speech' dealing with the hatred that he found a commonplace in Ireland:

> Out of Ireland have we come.
> Great hatred, little room,
> Maimed us at the start.
> I carry from my mother's womb
> A fanatic heart.[49]

But a few days before this, he had written the delicate and tenderly beautiful 'The Delphic Oracle Upon Plotinus';[50] which was modelled on Porphyry's *Life of Plotinus* prefixed to Stephen MacKenna's *Plotinus*:[51]

> Scattered on the level grass
> Or winding through the grove
> Plato there and Minos pass
> There stately Pythagoras
> And all the choir of Love.

Other August poems were 'The Dancer at Cruachan and Cro-Patrick'[52] and 'The Results of Thought' with again the contrast, the one a praise of vigorous life, the other a picture of images

> That turn dull-eyed away,
> Or shift Time's filthy load,
> Straighten aged knees,
> Hesitate or stay. . . .[53]

In September he wrote 'The Mother of God', in October 'Old Tom Again', 'a reply to the dancer's song' as he described it to Mrs Shakespear, and in November 'Quarrel in Old Age', a recording of some quarrel with Maud Gonne, probably over the treatment of women prisoners or Mary MacSwiney's hunger strike, which contained his old faith in her beauty and the hope of seeing her in her youth again:

> Somewhere beyond the curtain
> Of distorting days
> Lives that lonely thing
> That shone before these eyes
> Targeted, trod like spring.[54]

He reached new limits of outspokenness in two Crazy Jane poems also written in November, 'Crazy Jane and Jack the Journeyman' and 'Crazy Jane talks with the Bishop', with its startling lines:

> A woman can be proud and stiff
> When on love intent;
> But Love has pitched his' mansion in
> The place of excrement;

> For nothing can be sole or whole
> That has not been rent.[55]

Echoes of Blake emerge constantly in Yeats's verse, and these lines probably owe their inception to *Jerusalem*:

> For I will make their places of love and joy excrementitious.[56]

There came the reaction to be expected in Yeats's oscillating character. From Coole he wrote to his wife that he wanted to exorcise that slut, Crazy Jane, whose language had become unendurable, and to Mrs Shakespear that in the attempt to shake off his creation he had begun a longish poem called 'Wisdom'. The resulting poem, published as 'Vacillation', written in a time of excitement, intense, and thoughtful, is one of the clearest descriptions of Yeats's character that he has written. Letters to Mrs Shakespear set the scene. On the last Sunday in November he wrote to her from Coole:

> The night before letters came I went for a walk after dark and there among some great trees became absorbed in the most lofty philosophic conception I have found while writing *A Vision*. I suddenly seemed to understand at last and then I smelt roses. I realised the nature of the timeless spirit. Then I began to walk and in my excitement came—how shall I say—that old glory so beautiful with its autumnal tint—the longing to touch it was almost unendurable. The next night I was walking in the same path and now the two excitements came together. The autumnal tinge incredibly spiritual remote erect delicate featured and mixed with it the violent physical image the black mass of Eden. Yesterday I put my thoughts into a poem which I enclose but it seems to me a poor shadow of the intensity of the experience.

In January 1932 he wrote:

> You will be too quiet and lone if I get religion. I meant to write to you but thought of that sentence of yours then wrote a poem which puts clearly an argument that has gone on in my head for years—when I have finished the poem I began yesterday I will take up the theme in greater fullness. Here is the poem. Heart and Soul are speaking.
> HEART: What, be a singer born and lack a theme.
> SOUL: Search out reality, leave things that seem.
> SOUL: Ezekiel's coal and speech leaps out anew.
> HEART: Can there be living speech in Heaven's blue
> SOUL: Knock on that door, salvation waits within.
> HEART: And what sang Homer but original sin.
> I feel that this is the choice of the saint (St. Theresa's ecstasy, Gandhi's smiling face): comedy; and heroic choice: Tragedy (Dante and Don Quixote) live tragically but be not deceived (not the fool's tragedy). Yet I accept all the miracles. Why should not the old embalmers come back—as ghosts and bestow upon the saint all the care once bestowed upon Rameses: why should I doubt the tale that when St. Theresa's tomb was opened in the middle of the nineteenth century the still undecayed lady dripped with fragrant oil. I shall be a simple man to the end and think upon my death bed of all the nights I wasted in my youth. [57]

The poem is a masterly example of the thoughts which gave
Yeats drama.  The opening lines arrest the reader.  They are
a challenge:

> Between extremities
> Man runs his course[57a]

and a query:

> A brand or flaming breath,
> Comes to destroy
> All those antinomies
> Of day and night;
> The body calls it death,
> The heart remorse.
> But if these be right
> What is joy?

He answers with an image from *The Mabinogion* of the flaming
tree:

> And half is half and yet is all the scene;
> And half and half consume what they renew.[58]

Here is a simple and effective description of happiness in the
third section of the poem:

> While on the shop and street I gazed
> My body of a sudden blazed;
> And twenty minutes more or less
> It seemed, so great my happiness,
> That I was blessèd and could bless.

which is an echo of a fuller description in *Essays*[59] of a similar
experience.  And following this is a brief poem of the reverse
side of his character:

> But something is recalled
> My conscience or my vanity appalled.

The theme of the whole poem emerges in the seventh section
with its query:

> What theme had Homer but original sin?

This was suggested to him by a remark of Lady Gregory's
made a few weeks before her death.  He had shown her a book
by Day Lewis and she said she preferred the poems translated
from the Irish because they came out of original sin.[60]  From
original sin he returned in the last section of the poem to his
own conclusion, reached earlier in 'A Dialogue of Self and
Soul'.  Von Hügel, the author of *The Mystical Element of Religion*,
is taken as his symbol of Christianity—but though both believe
in miracles, Yeats must play his 'predestined part' for Homer
is his example.

During his last stay at Coole Yeats read all of Balzac and the autobiography of Shri Purohit Swami, an Indian monk he had met in London, who took much of his time from poetry.[60] He worked on the magnificent poetry of 'Coole and Ballylee, 1931'[61] during February. The poem's mood moves as swiftly as the river it describes, flowing past Yeats's tower before disappearing underground, emerging in Coole demesne, and flowing into the lake; yet this mood, swiftly evoked by the wintry scene, by the rising swan, a symbol of inspiration,[62] has all the breadth of vision which understands the tragedy of human life. Lady Gregory was

> a last inheritor
> Where none has reigned that lacked a name and fame
> Or out of folly into folly came.

Coole was sold to the Land Commission and the Department of Forestry in 1927 and she wrote a little sadly in her diary that the place

no longer belongs to anyone of our family or name, I am thankful to have been able to keep back a sale for these years past, for giving it into the hands of the Forestry people makes the maintenance of the woods secure and will give employment and be for the good and dignity of the country. As to the house I will stay and keep it as the children's home as long as I keep strength enough and can earn money enough. It had a good name before I came here, its owners were of good, even of high repute; and that has been continued, has increased, in Robert's time and mine. Perhaps some day one of the children may care enough for it to come back; they have been happy here.[63]

In 1929 Yeats had prophesied its coming ruin in verse, a dignified appeal to posterity:

> Here, traveller, scholar, poet, take your stand
> When all those rooms and passages are gone,
> When nettles wave upon a shapeless mound
> And saplings root among the broken stone,
> And dedicate—eyes bent upon the ground,
> Back turned upon the brightness of the sun
> And all the sensuality of the shade—
> A moment's memory to that laurelled head.[64]

Now Yeats feels the passing of glory. Lady Gregory is dying and he remembers their past work; they chose traditional sanctity and loveliness:

> But all is changed, that high horse riderless,
> Though mounted in that saddle Homer rode
> Where the swan drifts upon a darkening flood.

The poem bears the full result of Yeats's working over his material; the return to the swan and the flooded water is

masterly.  There is a subtle change.  The 'flooded lake' becomes 'a darkening flood'; the swan's 'sudden thunder' alters
to drifting.  Through these changes the emotional undertones
emerge, and stress the change that Yeats was experiencing, and
the loss not merely of his friend but of the dignity and loveliness he had found in the house that would die with her.  His
prophecies were fulfilled.  The Forestry Department sold the
house and it was pulled down.  Only the dignified grey stable-
yard remains to hint at the former presence of the house which
once had been a place

> Where travelled men and children found
> Content or joy.

# 10 (ii)

# AN OLD MAN'S EAGLE EYE
## (1932–1939)

*A mind Michael Angelo knew*
*That can pierce the clouds,*
*Or inspired by frenzy*
*Shake the dead in their shrouds;*
*Forgotten else by mankind,*
*An old man's eagle mind.*

W. B. YEATS[1]

*You think it horrible that lust and rage*
*Should dance attention upon my old age;*
*They were not such a plague when I was young;*
*What else have I to spur me into song?*

W. B. YEATS[2]

AFTER Lady Gregory's death Yeats stopped writing verse for some months, and even thought that the inner drama of his own life had gone with the passing of Lady Gregory and Coole. He needed the sense of a permanent home about him, and longed for quiet, which was 'part of the genius of that house'.[2a] A very suitable small estate was found at Rathfarnham, near Dublin, into which he moved in July:

> An old house in lovely grounds, a house built before cement took the place of stone and thin-walled clangour for the stately repose and long silence of continuous dwelling. His gate is on a bridge which spans a stream fresh from the golden granite of the hills. The walk rises through a well-gardened wilderness of flowering shrubs, and the cold grey house is screened by a blossoming orchard. His croquet lawn is beside it, and the hills form an everchanging picture as deep and as glowing in style as a picture by his brother, Jack Yeats, in his latest style. The door faces you. 'Yeats' on a heart-shaped brass knocker.[3]

This house had been envisaged long before: just as the tower had been the result of youthful dreaming, so Riversdale, the new house and grounds, symbolised a thought of middle age. In 1917 Yeats had written that the poet must ask himself as he grows old whether he can retain his mask and vision without new bitterness and disappointment:

> Surely, he may think, now that I have found vision and mask I need not suffer any longer. He will buy perhaps some small old house where like Ariosto he can dig his garden, and think that in the return of birds

and leaves, or moon and sun, and in the evening flight of the rooks he may discover rhythm and pattern like those in sleep and so never awake out of vision. Then he will remember Wordsworth withering into eighty years, honoured and empty-witted, and climb to some waste room and find, forgotten there by youth, some bitter crust.[4]

His own old age was anything but Wordsworthian. His energy remained, and in October he went to America on a last lecture tour which lasted several months. This was undertaken partially to earn money for some alterations to Riversdale, to make a playhouse in the yard for the children, and partially to raise funds for the newly launched Irish Academy of Letters. The tour was extremely successful. Yeats was always on time, sometimes lectured twice a day, and had reached a dignity and charm of manner which enhanced his now greater mental clarity and stronger powers of expression.

Coole had been a place of retreat from politics but once he was back in Dublin in 1933 he busied himself with Irish politics once more. His letters to Mrs Shakespear indicate the zest with which he re-entered upon an old interest. He thought he had to defend the new Academy of Letters from Catholic Action, while at the same time disliking Communism:

At the moment I am trying, in association with an ex-cabinet minister, an eminent lawyer and a philosopher, to work out a Social theory against Communism . . . what looks like emerging is fascism [sic] modified by religion. This country is exciting. I'm told Dev [De Valera] has said in private that in three years he will be torn in pieces. It reminds me of a saying of Kevin O'Higgins to his wife 'Nobody can expect to live who has done what I have'. No sooner does a politician get into power than he begins to seek unpopularity. It is the cult of sacrifice planted in the nation by the executions in 1916. Read O'Flaherty's novel *The Martyr*—a book forbidden by our censor and very mad at the end. Powerful and curious as an attack on the cult. I asked a high government officer if he could describe the head of the I.R.A. He began 'This is so-and-so who has a cult of suffering and is always putting himself in positions where he will be persecuted'.[5]

Although busy with various literary tasks he was always ready for some new experience and he wrote to Mrs Shakespear after meeting O'Duffy:

The papers . . . Blueshirts . . . Blueshirts . . . all for Independent Ireland within Commonwealth . . . it will certainly bring into discussion all the things I care for. Three months ago there seemed no trace of such a movement—and when it did come into existence it had little importance until that romantic dreamer I have described to you pitched on General O'Duffy for a leader. About him the newspapers have probably told you enough— He seemed to me a plastic man but I could not judge whether he could prove plastic to the opinion of others and obvious political currents or his own will ('Unity of Being'). The plastic man to his own will is always powerful. The opposite kind of man is like a mechanical toy. Lift him from the floor and he can but buzz. I have corrected the proofs of my new book *The Winding Stair* (not the little book published in America but all since I have written *The Tower*) 'Crazy Jane' poems (the origin of some of them you know) and the little group of love poems that follow are, I think, exciting or strange. Sexual abstinence fed their fire—I was ill and yet full of desire. They sometimes come out of the greatest mental excitement I am capable of. Now for a year I have written some twenty or thirty lines in all—result of recovered health, this crowded Dublin life which always incites me to prose and the turn given to my mind by lecture tour. When my essay for the Swami is finished I think of interpolating a little dance play in verse between this essay and my book about Lady Gregory. It does not matter whether I do or not, our life is a whole and my account of Coole will add to the solidity of what I have already written.[6]

At the time Yeats thought that the upper classes cared for nothing in Ireland but sport, while the rest of the inhabitants were steeped in political and religious fanaticism. His own hatred of the mob is described in a memory of Frank O'Connor, who met the poet coming home from the house of a friend. Yeats looked at the footpath, spread out his hand and exclaimed 'A wonderful phrase—he spoke of the lower classes, "their backs aching for the lash"'.[7] He considered that unity must be sought unless the State were to move from violence to violence or from violence to apathy. The mob seemed in command; and things would become worse. Parliament would disgrace and debauch all who entered it, and men of letters live like outlaws in their own country. The Government could only break the reign of the mob by seeking unity of culture. If any government or party undertook the work it would need force and must promise a disciplined way of life:

> When the nations are empty up there at the top
> When order has weakened or faction is strong
> Time for us all to pick out a good tune
> Take to the roads and go marching along.[8]

It seemed as if the Blueshirt Party might share or be persuaded to share Yeats's aims, and he wrote some marching songs for them,[8a] which, however, once he discovered that the new party had the usual elements of farce and tragedy about it,[9] were rewritten so that no political party could sing them. The question of Yeats's fascism has been raised by several critics;[10] but the essentially Irish trait of using a theory for a plaything must not be forgotten, especially in Yeats's case. It was an attitude to life which appeared when Edmund Gosse invited him to a dinner party some time before the first world war and whispered to him to avoid politics. He was then introduced to Lord Cromer who began to discuss that after-noon's debate in the House of Lords. Yeats, obeying his host's instructions, replied that he looked on English politics as a child does at a racecourse, taking sides by the colour of the jockey's coats, and often changing sides in the middle of a race, a remark that cooled the conversation.[11] His interest in fascism was no more to be blamed[11a] than the admiration afforded by countless English visitors to the public works achieved by Mussolini; he was interested in an aristocratic way of life and was always on the alert to resist any possible encroachment of government upon freedom of thought or action. One of the choruses to his 'Three Songs to the Same Tune':

> 'Drown all the dogs' said the fierce young woman,
> 'They killed my goose and a cat.'
> 'Drown, drown in the water-butt,
> Drown all the dogs,' said the fierce young woman[12]

was founded on an incident which happened at Riversdale, and a letter describing this to Mrs Shakespear not only reveals Yeats's skill in telling an anecdote but illustrates his own atti-tude to fascism:

Here is our most recent event. . . . Blueshirts are upholders of law, incarnations of public spirit, rioters in the cause of peace and George hates Blueshirts. She was delighted when she caught their [local Blueshirt family] collie-dog in our hen-house and missed a white hen. I was going into town and she said 'I will write and complain; if they do nothing I will go to the police'. When I returned in the evening she was plunged in gloom. Her letter sent by the gardener had been replied to at once in these words 'Sorry, have done away with collie-dog'—note the Hitler touch—a little later came the gardener and in his presence . . . [four dogs had been drowned]. . . . A fifth had revived when taken out of the water, and (as it was not their dog) but a stray —— had hunted it down the road with a tin can tied to its tail. There was a sixth dog, —— said, but as it had been with her for some time she would take time to think whether to send it to the dogs' home or drown it. I tried to console George . . . after all she was only responsible for the death of the collie and so on—but there was some-thing wrong and at last it came out. The white hen had returned. Was she to write and say so? I said 'You feel a multimurderess and if you write —— will too.' 'But she will see the hen.' 'Put it in the pot.' 'But it's my best layer.' However I insisted and the white hen went into the pot.[13]

This ironic attitude to the Blueshirts reveals the true Yeats, detached and merely playing with his thoughts, except for the intervals when he wanted to achieve complete directness and accuracy. These were not frequent in print; but he called Ezra Pound what Lewis termed a 'revolutionary Simpleton'[14] and wrote in a letter in 1933 that de Valera could be compared to Mussolini or Hitler—'all three have exactly the same aim as

far as I can judge. . . . The trouble is yet to come I suppose.'¹⁵
In 'A Prayer for Old Age' he asks God to keep him from thinking in the mind alone, from all that makes a wise old man
praised by everyone:

> I pray—for fashion's word is out
> And prayer comes round again—
> That I may seem, though I die old,
> A foolish passionate man.¹⁶

He did not want to be taken seriously, yet to be dubbed
'irresponsible' would not have pleased him. He expected his
hearers to discriminate between his varying moods. In a letter
to Dorothy Wellesley he recorded his shock at being understood
to hate England because of a political poem on which he
lavished some passion with an Irish sense of the past often
incomprehensible to his English friends.¹⁶ᵃ His was the old age
of Landor, rather than of Wordsworth, a possible mask he had
considered in middle age:

> Could he, if he would, knowing how frail his vigour from youth up, copy
> Landor who lived loving and hating, ridiculous and conquered, into
> extreme old age, all lost but the favour of his muses?
> The mother of the muses we are taught
> Is memory; she has left me; they remain
> And shake my shoulder urging me to sing.¹⁷

In August Yeats wrote to Mrs Shakespear that he had
written some twenty or thirty lines of verse in all in the last
year and said that this was a result of recovered health, a
significant remark when we consider the semi-feverish states in
which many of his poems were written, states of excitement
which prompted Lady Gerald Wellesley to point out that he
had many of the symptoms of tuberculosis, the rises and falls
of vitality and intense cerebral and often bodily excitement.¹⁸
But besides his state of recovered health there was the crowded
Dublin life which always incited him to prose and the thoughts
that had come to him on his American tour. His reading and
his other activities in 1933 are revealed in some of his letters to
Mrs Shakespear:

> . . . Have you read *Louis Lambert* in recent years? I have just reread it
> and think of making 'Michael Robartes' write an annotation or even of
> doing it myself. Perhaps *Faust, Louis Lambert, Seraphita* and *Axel* are our
> sacred books—man self sufficing and eternal though *Axel* is but a spectacle,
> an echo of the others. As *Louis Lambert* might have been an echo of that
> saying of Swendenborg's that the sexual intercourse of angels is a conflagra-
> tion of the whole being. . . . I have of late I think come to some coherent
> grasp of reality and whether that will make me write or cease to write I

do not know. I have learned a good deal from the Swami who suddenly makes all wisdom if you ask him the right question. . . .

. . . My two sensations at the moment are Hulme's *Speculations* and *Lady Chatterley's Lover*. . . . Get somebody to lend you the last if you've not read it. Frank Harris's Memoirs were vulgar and immoral—the sexual patches were like holes burned with a match in a piece of old newspaper. Their appeal to physical sensation was hateful but Lady Chatterley is noble. The description of the sexual act is more detailed than in Harris, the language is sometimes that of a cabman and yet the book is all fire. Those two lovers the gamekeeper and his employer's wife each separated from their class by their love and by fate are poignant in their loneliness; the coarse language of the one accepted by both becomes a forlorn poetry, uniting their solitudes, something ancient humble and terrible. . . .[19]

. . . Of course Lawrence is an emphasis directed against modern abstraction. I find the whole book interesting and not merely the sexual parts— they are something that he sets up as against the abstraction of an age that he thinks dead from the waist downward. Of course happiness is not where he seems to place it. We are happy when for everything inside us there is an equivalent something outside. I think it was Goethe said this— One should add the converse. It is terrible to desire and not possess, and terrible to possess and not desire. Because of these we long for an age which has that unity which Plato defined somewhere as sorrowing and rejoicing over the same things. How else escape the Bank Holiday crowd. I have bought a new suit of rough blue serge. . . . P.S. Read *Twenty Years Agrowing* —or some of it. I once told you that you would be happy if you had twelve children and lived on limpets. There are limpets on the Great Blaskets. . . .[20]

. . . Joyce and D. H. Lawrence have however almost restored to us the Eastern simplicity. Neither perfectly, for D. H. Lawrence romanticises his material with such words as 'essential fire' 'darkness' etc. and Joyce never escapes from his Catholic sense of sin. Rabelais seemed to escape from it by his vast energy—Yet why not take Swedenborg literally and think we attain in a partial contact what the spirits know by their being. He somewhere describes two spirits meeting and . . . they become a single conflagration. His vision may be true . . . Europe belongs to Dante and the Witches' sabbath not to Newton. . . .[21]

. . . Thank you for your praise of my book—the next book you will get from me will be my *Collected Poems* (all my lyrics in one volume) in the middle of November. I think I have finished with self-expression and if I write more verse it will be impersonal going back to my early self. I have a longing for remote beauty. I have been reading Morris' *Sigurd* to Anne and last night when I came to the description of the birth of Sigurd and that wonderful first nursing of the child I could hardly read for my tears. Then when Anne had gone to bed I tried to read it to George and it was just the same.[22]

. . . I am writing a dance play and I have just finished the verses for the opening of the curtain—here they are. The chiming bell is part of the play.

FIRST MUSICIAN (*singing*):

> I wait until the tower gives forth the chime;
> And dream of ghosts that have the speech of birds;
> Because they have no thought they have no words;
> No thought because no past or future; Time
> Comes from the torture of our flesh; and these
> Cast out by death and tethered there by love,
> Touch nerve to nerve throughout the sacred grove
> And (?) seem a single creature when they please.

SECOND MUSICIAN (*singing*):
> I call to mind the iron the bell
> And get from that my harsher imagery,
> All love is shackled to mortality;
> Love's image is a man-at-arms in steel;
> Love's image is a woman made of stone;
> It dreams of the unborn; all else is nought;
> Tomorrow and tomorrow fills its thought
> All tenderness reserves for that alone. [23]

The inner ideas in these lines are taken up later. One might say the love of the beloved seeks eternity, that of the child seeks time. Did I tell you that my apparitions [24] came a seventh time—as I awoke I saw a child's hand and arm and head—faintly self-luminous—holding above—I was lying on my back—a five of diamonds or of hearts I am not sure which. It was held as if the child was standing at the head of the bed. Is the meaning some fortuneteller's meaning attached to the card or does it promise me five months or five years? Five years would be about enough to finish my autobiography and bring out *A Vision*. [25]

My dear Olivia: I have come out of my reveries to write to you. I do nothing all day long but think of the drama I am building up in *Lady Gregory*. I have described Martyn and his house and Lady Gregory and here—have brought George Moore upon the scene [and] finished a long analysis of him which pictures for the first time that preposterous person. The first chapters are sensational and exciting and will bring George much money. I am just beginning on Woburn Buildings—alas the most significant image of those years must be left out . . . the past part will be probably made of extracts from letters of Lady Gregory and my comments. My first fifty pages probably to be published before the rest will bring me to 1900. They begin where my old autobiography ends. It is curious how one's life falls into definite sections. In 1897 a new scene was set, new actors appeared. [26]

Early in 1934 Yeats underwent the Steinach glandular operation, which had been described to him by a friend. The result was a fresh vitality and energy, though the effect of the operation upon his verse-writing can be overrated. He received a new self-confidence, his interest in sex was stimulated; and it continued to obsess him in varying degrees to the end of his life. For instance, he began to write, in the summer of 1934, a series of metaphysical poems, reminiscent of Donne's mixture of sacred and profane imagery, with the same delight in obscurity of thought [27] and arresting phrase:

> As man, as beast, as an ephemeral fly begets, Godhead begets Godhead,
> For things below are copies, the Great Smaragdine Tablet said. [28]

These poems might be thought to have been written as a result of the operation, especially when we read a letter to Mrs Shakespear written in July:

I have another poem in my head where a monk read his breviary at midnight on the tomb of long dead lovers on the anniversary of their death for on that night they are united above the tomb, their embrace being not partial but a conflagration of the entire body and so shedding the light he reads by. Strange that I should write these things in my old age when if I were to offer myself for new love I could only expect to be accepted by the very young wearied by the passive embrace of the bolster. That is why when I saw you last I named myself an uncle[29]

but for the fact that the germ of the poem's description of the lovers comes from his obsession with Swedenborg's description of the intercourse of angels which was included in the 1933 letters written to Mrs Shakespear before he had even thought or heard of the operation:

> The miracle that gave them such a death
> Transfigured to pure substance what had once
> Been bone and sinew; when such bodies join
> There is no touching here, nor touching there,
> Nor straining joy, but whole is joined to whole;
> For the intercourse of angels is a light
> Where for its moment both seem lost, consumed.[30]

There followed a period of intense activity in which he wrote 'Supernatural Songs'. These have directness, strength, and intellectual clarity, for the poet was sure of what he wanted to say, and the symbolism is clear in his own mind, even if the poems themselves appear mysterious at first reading. Once his aim is understood they stand as masterpieces of concise condensation. The meaning of 'The Four Ages of Man' must be discovered in letters to Mrs Shakespear:

. . . Note this symbolism.

Waters under the earth ⎫
The earth ⎬ the bowels etc.

The waters.              the blood and the sex organ. *Passion*.
The air.                 the lungs, logical thought, thought.
The fire.                spirit and soul. *Soul.    Thought*.

They are my four quarters—the Earth before 8, the Waters before 15, the Air before 22, the Fire before 1. (See *A Vision*, p. 86.) Note that on p. 85 of *A Vision* the conflict on which we now enter is 'against the soul', as in the quarter we have just left it was 'against the intellect'. The conflict is to restore the body.

The Earth = Every early Nature-dominated civilisation.
The Water = An armed sexual life, chivalry, Froissart's chronicles.
The Air   = From the Renaissance to the end of the 19th century.
The Fire  = The purging away of our civilisation by our hatred.[31]

. . . Yesterday I put into rhyme what I wrote in my last letter.

*The Four Ages*

> He with body waged a fight;
> Body won and walks upright.

> Then he struggled with the heart;
> Innocence and peace depart.
>
> Then he struggled with the mind;
> His proud heart he left behind.
>
> Now his wars with God begin;
> At stroke of midnight God shall win.

In the same way the meaning of 'Conjunctions' must be sought from his correspondence, when an apparently meaningless poem becomes clear:

They are the four ages of individual man; they are also the four ages of civilisation. You will find them in that book you have been reading— First Age; Earth, vegetable functions. Second Age; water, blood, sex. Third age; air, breath, intellect. Fourth Age; fire, soul etc. In the first two moon comes to the full—resurrection of Christ and Dionysos. Man becomes rational, no longer driven by below or above.[32]

I want to give you more rhymes—I was told that you may remember that my two children would be Mars conjunctive Venus; Saturn conjunctive Jupiter respectively and so they were. Anne the Mars Venus personality. Then I was [told] they would develop so that I could study in them the alternating dispositions Christian or Objective, then the Antithetical or subjective. The Christian is the Mars Venus, it is democratic. The Jupiter Saturn civilisation is born from among the most cultivated, out of tradition, out of rule.

> Should Jupiter and Saturn meet
> What a crop of mummy wheat
> The sword's a cross; thereon He died
> On breast of Mars the goddess sighed.

I wrote these lines because some days ago George said 'It is very strange but whereas Michael is always thinking about life Anne always thinks of death. Then I remembered the children were the two dispensations. Anne collects skeletons; she buries little birds and beasts and digs them up when worms and insects have eaten their flesh. She has a shelf of very white little skeletons. She had asked leave to go to the Zoological Museum to draw skeletons. Then she loves tragedies—has read all Shakespeare's and a couple of weeks ago was searching reference books to learn all about the poison that killed Hamlet's father. When she grows up she will either have some passionate love affair or else have some close friend that has—the old association of love and death.' I have written a lot of poetry of a passionate metaphysical sort—here is one on the soul, the last written.

> As the moon sidles up,
> She has sidled up,
> As trips the crazed moon
> Away must she trip.
> 'His light had struck me blind
> Dared I stop.'
> As sings the moon she sings
> 'I am I am I
> The greater grows my height
> The further that I fly
> All creation shivers
> With that sweet cry.

It is of course my central myth. When George spoke of Michael's pre-occupation with life or Anne's with death, she may have subconsciously remembered that her speech on a spoke of the centric movement and phase one as the kiss of life and the centric movements, and phase 15 (full moon) as the kiss of death. . . .[33]

In June Yeats went to Rapallo to collect furniture from the flat there. On this visit he showed the manuscript of *The King of the Great Clock Tower* to Ezra Pound and asked his opinion on it; the comment made was 'Putrid'. The play was produced in Dublin and turned out the most popular of Yeats's dance plays, with F. J. McCormick as the King, and Ninette de Valois, whose art Yeats valued highly, as the Queen:

> It has proved most effective; it was magnificently acted and danced. It is more original than I thought for when I looked up *Salome* I found that Wilde's dancer never danced with the head in her hands—her dance came before the decapitation of the Saint and is a mere uncovering of nakedness. My dance is a long expression of horror and fascination. She first bows before the head (it is on a seat) then in her dance lays it on the ground and dances before it then holds it in her hands.[34]

In the autumn Yeats was in Rome to deliver a lecture on the Irish theatre at a congress of the Alessandro Volta Foundation. The winter brought another collapse, from which he recovered sufficiently to work on the proofs of *Dramatis Personae,* his praise of Lady Gregory and attack on Martyn and Moore, and on the proofs of the final edition of *A Vision.* In June 1935 he celebrated his seventieth birthday, and was at work on the compilation of an anthology of modern verse for the Oxford Press. He wrote to Mrs Shakespear in November that he could not do any work unless he had a problem to solve:

> A Poet should live with sight and sound and that makes modern life a snare he has somehow to endure. My problem this time will be . . . How far do I like the Ezra Auden school and if I do not, why not? Then this further problem why do the younger generation like it so much? I am to write a long introduction, writing in the Arabian Nights manner. We must keep propaganda out of our own blood because three important persons know nothing of it—a man modelling a statue, a man playing a flute, and a man in a woman's arms.[35]

The winter of 1935-6 was spent at Majorca in the company of Shri Purohit Swami, with whom he was collaborating in a translation of the Upanishads, which meant correcting the Swami's over-ornate English, much to Mrs Yeats's disgust, for she grudged the waste of time that could have been given to poetry. Yeats had a great enthusiasm for the Swami. In 1934 he had written to Mrs Shakespear of his work:

I have just sent back final proofs of *The Holy Mountain* and have just read it all through. It seems to me one of those rare books that are fundamental. For generations writers will refer to it as they will to *An Indian Monk*. The Swami will fulfil the prophecy of his astrologer 'Preach to the whole world' though not as did — — whose eloquence bores me. Of course 'All the world' is a vague phrase like 'the world and his wife'. Two such books will shift for those who move others the foundation of their thought but it will take years. I cannot write—I have so much queer information. [35a]

In another letter he wrote that he had learned a good deal from the Swami, 'who suddenly makes all wisdom if you ask him the right question'. [35b] By January 1936, Yeats had become seriously ill again and wrote to Lady Gerald Wellesley:

I have had an unexpected attack, breathing became difficult and painful. I sent for a very able Spanish doctor, who stopped all writing and cured me by more or less drastic treatment. He says that the enlargement of my heart is very slight but that my heart misses a beat and that this has come about through the overwork of years and should not be incurable. . . . The Swami is a constant instruction and delight. He puts sugger [*sic*] in his soup, in his salad, in his vegetables, and then unexpectedly puts salt on stewed pares [*sic*]. Sometimes he picks salt, sugger and pepper merely I think because his eyes light on them. He says 'I like all six flavours but prefer sugger.' Our translation of the *Upanishads* is going to be the classic translation. . . . [35c]

Mrs Yeats travelled to Majorca to see that he was properly looked after. She wrote to Lady Gerald Wellesley in February:

Willy is better I think, but is going to be a long business. He has kidney trouble (Nephritis) and his heart is not good, also his lungs do not expand as they should although there is no congestion. Today his breathing is very much easier. He had two bad days of gasping this last week. [35d]

She took him in April to a bungalow overlooking the Mediterranean when he recovered sufficiently to resume work. From there he had unexpectedly to go to Barcelona to look after Margot Ruddock who had arrived at Majorca to find out whether her verse was any good:

I had known her for some years and had told her to stop writing as her technique was getting worse. I was amazed by the tragic magnificence and said so. She went out in pouring rain, thought, as she said afterwards, that if she killed herself her verse would live instead of her, went to the shore to jump in, then thought she loved life and began to dance. She went to the lodging house where Shri Purohit Swami was, to sleep. She was wet through so Swami gave her some of his clothes, she had no money, he gave her some. Next day she went to Barcelona and there went mad, climbing out of a window, falling through a broken roof, breaking a knee cap, hiding in a ship's hold, singing her own poems most of the time. [36]

He went to Barcelona with his wife and they found Miss Ruddock with recovered sanity giving an account of her madness at a clinic:

> That crazed girl improvising her music,
> Her poetry, dancing upon the shore,
> Her soul in division from itself
> Climbing, falling she knew not where,
> Hiding amid the cargo of a steamship,
> Her knee-cap broken, that girl I declare
> A beautiful lofty thing, or a thing
> Heroically lost, heroically found.[37]

He was back in Dublin in June, and began writing the series of poems which appear in *Last Poems* and *Letters on Poetry to Dorothy Wellesley* on the subject of the Lady, the chambermaid and the lover. He had made the acquaintance of Lady Gerald Wellesley the previous year and the friendship ripened quickly, its fruit being the collection of letters published by Lady Gerald, which give glimpses of the strange qualities of Yeats's mind, and his mental activity. In conversation she wrote:

> Sex, philosophy and the occult preoccupy him. He strangely intermingles the three. The old masters, the dead accepted poets about which I much desire his opinion, appear to weary him. He seems to have passed through all these, and out beyond.[38]

But the letters cast a useful light on his opinions on poetry as, for instance, his praise of Archibald MacLeish's[39] article in *The Yale Review* which commended his work because its language was 'public'.

He had come to a fresh simplicity. The extraordinary nature of his poetic vitality came from his ability to remodel his personality, perhaps even on a model which he had used before, but never quite in the same way:

> Grant me an old man's frenzy,
> Myself must I remake
> Till I am Timon and Lear
> Or that William Blake
> Who beat upon the wall
> Till Truth obeyed his call.[40]

He became interested in the ballad form yet again, and the opportunity presented itself for a vigorous use of it. Though officially an invalid he saw whom he wanted, and one of his visitors was Henry Harrison, a devotee of Parnell, who asked Yeats to write something in praise of Parnell. The excitement of this visit caused a relapse, but out of it came the rollicking ballad 'Come gather round me, Parnellites' with its keynote of pride:

> Every man that sings a song
> Keeps Parnell in his mind.
> For Parnell was a proud man,

> No prouder trod the ground,
> And a proud man's a lovely man
> So pass the bottle round.[41]

He had reverted to an outspoken dislike of 'the English' for which Lady Gerald Wellesley reproved him.[41a] Then he read Dr Maloney's *The Forged Casement Diaries*, and burst into angry bitterness with 'Roger Casement' and 'The Ghost of Roger Casement', with its attack on 'John Bull' made the more savage by its adaptation of Gray's 'Elegy'[42] for its last verse:

> I poked about a village church
> And found his family tomb
> And copied out what I could read
> In that religious gloom;
> Found many a famous man there;
> But fame and virtue rot.[43]

'The O'Rahilly' was another political ballad dealing with the 1916 rebellion in a tone vastly different to the sorrow of the poetry written contemporaneously. There were ballads on other than political subjects. Love was, of course, another theme. 'The Wild Old Wicked Man' had a certain auto-biographical flavour, being written to a friend of his:

> Who can know the year, my dear,
> When an old man's blood grows cold?
> I have what no young man can have
> Because he loves too much.
> Words I have that can pierce the heart,
> But what can he do but touch.
> *Daybreak and a candle-end.*[44]

but 'Colonel Martin'[44a] was founded on a Ballina legend. His emphasis on sensuality has a direct violence:

> We'd drink a can or two
> And out and lay our leadership
> On country and on town,
> Throw likely couples into bed
> And knock the others down.[44b]

There was no restriction on the expression of his feelings. If anything interested him then he wrote about it. King Edward's abdication provoked 'Model for the Laureate' while his rage against the intelligentsia produced 'The Curse of Cromwell', whom he regarded as 'the Lenin of his day'.[45] In this poem his refrain, unlike some of the simpler refrains in such poems as 'The O'Rahilly' with its '*How goes the weather?*', does add to the emotional atmosphere he wished to create.[45a] He spoke through the mouth of some wandering peasant poet in Ireland, and the refrain has a haunting air to it:

> *O what of that, o what of that,*
> *What is there left to say?*[46]

His spleen was excited by statesmen, journalists, and, especially, actors lacking music, and produced a tirade on the subject in 'The Old Stone Cross'.

'The Curse of Cromwell' contained an idea that possessed Yeats at many times, the cycle of change:

> All neighbourly content and easy talk are gone,
> But there's no good complaining, for money's rant is on.
> He that's mounting up must on his neighbour mount,
> And we and all the Muses are things of no account.

This idea, based on *A Vision*, was given frequent and often grim expression, in political guise in 'The Great Day':

> Hurrah for revolution and more cannon-shot!
> A beggar on horseback lashes a beggar on foot.
> Hurrah for revolution and cannon come again!
> The beggars have changed places, but the lash goes on.[47]

with 'the heroic cry in the midst of despair' in 'Lapis Lazuli':

> On their feet they came, or on shipboard,
> Camel-back, horse-back, ass-back, mule-back,
> Old civilisations put to the sword.
> Then they and their handiwork went to rack . . .
> All things fall and are built again,
> And those that build them again are gay.[48]

The most effective expression of this thought came in 'The Gyres'[49] where a terrifying atmosphere is produced by the acceptance of this inevitable change. There is an intensity of passionate feeling in the cry with which the poem opens, apostrophising the gyres, and calling to 'Old Rocky Face' to look forth. Old Rocky Face is Shelley's Jew[50] who lived in a cavern amid the Demonesi:

> Some feign that he is Enoch: others dream
> He was pre-Adamite, and has survived
> Cycles of generation and of ruin.
> The sage, in truth, by dreadful abstinence
> And conquering penance of the mutinous flesh,
> Deep contemplation and unwearied study,
> In years outstretched beyond the date of man,
> May have attained to sovereignty and science
> Over those strong and secret things and thoughts
> Which others fear and know not.

and he has seen the cycles of generation and ruin which the poem contemplates in tragic joy:

> What matter though numb nightmare ride on top,
> And blood and mire the sensitive body stain?

> What matter? Heave no sigh, let no tear drop,
> A greater, a more gracious time has gone;
> For painted forms or boxes of make-up
> In ancient tombs I sighed, but not again;
> What matter? Out of cavern comes a voice,
> And all it knows is that one word 'Rejoice'!

There is an inhuman remoteness from ordinary life in the poem
with its insistence achieved by a repetition of key words:
'The gyres', 'The gyres!', 'For beauty dies of beauty, worth
of worth', 'What matter' (repeated four times) and the
culminating

> Conduct and work grow coarse, and coarse the soul,
> What matter?

The underlying joyous emotion of the poem was one which
Yeats often experienced when he let himself think of the idea
of continuity of life. He described it in the introduction to
*A Vision*, and this setting makes it the easier to comprehend
'The Gyres':

> Yesterday when I saw the dry and leafless vineyards at the very edge of
> the motionless sea, or lifting their brown stems, from almost inaccessible
> patches of earth high up on the cliff side or met at the turn of the path the
> orange and lemon trees in full fruit, or the crimson cactus flower, or felt
> the warm sunlight falling between blue and blue, I murmured, as I have
> countless times 'I have been part of it always and there is may be no escape,
> forgetting and returning life after life like an insect in the grass'. But
> murmured it without terror,[51] in exultation almost.[52]

In the summer of 1936 Yeats planned a visit to England.
The appearance of the controversial and commercially successful[52a] *Oxford Book of Modern Poetry* was followed by a broadcast
talk on modern poetry from London in October. He became
interested in the technique of speaking verse on the radio and
arranged to collaborate in programmes of modern poetry.
They incorporated his ideas on the accompaniment of verse-
speaking: drums between verses or hand-clapping, perhaps a
whistle or a concertina; no background of music while the
poetry is spoken; and unaccompanied singing of refrains, in
which Margot Ruddock excelled. His second programme, 'The
Poets' Pub', was on 22 April 1937, with music arranged by
W. J. Turner, his third, 'My own Poetry', with music arranged
by his friend Edmund Dulac, took place in July, while another
with the same title followed in September. After this he realised
that his health would not permit him to take part in any more
of the programmes, and when the 'Poets' Pub' was to be produced again he wrote to the B.B.C. producers that his broadcasting was finished.

During the summer of 1937 he stayed at the Athenaeum
instead of the Savile Club. He had been elected a member of
the Athenaeum earlier but had refused, finding the entrance
fee too high. When the entrance fee was later abolished he was
re-elected on Sir William Rothenstein's suggestion, and grati-
fied 'a childish desire to walk up those steps and under that
classical façade'.[53]   In June and July he also visited Lady
Gerald Wellesley at Penns-in-the-Rocks and there discussed the
association of poetry and music with Hilda Matheson and
W. J. Turner.

A testimonial committee of fifty members was formed in
America in 1937 and this established a fund which would
guarantee Yeats a sufficient income for the rest of his life. He
decided that he would use the money for spending his winters
in warmer climates. He made the matter public at a banquet of
the Irish Academy of Letters in August, and published *A Speech
and Two Poems* as a gift for the members of the Committee.
One of these poems was 'The Municipal Gallery Revisited',
which is one of the best examples of Yeats's final blending of
simplicity and grandeur. He could elevate his friends to
Olympian heights, and remain direct and clear. In his rare
poetic moods of unity he could achieve the strength of greatness:

> Heart-smitten with emotion I sink down,
> My heart recovering with covered eyes;
> Wherever I had looked I had looked upon
> My permanent or impermanent images:
> Augusta Gregory's son; her sister's son,
> Hugh Lane, 'onlie begetter' of all these;
> Hazel Lavery living and dying, that tale
> As though some ballad-singer had sung it all.
>
> Mancini's portrait of Augusta Gregory,
> 'Greatest since Rembrandt', according to John Synge;
> A great ebullient portrait certainly;
> But where is the brush that could show anything
> Of all that pride and that humility?
> And I am in despair that time may bring
> Approved patterns of women or of men
> But not that selfsame excellence again.
>
> . . . And here's John Synge himself, that rooted man,
> 'Forgetting human words', a grave deep face.
> You that would judge me, do not judge alone
> This book or that, come to this hallowed place
> Where my friends' portraits hang and look thereon;
> Ireland's history in their lineaments trace;
> Think where man's glory most begins and ends,
> And say my glory was I had such friends.[54]

He wrote 'Beautiful Lofty Things'[55] in the same spirit.  It
does not matter that the lines:

> My father upon the Abbey stage, before him a raging crowd:
> 'This Land of Saints', and then as the applause died out,
> 'Of plaster Saints', his beautiful mischievous head thrown back

do not resemble his father's remembrance of the incident:

> Here is what I said.  I began with some information about Synge which
> interested my listeners and then 'Of course I know Ireland is an island of
> Saints, but thank God it is also an island of Sinners—only unfortunately in
> this country people cannot live or die except behind a curtain of deceit'.
> At this point the chairman and my son both called out 'Time's up, Time's
> up'.  I saw the lifted sign and like the devil in *Paradise Lost* I fled.[56]

No matter also that Lady Gregory was not near eighty when
her life was threatened, but seventy.[57]  The attitude of mind is
accurately recorded, and the significance of these friends[57a] in
the poet's life stated simply:

> Maud Gonne at Howth station waiting a train,
> Pallas Athene in that straight back and arrogant head:
> All the Olympians, a thing never known again.

In the autumn Macmillan published the revised edition of
*A Vision*, and the Cuala Press *Essays 1931–1936*, while *The
Herne's Egg* appeared in January 1938.  An introduction to the
Swami's translation of the *Aphorisms* of Patanjali was written
and there was much activity on the subject of the Cuala Press
Broadsides, before Yeats and his wife left to spend the winter
at Mentone, on the Riviera, where they stayed until March.
Here he revised the proof sheets of *New Poems* (mainly those
included in the posthumous *Last Poems and Plays*) and began
to write part of *On the Boiler*:

> A *Fors Clavigera* of sorts—my advice to the youthful mind on all manner of
> things and poems.  After going into accounts I find that I can make *Cuala*
> prosperous if I write this periodical and publish it bi-annually.  It will be
> an amusing thing to do—I shall curse my enemies and bless my friends.  My
> enemies will hit back and that will give me the joy of answering them.[58]

In this 'big essay' he thought he would sketch out the fundamental principles, as he saw them, on which literature and
politics should be based:

> I need a new stimulus now that my life is a daily struggle with fatigue.
> I thought my problem was to face death with gaiety, now I have learnt it
> is to face life.[59]

The completion of *On the Boiler* was delayed.  It was mainly
concerned with Ireland: its lack of proper education, and its

need for able men with public minds upon whom the country's system should be moulded. In addition, eugenics, politics, history, the Abbey Theatre, Cuala embroidery, all received his pungent comment.

He returned from Mentone in March 1938 and spent some time at Penns-in-the-Rocks, then at Steyning, at the home of Edith Shackleton Heald, to whom he had earlier been introduced by Dulac, and then at Penns again in April. He returned to Ireland, again full of mental energy:

> In the last fortnight I have come to understand the reason why people think certain things, with the result that I have new poems that I long to write. I have grown abundant and determined in my old [age] as I never was in youth.[60]

He was still as concerned as ever over what people thought of him; it was an essential part of his character and perhaps an essentially Irish trait. In 1930 he had written in his Diary:

> I have talked most of a long motor journey, talked even when I was hoarse. Why? Surely because I was timid, because I felt the other man was judging me, because I endowed his silence with all kinds of formidable qualities. Being on trial I must cajole my judge.[60a]

Now, in July 1938, he sent a note back to Lady Gerald Wellesley by the chauffeur who had driven him to Steyning:

> I have borrowed the money and tipped him, I could not endure the thought of his meditating on my meanness all that long journey back. I would not have minded if it was half that distance.[60b]

In the summer Maud Gonne came to visit him at Riversdale, and to her immense surprise and pleasure he said, as she was leaving, 'Maud, we should have gone on with our Castle of the Heroes'. He wanted Sir William Rothenstein to portray her statuesque old age:

> I wish you would find some way of making a drawing of Maud Gonne. No artist has ever drawn her, and just now she looks magnificent. I cannot imagine anything but an air raid that could bring her to London. She might come to see the spectacle.[61]

A head of 'his phoenix' by Lawrence Campbell in the Dublin Municipal Gallery inspired that fine poem 'A Bronze Head'[62] which left the subject of her human and superhuman qualities and yet again (in an unpublished verse) faced death triumphantly:

> But even at the starting post, all sleek and new,
> I saw the wildness in her and I thought
> A vision of terror that it must live through

Had shattered her soul.  Propinquity had brought
Imagination to that pitch where it casts out
All that is not itself: I had grown wild
And wandered murmuring everywhere, 'My child, my child!'

Or else I thought her supernatural;
As though a sterner eye looked through her eye
On this foul world in its decline and fall;
On gangling stocks grown great, great stocks run dry,
Ancestral pearls all pitched into a sty,
Heroic reverie mocked by clown and knave,
And wondered what was left for massacre to save.

O Hour of triumph, come and make me gay.
If burnished chariots are put to flight
Why brood on old triumph; prepare to die.
Even at the approach of the un-imaged night
Man has the refuge of his gaiety.
A dab of black enhances every white.
Tension is but the rigour of the mind
Cannon the god and father of mankind.

His moods were judicial.  In 'Are You Content?' he called on
his ancestors to judge what he had done.  He could not, but
was not content.  The prospect of normal old age still horrified
him:

> Infirm and aged I might stay
> In some good company,
> I who have always hated work,
> Smiling at the sea,
> Or demonstrate in my own life
> What Robert Browning meant
> By an old hunter talking with Gods;
> But I am not content.[63]

These thoughts on old age are also to be found in 'An Acre
of Grass'[64] and 'What Then?'[65] but these poems differ in their
treatment of the theme.  In 'An Acre of Grass' the second
stanza implied that neither imagination nor the rags and bones
of old memory, so magnificently, so dramatically, so accurately
described in the rhetoric of 'The Circus Animals' Desertion',
can make truth known.  The third stanza shouts in reply that
frenzy can create truth.  Truth, as represented by the frenzy of
an old man, means a position with the great frenzied minds of
the past—'forgotten else by mankind'.  This thought was
suggested by Nietzsche to whom Yeats had returned at the end
of the nineteen-thirties; it is an echo of passages in *The Dawn
of Day*: which state that elderly people, through a love of
enjoyment, wish to enjoy the results of their thinking rather
than testing them:

This leads them to make their thoughts palatable and enjoyable and to take away their dryness, coldness and want of flavour; and thus it comes about that the old thinker apparently raises himself above his life's work, while in reality he spoils it by infusing into it a certain amount of fantasy, sweetness, flavour, poetic mists, and mystic lights. This is how Plato ended and . . .[66]

This passage probably inspired the refrain of 'What Then?':

*' What then?' sang Plato's ghost. ' What then?'*

which does not carry its thought as far as 'An Acre of Grass', remaining content with the description of his achievements and the realisation of his happier dreams. The ultimate question of 'What Then?' is an echo of Nietzsche's repeated questioning in *The Dawn of Day*, where he describes the argonauts of the intellect flying further into space, but eventually compelled to cease their flight and rest on a mast or narrow ledge; and asks who could conclude from this that there was no endless clear space before them. Other birds will fly further; but where, and why? And he asks if the fate of man is to be wrecked on the infinite, or——? The 'or' is recaptured in the final crescendo of the refrain in Yeats's poem:

*But louder sang that ghost ' What then?'*

August saw his last public appearance, at the Abbey for a performance of *Purgatory*. After this a holiday in Sussex, and he returned to Ireland where he wrote 'Under Ben Bulben', a long poem, containing all the magic with which he was himself spellbound. He swears by his images—Shelley's Witch of Atlas, an interest in the sages in Egypt of whom he had read in the early nineteen-twenties in one of George A. Birmingham's serious works,[67] the spirits seen by country folk near Ben Bulben, which symbolise the ideas on which his mind had fixed its concentration. Their meaning is that Man lives and dies between two eternities, of race and soul:

Though grave-diggers' toil is long,
Sharp their spades, their muscles strong,
They but thrust their buried men
Back in the human mind again.[68]

The fifth section of the poem is Yeats's admiration of the three classes of society that gave life vigour and strength: the aristocrat, the poet, and the peasant. His love of Ireland went with these. Did not his life centre in Ireland always? The night before he left Ireland for ever he chanted to his friend, the poet F. R. Higgins:

After midnight we parted on the drive from his house. The head of the
retiring figure, erect and challenging, gleamed through the darkness, as I
looked back; while on the road before me, my thoughts were still singing
with the slow powerful accents of his chanting:

> Irish poets, learn your trade,
> Sing whatever is well made,
> Scorn the sort now growing up
> All out of shape from toe to top,
> Their unremembering hearts and heads
> Base-born products of base beds.
> Sing the peasantry, and then
> Hard-riding country gentlemen,
> The holiness of monks, and after
> Porter-drinkers' randy laughter;
> Sing the lords and ladies gay
> That were beaten into the clay
> Through seven heroic centuries;
> Cast your mind on other days
> That we in coming days may be
> Still the indomitable Irishry.[69]

He set out for the Riviera for the winter. On the way he
stayed at Chantry House, where he made the prose draft of his
last play, *The Death of Cuchulain*, and then left for Cap Martin,
where he and Mrs Yeats stayed in the Hotel Idéal Séjour. At
Christmas Michael came for his holidays. There were many
friends in the neighbourhood; the Misses Heald, Dermod and
Mrs O'Brien, and Lady Gerald Wellesley, and these he saw
frequently. His health had greatly deteriorated. In his last
years he had disliked admitting illness, while acknowledging
its presence where the honesty of his verse demanded:

> Heart-smitten with emotion I sink down
> My heart recovering with covered eyes.[70]

Yet he had been preparing himself for death for some time.
More than a year before he had written in a letter that, once
he had put the Cuala Press in order that it could continue after
his death, he might fold his hands 'and be a wise old man and
gay'.[71] In July he had written a poem which must be read
aloud for its exquisite verbal music to be valued. In this poem,
'The Man and the Echo',[72] he sees himself without trappings,
sees the naked truth of what his life had been

MAN:
> And all seems evil until I
> Sleepless would lie down and die.

ECHO:
> Lie down and die.

MAN:
>      That were to shirk
> The spiritual intellect's great work,
> And shirk it in vain.  There's no release
> In a bodkin or disease,
> Nor can there be work so great
> As that which cleans man's dirty slate.
> While man can still his body keep
> Wine or love drug him to sleep,
> Waking he thanks the Lord that he
> Had body and its stupidity,
> But body gone he sleeps no more,
> And till his intellect grows sure
> That all's arranged in one clear view,.
> Pursues the thoughts that I pursue,
> Then stands in judgment on his soul,
> And, all work done, dismisses all
> Out of intellect and sight
> And sinks at last into the night.

ECHO:
> Into the night. . . .

In January Yeats was certain he had not much longer to live. After writing much verse he decided to rest two or three weeks so that he could use his overflowing energy to write his most fundamental thoughts and the arrangement of thought which would complete his studies:

> I am happy and I think full of an energy, of an energy I had despaired of.  It seems to me that I have found what I wanted.  When I try to put all into a phrase I say, 'Man can embody truth but he cannot know it'.  I must embody it in the completion of my life.[73]

He wrote 'The Black Tower', his last poem, on the subject of political propaganda:[74]

> Those banners come to bribe or threaten,
> Or whisper that a man's a fool
> Who, when his own right king's forgotten,
> Cares what king sets up his rule.
> If he died long ago
> Why do you dread us so?[75]

His condition worsened on Thursday, 26th January, but he recovered sufficiently to correct portions of 'Under Ben Bulben' and 'The Death of Cuchulain'.  On Friday he was in some pain and suffered from the breathlessness which had been affecting him intermittently for some time.  On Saturday, 28 January 1939, he died.

He was buried in the cemetery at Roquebrune, but his body has been brought back to Drumcliffe Churchyard in Sligo, where his ancestor had been rector.  He had wished to be buried there 'under bare Ben Bulben's head', and his epitaph, with its consistent emphasis on the unusual, the inhuman, was written for this place he loved:

> No marble, no conventional phrase;
> On limestone quarried near the spot
> By his command these words are cut:
>
> Cast a cold eye
> On life, on death.
> Horseman, pass by![76]

He had made himself a great poet.

# NOTES

1. Information from family papers in the possession of Miss Lily Yeats.
2. W. Harris, *The History and Antiquities of Dublin*, p. 93.
3. J. T. Gilbert, *A History of the City of Dublin*, vol. i, p. 346.
4. J. T. Gilbert, ibid., p. 350.
5. J. T. Gilbert, ibid., p. 354.
6. Miss Yeats obtained this information from the Genealogical Office, Dublin. It is impossible to decide which name is correct as the writing is blurred and blotted.
7. Number Fifteen.
8. Alexander Pope, Epilogue to the *Satires*, i, 70 (p. 341, Oxford edition).
9. J. T. Gilbert, *A History of the City of Dublin*, vol. iii, p. 350.
10. Subsequent information on the Butler connection is derived from family papers in the possession of Miss Lily Yeats.
11. Not much is known about the Huguenot connection. The scanty family information is that Claude Voisin married Catherine Ruaut (spelling uncertain) and emigrated to London, where his son Abraham Voisin, born in 1637, married Ann Heath (spelling again uncertain). Edmond Butler had married their daughter Mary Voisin in 1696. (She was a friend of Stella, and was buried in Donnybrook Church, Dublin. *Vide* W. B. Yeats, *Wheels and Butterflies*, p. 7, and *Pages from a Diary Written in 1930*, p. 6.)
12. Their host was Gideon Tabuteau, of 'Southampton', Tullamore.
13. W. B. Yeats, *Autobiographies*, p. 23.
14. Two copies of the *Almanack* which were bought on a second-hand bookstall by Miss Lily Yeats provided the information incorrectly used by the poet in his 'Prologue' to *Responsibilities, Collected Poems*, p. 113. There was a family tradition that Benjamin's business failed.
15. He received his early education at Samuel Whyte's school in Grafton Street, Dublin. The Duke of Wellington was another (almost contemporary) pupil of the minor poet.
16. G. D. Burtchaell and T. U. Sadleir, *Alumni Dublinenses*. Confirmed by family papers.
17. The office was held by this family for five generations. *Vide* obituary notice of William Taylor, *Dublin Evening Post*, 8 July 1817. Other information from Miss Lily Yeats.
18. Rev. T. F. O'Rorke, *History of Sligo: Town and Country*, vol. ii, p. 27.
19. There is some difficulty in determining the correct dates for William Butler Yeats's birth and the time that he spent at Dublin University. Burtchaell and Sadleir, *Alumni Dublinenses*, give the date of his birth as 1808, and his time at college as 1828–33 (B.A.). Hone, *W. B. Yeats, 1865–1939* p. 5 gives his B.A. date as 1831. Miss Lily Yeats supports this date for his B.A., but gives the date of birth as 1806. It seems more reasonable to accept her dates, as William Butler Yeats became a curate in 1831 and must have taken his B.A. degree that year. Miss Yeats wrote to the Trinity College authorities to correct the dates given in *Alumni Dublinenses* on the evidence of family papers.

20. Cf. J. B. Yeats, *Letters to His Son W. B. Yeats and Others*, p. 79, for an explanation of this:
Sir W. Wilde never met me without asking for my Uncle and saying 'Fancy Tom Yeats buried in Sligo'. Tom Yeats was buried in Sligo because at his father's death he gave himself up to the immediate support of near relations—in those days women did not support themselves, and I could give you lots of other instances in our family.

21. He lived with his Butler grandmother, who died in 1834. She supplied him with an allowance of two hundred pounds a year, kept a horse for him and provided many luxuries during his time at college.

22. J. B. Yeats, *Early Memories: Some Chapters of Autobiography*, p. 39.

23. Her father was a Captain Armstrong who died in 1797; her mother a daughter of Colonel Young, of Lahard, Queen's County. Captain Armstrong was a nephew of Major-General Sir John Armstrong who died in 1742. Cf. J. B. Yeats, *Letters to His Son W. B. Yeats and Others*, p. 268. Cf. Cannon, *Historical Record of the King's Liverpool Regiment of Foot*, pp. 374 and 441. Another relative was Bigoe Armstrong, Colonel of the 83rd, who died in his Wimpole St. House in 1794. The Corbets also provided soldier ancestors for the poet. William Corbet (1757–1824) married Grace Armstrong in County Cavan in 1791: the glamorous members of this family included Patrick Corbet, a Lieutenant in the 8th Madras Native Infantry, 'the possessor of a scarlet and bright yellow uniform laced with silver', who was created a Major on the field of battle, and later became Governor of Penang. Yeats has given a brief account of these relatives in *Autobiographies*, pp. 25 *seq*.

24. His wife's uncle, the Rev. Beattie, had retired in his favour.

24A. W. B. Yeats, *Last Poems and Plays*, p. 51.

25. Oliver Edwards, 'W. B. Yeats and Ulster; and a thought on the future of the Anglo-Irish tradition', *The Northman*, vol. xiii, no. 2, p. 16.

26. J. B. Yeats, *Early Memories: Some Chapters of Autobiography*, p. 5.

27. J. B. Yeats, ibid., p. 2.

28. J. B. Yeats, ibid.. p. 35.

29. J. B. Yeats, ibid., p. 6.

30. J. B. Yeats, *Essays Irish and American*, p. 25. Cf. *Early Memories: Some Chapters of Autobiography*, p. 33.

31. J. B. Yeats, ibid., pp. 84 *seq*.

32. Robert Corbet had been a subaltern; when quartered at Hastings he had been in charge of a French officer. He and his prisoner enjoyed a round of balls and parties together. When he left the army he became a stockbroker, and eventually drowned himself after he had lost his money.

33. J. Hone, *W. B. Yeats, 1865–1939*, p. 13, is incorrect in stating that he was buried at Berwick.

34. William Middleton was forty-five and had been married before. He was a smuggler with a depot in the Channel Isles, and carried most of his goods to and from South America, where he was once captured and made his escape by night under thrilling circumstances. The smuggling later petered out into a carrying trade in salt and general cargoes between Sligo and the Iberian Peninsula.

35. Information from family documents and Miss Lily Yeats's memories of family traditions. She has a family tree showing the Pollexfen connections with the Drake family. Sir Francis Drake, the third Baronet, married as his third wife Elizabeth, the daughter of Sir Henry Pollexfen of Nutwell Court but it is not certain that the Sligo Pollexfens were connected with this Sir Henry Pollexfen.

36. Rev. T. F. O'Rorke, *History, Antiquities and Present State of the Parishes of Ballysadare and Kilvarnet, in the County of Sligo*, pp. 527–9.

37. W. B. Yeats, *Autobiographies*, p. 7.
38. W. B. Yeats, ibid., p. 19.
39. W. B. Yeats, ibid., p. 27. Cf. J. B. Yeats, *Early Memories: Some Chapters of Autobiography*, p. 20.
40. This fact is not to be confirmed and rests upon hearsay. Terence de Vere White is of the opinion that J. B. Yeats devilled for Butt. (Cf. *The Road of Excess*, p. 161.) A passage in *Early Memories: Some Chapters of Autobiography*, p. 62, suggests that if Yeats did work with Butt the association was not very important. J. B. Yeats was called to the Irish Bar in 1866, and shortly before he left Dublin and law for London and art the butler at Sandymount Castle said to Butt:
'Now Sir, Mr Johnnie is a Barrister, and you ought to do something for him', and Butt answered 'Michael, I will'. And he did, in a way that, because of my resolution to go to England, was vain, but it would have been a substantial help to me.
41. J. B. Yeats to W. B. Yeats. Cf. J. Hone, *W. B. Yeats, 1865–1939*, p. 11. Cf. T. de Vere White, *The Road of Excess*, pp. 287–8.
41A. J. B. Yeats, letter in National Library, Dublin, to Frank Mac-Donagh, 16 April 1913.
42. W. B. Yeats, *Autobiographies*, p. 5.
43. J. B. Yeats, *Essays Irish and American*, p .9.
44. J. B. Yeats, ibid., p. 14.
45. Letter to his wife from 23 Fitzroy Road, dated 1 November 1872.
46. For subsequent information on the Pollexfen household I am indebted to Miss Lily Yeats, who allowed me to read her own unpublished memoirs on the subject and supplemented these in many cases with personal recollections. The description of Mrs Pollexfen is taken from these memoirs.
47. W. B. Yeats, *Autobiographies*, p. 21.
48. W. B. Yeats, ibid., p. 13.
49. W. B. Yeats, *Collected Poems*, p. 266.
50. Cf. Stephen Gwynn, *Oliver Goldsmith*, p. 21.
51. W. B. Yeats, *Autobiographies*, p. 29.
52. W. B. Yeats, ibid., p. 56.
53. W. B. Yeats, ibid., p. 53.
54. Letter to Katherine Tynan, 2 December 1891.
55. W. B. Yeats, *Autobiographies*, p. 38.
56. J. Hone, *W. B. Yeats, 1865–1939*, p. 26.
57. W. B. Yeats, *Autobiographies*, p. 37.
58. Cf. W. B. Yeats, ibid., pp. 38–51, for the information on his experiences at the Godolphin School.
59. These documents are in the possession of Mrs W. B. Yeats.
60. W. B. Yeats, *Autobiographies*, p. 60.
61. The house still stands, the squireen referred to was a Mr Ormsby.
62. Oscar Wilde reacted in the same manner to schooling. *Vide* Hesketh Pearson, *The Life of Oscar Wilde*, pp. 18–19. Shaw's education at Wesley College, Dublin (it stands in the next street to Harcourt Street, on Stephen's Green) produced the same comment. *Vide* Hesketh Pearson, *Bernard Shaw: His Life and Personality*, p. 26:
I cannot learn anything that does not interest me. My memory is not indiscriminate: it rejects and selects; and its selections are not academic.
63. W. B. Yeats, *Autobiographies*, p. 72.
64. W. B. Yeats, ibid., p. 73. Cf. Miss Gerta Hütteman, *Wesen der Dichtung und Ausgabe bei William Butler Yeats*, chap. viii, where she speaks of his innate religious temperament; and D. S. Savage, *The Personal Principle*, p. 90:

In default of a principle of personal dynamism within himself and of such a classical stable order and accepted orthodoxy, Yeats assembled a home-made, gimcrack order and 'religious' system out of the exotic fragments he found here and there beyond the borders of commonplace life; thus his apparent romanticism.

65. W. B. Yeats, *Autobiographies*, pp. 76–9.
66. J. B. Yeats, *Essays Irish and American*, p. 30.
67. W. B. Yeats, *Autobiographies*, p. 143.

CHAPTER II

1. Anonymous article in *T.P.'s Weekly*, 'W. B. Yeats at School', 7 June 1912.
2. Katharine Tynan, *Twenty-five Years*, p. 144.
3. W. B. Yeats, *Last Poems and Plays*, p. 18. J. Hone, *W. B. Yeats, 1865–1939*, p. 450, gives an inaccurate account of how Yeats was asked for the poem. Early in 1937 A. Norman Jeffares, then editing *The Erasmian*, telephoned Yeats and asked him if he would give a poem to a new series of contributions from ex-pupils. He was not sufficiently well to undertake the strain of writing a new poem but said he would search for some unpublished poem among his recent writings which would be suitable for a school magazine. Jeffares subsequently called at Riversdale for 'What Then?' which was published in the April issue of *The Erasmian*, 1937.
4. He had a studio constructed later in 7 St Stephen's Green. Cf. Katharine Tynan, *Memories*, pp. 276 *seq.* for aspects of the life of his salon.
5. W. B. Yeats, *Autobiographies*, p. 81.
6. Katharine Tynan, *The Middle Years*, p. 51.
7. W. B. Yeats, *Autobiographies*, p. 91.
8. W. B. Yeats, ibid., p. 82.
9. W. B. Yeats, ibid., pp. 105 *seq.*
10. This probably refers to 'Time and the Witch Vivien', included in *The Wanderings of Oisin and Other Poems* (1889).
11. Quoted by J. Hone, *W. B. Yeats, 1865–1939*, p. 43. Date of letter, 7 January 1884. Willie entered the School of Art in May 1884, and attended day classes until July 1885. His sisters Susan and Elizabeth were pupils at the same time. Information confirmed by a letter from the Registrar of the National College of Art to me, 10 January 1947.
12. Information from Miss Lily Yeats used here.
13. W. B. Yeats, *Autobiographies*, p. 58.
14. Information from Miss Cathleen Sheppard. Cf. J. Hone, *W. B. Yeats, 1865–1939*, p. 42.
15. W. B. Yeats, *Autobiographies*, p. 103.
16. Later Professor of Economics at the Royal University of Ireland.
17. Rev. T. F. O'Rorke, *History of Sligo: Town and County*, vol. ii, p. 331. The reference is to the Ballisodare property of the firm.
18. W. B. Yeats, *Autobiographies*, p. 88. For a description of George Pollexfen, *vide* pp. 84–8 of that work, also pp. 316–18.
19. W. B. Yeats, *Autobiographies*, p. 92.
20. W. B. Yeats, *Last Poems and Plays*, p. 32.
21. W. B. Yeats, *Fairy and Folk Tales of the Irish Peasantry*, p. xii.
22. W. B. Yeats, *Autobiographies*, pp. 319–32.
23. W. B. Yeats, ibid., p. 95.
24. W. B. Yeats, ibid., p. 97.
25. W. B. Yeats, 'Song of the Faeries', *Dublin University Review*, March

1885. This poem is part of 'The Island of Statues', included in *The Wanderings of Oisin and Other Poems* (1889).
26. Cf. W. B. Yeats, *Collected Poems*, pp. 8, 9, 225, and 291, also a passage from 'The Island of Statues', *Dublin University Review*, June 1885:
> As the sea's furrows on a sea-tost shell
> Sad histories are lettered on thy cheek.
27. W. B. Yeats, *Collected Poems*, p. 197.
28. W. B. Yeats, 'The Island of Statues', *The Wanderings of Oisin and Other Poems* (1889).
29. Miss P. Gurd, *The Early Poetry of W. B. Yeats* (Lancaster, U.S.A., 1916).
30. W. B. Yeats, *Collected Poems*, p. 8.
31. P. B. Shelley, *Prometheus Unbound*, Act III, scene iii.
32. W. B. Yeats, *Collected Poems*, p. 9.
32A. Cf. W. B. Yeats, *Mosada* (*Dublin University Review*, June 1886):
> Dear heart, there is a secret way that leads
> Its paved length towards the river's marge,
> Where lies a shallop in the yellow reeds.
> Awake, awake, and we will sail afar,
> Afar along the fleet white river's face.
33. W. B. Yeats, *Autobiographies*, p. 109.
34. E. A. Boyd, *Ireland's Literary Renaissance*, p. 213.
35. W. B. Yeats, *Essays*, p. 79.
36. John Eglinton, *A Memoir of Æ*, p. 10. Katherine Tynan, *Twenty-five Years*, p. 248.
37. W. B. Yeats, *Autobiographies*, p. 110.
38. W. B. Yeats, *Collected Works*, vol. viii, p. 279.
39. W. B. Yeats, 'Kanva on Himself', *The Wanderings of Oisin and Other Poems* (1889).
40. W. B. Yeats, *Collected Poems*, p. 279.
41. Katharine Tynan, *Twenty-five Years*, p. 145.
42. W. B. Yeats, *The Celtic Twilight*, pp. 45-51. Cf. W. B. Yeats, 'An Impression', *The Speaker*, 21 October 1893.
43. Information from Miss Lily Yeats.
44. W. B. Yeats, *Autobiographies*, p. 126.
45. W. B. Yeats, ibid., p. 111.
46. Information from Miss Lily Yeats.
47. W. B. Yeats, *Autobiographies*, p. 115.
48. W. B. Yeats, ibid., p. 123. Shaw began his speechifying for the same purpose.
49. This shyness and lack of self-confidence is paralleled by that of Shaw. Hesketh Pearson has a similar story to tell in *Bernard Shaw: His Life and Personality*, p. 59.

'An abnormal shyness, which is the form vanity takes in youth, tormented him on these occasions and made him unmannerly and arrogant in social intercourse. "I suffered such agonies of shyness that I sometimes walked up and down the Embankment for twenty minutes or more before venturing to knock at the door: indeed I should have funked it altogether and hurried home asking myself what was the use of torturing myself when it was so easy to run away, if I had not been instinctively aware that I must never let myself off in this manner if I meant ever to do anything in the world. Few men can have suffered more than I did in my youth from simple cowardice or been more horribly ashamed of it. I shirked and hid when the peril both real or imaginary was of the sort that I had no vital interest in facing; but when an interest was at stake, I went ahead and suffered accordingly. The worst of it was that when I appeared in the Lawsons'

drawing-room I did not appeal to the good nature of the company. I had
not then tuned the Shavian note to any sort of harmony; and I have no
doubt the Lawsons found me discordant, crudely self-assertive, and
insufferable." '

50. W. B. Yeats, *Autobiographies*, p. 116.
51. Katharine Tynan, *Twenty-five Years*, p. 209.
52. W. B. Yeats, *Autobiographies*, pp. 127 *seq*.
53. W. B. Yeats, *Essays*, p. 3.
54. W. B. Yeats, ibid., p. 5.
55. The editor was Father Matthew Russell, a friend of Katharine Tynan,
and an encourager of the younger poets. *Vide* W. B. Yeats, *Letters to the
New Island*, p. 88.
56. W. B. Yeats, *The Bookman*, May 1896.
57. W. B. Yeats, *Essays*, p. 4.
58. W. B. Yeats, *Autobiographies*, p. 127.
59. W. B. Yeats, *Collected Poems*, p. 20.
60. W. B. Yeats, ibid., p. 17. The 1889 version is quoted here.
61. She found him 'fond of mysticism and extraordinarily interesting.
Another William Blake.' *Twenty-five Years*, p. 248.
62. W. B. Yeats, *Autobiographies*, p. 139.
63. Information from·Miss Lily Yeats.
64. Katharine Tynan, *The Middle Years*, p. 34.
65. Katharine Tynan, ibid., p. 71.
66. W. B. Yeats, *Autobiographies*, p. 47.
67. Katharine Tynan, *The Middle Years*, p. 41. She was one of those
who attempted to urge the poet into profitable work. Cf. *Memories*, p. 232.
68. W. B. Yeats, *Autobiographies*, p. 190. Cf. J. Hone, *W. B. Yeats, 1865–
1939*, p. 60. R. McHugh, *W. B. Yeats Letters to Katharine Tynan* (1953),
p.172, clears up the dates of these visits.
69. Katharine Tynan, ibid., p. 43.
70. Katharine Tynan, ibid., p. 46.
71. Katharine Tynan, ibid., p. 47.
72. He realised the unreality of this poetry himself. He wrote to Katharine
Tynan when he was preparing and revising poems for the 1889 volume:
'I have much improved "Mosada" by polishing the verse here and there.
I have noticed some things about my poetry that I did not know before in
this process of correction, for instance, that it is almost all a flight into fairy
land from the real world and a summons to that flight. The chorus to
"The Stolen Child" sums it up. That it is not the poetry of insight and
knowledge but of longing and complaint—the cry of the heart against
necessity. I hope some day to alter that and write poetry of insight and
knowledge.'
Katharine Tynan, *The Middle Years*, p. 39.
73. W. B. Yeats, *Collected Poems*, p. 23. *Vide*, for source, notes to *Poems*
(1899).
74. The dangers of neglecting aspects of biography in any study of
Yeats's work are illustrated by Miss P. Gurd, *The Early Poetry of W. B.
Yeats*, p. 43, who states that the connection between Yeats's poem and
Lady Gregory's *Gods and Fighting Men* is obvious. Lady Gregory's book was
published in 1904, but Miss Gurd, unaware that Yeats first met Lady
Gregory in 1896, asserts that Lady Gregory's account 'must have been
accessible to Mr. Yeats as far back as 1889'. In my discussion of the sources
of the poem I have taken much information from Russell K. Alspach's
article 'Some sources of Yeats's The Wanderings of Oisin', *P.M.L.A.*,
September 1943, p. 849 *seq*.
75. W. B. Yeats, *Collected Poems*, p. 327.

76. *Trans. Ossianic Society*, vol. iv, 1859, pp. 21–5, 117–18, 249. David Comyn, *Gaelic Union Publications*, 1880.

77. W. B. Yeats, *Fairy and Folk Tales of the Irish Peasantry*, p. 200.

78. C. H. Foote, *Folk Lore Record*, vol. ii, 9 November 1879, to which Yeats refers, *Fairy and Folk Tales of the Irish Peasantry*, p. 326.

79. Crofton Croker, *Fairy Legends and Traditions of the South of Ireland*, vol. i, p. 317.

80. W. B. Yeats, *Fairy and Folk Tales of the Irish Peasantry*, p. 212.

81. Sir Samuel Ferguson, *Lays of the Western Gael*, 'Aideen's Grave', II, pp. 12–15.

82. W. B. Yeats, *Collected Poems*, p. 324.

83. E. Dowden. Cf. Lady Ferguson's material in *Sir Samuel Ferguson in the Ireland of His Day*.

84. Later he wrote (*Essays*, p. 5):

'When I found my verses too full of the reds and yellows Shelley gathered in Italy, I thought for two days of setting things right, not as I should now by making my rhythm faint and nervous and filling my images with a certain coldness, a certain wintry wildness, but by eating little and sleeping on a board.

There is also the influence of Morris's narrative poetry to be found in *The Wanderings of Oisin*.

85. Katharine Tynan, *The Middle Years*, p. 45.

86. Katharine Tynan, ibid., p. 47.

87. W. B. Yeats, *Collected Poems*, p. 325.

88. W. B. Yeats, *Last Poems and Plays*, p. 59.

89. W. B. Yeats, ibid., p. 80.

## Chapter III

1. Cf. the portrait by H. M. Paget, frontispiece to W. B. Yeats, *Letters to the New Island*.

1A. W. B. Yeats, *Autobiographies*, p. 141.

2. This account is taken from unpublished material. A similar description is included in *Autobiographies*, pp. 177 seq.

3. Parts of this Diary, which is in the possession of Miss Lily Yeats, were printed by J. Hone, 'A scattered fair', *The Wind and the Rain*, vol. iii, no. 3, autumn 1946. Permission to examine the Diary has since been refused to other investigators.

4. W. B. Yeats, *Autobiographies*, p. 174.

5. W. B. Yeats, *Essays*, p. 73.

5A. W. B. Yeats, *Autobiographies*, p. 165.

5B. J. B. Yeats, *Early Memories: Some Chapters of Autobiography*, p. 57.

6. W. B. Yeats, *Autobiographies*, p. 214.

7. Apparently unaware of the classical meaning of the word Horace Reynolds makes this comment on Yeats's attitude to Madame Blavatsky:

'It is difficult to judge from what Yeats has written about this woman just how seriously he took her and her doctrines. Not very seriously, I am sure: one does not call the high priestess of a belief one reverences, a pythoness. (*Letters to the New Island*, p. 39.)

8. P. B. Shelley, *Hellas*, ll. 159 seq.

9. Cf. J. Hone, *W. B. Yeats, 1865–1939*, p. 70.

10. Lady Gregory's *Journals* (ed. Lennox Robinson), p. 263.

11. W. B. Yeats, unpublished material.

12. W. B. Yeats, *Autobiographies*, pp. 226 seq.

13. Yeats's knowledge of the society is given in Notes to *Autobiographies* (1926), p. 471.

14. W. B. Yeats, *Autobiographies*, p. 230.
15. W. B. Yeats, unpublished material.
16. W. B. Yeats, *Autobiographies*, p. 31.
17. David Daiches, *Poetry and the Modern World*, p. 131.
18. Katharine Tynan, *The Middle Years*, p. 70.
19. W. B. Yeats, unpublished material and *Autobiographies*, p. 181.
19A. Cf. Sir William Rothenstein, *Men and Memories*, p. 132, for the effect of Wilde upon Le Gallienne.
19B. Cf. Hesketh Pearson, *The Life of Oscar Wilde*, p. 306, for Yeats's activity in bringing letters of sympathy to Wilde at the time of his trial.
20. W. B. Yeats, unpublished material and *Autobiographies*, pp. 160–72.
21. W. B. Yeats, unpublished material.
'I was greatly troubled because I was making no money. I should have gone to the Art School but with my memory of the Dublin Art School put off the day. I wanted to do something that would bring in money at once for my people were poor. I saw my father sometimes sitting over the fire in great gloom, and yet I had no money-making faculty. Our neighbour York Powell at last offered to recommend me for the sub-editorship of, I think, the *Manchester Courier*. I took some days to think it over. It meant an immediate income but it was an unknown paper. At last I told my father that I could not accept and he said "You have taken a great weight off my mind".'
22. W. B. Yeats, *Autobiographies*, pp. 192 *seq.*
23. W. B. Yeats, ibid., pp. 192 *seq.*
24. W. B. Yeats, *Dublin University Review*, April 1886.
25. W. B. Yeats, *Autobiographies*, p. 199 *seq.*
26. Katharine Tynan, *The Middle Years*, pp. 64, 67.
27. W. B. Yeats, unpublished material.
28. W. B. Yeats, *Autobiographies*, p. 79.
29. W. B. Yeats, ibid., p. 93.
30. See R. McHugh, *W. B. Yeats Letters to Katharine Tynan*, 1953.
31. Hesketh Pearson, *Bernard Shaw: His Life and Personality*, pp. 120–1. But cf. the Introduction by Shaw to *Florence Farr, Bernard Shaw and W. B. Yeats* (ed. Clifford Bax), where 12 not 14 are mentioned.
32. Mrs W. B. Yeats, *Letters to Miss Florence Farr, from Bernard Shaw and W. B. Yeats*, p. 43.
33. Hesketh Pearson, *Bernard Shaw: His Life and Personality*, p. 36.
34. W. B. Yeats, unpublished material.
35. Maud Gonne was a woman with revolutionary aims who devoted herself to the cause of Ireland's independence and the destruction of the British Empire. She was influenced in her decision to take up this work partially by the death of her father, who intended to stand as a Home Rule candidate after he had resigned his Colonelcy in the British Army, a plan which was cut short by his death from cholera in Dublin: partially by the influence of her friend Millevoye, the French orator and editor of *La Patrie* with whom she had a secret pact designed to damage England's power. Immediately after her father's death she had a brief experience of acting, fell ill, and then discovered that there was enough money for her sister and herself to live comfortably.
35A. According to Miss Lily Yeats she called 'on Willie, of course, but apparently on Papa. . . . She is an immense height and very stylish and well dressed in a careless way. . . . She has a rich complexion, hazel eyes.' Miss Elizabeth Yeats described her as 'the Dublin beauty who is marching on to glory over the heads of the Dublin youth'. Cf. J. Hone, *The Wind and the Rain*, Autumn 1946.

36. W. B. Yeats, *Letters to the New Island*, pp. 112 *seq.*, and *Autobiographies*, p. 148.

37. W. B. Yeats, *Letters to the New Island*, p. 104.

38. W. B. Yeats, ibid., pp. 95, 165. Cf. W. Allingham, *Sixteen Poems*, p. 1.

39. W. B. Yeats, *Letters to the New Island*, p. 103.

40. W. B. Yeats, ibid., p. 106.

41. W. B. Yeats, ibid., p. 165.

42. W. B. Yeats, unpublished material.

43. W. B. Yeats, *Autobiographies*, p. 192.

44. W. B. Yeats, unpublished material.

45. W. B. Yeats, *John Sherman*, p. 130 (or *Collected Works*, vol. vii, p. 259).

46. Katharine Tynan, *The Middle Years*, p. 67. Cf. Cyril Connolly, *Enemies of Promise*, p. 198, for the Anglo-Irish reaction to the differences between England and Ireland.

47. *Vide* W. B. Yeats, *Autobiographies*, p. 88, for the suggestion that the attraction of the solitary life owed something to Thoreau:
'My father had read to me some passage out of *Walden*, and I planned to live some day in a cottage on a little island called Innisfree, and Innisfree was opposite Slish Wood. . . . I thought that having conquered bodily desire and the inclination of my mind towards women and love, I should live, as Thoreau lived, seeking wisdom.'
Katharine Tynan, 'Thoreau at Walden', *Louise de la Vallière and Other Poems* (1885), p. 90, has a similar subject in:

A little log hut in the woodland dim
A still lake, like a bit of summer sky

and the poet inhabitant 'fair Nature's knight' who

Heard the unborn flowers' springing footsteps light
And the winds' whisper of the enchanted sea,
And the birds sing of love, and pairing time.

47A. W. B. Yeats, *John Sherman*, p. 122.

48. Katharine Tynan, *The Middle Years*, p. 68.

49. E. Rhys, 'W. B. Yeats: Early Recollections', *Fortnightly Review*, July 1935. Cf. also 'Invoking the Irish Fairies', *The Irish Theosophist*, October 1892, probably by Yeats, who later used the initials D.E.D.I. in one of his secret societies.

50. W. B. Yeats, *Autobiographies*, p. 204.

51. W. B. Yeats, ibid., p. 206.

52. Maud Gonne MacBride, *A Servant of the Queen*, p. 92.

53. W. B. Yeats, *Autobiographies*, p. 152.

54. W. B. Yeats, *Letters to the New Island*, p. xii.

54A. A letter written by Sarah Purser to Yeats is in the possession of Mr Geoghan, her nephew. This was a letter of advice which was never sent to the poet.

55. W. B. Yeats, unpublished material.

56. W. B. Yeats, *Letters to the New Island*, p. 137. He was obviously thinking of Maud Gonne when there; even his article on the ballad singer whose plaintive lament he overpraised was interrupted by reveries. Apple blossom was always associated with his early memories of Maud's appearance, and his reading of *Marius the Epicurean* was desultory:
'I have been reading slowly and fitfully since morning, taking the book up for a moment and then laying it down again, and letting my mind stray off to the red apples and the shadowing leaves before me.'

57. W. B. Yeats, unpublished material.

58. Maud Gonne MacBride, *A Servant of the Queen*, p. 17.

59. W. B. Yeats, unpublished material. H. Reynolds, *Letters to the New Island*, p. 56, is not correct in stating that it was Florence Farr's image that Yeats saw and her voice that he heard when composing *The Countess Kathleen*. Vide Maud Gonne MacBride's statement, *A Servant of the Queen*, p. 176:
'He said he had written the part of the Countess Kathleen for me and I *must* act it.'
60. Cf. Maud Gonne MacBride, *A Servant of the Queen*, p. 255.
61. W. B. Yeats, unpublished material.
62. *Vide* Maud Gonne MacBride, *A Servant of the Queen*; information also from conversation with Madame MacBride.
63. W. B. Yeats, *Dramatis Personae*, p. 18.
63A. Kathleen appears as Cathleen from 1895 onwards.
64. W. B. Yeats, *Last Poems and Plays*, p. 80.
65. Maud Gonne MacBride, *A Servant of the Queen*, p. 147.
66. Maud Gonne Macbride, ibid., pp. 131–44.
67. W. B. Yeats, *Autobiographies*, p. 153.
68. W. B. Yeats, ibid., p. 314.
69. W. B. Yeats, *Collected Poems*, p. 41.
To add to the certainty of the poem being written for Maud Gonne an anecdote told me by Professor E. R. Dodds must be cited. The poem was first composed of two stanzas. Yeats recited it to Æ and some friends in this form after he and Maud had returned from tramping the Dublin mountains. Yeats was upset that she had been tired by walking on the rough roads and added the third stanza, to Æ's disapproval. The latter told Professor Dodds that he disliked these sentimental lines, especially for the incongruity of the words 'weary and kind'. He thought the word 'kind' meaningless in its context and explained that it was there because after the long walk Maud Gonne, though footsore, was in a gentler mood than usual. He also thought it ridiculous to call the world of human experience 'a grassy road'; and told the story to illustrate how fine poetry can be ruined by the intrusion of the transient and incidental.
70. Troy was a likely subject for his verse; at the time he was full of Todhunter's *Helen of Troy*. *Letters to the New Island*, p. 174.
71. 'Intellectual' in the sense that Yeats thought them so, and they partook of his often inchoate ideas founded upon fragments of unsound sources. Cf. his note to *The Countess Kathleen and Various Legends and Lyrics* (1892), p. 140:
'The Rose is a favourite symbol with the Irish poets. It has given a name to more than one poem, both Gaelic and English, and is used, not merely in love poems, but in addresses to Ireland, as in de Vere's line "The Little Black Rose shall be red at last", and in Mangan's "Dark Rosaleen". I do not, of course, use it in this sense.' Cf. the comment of E. A. Boyd, *Ireland's Literary Renaissance*, p. 185:
'The last verse empties the poem of any intellectual content. [His] mysticism is not an intellectual belief but an emotional or artistic refuge.'
72. W. B. Yeats, *United Ireland*, 15 October 1892.
73. W. B. Yeats, *Collected Poems*, p. 41.
74. W. B. Yeats, ibid., p. 35.
75. W. B. Yeats, ibid., p. 56.
76. W. B. Yeats, ibid., pp. 46, 45, 45, 47, 48, 46, 54.
77. W. B. Yeats, ibid., p. 36.
78. W. B. Yeats, *The Countess Kathleen and Various Legends and Lyrics*, p. 140.
79. W. B. Yeats, *Collected Poems*, p. 43.
80. W. B. Yeats, ibid., p. 49. It is possible that the line:
He stood among a crowd at Drumahair

has some connection with the fact that there were Middletons in Dromohair, Co. Leitrim. Cf. J. Hone, *W. B. Yeats, 1865-1939*, p. 13.

81. W. B. Yeats, *Autobiographies*, p. 249.

82. Cf. W. B. Yeats, notes to *The Countess Kathleen and Various Legends and Lyrics*, and to *Collected Works*, 1908.

83. Letter to Katharine Tynan, *The Middle Years*, p. 49. The various versions of the poem have been discussed by Forrest Reid, *W. B. Yeats: A Critical Study*, pp. 42, 50–4.

84. W. B. Yeats, *The Countess Kathleen and Various Legends and Lyrics*, vide note on p. 128.

85. W. B. Yeats, *The Celtic Twilight* (1893), p. 23.

86. W. B. Yeats, *The Countess Kathleen and Various Legends and Lyrics*, p. 128.

87. Cf. G. D. P. Allt, 'Yeats and the Revision of his Early Verse', *Hermathena*, vol. lxiv, November 1944.

88. W. B. Yeats, *Collected Poems*, p. 52.

89. W. B. Yeats, *Fairy and Folk Tales of the Irish Peasantry*, p. 324. The source is to be found in Rev. T. F. O'Rorke, *The History, Antiquities and Present State of the Parishes of Ballisadare and Kilvarnet*, pp. 198, 206.

90. Cf. for source W. B. Yeats, notes to *The Countess Kathleen and Various Legends and Lyrics* (1892), p. 116. The reference is to C. J. Kickham, *Knocknagow* (1887), pp. 482–86. Yeats read *Knocknagow* when preparing *Representative Irish Tales*, and included selections from Kickham in this work. Russell K. Alspach has discovered that some of the material from *Knocknagow* was used in *The Wanderings of Oisin*. Cf. P.M.L.A., September 1943, p. 858. In the notes to *The Countess Kathleen* referred to above he misspells Kickham's title as 'Knockangow'.

91. Forrest Reid, *W. B. Yeats: A Critical Study*, p. 48.

92. W. B. Yeats, *Collected Poems*, p. 46. Cf. W. F. Mackay, 'Yeats's Debt to Ronsard on a Carpe Diem Theme', *Comparative Literature Studies*, vol. xix, p. 4. The Ronsard source is *Sonnets pour Hélène*, ii, 1578.

93. Maud Gonne MacBride, *A Servant of the Queen*, p. 308.

94. W. B. Yeats, *Collected Poems*, p. 54.

95. Cf. his letter to Katharine Tynan, chapter 2, note 72.


## CHAPTER IV

1. W. B. Yeats, *Autobiographies*, p. 245.

2. W. B. Yeats, *Collected Poems*, p. 103.

3. W. B. Yeats, letter to Katharine Tynan, December 1891: 'I am busy getting up a London Irish Literary Society—to be a branch ultimately of Y.I. League—we are asking Gavan Duffy to be President and are hoping to get Stopford Brooke for one of the Vice-Presidents, and Rolleston promises to be another.'

3A. Cf. C. H. Rolleston, *Portrait of an Irishman*, p. 10.

4. W. B. Yeats, *Autobiographies*, p. 252.

5. W. B. Yeats, ibid., p. 281.

6. W. B. Yeats, ibid., p. 283.

7. W. B. Yeats, ibid., p. 282.

8. W. B. Yeats, unpublished material.

9. Cf. Chapter 3, note 54B.

10. Madame MacBride's account of the grey lady, given in *A Servant of the Queen*, p. 255, may reveal some of her mental unrest at the time: 'They said she had confessed to having killed a child and wrung her hands in sorrow and remorse. After this I began to think she must be evil

and decided to get rid of her. It seemed to me I might not be able to control her, so, resolutely, I put on the blinkers and denied her existence.'
11. Rev. T. F. O'Rorke, *The History of Ballysadare and Kilvarnet*, p. 198.
12. W. B. Yeats, *Collected Poems*, p. 27.
13. W. B. Yeats, *Essays, 1931–1936*, p. 7.
14. Ernest Rhys, *Everyman Remembers*, p. 105.
15. W. B. Yeats, *Essays, 1931–1936*, p. 8.
16. This attention paid to scholarship was largely inspired by Pater who was the oracle of the Rhymers, to whom Symons and Johnson paid frequent visits from which they returned with *obiter dicta* for the other rhymers. Cf. W. B. Yeats, *Autobiographies*, pp. 372 *seq.*
17. W. B. Yeats, ibid., p. 273.
17A. He is no longer Willie Yeats of Dublin, but 'Yeats' or 'W. B. Yeats', a result of the slightly distant manner he had cultivated.
18. W. B. Yeats, *Autobiographies*, p. 207.
18A. Cf. his notes in *Collected Works*.
18B. He had an income of 30s. a week. Cf. W. B. Yeats, *Autobiographies*, p. 344.
19. Cf. W. B. Yeats, *Collected Works*, vol. v, p. 106:
'It is one of the great troubles of life that we cannot have any unmixed emotions. There is always something in our enemy that we like, and something in a sweetheart that we dislike. It is this entanglement which makes us old and puckers our brows and deepens the furrows about our eyes.'
20. W. B. Yeats, *Collected Poems*, p. 62.
21. W. B. Yeats, *Collected Plays*, p. 70.
21A. He used to compose poems in a garden built on a hill at Ballygawley overlooking woods and a lake
22. W. B. Yeats, *Autobiographies*, p. 320.
23. W. B. Yeats, ibid., p. 321.
24. W. B. Yeats, ibid., p. 333.
25. W. B. Yeats, *Collected Poems*, p. 71. His sister remembers him recounting the dream the morning that he had dreamed it.
26. From original in the possession of Mr A. Earle.
27. W. B. Yeats, *Collected Poems*, p. 148.
28. Cf. Hugh Law, *Anglo-Irish Literature*, p. 282.
29. W. B. Yeats, unpublished material.
30. W. B. Yeats, *Autobiographies*, p. 397.
31. W. B. Yeats, ibid., p. 394.
31A. For an example of their discussing various subjects together cf. Sir William Rothenstein, *Men and Memories*, p. 330.
32. W. B. Yeats, *Autobiographies*, p. 189.
33. Cf. a review of Louis MacNeice, 'The Poetry of W. B. Yeats', *English Studies*, December 1945.
34. W. B. Yeats, *Collected Poems*, p. 69.
35. W. B. Yeats, ibid., p. 78.
36. P. More, *Shelburne Essays* (First Series), pp. 181–2. Gaelic poetry, however, often praises the hair. Cf. Robin Flower, *The Irish Tradition*, p. 151.
37. *The Savoy*, September 1896, p. 18.
38. Ibid., August 1896, p. 24.

CHAPTER V

1. Letter to Mrs Shakespear, 27 February 1934.
1A. Cf. W. B. Yeats, *Letters on Poetry to Dorothy Wellesley*, p. 51.

1B. W. B. Yeats, *Autobiographies*, pp. 401, 402.
1C. Cf. Osbert Burdett, *The Beardsley Period*, p. 8.
1D. Perhaps the best account of his use of magical symbols is given by W. S. Blunt, *My Diaries, 1888–1914*, 1 April 1898:
'Yeats experimented magically on me. He first took out a notebook and made what he called a pyramid in it which was a square of figures, then he bade me think of and see a square of yellow as it might be a door, and walk through it and tell him what I saw beyond. All that I could see at all clearly was that I seemed to be standing on a piece of green rushy grass, in front of me a small pool from which issued two streams of very blue water to right and left of me. He then bade me turn and go back through the door, and told me I should see either a man or a woman who would give me something. I failed to see anything but darkness but at last with some effort I made out the indistinct figure of a child which offered me with its left hand some withered flowers. I could not see its face. Lastly he bade me thank the person to whose intervention the vision was due, and read from his notebook some vague sentences prefiguring this vision. The performance was very imperfect, not to say dull.'
2. Information from private papers for foregoing statements.
3. The story of this vision is given in *Autobiographies*, pp. 457 *seq.*, and annotated on p. 473 on that work. Cf. also W. B. Yeats, 'A Biographical Fragment', *The Criterion*, July 1923, pp. 315 *seq.*
4. For a detailed account of the house *vide* Lady Gregory's *Coole*.
5. W. B. Yeats, unpublished material.
6. W. B. Yeats, *Autobiographies*, p. 423.
7. W. B. Yeats, ibid., p. 424.
8. W. B. Yeats, *Collected Poems*, p. 62.
8A. This order of mysteries was regarded as an escape from active life and politics as well as a means of gaining Maud's love. Cf. a passage in a letter to Æ dated Saturday, 23 January 1898 where the dashes seem to represent Maud Gonne. *Dublin Magazine*, July-September 1939:
'I am deep in "Celtic Mysticism" the whole thing is forming an elaborate vision — — and myself are going for a week or two perhaps to some country place in Ireland to get as you do the forms and gods and spirits and to get some sacred earth for our evocation. Perhaps we can arrange to go somewhere where you are so that we can all work together — — has seen the vision of a little temple of the elements which she proposes to build somewhere in Ireland when '98 is over and to make it the centre of our mystical and literary movements.'
9. W. B. Yeats, unpublished material. Cf. *Autobiographies*, pp. 313 *seq.*
10. W. B. Yeats, *Autobiographies*, p. 418.
11. W. B. Yeats, unpublished material.
12. W. B. Yeats, *Collected Poems*, p. 256.
13. W. B. Yeats, ibid., p. 73. Cf. notes to this work, p. 442
14. W. B. Yeats, ibid., p. 440.
15. W. B. Yeats, *Autobiographies*, p. 415.
16. W. B. Yeats, *Collected Poems*, p. 73.
17. W. B. Yeats, *The Wind Among the Reeds* (1899), p. 73.
17A. W. B. Yeats, *Poems* (1899), p. 292.
18. Mrs Joseph (Mary Davenport) O'Neill.
19. W. B. Yeats, *Collected Poems*, p. 81.
20. W. B. Yeats, ibid., p. 80.
21. W. B. Yeats, ibid., p. 75.
22. W. B. Yeats, ibid., p. 68.
23. W. B. Yeats, ibid., p. 80.
24. W. B. Yeats, ibid., p. 71.

25. W. B. Yeats, ibid., p. 80.
26. W. B. Yeats, notes to *The Wind Among the Reeds* (1899).
27. W. B. Yeats, *The Adoration of the Magi*, p. 47.
28. W. B. Yeats, *Collected Poems*, p. 41.
29. C. L. Wrenn, *Durham University Journal*, July 1919.
30. W. B. Yeats, *Collected Poems*, p. 75.
30A. Cf. W. T. Horton, *A Book of Images*, p. 13.
31. W. B. Yeats, *Collected Poems*, p. 77.
32. Cf. Frank Hugh O'Donnell, *The Stage Irishman of the Pseudo-Celtic Revival* (1904).
33. W. B. Yeats, unpublished material.
33A. Lady Gregory, *Coole*, p. 39
33B. For the pictures which Yeats admired at Coole, cf. *Estrangement*, pp. 3, 5.
33C. Lady Gregory, *Coole*, p. 2.
34. W. B. Yeats, *Collected Poems*, p. 75.
35. W. B. Yeats, notes to *The Wind Among the Reeds* (1899). Cf. 'Song of Mongan', *The Dome*, October 1898, and 'Aodh pleads with the Elemental Powers', *The Dome*, December 1898.
36. W. B. Yeats, *Collected Poems*, p. 81.
37. Information from Mrs Yeats, and unpublished material. Cf. *Autobiographies*, p. 462.
37A. Their work formed part of Lady Gregory's *Visions and Beliefs in the West of Ireland*.
37B. The rest from reading was good for his sight. His right eye was astigmatic, his left almost sightless, this being due to a conical cornea. Cf. a letter to Sir William Rothenstein, *Men and Memories*, vol. ii, p. 20, alluding to his eyes being 'too bad to read MSS.'.
37C. There was also a respite from financial cares which was important. He was still very poor and writes somewhat anxiously to George Russell in January 1898 (*Dublin Magazine*, July 1939):
'How much a week could I live for in the country, if I stayed a couple of weeks or so? Could I do it for 30/-? Please let me know about this soon.'
38. W. B. Yeats, *Autobiographies*, p. 463.
39. W. B. Yeats, ibid., p. 287.
40. W. B. Yeats, ibid., p. 288. Cf. E. R. W.'s 'Reminiscences of W.B.', *The Irish Times*, 10 February 1940:
'In the early days of our acquaintance he knew few people in Dublin for his strong nationalism excluded him from the ruling Anglo-Irish Society. Lady Lyttelton, the wife of the Commander-in-Chief, a very cultured woman, used to invite him sometimes to dinner. But even then she had to be careful about the guests she asked to meet him. He was, therefore, rather a lonely man, for the merely bohemian company he might have joined had no attraction for him; but I never heard him complain on this account.'
'E. R. W.' is Mr E. R. Walsh.
40A. After his first visit Æ told Maud Gonne that he thought Lady Gregory patronising and that he would not go back again.
41. W. B. Yeats, unpublished material.
42. W. B. Yeats, *Autobiographies*, p. 465.
43. W. B. Yeats, *Essays*, p. 248.
44. W. B. Yeats, ibid., p. 140.
45. W. B. Yeats, ibid., p. 237.
46. W. B. Yeats, ibid., p. 253.
47. W. B. Yeats, ibid., p. 263. The effect of the meetings of '97 and '98 upon him was not to shatter his belief in Ireland completely (despite a later account of them:

'All the while I worked with this idea founding societies that became quickly or slowly everything I despised, one part of me looking on mischievous and mocking, and other part spoke words which were more and more unreal.')

For instance, the idealism of his views on poetry and politics can be seen in a generous and encouraging letter which he wrote to George Russell on 23 January, 1898 (*Dublin Magazine*, July 1939)—presumably to persuade Russell of the value of his work with the Co-operative movement:

'I feel certain that things will greatly improve with you in a month or so. I do intreat you to give this work a fair trial. . . . But remember always that now you are face to face with Ireland, its tragedy and its poverty and if we would express Ireland we must know her to the heart and in all her moods. You will be a far more powerful mystic and poet and teacher because of this knowledge. This change of life will test you as a man and a thinker and if you can gradually build up a strong life out of it you will be a bigger soul in all things.

'You are face to face with the heterogeneous and the test of one's harmony is our power to absorb it and make it harmonious. Gradually these banks, hotels and cottages, and strange faces will become familiar, gradually you will come to see them through a mist of half-humourous, half-comical, half-poetical, half-affectionate memories and hopes. The arguments you use, and the methods you adopt, will become familiar and then your mind will be free again. . . . Absorb Ireland and her tragedy and you will be the poet of a people, perhaps the poet of a new insurrection.'


## Chapter VI

1. W. B. Yeats, *Essays*, p. 232.

2. John Eglinton, W. B. Yeats, Æ, W. Larminie, *Literary Ideals in Ireland*, p. 37.

2A. He had, of course, altered already. Cf. a letter written to Æ in 1904 (*Dublin Magazine*, July 1939):

'In my "Land of Heart's Desire" and in some of my lyric verse of that time there is an exaggeration of sentiment and sentimental beauty which I have come to think unmanly. The popularity of "The Land of Heart's Desire" seems to me to have come not from its merits but because of this weakness. I have been fighting the prevailing decadence for years, and have just got it under foot in my own heart—it is sentiment and sentimental sadness, a womanish introspection—my own early subjectiveness at rare moments and yours nearly always rises above sentiment to a union with a pure energy of spirit, but between this energy of the spirit and the energy of the will out of which epic and dramatic poetry comes there is a region of brooding emotions full of fleshly waters and vapours which kill the spirit and the will, ecstasy and joy equally. Yet this region of shadows is full of false images of the spirit and of the body. I have come to feel towards it as O'Grady feels towards it sometimes and even a little as some of my stupidest critics feel. As so often happens with a thing one has been tempted by and is still a little tempted by I am roused by it to a kind of frenzied hatred which is quite out of my control. Beardsley exasperated some people in this way but he has never the form of decadence that tempted me and so I am not unjust to him but I cannot probably be quite just to any poetry that speaks to me with the sweet insinuating feminine voice of the dwellers in that country of the shadows and hollow images. I have dwelt there too

long not to dread all that comes out of it. . . . P.S.—Let us have no
emotions, however abstract, in which there is not an athletic joy.'
  3. W. B. Yeats, *Essays*, p. 432.
  4. W. B. Yeats, ibid., p. 337.
  4A. One of his essays in *Ideas of Good and Evil* (1903), 'The Return of
Ulysses', states his belief clearly as he held it in 1896:
  'The more a poet rids his verses of heterogeneous knowledge and irrelevant analysis, and purifies his mind with elaborate art, the more does the
little ritual of his verse resemble the great ritual of Nature and become
mysterious and inscrutable.' (*Essays*, p. 248.)
  5. John Dryden, *The Sec. Masque*, p. 142.
  6. W. B. Yeats, *Dramatis Personae*, p. 18.
  7. W. B. Yeats, *Autobiographies*, p. 447.
  8. Information from Madame MacBride. Cf. J. Hone, *W. B. Yeats,
1865–1939*, p. 152.
  9. W. B. Yeats, *Collected Poems*, p. 87.
  9A. W. Blake, *Works* (Nonesuch edition), p. 86.
  10. W. B. Yeats, *Collected Poems*, p. 85.
  11. W. Blake, *Works* (ed. Ellis and Yeats), vol. ii, p. 263. Cf. for arrow
symbolism, vol. iii, p. 5. Cf. Grace Jackson, *Mysticism in Æ and Yeats in
Relation to Oriental and American Thought*, p. 163.
  12. W. B. Yeats, *Autobiographies*, p. 152, and 'A Dream of the World's
End', *The Green Sheaf*, No. 2, p. 6.
  13. W. B. Yeats, *Collected Poems*, p. 86.
  14. W. B. Yeats, ibid., p. 88.
  14A. Reputedly the coronation stone of the ancient Irish kings.
  15. Maud Gonne MacBride, *A Servant of the Queen*, p. 328.
  15A. Cf. *Letters to Miss Florence Farr from Bernard Shaw and W. B. Yeats*, p. 52:
  'The play is now set upon a single idea—which is in these new lines—
        When the world ends
        The mind is made unchanging for it finds
        Miracle, ecstacy, the impossible joy,
        The flag stone under all, the fire of fires,
        The root of the world. . . .
The play as it was came into existence after years of strained emotion, of
living upon tip-toe, and is only right in its highest moments, the logic and
circumstances are all wrong.'
  The pre-Raphaelite touch is apparent in Forgael's speech (*Collected
Works*, vol. ii, p. 192):
        Now the secret's out
        For it is love that I am seeking for,
        But of a beautiful unheard-of kind
        That is not in the world.
There is more than a little Blake to be discovered in the play, for instance,
these lines:
        Do what you will,
        For neither I nor you can break a mesh
        Of the great golden net that is about us
seem to owe something to Blake's 'The Golden Net'. (Nonesuch edition),
p. 110.
  16. W. B. Yeats, *Autobiographies*, p. 467.
  17. Lady Gregory, *Our Irish Theatre*, p. 6.
  17A. He had met Moore at the Cheshire Cheese before 1893 (*vide*
J. Hone, *The Life of George Moore*, p. 213) and was, according to Sir William
Rothenstein, *Man and Memories*, p. 282, 'the pied piper who played Moore
into Dublin', an account confirmed in *Hail and Farewell*.

18. Cf. A. E. Malone, *The Irish Theatre* (ed. Lennox Robinson), p. 13.
19. In *Dramatis Personae*.
20. Information from Madame MacBride.
20A. She used to demonstrate this verse-speaking at Yeats's 'Mondays'. Cf. Sir William Rothenstein, *Men and Memories*, p. 282.
21. W. S. Blunt, *My Diaries, 1888–1914*, p. 28.
22. J. Hone, *W. B. Yeats, 1865–1939*, p. 191.
23. W. B. Yeats, *Essays*, p. 18.
24. Cf. J. Hone, *The Life of George Moore*, p. 221.
25. Cf. J. Hone, ibid., p. 239.
25A. W. B. Yeats, *Plays in Prose and Verse*, p. 425.
25B. W. B. Yeats, *The Irish National Theatre*, Rome, 1935.
25C. Cf. *Some Passages from the Letters of Æ to W. B. Yeats*, p. 27. Date of letter, 28 January 1902.
26. W. B. Yeats, *Collected Plays*, p. 86.
27. *Vide* Stopford Brooke and Rolleston, *A Treasure of Irish Poetry*, p. 22. Here the date of the song is given (cf. E. Curtis, *A History of Ireland*, p. 338) as 1796, the year of the French expedition to Bantry Bay. A second expedition assembled off the Texel in June 1797 and was defeated at Camperdown in October. Stephen Gwynn, *Irish Literature and Drama*, p. 160, connects the song with the expedition of 1798, commanded by General Humbert, who landed his men at Killala and later surrendered at Ballinamuck. Yeats, it seems, also connected the song with this expedition.
27A. Cf. W. B. Yeats, *Plays in Prose and Verse*, p. 419:
'My dear Lady Gregory . . . One night I had a dream almost as distinct as a vision, of a cottage where there was well-being and talk of a marriage, and into the midst of that cottage there came an old woman in a long cloak. She was Ireland herself, that Cathleen ni Houlihan . . . we turned my dream into the little play Cathleen-ni-Houlihan. . . .'
28. Stephen Gwynn, *Irish Literature and Drama*, p. 158.
29. W. B. Yeats, *Last Poems and Plays*, p. 83.
30. W. B. Yeats, *Collected Poems*, p. 90.
31. The poem appears in *Irish Minstrelsy*, p. 141, a copy of which was given to Yeats by its compiler, H. Halliday Sparling, in 1888. The volume included a poem by Yeats.
32. W. B. Yeats, *Autobiographies*, p. 240.
33. Maud Gonne MacBride, *Scattering Branches*, p. 22. George Moore's malicious account of a conversation gives one angle on Yeats's love that must have irritated him when he saw it in print; the quotation is from *Vale*, p. 168:
'We talked of her whom he had loved always, the passionate ideal of his life, and why this ideal had never become a reality to him as Mathilde had become to Roland. Was it really so? was my pressing question and he answered me:
' "I was very young at the time and was satisfied with . . ." My memory fails me, or perhaps the phrase was never finished. The words I supply "the spirit of sense", are merely conjectural.
' "Yes, I understand, the common mistake of a boy." And I was sorry for Yeats and his inspiration which did not seem to have survived his youth because it had arisen out of an ungratified desire. Hyacinths grown in a vase only bloom for a season.'
34. Yeats was about to lecture at the time, and the telegram arrived just before his lecture. He spoke, but could never remember what he said, and after the lecture walked endlessly about the streets. (Information from Mrs Yeats.) The tour had a stimulating effect on him, however. Cf. W. S. Blunt, *My Diaries, 1888–1914*, entry for 10 May 1904:

'Yeats is just back from America where they have made a great fuss of
him, and he takes himself very seriously in consequence.'
35. W. B. Yeats, *Collected Poems*, p. 102.
36. C. M. Bowra, *The Heritage of Symbolism*, p. 199.
37. W. B. Yeats, *Collected Poems*, p. 103.
37A. Cf. Chapter 5, note 8A.
38. Cf. Maud Gonne MacBride, *Scattering Branches*, p. 24.
39. W. B. Yeats, *Collected Poems*, p. 102.
40. W. B. Yeats, ibid., p. 103.
41. Maud Gonne MacBride, *Scattering Branches*, p. 27.
42. W. B. Yeats, *Collected Poems*, p. 100.
43. W. B. Yeats, ibid., p. 101.
44. W. B. Yeats, unpublished material.
44A. Cf. a passage marked 172 in his 1908–12 Diary:
'I do not listen enough. I meant to write down much of Dunsany's
thought. It is not merely that I talk, for if I am silent in a room I do not
really listen. A word suggests something and I follow that—I am always
like a child playing with bricks in a corner.'
44B. Cf. George Moore, *Vale*, pp. 163–6.
45. George Moore, ibid.
46. *W. B. Yeats: A Critical Study* (1915).
47. V. K. Menon, *The Development of William Butler Yeats*, p. 44.
48. Cf. W. B. Yeats, *Collected Poems*, p. 85:
           . . . new commonness
     Upon the throne and crying about the streets
     And hanging up its paper flowers from post to post.
49. Diary version quoted.
49A. Cf. Arnold Bax, *Farewell my Youth*, p. 98.
But Yeats was never there (Æ's house in Rathgar, Dublin) for he and
Russell were estranged from one another at that period. The former
though he thought well of Colum and Stephens had no patience with
kindhearted Æ's spoonfeeding of fledgling poets and satirised them in an
epigram.
49B. A. E. Malone, *The Irish Theatre*, p. 20.
49C. Cf. Frank O'Connor, 'A Classic One-Act Play', *The Radio Times*,
5–11 January 1947:
'Critics of the Irish Theatre would do well to note that round the beginning of the century anyone who became friendly with Yeats was liable to
break out in one-act plays. The one-act play, usually set in a cottage
interior, is the characteristic form of the movement, which was a revolt
against the commercialism of the English Theatre with its lavish and taste-
less settings. To be practical, an Irish play had to be simple and cheap to
produce. . . . Yeats was a masterful man, and the inspiration is all his.
Many of these little plays are "miracles" (he was a mystic); some legendary
(he was a disciple of Morris); several nationalistic (he was a member of a
secret revolutionary organisation). All are marked in style, in treatment,
by careful exclusion of the trivial and occasional.'
49D. J. B. Yeats, *Letters to His Son W. B. Yeats and Others*, p. 151.
50. W. B. Yeats, *Collected Poems*, p. 104.
51. Sturge Moore, *Art and Life*, p. 38.
52. Heinrich Heine, *Atta Troll*, iii, p. 9.
53. Letter to Sir William Rothenstein, *Scattering Branches*, p. 40.  Cf. Sir
William Rothenstein, *Men and Memories*, pp. 282 and 329. He calls Yeats's
interests 'nonsense' in connection with Yeats meeting Stephen Philips,
ibid., p. 283.
54. W. B. Yeats, *Collected Poems*, p. 263.

54A. Sir William Rothenstein, *Men and Memories*, p. 373. Binyon and Yeats encouraged Masefield's adventures in poetry. Cf. ibid., vol. ii, p. 20 for Yeats's attitude to Stirling, author of *The Canon*.

54B. Cf. Sir William Rothenstein, *Men and Memories*, pp. 282 *seq.* for a description of Yeats's 'Mondays' where 'every week he held forth on fairies and magic, the Cabbala, and the philosophical stone'.

55. W. B. Yeats, *Collected Poems*, p. 109.

56. W. B. Yeats, unpublished material.

57. Maud Gonne MacBride, *Scattering Branches*, p. 28.

57A. Cf. W. B. Yeats, *Estrangement*, p. 39.

58. These lines in the poem:

How should the world be luckier if this house
Where passion and precision have been one
Time out of mind, became too ruinous
To breed the lidless eye that loves the sun?
And the sweet laughing eagle thoughts that grow
Where wings have memories, and all
That comes of the best knit to the best?

are echoes of Blake's imagery. Cf.

The eagle that doth gaze upon the sun.

('King Edward the Third', poetical sketches, *The Poems of William Blake* (ed. Yeats), p. 13.)

As the winged eagle scorns the towery fence . . .
Then, bosomed in an amber cloud, around
Plumes his wide wings, and seeks Sol's palace high.

('An Imitation of Spenser', poetical sketches, ibid., p. 29.)

And the eagle returns—
Shaking the dust from his immortal pinions to awake
The sun that sleeps too long.

('Visions of the Daughters of Albion', The Prophetical Books, ibid., p. 181, or *Blake*, Nonesuch edition, p. 195.)

Ask the winged eagle why he loves the sun?

(Ibid., p. 182, or *Blake*, Nonesuch edition, p. 196..) Yeats used the eagle as a symbol of objectivity and the sun is also regarded as objective (cf. *A Vision*) but the poetical value of the symbolism of the eagle and the sun seems due to Blake.

58A. *Letters to Miss Florence Farr from Bernard Shaw and W. B. Yeats*, p. 52.

58B. Wilfrid Blunt, *My Diaries, 1888–1914*, p. 252, 9 June 1909. Cf. J. B. Yeats, *Letters to His Son W. B. Yeats and Others*, p. 175.

59. Frank O'Connor, *The Irish Theatre*, p. 51.

60. W. B. Yeats, *Last Poems and Plays*, p. 49.

60A. But cf. for an earlier interest in the Celtic notion of the fool's wisdom, *The Wind Among the Reeds* (1890), p. 68.

61. In *The Hour Glass*.

62. J. B. Yeats, *Letters to His Son W. B. Yeats and Others*, p. 97.

63. W. B. Yeats, *Collected Poems*, p. 113.

64. Gaelic Society, *Transactions*, vol. i, 1808. Cf. for sources of the legend O. Bergin, introduction to *Stories from Keating's History of Ireland*.

65. *Atlantis*, vol. iii, 1862.

66. Cf. note 67A.

67. Sir Samuel Ferguson, *Poems*, p. 140.

67A. I am greatly indebted to Mr Casey's discussion of the Irish sources of the legend in an unpublished M.A. thesis on Sir Samuel Ferguson's poetry, the National University of Ireland, University College, Dublin, 1945.

68. J. MacPherson, 'Dar Thula', *Ossian*, p. 342.

69. W. B. Yeats, *Plays in Prose and Verse*, p. 192.

69A. W. B. Yeats, ibid., p. 219.
70. W. B. Yeats, *The Arrow*, No. 3.
70A. There is an interesting unpublished fragment dated October (probably 1913) which records some of his views on the drama after the first flush of enthusiasm was over:
'Great art, great poetic drama is the utmost of nobility and the utmost of reality. The passions and drama fall into two groups commonly the groups where nobility predominates and the group where reality predominates. If there is too much of the first all becomes sentimental, too much of the second all becomes sordid. Nobility struggles with reality, the eagle and the snake. . . . The nobility is never all personal—In Shakespeare where it is often intermixed with reality in the same characters—Macbeth for instance—it is hard and separate, it is largely a Roman tradition with a passion that is not Roman and a far more powerful context of reality. In modern work . . . Faust . . . the plays of D'Annunzio . . . the two groups are more distinct. We have grown self-conscious, more like the Greeks and Romans in this, but the idealism now [is] no longer their [s? or 'there'?]. It is I think more Christian. We are further from the rediscovery of learning.'
71. W. B. Yeats, *Collected Poems*, p. 107.
72. W. B. Yeats, unpublished material.
73. For Yeats's activity in this matter cf. W. S. Blunt, *My Diaries, 1888–1914*, entry for 10 May 1904.

## CHAPTER VII

1. W. B. Yeats, unpublished material.
2. Louis MacNeice, *The Poetry of W. B. Yeats*, p. 127, calls it his basic principle.
3. W. B. Yeats, *Essays*, p. 492.
4. W. B. Yeats, *Collected Poems*, p. 109.
5. He dealt with contraries in the 1893 edition of Blake. Opposite this passage in Denis Saurat's *Blake and Modern Thought*, p. 19:
'Without contraries there is no progression. Attraction and Repulsion, Love and Hate, are necessary to Human existence. From these contraries spring what the religious call Good and Evil. Good is the passive that obeys Reason. Evil is the active springing from Energy. Good is Heaven. Evil is Hell.' he pencilled the comment:
'I think there was no such thought known in England in Blake's day. It is fundamental in Blake.' The qualification 'in England' suggests that Yeats knew the idea in Boehme whom he had studied in some detail. For the occurrence of the idea in Boehme cf. H. L. Martensen, *Jacob Boehme: his life and teaching*, p. 77.
6. J. Hone, *W. B. Yeats, 1865–1939*, p. 114.
7. Cf. W. B. Yeats, *Collected Poems*, p. 209:
> While round the shore a million stood
> Like drops of frozen rainbow light,
> And pondered in a soft vain mood
> Upon their shadows in the tide.
7A. The idea may have owed something to the Yeats–Pollexfen extremes amongst which he grew up. Cf. a passage in *John Sherman*, p. 130, quoted in Chapter 3, note 45.
8. W. B. Yeats, *Collected Poems*, p. 36.

9. James Joyce, *A Portrait of the Artist as a Young Man*, p. 286. The sentence begins with the title of the poem in *The Wind among the Reeds* (1899).

10. He first appears in *The Secret Rose* (1897). Another imaginary figure was Owen Aherne (described to me by Mrs Joseph O'Neill as representing the Christian elements in Yeats); they are both part of 'Ego Dominus Tuus', completed in 1915. Perhaps the best way to describe them is to use Mrs O'Neill's explanation that they resembled the imaginary friends that sensitive children will create and hold conversations with, until they become more important than real persons. Yeats invested his creations with much detail. Robartes is probably based on MacGregor Mathers who had 'a gaunt resolute face and an athletic body' (*Autobiographies*, p. 226).

11. W. B. Yeats, *The Secret Rose*, p. 241.

12. W. B. Yeats, *Estrangement*, p. 11.

12A. Presumably 'mask' here is a misspelling for 'masque'.

12B. Cf. a passage in the unpublished autobiography:
'It was only during recent years that the thought that I was working steadily more than two hours original composition brings me almost at once to nervous breakdown. . . . I was always conscious of something helpless or even perhaps [indecipherable] in myself, I could not hold to my opinions among people who would make light of them. I would often accuse myself of disloyalty to some absent friend, I had it seems an incredible timidity—sometimes this became respectable and still explicable and painful to the memory.'

12C. It was in the United Arts Club that he ate two dinners without noticing the fact, so absorbed was he in his talk. P. L. Dickinson, *The Dublin of Yesterday*, p. 54.

13. W. B. Yeats, *Collected Poems*, p. 115.

14. J. Bronowski, *The Poet's Defence*, p. 233.

14A. W. B. Yeats, *Essays*, pp. 479 *seq.*

14B. W. B. Yeats, *Plays in Prose and Verse*, p. 428.

15. W. B. Yeats, ibid., p. 219.

16. W. B. Yeats, *Essays*, p. 292.

17. W. B. Yeats, ibid., p. 277.

18. Lennox Robinson, *Scattering Branches*, p. 108.

18A. This had been of increasing importance to him. Cf. E. R. Walsh, 'Reminiscences of W. B.', *The Irish Times*, 10 February 1940, where an incident of some significance is described:
'He had called, carelessly dressed, at Sutherland House one afternoon to see the Duchess, who had been a constant friend to him. Ushered into her great drawing-room he noticed a small group standing apart round a lady. The Duchess came forward to greet him, and immediately said: "I want to present you to Her Majesty", and, before he had time to gather his wits together, he found that he was talking to Queen Alexandra. He did most of the conversation, however, contrary to the tradition of etiquette, but he learned afterwards that the Queen was very pleased with him. The ease and lack of self-consciousness of the party strengthened his desire for a polished society, and the disdain he felt for the bourgeoisie, whose lives were ruled by convention and fear. "There are only three classes I respect," he exclaimed, "the aristocracy who are above fear; the poor who are beneath it, and the artists whom God has made reckless!"'

18B. Cf. J. Hone, *W. B. Yeats, 1865-1939*, p. 260, for General Sir Ian Hamilton's recollections of the poet there—'His milieu was the centre of a small band of admirers'. Yeats preferred women listeners. Cf. Sir William Rothenstein, *Men and Memories*, p. 282:
'Yeats impressed me. True, he had an artificial manner, and when he was surrounded by female admirers his sublimity came near to the ridicu-

lous at times; but he was a true poet and behind the solemn mask of the mystic there was a shrewd wisdcm. Yeats, like Shaw, was a man of great courage, who championed losing causes, and men who were unfairly assailed. Moreover, he maintained the dignity of literature and even in the midst of his lady admirers he was a really fine talker.'

19. W. B. Yeats, *Collected Poems*, p. 177.

19A. In Dublin he was at home to his friends on Sunday evenings in the hotel in South Frederick Street where Maud Gonne had been accustomed to stay when she was in Dublin. Lady Gregory used the hotel as a residence as well as Yeats (and Maud was not a little irritated at first when she found that the suite of rooms she normally occupied was taken by Lady Gregory), and the hotel became, in a sense, the headquarters of the dramatic movement. Cf. E. R. Walsh, 'Reminiscences of W.B.', *The Irish Times*:

'I was generally the first to arrive, and was greeted with a reassuring courtesy which removed a great deal of the diffidence I felt at first in expressing my opinions. Lady Gregory usually retired early, and until she left the conversation centred round Abbey Theatre affairs, Hugh Lane's modern gallery, current literary matters or French literature with which she was deeply acquainted. After she retired talk became less formal, and Yeats took a larger part in it. John Synge, a frequent visitor, spoke least, but there was a reserved power about him which impressed me, and I noticed a shade of deference in Yeats's manner when he asked for Synge's opinion. When he became really interested in a topic Yeats would walk about the room, with head thrown back, and pour forth in his beautiful voice comment or interesting experiences. He loved to talk of the Rhymers' Club; for he knew Beardsley, Dowson and Lionel Johnson well, and the early brilliance and subsequent tragic failure of their lives had touched him deeply.'

20. Rabindranath Tagore, *Gitanjali*, 1913.

20A. Rothenstein introduced Tagore to Yeats, cf. *Men and Memories*, vol. ii, pp. 262, 263, and 266.

20B. Cf. for Ezra Pound's influence on Yeats, Ernest Boyd, *Portraits: Real and Imaginary*, p. 238.

20C. Yeats had many Indian friends at the time, including the poetess Sarojini Naidu. Cf. J. Hone, *W. B. Yeats, 1865–1939*, p. 264.

21. Douglas Goldring, *South Lodge*, p. 48.

21A. In 'Notes of the Month', *Dublin Magazine*, May 1924, p. 854, mention is made of Yeats again re-reading Swedenborg. On 19 November (1913) he wrote in a manuscript-book given to him by Maud Gonne:

'I dreamed last night that Lady Gregory and I were talking to Moran, the most offensive of Irish clerical personalities but an amiable fat man in presence. He spoke of the arts at Jerusalem and said: "There, there is no one but ourselves and the Pope". I thought the arts thrived there and thought "so he does not class himself with the bourgeoisie" and said "We make fine things if we are rich or poor but not if we have just enough to be always afraid of losing it". He said, "We are harassed but we are able to put that thought away". He then said something I could not quite hear; but I understood that he was going to ask Lady Gregory and myself to advise some of his visitors. I looked towards Lady Gregory and wondered what I could say that would not offend him and then, resolved to speak the truth, said "The first condition of great writing is to have, as a writer, beautiful manners". I then half-woke and in the half-waking state told myself that the dream was a warning to avoid religious controversy. That day I had said at Mrs. Fowler's: "I have thought for some time that I should be drawn into religious controversy by the natural development of things in Dublin. A mystical religious movement would be better than anticlericalism if the clericals attack us."'

22. W. B. Yeats, *Collected Poems*, p. 136. An earlier poem on the Rosicrucian theme was published in *The Bookman*, October 1895 under the title 'A Song of the Rosycross'.

23. W. B. Yeats, *Essays*, p. 241.

24. Douglas Goldring, *South Lodge*, pp. 157-9.

25. Cf. W. B. Yeats, *Collected Poems*, p. 257:
> He loved strange thought
> And knew that sweet extremity of pride
> That's called platonic love.

26. W. B. Yeats, *Essays*, p. 278.

27. J. Hone, *W. B. Yeats, 1865-1939*, p. 294.

28. W. B. Yeats, *Collected Poems*, p. 175.

29. He wrote in his manuscript-book in September 1913:
> The riddle is half-mastered, when
> Our pride and humbleness are such
> That we claim little of other men
> And of ourselves claim much.

30. Desmond MacCarthy, 'Living Records', *The Sunday Times*, 2-9 February 1947.

31. W. B. Yeats, letter to Hugh Lane, 1 January 1913, asking him if he thought the poem 'politic':
'I have tried to meet the argument in Lady Ardilaun's letter to somebody, her objection to giving because of Home Rule, and Lloyd George and still more to people like Ardilaun that they should not give unless there is public demand.'

32. Cf. W. B. Yeats, *Estrangement*, p. 20, for one of the frequent allusions to Castiglione in his private diaries of the 1909 period.

33. W. B. Yeats, *The Bounty of Sweden*, p. 18.

34. W. B. Yeats, *Collected Poems*, p. 169.

35. Cf. note to Count Baldesar Castiglione, *The Courtier*, No. 203, p. 129, which describes Duke Ercole as a special patron of the theatre, 'no less than five plays of Plautus being performed during the wedding of his son Alfonso in 1502', a feature of the Duke's character likely to commend itself to Yeats and Lady Gregory, which probably begot the lines:
> What cared Duke Ercole, that bid
> His mummers to the market-place,
> What the onion sellers thought or did
> So that his Plautus set the pace
> For the Italian comedies?

36. Count Baldesar Castiglione, ibid., p. 9.

37. W. B. Yeats, *Essays*, p. 360. Count Baldesar Castiglione, *The Courtier*, No. 203, p. 8.

38. C. M. Bowra, *The Heritage of Symbolism*, p. 121.

39. W. B. Yeats, *Autobiographies*, p. 118.

40. C. M. Bowra, *The Heritage of Symbolism*, p. 120.

41. A. C. Swinburne, *William Blake*, pp. vi, vii.

42. J. B. Yeats, *Letters to His Son W. B. Yeats and Others*, p. 92.

43. W. B. Yeats, *Collected Poems*, p. 444.

44. W. B. Yeats, ibid., p. 122.

45. W. B. Yeats, ibid., p. 444, cf. Lady Gregory, *Hugh Lane*, p. 138.

46. W. B. Yeats, *Collected Poems*, p. 123.

47. This passage illustrates how intimately Yeats's rage was bound up with the earlier controversy. In *Autobiographies*, p. 390, he wrote:
'During the quarrel over Parnell's grave a quotation from Goethe ran through the papers, describing our Irish jealousy: "The Irish seem to me like a pack of hounds, always dragging down some noble stag."' Cf. Ecker-

mann, *Conversations with Goethe*, 7 April 1829. For Yeats's use of Eckermann cf. Oliver St John Gogarty, *As I was going down Sackville Street*, p. 110.

48. W. B. Yeats, *Collected Poems*, p. 166.

49. For a different interpretation *vide* Edmund Wilson, *Axel's Castle*, p. 36, and L. A. G. Strong, *Scattering Branches*, p. 200. Cf. A. Norman Jeffares, 'W. B. Yeats and his Methods of Writing Verse', *Nineteenth Century*, March 1946. A similar explanation is given by Miss Babette Deutsch, *This Modern Poetry*, p. 217.

50. His dreams seemed to be filled with concern for her; many of these are recorded in his Diaries from 1908 (when he visited her in Paris) onwards.

51. W. B. Yeats, *Collected Poems*, p. 138.

52. W. B. Yeats, ibid., p. 140.

53. Information from Mrs W. B. Yeats.

54. W. B. Yeats, *Collected Poems*, p. 139.

55. Information from Oliver Edwards and Mrs W. B. Yeats.

56. W. B. Yeats, *Collected Poems*, p. 128.

57. W. B. Yeats, ibid., p. 124. There is a certain similarity between this poem and 'The Grey Rock' (ibid., p. 115) in that each falls into two separate parts. The poets of the Cheshire Cheese who remain loyal to their trade are contrasted with the heroic story of Aoife, told with mocking refusal to subscribe to the old standards; 'The Three Beggars' replaces the poets by the solitary heron while the heroic story was settled at a considerably lower level with Guare and the beggars. The earlier mockery is now probably a satire upon the avarice which Yeats despised in his contemporary setting. He is to be associated with the poets and the heron, being himself poet and solitary.

58. W. B. Yeats, *Collected Poems*, p. 127.

59. W. B. Yeats, *Essays*, p. 500.

60. W. B. Yeats, *Collected Poems*, p. 156.

61. Information from Mrs W. B. Yeats, from conversations with both Yeats and Pound who were both living in Sussex at the time.

62. W. B. Yeats, *Collected Poems*, p. 129.

63. W. B. Yeats, ibid., p. 130.

64. Louis MacNeice, *The Poetry of W. B. Yeats*, p. 113.

65. J. M. Synge, *The Shadow of the Glen, Plays* (1915), p. 26.

66. W. B. Yeats, *Collected Poems*, p. 141.

67. J. M. Synge, *The Aran Islands*, p. 37.

68. W. B. Yeats, *Collected Poems*, p. 142.

69. *The English Review*, vol. xvi, 1914.

70. George Moore, *Ave*.

71. W. B. Yeats, *Collected Poems*, p. 113.

72. W. B. Yeats, ibid., p. 443.

73. *Vide* the discussion of this matter in Chapter 1. Yeats got his information from the two copies of the *Gentleman's Almanack* in his sister's possession.

74. Lady Gregory's *Journals*, p. 264.

75. W. B. Yeats, *Collected Poems*, p. 108.

76. W. B. Yeats, ibid., p. 175.

77. W. B. Yeats, ibid., p. 149.

77A. J. B. Yeats, *Letter to His Son W. B. Yeats and Others*, p. 193.

77B. W. B. Yeats, *Collected Poems*, p. 172.

78. W. B. Yeats, ibid., p. 136.

79. W. B. Yeats, ibid., p. 137.

80. W. B. Yeats, ibid., p. 174.

81. All dates given for poems have been obtained from manuscripts and diaries, and checked by Mrs W. B. Yeats with other information in her possession. The order in which many poems were published is not con-

secutive. 'I don't want them to know all about everything', he said to his wife, when deliberately placing some poems out of chronological order.

82. W. B. Yeats, *Collected Poems*, p. 168.
83. W. B. Yeats, ibid., p. 169.
84. W. B. Yeats, ibid., p. 170. The length of line in Yeats's poem suggests that a possible source might be a ballad 'The Red Man's Wife':

> My darling sweet Phoenix, if now you will be my own
> For the patriarch David had a number of wives it's well known.

*Irish Street Ballads* (ed. Colm O'Lochlain), p. 193. (Cf. also p. 49 for another use of phoenix for the poet's love.)

85. W. B. Yeats, *Collected Poems*, p. 172.


## Chapter VIII

1. From the Royal Societies Club, 12 May 1916.
2. W. B. Yeats, *Collected Poems*, p. 120.
3. W. B. Yeats, ibid., p. 202. Cf. *Essays*, p. 389.
3A. Cf. Sir William Rothenstein, *Men and Memories*, vol. ii, p. 321.
4. W. B. Yeats, *Estrangement*, p. 31.
5. W. B. Yeats, *Collected Poems*, p. 205.
6. W. B. Yeats, ibid., p. 206.
7. To Mrs. W. B. Yeats, from Lucan, 1918. The poem was completed in January 1919.
8. W. B. Yeats, *Collected Poems*, p. 206.
9. Cf. W. B. Yeats, unpublished material quoted in chapter 5, for the lofty dignity of the county houses.
10. W. B. Yeats, *Collected Poems*, p. 207.
11. Information from Mrs Francis Stuart. Cf. also a letter from W. B. Yeats to Lady Gregory, August 1916, from Normandy, quoted by J. Hone, *W. B. Yeats, 1865–1939*, p. 303:

'I believe I was meant to be the father of an unruly family. I did not think I liked little boys but I liked Shawn (the son of Maud Gonne and John MacBride) I am really managing Iseult very well. The other night she made a prolonged appeal for an extra cigarette. . . . I have stayed on longer than I intended but I think you will forgive me under the circumstances—as father, but as father only, I have been a great success.

12. W. B. Yeats, *Essays*, p. 537.
13. Yeats had never a bohemian contempt for marriage—except perhaps in moments of depression when he would stare:

> At the old bitter world where they marry in churches,
> And laugh over the untroubled water
> At all who marry in churches,
> Through the white thin bone of a hare.

*Collected Poems*, p. 153. Initially he had thought Maud Gonne an unsuitable wife and therefore had endeavoured to suppress his love for her. Later he wrote to Æ at a time of growing personal disillusionment (cf. *Dublin Magazine*, July 1939):

'I congratulate you on the birth of your son of which I have heard from Lady Gregory. I think that a poet, or even a mystic, becomes a greater power from understanding all the great primary emotions and these one only gets out of going through the common experiences and duties of life.'

14. Information from Madame MacBride.

15. W. B. Yeats, *Collected Poems*, p. 136.
16. W. B. Yeats, ibid., p. 137.
17. W. B. Yeats, ibid., p. 174.
18. W. B. Yeats, ibid., p. 156.
19. Cf. J. Hone, *W. B. Yeats, 1865–1939*, p. 303.
20. Cf. A. Norman Jeffares, 'Two Songs of a Fool and their Explanation'. *English Studies*, December 1945. The first section was written at Coleman's Hatch, Sussex on 24 October, the second section on 27 October 1917.
21. The tin boxes which house the script are still in the possession of Mrs W. B. Yeats.
22. Quoted by J. Hone, *W. B. Yeats, 1865–1939*, p. 307.
23. The first edition is dated 1925, but it was published in January 1926. Cf. W. Roth, *A Catalogue of the Writings of William Butler Yeats*, p. 60.
24. W. B. Yeats, *A Vision*, Introduction, p. xvi.
25. W. B. Yeats, ibid., p. xvii.
26. W. B. Yeats, *A Packet for Ezra Pound*, p. 25.
27. Information from Professor G. A. T. O'Brien.
28. Quoted J. Hone, *W. B. Yeats, 1865–1939*, p. 305.
29. W. B. Yeats, *Collected Poems*, p. 180.
30. W. B. Yeats, *Essays*, p. 485.
31. The image of the Bedouin was probably taken from Shelley's *Queen Mab*:

Behold yon sterile spot
Where now the wandering Arab's tent
Flaps in the desert breeze.

In describing an odd personage (*Autobiographies*, p. 105) whom he had seen in the days of his Shelley worship he again mentions the image. The old man kept up the illusion of living under canvas in the desert.
32. W. B. Yeats, *Essays*, p. 496.
33. W. B. Yeats, ibid., p. 493.
34. Chaucer, *The Complete Works* (ed. F. N. Robinson), p. 168, and *The Complete Works* (ed. W. W. Skeat), notes.
35. W. B. Yeats, *A Vision*, 'Dedication to Vestigia' (Mrs MacGregor Mathers), p. 12.
36. In *Michael Robartes and the Dancer* (Cuala Press), 1920.
37. W. B. Yeats, *Collected Poems*, p. 183.
38. W. B. Yeats, *A Vision*, p. 38.
39. W. B. Yeats, ibid., p. 69.
40. W. B. Yeats, ibid., p. 61.
41. W. B. Yeats, ibid., p. 64.
42. W. B. Yeats, ibid., p. 69. Yeats's own phase was seventeen. He lists as examples of it both Dante and Shelley.
43. W. B. Yeats, *Collected Poems*, p. 192.
44. W. B. Yeats, ibid., p. 189.
45. W. B. Yeats, *A Vision*, pp. 115 *seq*.
46. For a fuller discussion *vide* A. Norman Jeffares, 'Gyres in the Poetry of W. B. Yeats', *English Studies*, June 1946.
47. He read *La Spirale* after he had written the section of *A Vision* dealing with gyres. The book was given to him by Sturge Moore.
47A. Cf. J. P. Mahaffy, *Descartes*, p. 159.
48. Cf. E. Swedenborg, *Diarium Maius*, paragraphs 1015, 1015½, 1016, 1017, 2920, and 2921; *The Principia*, 38 and 39; *Arcana Coelestia*, 1571, 5181, 15182, and 5183.
49. Cf. H. L. Martensen, *Jacob Boehme*, pp. 31, 33, 62, and 258, for the ideas of the tinctures, of the will fashioning itself a mirror, of contraries, and of the inevitability of change.

50. Yeats read William Law's *An Illustration of the Deep Principles of Jacob Boehme the Teutonic Philosopher in Thirteen Figures,* referred to in *A Packet for Ezra Pound,* p. 31.

51. W. B. Yeats, *The Celtic Twilight* (1902), p. 205.

52. W. B. Yeats, *Collected Poems,* p. 210. The idea of falconer and falcon probably comes from Dante, *vide* note 53, ibid., pp. 74, 129 *seq.*

53. Dante, *The Vision of Hell,* canto xvii, Cary's translation (Dent, 1908 and 1909), pp. 73, 128 *seq.*

54. W. B. Yeats, *Last Poems and Plays,* p. 76.

54A. *Vide* Dante's *Vision of Hell* (illustrated by Doré), illustration facing p. 88, cf. also p. 91.

55. W. B. Yeats, *A Vision,* p. 183.

56. W. B. Yeats, ibid., p. 213.

56A. P. Ure, *Towards a Mythology,* connects this beast with the visions called up by Mather's symbols. Cf. *Autobiographies,* p. 230:
'He gave me a cardboard symbol and I closed my eyes. Sight came slowly, there was not that sudden miracle as if the darkness had been cut with a knife for that miracle is mostly a woman's privilege, but there rose before me mental images I could not control: a desert and black Titan raising himself up by his two hands from the middle of a heap of ancient ruins. Mathers explained that I had seen a being of the order of Salamanders. . . .'

57. J. B. Yeats, *Letters to His Son W. B. Yeats and Others,* p. 97. Letter from 7 Stephen's Green, 1906.

57A. A passage probably written after his visit to Paris in 1908 illustrates this clearly:
'The other day in Paris I found that for days I lost all social presence of mind through the very ordinary folly of a very ordinary person. I heard in every word she spoke ancient enemies of vanity and sentimentality and became rude and accordingly miserable. This is my worst fault rooted in ♂ ☍ ☽ ). I must watch myself carefully recording errors that I may become interested in their cure perhaps I ought [to] seek out people I dislike till I have conquered this petulant combativeness. It is always inexcusable to lose self-possession. It always comes from impatience from a kind of spiritual fright of someone who is here and now more powerful even if only from stupidity. I am never angry with those in my power. I fear strangers and I fear the representatives of the collective opinion and so rage stupidly and rudely exaggerating what I feel and think.

57B. Cf. his use of the word for this purpose in *Wheels and Butterflies,* p. 120.

58. J. Hone, *W. B. Yeats, 1865–1939,* p. 326.

59. W. B. Yeats, *Essays,* p. 508.

60. W. B. Yeats, *Collected Poems,* p. 158.

61. W. B. Yeats, *Essays,* p. 509.

62. W. B. Yeats, *Collected Poems,* p. 152.

63. W. B. Yeats, ibid., p. 156.

64. W. B. Yeats, ibid., p. 155.

65. W. B. Yeats, ibid., p. 199. Another poem 'On Woman' does not refer to Mrs Yeats, being written before his marriage in the same mood of disillusionment as 'Beggar to Beggar Cried' (ibid., p. 128). Solomon and Sheba occur as symbols of perfect love in the 1909–12 diaries.

66. W. B. Yeats, *Collected Poems,* p. 200.

67. Cf. P. More, *Shelburne Essays,* series i, p. 182.

68. In *Michael Robartes and the Dancer* (Cuala Press), 1920.

69. W. B. Yeats, *Collected Poems,* p. 208. The poem is an actual record of the dreams experienced by the poet and his wife when they were staying

in the Powerscourt Arms Hotel, Enniskerry, Co. Wicklow, in January 1919. Cf. for a similar description of touching, R. Jefferies, *The Story of My Heart*, p. 20.

70. W. B. Yeats, *A Vision*, p. 173.
71. W. B. Yeats, *Collected Poems*, p. 209.
72. Information from Mrs W. B. Yeats.
73. W. B. Yeats, *Collected Poems*, p. 190. The poem was written between July and September 1918 when Yeats and his wife were living at Ballinamantane House, near Gort.
74. W. B. Yeats, ibid., p. 157.
74A. This word lineaments was one which Blake used frequently. (Cf. for its use in a passage selected by Yeats, *The Poems of William Blake* (1893 and 1906), p. 141.) Yeats praised another word 'copulate' (*Letters on Poetry to Dorothy Wellesley*, p. 173) also used frequently by Blake. (Cf. *The Poems of William Blake*, 1893, pp. 186–7.)

75. W. B. Yeats, *Collected Poems*, p. 197. The first MS is dated April 1919; the poem was completed in June 1919.

76. W. B. Yeats, ibid., p. 211.
77. This was an old complaint about Maud. Cf. a passage in his Diary 1910:
'I fear for her any renewed devotion to any opinion. Women because the main event of their lives has been a giving of themselves give themselves to an opinion as if it were a stone doll—women should have their play with dolls finished in childhood, for if they play with ideas again it is amid hatred and malice.'
The idea that over-much beauty brought bad luck was an intermittent one, varying according to his moods. Cf. a line in *Deirdre* (*Plays in Prose and Verse*, p. 192):
But that she'd too much beauty for good luck.

## Chapter IX

1. W. B. Yeats, *Collected Poems*, p. 229.
2. W. B. Yeats, Letter to Mrs Shakespear, from Thoor, Ballylee, dated 25 May 1926.
2A. Cf. Chapter 8, note 13.
3. W. B. Yeats, *The Celtic Twilight*, pp. 35 seq.
4. W. B. Yeats, *Collected Poems*, p. 124.
5. W. B. Yeats, ibid., p. 219.
6. W. B. Yeats, ibid., p. 180.
7. W. B. Yeats, ibid., p. 183.
8. John Milton, *Il Penseroso*, vol. i, pp. 85 seq.
9. P. B. Shelley, *Laon and Cythna*, *Prince Athanase*, part II, fragment 11.
For a fuller discussion of the literary sources of Yeats's tower poetry cf. A. Norman Jeffares, 'Thoor Ballylee', *English Studies*, December 1947. The general influence of Shelley on Yeats has been stressed in an article by Professor Häusermann in *The Mint* (ed. G. Grigson), 1946.
10. Cf. Count Villiers de l'Isle Adam, *Axel*, p. 94, where Axel, Count of Auersperg, studies ancient manuscripts by lamplight in his tower. Yeats wrote a note on the performance of *Axel* in *The Bookman*, April 1894, and recalled the first impression the play had then made on him in his Introduction to the translation made by H. P. R. Finberg in 1925. He wrote that the symbols became a part of him and for years to come dominated his thought.
11. Cf. J. B. Yeats's letter mentioning Charles Johnston's description of

W. B. Y. as 'the most self-centred man I ever knew, but not in the least selfish', footnote to p. 120, *Letters to His Son W. B. Yeats and Others.*
12. W. B. Yeats, *Essays*, p. 137.
13. W. B. Yeats, ibid., p. 106.
14. W. B. Yeats. *Collected Poems*, p. 184.
15. J. Hone, *W. B. Yeats, 1865–1939*, p. 310, dates the purchase of the castle as 'some years before his marriage'. A letter from Yeats to Lady Gregory, dated 30 June 1917, mentions that he has just paid for the castle.
16. Memo dated 19 February 1917, from H. R. Vereker to Sir Henry Doran. This raised objections to the sale of the castle, as the bridge leading into the castle could be used as a public road instead of the existing system of a ford:
'When the river is low it is shallow enough for carts to go across, and the primitive arrangement of flags laid on dry stone piers enables foot passengers to cross.' Eventually the price of £80 was reduced on condition that the bridge leading to the castle be utilised as a thoroughfare, as otherwise the Board would have had to build a bridge on the site of the ford. The final arrangement between the Board and Yeats was made on 31 March 1917.
17. W. B. Yeats, *Collected Poems*, p. 159.
18. W. B. Yeats, ibid., p. 202.
19. W. B. Yeats, ibid., p. 183.
20. W. B. Yeats, ibid., p. 148.
21. W. B. Yeats, ibid., p. 211.
22. Douglas Goldring, *South Lodge*, p. 124.
23. W. B. Yeats, *Collected Poems*, p. 232.
24. Cf. his translation of the Sophoclean chorus which describes the sacred olive, ibid., p. 245. The destruction is the Persian sack of the city which could not destroy the plant.
25. When the thought of *A Vision* is referred to the thoughts are meant which were occupying him from the time of his marriage onward (if not before) which can be best described under this heading. References in the notes are, unless otherwise stated, to the 1925 edition.
26. The spirits who gave the messages to Mrs Yeats told him that they had come to give him metaphors for poetry. Cf. *A Packet for Ezra Pound*, p. 2.
27. W. B. Yeats, *Collected Poems*, p. 157.
28. W. B. Yeats, *A Vision*, pp. 155 and 157.
29. Statement made in a conversation with Professor H. O. White. In notes made by the latter of a broadcast by Yeats (2 July 1937) 'The Wild Swans at Coole' is described as a criticism of life, not a dream.
30. W. B. Yeats, *Collected Poems*, p. 147.
31. P. B. Shelley, *Alastor*, vol. i, pp. 282 seq.
31A. W. B. Yeats, *Collected Poems*, p. 275. Letter to Mrs W. B. Yeats from Coole, 3 February 1932.
32. W. B. Yeats, 'Dove or Swan', *A Vision*.
33. He gave it to a short-lived magazine founded by Francis Stuart and Lennox Robinson.
34. W. B. Yeats, *The Cat and the Moon and Certain Poems*, p. 37.
35. W. B. Yeats, *Collected Poems*, p. 241.
36. Information from Mrs W. B. Yeats.
37. W. S. Landor, *Imaginary Conversations, Collected Works*, vol. iii, p. 127.
38. W. Blake, *Poetical Works* (ed. W. B. Yeats), p. 108. *Works* (Nonesuch edition), p. 107.
39. J. C. Mangan, *Poems* (ed. D. J. O'Donoghue), p. 249.
40. Cf. Stephen Gwynn, *Irish Literature and Drama*, p. 86.

40A. The word was used frequently by Blake. Cf. for an example his *Poems* (ed. Yeats), p. 127.

41. W. B. Yeats, *Seven Poems and a Fragment*, p. 23. *Collected Poems*, p. 448.

42. Arthur Symons, *Poems*, vol. ii, p. 103.

43. Information from Mr Austin Clarke.

44. Yeats read of the case in the Rev. Dr Carrigan's *History of the Diocese of Ossory* (*vide* note 43) and St John D. Seymour's *Irish Witchcraft and Demonology* (information from Mr Austin Clarke).

45. Quoted by J. Hone, *W. B. Yeats, 1865–1939*, p. 326.

46. W. B. Yeats, *Seven Poems and a Fragment*, p. 6.

47. W. B. Yeats, *Collected Poems*, p. 242.

48. W. B. Yeats, ibid., p. 256.

49. The speech was made on 17 February. The motion 'That this House would welcome complete Self Government in Ireland, and condemns reprisals' was carried by 219 votes to 129. Yeats spoke fifth. I am indebted to the Secretary of the Oxford Union for the following press cutting which illustrates Yeats's sincere and rhetorical approach to the problem:

'Mr W. B. Yeats said the law had never broken down in Ireland. English law had broken down, but though he was not a Sinn Feiner he would say that Sinn Fein justice was real justice, and in many places in Ireland real justice had come for the first time. Hon. Members opposite did not like reprisals any more than he did, but their country was in such a position that they felt bound to support them. The causes which made the Germans act so in Belgium were the same precisely as those which were making officers—the Black and Tans—act madly and brutally in Ireland to-day, and those causes were drink and hysteria. The rural policeman who attended to take the dying depositions of the women shot from a passing lorry in Galway, was not allowed to do so, and the man who went for the doctor was shot. The verdict of the military enquiry was that the women was struck by a descending bullet fired from the lorry "as a precautionary measure". Ireland had long ceased to expect mercy for her men; she had expected it for her women. From every part of his own district in Galway came the complaint of ordinary law-abiding people about horrible things done by these maddened men, and it was not true to say that their nerves had been overwrought and had given way. The troops had been there longer, and their nerves had been severely tried, but with very few exceptions such things had not happened where they had been in charge. "I do not know" declared Mr Yeats "which lies heaviest on my heart—the tragedy of Ireland or the tragedy of England." Ireland would come through it all strengthened by suffering, but what of England? Where was the England of Gladstone and Disraeli, to let such things be done in England's name? Only when England realised would she hold the necessary enquiry and be done with things which dishonoured her once great name, the Mother of Freedom.'

50. *Vide* Lady Gregory's *Journals*, pp. 127–65. For the incident of the woman shot by the soldiers, p. 137. This is what Yeats referred to in 'Nineteen Hundred and Nineteen', stanza four, *Collected Poems*, p. 232. He wrote a bitter poem on the subject for *The Nation* in 1921 (Lady Gregory also wrote in this, but anonymously, *vide* her *Journals*, pp. 129 and 139) which contrasts with 'An Irish Airman foresees his Death', *Collected Poems*, p. 152. Both poems are written in appreciation of Robert Gregory (that written for *The Nation* was withheld from publication by Yeats as he thought it might hurt Gregory's widow) but the treatment of Kiltartan in the two poems is different. In the earlier published poem, written before any atrocities had taken place, Yeats uses the village as the real object of Gregory's patriotism:

Those that I fight I do not hate
Those that I guard I do not love.
But in the second the village has achieved martyrdom:
... Yet rise from your Italian tomb
Flit to Kiltartan Cross and stay
Till certain second thoughts have come
Upon the cause you served, that we
Imagined such a fine affair:
Half drunk or whole mad soldiery
Are murdering your tenants there
Men that revere your father yet
Are shot at on the open plain.
Where may new married women sit
And suckle children now? Armed men
May murder them in passing by
Nor law nor parliament take heed—
Then close your eyes with dust and lie
Among the other cheated dead.

51. These poems, first published in January 1923, were included in *The Cat and the Moon*, 1924. *Collected Poems*, p. 232.

52. Information from Mrs W. B. Yeats.

53. W. B. Yeats, *Essays*, p. 103.

54. W. B. Yeats, ibid., p. 106.

55. W. B. Yeats, *Collected Plays*, p. 281.

56. W. B. Yeats, *Collected Poems*, p. 238.

57. Letter from 4 Broad Street, Oxford. Cf. J. Hone, *W. B. Yeats, 1865–1939*, p. 340.

58. W. B. Yeats, *The Bounty of Sweden*, p. 50.

59. 'The Lonely Tower', *The Minor Poems of John Milton* (illustrated Samuel Palmer), p. 30.

60. Sir William Rothenstein, *Scattering Branches*, p. 46.

61. W. B. Yeats, *Collected Poems*, p. 207.

62. From 82 Merrion Square, Dublin, 28 June 1923.

Yeats's growing pride in his Anglo-Irish family was reinforced by the actual possession of the tower, of a part of Irish soil. He had become a part of the countryside, far more perhaps in his character of poet than if he had been a member of the county society which had seemed another world to him in his boyhood. Cf. his idea of family continuity in 'Meditations in Time of Civil War', *Collected Poems*, pp. 227 and 228. He had 'founded' there:

that after me
My bodily heirs may find,
To exalt a lonely mind,
Befitting emblems of adversity

and

Having inherited a vigorous mind
From my old fathers, I must nourish dreams
And leave a woman and a man behind
As vigorous . . .

63. Cf. W. B. Yeats, *On the Boiler*, p. 12.

64. W. B. Yeats, *Collected Poems*, p. 427.

64A. There is a note to the poem included in *The Cat and the Moon and Certain Poems*, p. 38, which gives a flippant account of his marriage:

(Harun has presented Kusta, symbolising Yeats, with a new bride.) 'According to one tradition of the desert, she had, to the great surprise of her friends, fallen in love with the elderly philosopher but according to another Harun bought her from a passing merchant. Kusta, a christian like the Caliph's own physician, had planned, one version of the story says, to end his days in a Monastery at Nisibis, while another story has it that he was deep in a violent love affair that he had arranged for himself. The only thing upon which there is general agreement is that he was warned by a dream to accept the gift of the Caliph, and that his wife a few days after the marriage began to talk in her sleep, and that she told him all those things which he had searched for vainly all his life in the great library of the Caliph and in the conversation of wise men.'

65. Letter to Mrs Shakespear, 23 August (1934) from Riversdale, Rathfarnham:

'I had a Swedish compliment the other day—that has pleased better than [any] I have ever had. Some Swede said to my wife "Our Royal Family liked your husband better than any other Nobel Prize Winner, they said he had the manners of a courtier". I would like to think this true but I doubt—my kind of critical mind creates harshness and roughness which somehow reminds me—Have you read *Hadrian the Seventh* by Lionel's friend and acquaintance Baron Corvo. It is quite cheap and nearly a great work— my sort of book—the love of the ruling mind, the ruling race—an imaginary Pope is the theme with enough evil to be a great man. I hate the pale victims of modern fiction—but suppose that they may have minds like photographic plates.'

Lionel is Mrs Shakespear's relative, Lionel Johnson. For details of Baron Corvo's life, *vide* A. J. A. Symonds, *The Quest for Corvo*.

65A. W. B. Yeats, *The Bounty of Sweden*, p. 11.
65B. W. B. Yeats, ibid., p. 13.
66. The Nobel Prize brought him £7,500. He spent some of this on books, mainly expensive histories and works of reference, and invested the larger part of it. The salary of a Senator was £360 a year, free of income tax.
67. W. B. Yeats, *Collected Poems*, p. 237.
68. W. B. Yeats, ibid., p. 217.
69. W. B. Yeats, ibid., p. 218.
69A. Cf. W. B. Yeats, *John Sherman*, p. 122.
70. Cf. W. B. Yeats, *Collected Poems*, p. 447.
71. W. B. Yeats, *Letters to the New Island*, p. 42.
72. Cf. his article in *United Ireland*, 12 December 1891.
73. W. B. Yeats, *Collected Poems*, p. 21.
74. W. B. Yeats, ibid., pp. 150, 183, 184, 212, 226.
75. W. B. Yeats, ibid., pp. 150, 183, 211, 212, 219, 226, 231, 230.
76. W. B. Yeats, ibid., pp. 151, 180, 211, 212, 226, 230, 231, 267.
77. W. B. Yeats, ibid., pp. 183, 226 (a farmhouse), 267.
78. W. B. Yeats, ibid., pp. 150, 184, 226, 230, 275.
79. W. B. Yeats, ibid., pp. 150, 180, 182, 184, 212, 213, 275.
80. W. B. Yeats, ibid., pp. 148, 221, 227, 228, 232, 265, 268, 269.
81. W. B. Yeats, ibid., p. 227, 230.
82. W. B. Yeats, ibid., pp. 180, 182, 184, 186, 188, 227.
83. W. B. Yeats, ibid., pp. 219, 265.
84. W. B. Yeats, ibid., pp. 231, 267, 269.
85. From notes 74–84 it will be seen that Yeats was remembering 'Shelley's continually repeated symbols' (*Essays*, p. 290).

The use which is made of the tower as a symbol varies. There is the meaning carried on from Milton, Shelley, and de l'Isle Adam:
          'an image of mysterious wisdom won by toil'
(*Collected Poems*, p. 184). It is also used as a setting for the poet's life and ideas; it is mentioned because it was there, because he was recording it as a part of the scenery in the same way that he mentions the bridge, the trees, the water-hens, the river, etc. It serves as symbol of antiquity, and is des-

cribed as ancient (*Collected Poems*, p. 226, cf. 'A Prayer on going into my House', ibid., p. 183) a use which carries the poet back to the Anglo-Irish stock (*Collected Poems*, pp. 221, 267, 268). It serves also as a symbol of the contemporary world (*Collected Poems*, pp. 267, 269). These symbolisms are hard to distinguish; the first and the second are akin, for when Yeats was living in the tower he was to, a certain extent, symbolising the Shelleyan character. The third and fourth are also blended in meaning, for Yeats was constantly referring the present to the past. First and second blend into the uses of third and fourth, the link being the poet's own Protean personality.

86. Cf. W. B. Yeats, *Collected Poems*, p. 242, and the later emergence of the phrase in *A Full Moon in March*, p. 69.

87. W. B. Yeats, *Collected Poems*, p. 21, previously quoted, note 73.

88. W. B. Yeats, ibid., p. 166.

89. A. Norman Jeffares has quoted and discussed the drafts and sources of the two Byzantine poems in an article in *The Review of English Studies*, January 1946.

89A. See Bibliography.

90. Letter from 82 Merrion Square, 28 June 1923.

91. Letter from 82 Merrion Square, 22 April 1926.

92. Letter from Thoor Ballylee, 25 May 1926.

93. *Journal and Letters* of Stephen MacKenna (ed. E. R. Dodds), p. 235.

94. Cf. note 70.

95. Letter to Mrs Shakespear from Ballylee, 2 July 1926.

96. Letter to Mrs Shakespear from Thoor, Ballylee, 24 September 1926.

97. Letter from 82 Merrion Square, 24 March 1927.

98. W. B. Yeats, *Collected Poems*, p. 240.

99. Letter to Sturge Moore, undated but obviously 1926 and previous to another letter to the same, dated 27 May 1926. Cf. J. Hone, *W. B. Yeats, 1865–1939*, p. 377.

100. Another reason that might be put forward for the change in his own admiration that he had come to a greater admiration of the classical English poets. For instance, he had studied Chaucer in 1910 and 1913 (the time that there was a chance of his getting the Professorship of English at Dublin University). A letter to Lady Gregory from 18 Woburn Buildings, dated 7 May 1913, tells of Gogarty advising him to go to Dublin, but the very thought of going there (he had written two lyrics, one in six weeks, one at a sitting):

'instead of starting another lyric fills me with gloom and fury'.

In January (letter to Lady Gregory from 18 Woburn Buildings, dated 3 January 1913) he had read Milton, and was

'writing with a new confidence having got Milton off my back'.

Austin Clarke has made this conjecture in *The Dublin Magazine*, April–June 1939.

101. W. B. Yeats, *Wheels and Butterflies*, p. 7.

102. W. B. Yeats, *1930 Diary*, p. 10.

103. Unpublished material.

104. W. B. Yeats, *Collected Poems*, p. 255.

105. For a concise account of the Academy, founded in 1932, *vide* Stephen Gwynn, *Irish Literature and Drama*, pp. 232–6. The letter sent to those invited to become 'founder members' was signed by Shaw and Yeats, the plan having previously been discussed at Coole by Yeats and Russell.

106. W. B. Yeats, 'Irish Censorship', *The Spectator*, 29 September 1928. The one good of the Bill was, he thought, that it united Irish intellectuals. It would mean control of thought if pushed to extremes.

107. Letter from 82 Merrion Square.

108. Unpublished material.

109. W. B. Yeats, *Collected Poems*, p. 242.

110. Cf. A. Norman Jeffares, 'W. B. Yeats and His Methods of Writing Verse', *Nineteenth Century*, March 1946, where the variants of this poem are discussed.

110A. It is probable that his knowledge that Aristotle was Alexander's tutor came from Castiglione's *The Courtier*, p. 284:

'Aristotle so well knew the character of Alexander and tactfully fostered it so well, that he was loved and honoured more than a father by Alexander. . . . Aristotle so instructed him in the natural sciences and in the virtues of the mind as to make him most wise, brave, continent, and a true moral philosopher not only in words but in deeds; for a nobler philosophy cannot be imagined than to bring into civilized living such savage people as those who inhabited Bactria and Caucasia, India, Scythia. . . . So that countless men were by his laws reduced from savage life to civilization. And of these achievements of Alexander the author was Aristotle, using the means of a good courtier.'

Yeats, admittedly, hardly attributed him with the normal means of a good courtier.

111. Letter from Thoor, Ballylee, 25 May 1926.

112. Letter from Thoor, Ballylee, 2 July 1926.

113. W. B. Yeats, *Collected Poems*, pp. 249 *seq.*

114. W. B. Yeats, ibid., pp. 308 *seq.*

115. W. B. Yeats, ibid., p. 190.

116. W. B. Yeats, *Last Poems and Plays*, p. 76.

117. Letter from Thoor, Ballylee, 25 May 1926.

118. F. R. Higgins, *Scattering Branches*, p. 152.

119. Letter to Mrs Shakespear, from 82 Merrion Square, 23 June. The phrase about the Prince Consort appears more formally in *Wheels and Butterflies*, p. 25:

'Some obscure person somewhere inventing the spinning-jenny, upon his face that look of benevolence kept by painters and engravers, from the middle of the eighteenth century to the time of the Prince Consort.'

120. *Vide* note 89.

121. Letter from 82 Merrion Square, 27 October.

122. Letter from 82 Merrion Square, 7 December 1926.

122A. George is Mrs W. B. Yeats.

123. Letter from 82 Merrion Square, 2 October, to Mrs Shakespear.

124. Cf. J. Hone, *W. B. Yeats, 1865–1939*, p. 383.

125. W. B. Yeats, *Collected Poems*, p. 264.

126. W. B. Yeats, ibid., p. 267.

127. Although he was the successor of the Anglo-Irish he was poet, not politician; his being alive did not, therefore, affect the state of the tower being half-dead at the top.

128. W. B. Yeats, *On the Boiler*, p. 30.

129. W. B. Yeats, ibid., p. 12.

129A. He possibly got his hatred of Newton from Blake. Cf. his edition of Blake's *Poems*, p. 138, and Blake's *Works* (Nonesuch edition), p. 927:

'I know too well the majority of Englishmen are fond of the indefinite which they measure by Newton's doctrine of the fluxions of an atom, a thing that does not exist.'

Cf. also Nonesuch edition, p. 107.

130. W. B. Yeats, *Essays, 1931–1936*, p. 36.

130A. Cf. A. A. Luce, *Berkeley's Immaterialism*, p. ix.

131. W. B. Yeats, *Collected Poems*, p. 265.

132. Cf. J. Hone, *W. B. Yeats, 1865–1939*, p. 359.

133. Letter to Mrs Shakespear (82 Merrion Square), 4 March 1926.

133A. Cf. for repetition of images, *Autobiographies*, p. 143.

134. Letter from 82 Merrion Square, 7 September.
135. Letter from 82 Merrion Square, 2 October 1927.
136. W. B. Yeats, *Collected Poems*, p. 278.
137. W. B. Yeats, ibid., p. 263.
138. Letter from 82 Merrion Square, 25 April 1928, to Mrs Shakespear.

CHAPTER X

*Section 1*

1. W. B. Yeats, *Collected Poems*, p. 285.
2. W. B. Yeats, ibid., p. 271.
3. W. B. Yeats, Letter to Mrs Shakespear, dated 29 March 1929.
4. W. B. Yeats, *Collected Poems*, p. 278.
5. Letter dated 12 January 1928. From Cannes.
6. W. B. Yeats, *Collected Poems*, p. 287.
7. W. B. Yeats, *A Packet for Ezra Pound*.
8. Letter dated 25 April 1928.
9. Letter dated 2 March 1929. From Rapallo.
9A. This poem was written out of terror at the power of great geniuses. What destruction, he thought, would come on us if the mediocrity of journalists who brought the work of genius down to one level were to fail us. Notes made by Professor H. O. White of Yeats's broadcast in July 1937.
10. Letter dated 21 January 1929.
11. W. B. Yeats, *Collected Poems*, p. 295.
11A. A possible germ of the idea can be found in one of Synge's translations from Villon, 'An Old Woman's Lamentations', *Poems and Translations*, p. 44:
'The man I had a love for—a great rascal would kick me in the gutter—is dead thirty years and over it, and it is I am left behind, grey and aged. When I do be minding the good days I had, minding what I was one time, and what it is I'm come to, and when I do look on my own self, poor and dry, and pinched together, it wouldn't be much would set me raging in the streets.
'Where is the round forehead I had, and the fine hair, and the two eyebrows, and the eyes with a big gay look out of them would bring folly from a great scholar? Where is my straight shapely nose, and two ears, and my chin with a valley in it, and my lips were red and open?
'Where are the pointed shoulders that were on me, and the long arms and nice hands to them? Where is my bosom was as white as any, or my straight rounded sides?
'It's the way I am this day—my forehead is gone into furrows, the hair of my head is grey and whitish, my eyebrows are tumbled from me, and my two eyes have died out within my head—those eyes that would be laughing to the men—my nose has a hook on it, my ears are hanging down, and my lips are sharp and skinny.
'That's what's left over from the beauty of a right woman—a bag of bones, and legs the like of two shrivelled sausages going beneath it.
'It's the like of what we old hags do be thinking, of the good times that are gone away from us, and we crouched on our hunkers by a little fire of twigs, soon kindled and soon spent, we that were the pick of many.'
12. Letter from Coole Park, dated 'Last Sunday in November'.
13. J. Hone, *W. B. Yeats, 1865–1939*, p. 401.
14. Letter dated 29 March 1929.

15. F. R. Higgins, *Scattering Branches*, 'Yeats as Irish Poet', p. 152.
16. W. B. Yeats, *Collected Poems*, p. 300.
17. Letter dated 2 July 1929.
18. W. B. Yeats, *Collected Poems*, p. 273. The poem was begun in 1928.
19. W. B. Yeats, ibid., p. 301.    A letter, written to Mrs Shakespear in 1933, tells how a number of reviewers had quoted the poem written after he had arrived in Rapallo (the final dating is December 1929) and reminds her of its personal meaning:
'I wonder if you remember those autumn evenings when I was on my way to Rapallo.'
20. W. B. Yeats, *Pages from a Diary written in 1930*, p. 1.
21. W. B. Yeats, ibid., p. 2.
22. W. B. Yeats, *Collected Poems*, p. 451.
22A. J. Crowe Ransom, *The Southern Review*, Winter 1942, 'The Irish, the Gaelic, the Byzantine', complains of the difficulty of immediate assimilation of all the magnificence of Yeats's Byzantium.
23. W. B. Yeats, *A Vision*, p. 191.
24. W. B. Yeats, *Collected Poems*, p. 280.
25. Cf. A. Norman Jeffares's article, *The Review of English Studies*, January 1946.
25A. He had not read his authorities on Byzantium sufficiently thoroughly. Cf. W. G. Holmes, ibid., p. 119, for a description of the dissolute ways of the Byzantine youth.
26. W. B. Yeats, *Pages from a Diary Written in 1930*, pp. 1-2.
27. W. B. Yeats, ibid., p. 3. Salome is referred to. Cf. *A Vision* (1937), p. 273.
28. W. B. Yeats, *Pages from a Diary Written in 1930*, p. 5.
29. W. B. Yeats, ibid., p. 21.
29A. Cf. W. B. Yeats, *Wheels and Butterflies*, p. 7:
'Swift haunts me; he is always just around the corner. Sometimes it is a thought of my great-great-grandmother, a friend of that Archbishop King who sent him to England about the "First Fruits", sometimes it is St Patrick's where I have gone to wander and meditate, that brings him to mind, sometimes I remember something hard or harsh in O'Leary or in Taylor, or in the public speech of our statesmen, that reminds me by its style of his verse or prose.'
30. W. B. Yeats, ibid., p. 7.
31. W. B. Yeats, ibid., p. 18.
32. W. B. Yeats, ibid., p. 19.
33. W. B. Yeats, ibid., p. 5.
34. *Dublin Magazine*, October-December 1931.
35. W. B. Yeats, *Pages from a Diary Written in 1930*, pp. 4, 5.
36. W. B. Yeats, ibid., p. 34.
37. W. B. Yeats, ibid., p. 38.
38. W. B. Yeats, ibid., p. 41. Cf. A. A. Luce, *Berkeley's Immaterialism*, Preface.
38A. Cf. Blake (Nonesuch edition), p. 430: 'To cast Bacon, Locke and Newton from Albion's covering.'
39. W. B. Yeats, *Collected Poems*, p. 271.
40. I am greatly indebted to Mr Sparrow for the use of his notes made after this conversation.
41. Letter from Coole Park, Gort, 2 August 1931.
42. W. B. Yeats, *A Vision*, p. 149.
43. W. B. Yeats, *Collected Poems*, p. 239.
44. W. B. Yeats, *Wheels and Butterflies*, p. 109.
45. Virgil, Eclogue iv, 31-6.

46. P. B. Shelley, *Hellas*, concluding chorus. E. M. Tillyard, *Poetry Direct and Oblique*, p. 74, has also drawn attention to the similarity of the passages in Yeats and Shelley:
'The effect is tremendous. It is only when Yeats's fierce irony is set against the background of Shelley's most serene and passionate idealism that it gets its full force.'
Yeats had earlier used the idea in *Samhain*, December 1904, p. 17.
47. W. B. Yeats, *Wheels and Butterflies*, p. 107.
48. W. B. Yeats, *Collected Poems*, p. 305.
49. W. B. Yeats, ibid., p. 287.
50. W. B. Yeats, ibid., p. 306.
51. S. MacKenna, *Plotinus*, pp. 23–4.
52. W. B. Yeats, *Collected Poems*, p. 304. The Saint was Cellach. Information from Mrs Yeats. Cf. *Essays, 1931–36*, p. 80, for a statement he has forgotten the saint's name who sang that there is one perfect among beasts and fish and men. . . .
53. W. B. Yeats, *Collected Poems*, p. 287.
54. W. B. Yeats, ibid., p. 286.
55. W. B. Yeats, ibid., p. 294.
56. W. Blake, *Jerusalem*, IV. 88. (Nonesuch Blake, p. p. 553.)
57. Letter dated 3 January 1932. From Coole.
57A. A passage from one of his diaries illustrates his thoughts:
'The antithetical man works by flashes of lightning. He was the burden of himself and must lose himself to rest—Primary man does not lose himself, he may be perfect, a saint or sage. He has always an authority to obey and so can rest. Does not Crashaw seem to suspect that St Theresa was once Sappho? St Theresa says God desires the soul to be pure and lovely— but she has always the family. · The antithetical man is always impure and lonely—though pure in the lightning flash.'
58. Lady Charlotte Guest, *The Mabinogion*, p. 86.
59. W. B. Yeats, *Essays*, p. 533.
60. Frank O'Connor, *The Irish Theatre*, 'Synge', p. 38.
60A. The introduction which he wrote to *An Indian Monk, The Holy Mountain*, and *Aphorisms of Yoga* did not take as much time as revision of the Swami's English. *The Ten Principal Upanishads* was a translation under taken in collaboration.
61. W. B. Yeats, *Collected Poems*, p. 275.
62. Letter to Mrs W. B. Yeats, dated 3 February 1932.
63. Lady Gregory's *Journals*, p. 39.
64. W. B. Yeats, ibid., p. 273.

## Chapter X

### Section 2

1. W. B. Yeats, *Last Poems and Plays*, p. 17.
2. W. B. Yeats, ibid., p. 37.
2A. W. B. Yeats, *Letters on Poetry to Dorothy Wellesley*, p. 68.
3. Oliver St John Gogarty, *As I was going down Sackville Street*, p. 109.
4. W. B. Yeats, *Essays*, p. 506.
5. Letter from Riversdale, dated April 1933.
6. Letter from Riversdale, dated 17 August 1933.
7. Frank O'Connor, 'The Old Age of a Poet', *The Bell*, February 1941.
8. W. B. Yeats, *A Full Moon in March*, p. 52.

8A. W. B. Yeats, *The King of the Great Clock Tower*, p. 38.
9. Letter to Mrs Shakespear from Riversdale, dated 20 September 1933.
10. Initially by Louis MacNeice, *The Poetry of W. B. Yeats*. Cf. a review of that work in *English Studies*, February 1946.
11. Cf. J. Hone, *W. B. Yeats, 1865–1939*, p. 234.
11A. Cf. L. C. Knights, *Explorations*, p. 171.
12. W. B. Yeats, *A Full Moon in March*, p. 50.
13. Letter from Riversdale, dated 1 May 1934.
14. Comparing him to Maud Gonne, cf. J. Hone, *W. B. Yeats, 1865–1939*, p. 394.
15. Letter from Riversdale to Mrs Shakespear, dated 21 February 1933. Cf. Appendix, a document found among his private papers which reveals his attitude to both fascism and communism.
16. W. B. Yeats, *A Full Moon in March*, p. 59.
16A. Cf. W. B. Yeats, *Letters on Poetry to Dorothy Wellesley*, pp. 122, 138, 143, and for her serious-mindedness cf. p. 196.
17. W. B. Yeats, *Essays*, p. 506.
18. W. B. Yeats, *Letters on Poetry to Dorothy Wellesley*, p. 189.
19. Letter from Riversdale, dated 21 February 1933
20. Letter from Riversdale, dated 25 May 1933.
21. Letter from Riversdale, dated 9 March 1933.
22. Letter from Riversdale, dated 24 October 1933.
23. These, intended for *The King of the Great Clock Tower*, were rewritten.
24. A letter of January 27 [1934] also deals with these.
25. Letter from Riversdale, dated 11 November 1933.
26. Letter from Riversdale, dated 27 February 1934.
27. W. B. Yeats, *The King of the Great Clock Tower*, p. 44.
28. W. B. Yeats, *A Full Moon in March*, p. 63. The point of the poem according to a letter (see following note for date) is that 'we beget and bear because of the incompleteness of our love'.
29. Letter from Riversdale, dated 24 July 1934.
30. W. B. Yeats, *A Full Moon in March*, p. 61.
31. Letter from Riversdale, dated 24 July 1934.
32. Letter from Riversdale, dated 7 August 1934.
33. Letter from Riversdale, dated 23 August 1934.
34. Letter from Riversdale, dated 7 August 1934.
35. Letter from Riversdale, dated 28 November 1935.
35A. Letter from Riversdale, dated 8 May 1934.
35B. Letter from Riversdale, dated 21 February 1933.
35C. W. B. Yeats, *Letters on Poetry to Dorothy Wellesley*, p. 54.
35D. W. B. Yeats, ibid., p. 57.
36. Letter to Mrs Shakespear, quoted J. Hone, *W. B. Yeats, 1865–1939*, p. 446.
37. W. B. Yeats, *Last Poems and Plays*, p. 20.
38. W. B. Yeats, *Letters on Poetry to Dorothy Wellesley*, p. 191.
39. Archibald MacLeish, 'Public Speech and Private Speech in Poetry', *Yale Review*, Spring 1938.
40. W. B. Yeats, *Last Poems and Plays*, p. 17.
41. W. B. Yeats, ibid., p. 29.
41A. Without understanding his attitude in the least, cf. *Letters on Poetry to Dorothy Wellesley*, pp. 122, 124, 140, 143.
42. Cf. A. Norman Jeffares, 'W. B. Yeats and His Methods of Writing Verse', *The Nineteenth Century*, March 1946. Additional proof that Yeats was reading the Elegy at the time can be found in *On the Boiler*, p. 17.
43. W. B. Yeats, *Last Poems and Plays*, p. 26.
44. W. B. Yeats, ibid., p. 31. Poem written to Lady Elizabeth Pelham.

44A. W. B. Yeats, *Last Poems and Plays*, p. 44.

44B. W. B. Yeats, ibid., p. 52.

45. W. B. Yeats, *Letters on Poetry to Dorothy Wellesley*, p. 131.

45A. The O'Rahilly 'a strikingly handsome young man always dressed in a saffron kilt who was destined to be killed in O'Connell Street during Easter week'. Cf. Sir Arnold Bax, *Farewell my Youth*, p. 100.

46. W. B. Yeats, *Last Poems and Plays*, p. 22.

47. W. B. Yeats, ibid., p. 34.

48. W. B. Yeats, ibid., p. 4.

49. W. B. Yeats, ibid., p. 3.

50. P. B. Shelley, *Hellas*. The Jew is described after the entrance of Hassan. The theme of a chorus 'Worlds on worlds are rolling ever/From creation to decay' and speeches of Mahmud and Ahasuerus on the future are not dissimilar to Yeats's basic ideas. See A. Norman Jeffares, 'Yeats's "The Gyres": sources and symbolism', *Huntington Library Quarterly*, XV, I, November 1951.

51. Yet note that the idea of terror was present in his mind when he was writing *A Vision*, cf. *On the Boiler*, p. 19.

52. W. B. Yeats, *A Vision*, p. xiii.

52A. W. B. Yeats, *Letters on Poetry to Dorothy Wellesley*, p. 124.

53. Cf. Sir William Rothenstein, *Scattering Branches*, p. 50. W. B. Yeats, *Letters on Poetry to Dorothy Wellesley*, p. 140.

54. W. B. Yeats, *Last Poems and Plays*, p. 48.

55. W. B. Yeats, ibid., p. 19.

56. J. B. Yeats, *Letters to His Son W. B. Yeats and Others*, p. 214.

57. She was born in 1852.

57A. Mary Colum, *Life and the Dream*, pays tribute to the extravagance with which Yeats would spend himself in battle for a cause or a friend:
'He was always overpraising his friends; some of his swans were certainly geese; but at the same time if anybody injured or hurt him or someone close to him he never forgot or forgave.'

58. W. B. Yeats, *Letters on Poetry to Dorothy Wellesley*, p. 163.

59. W. B. Yeats, ibid., p. 164.

60. W. B. Yeats, ibid., p. 179.

60A. W. B. Yeats, *Pages from a Diary Written in 1930*, p. 25.

60B. W. B. Yeats, *Letters on Poetry to Dorothy Wellesley*, p. 200.

61. Sir William Rothenstein, *Scattering Branches*, p. 51.

62. W. B. Yeats, *Last Poems and Plays*, p. 67.

63. W. B. Yeats, ibid., p. 51.

64. W. B. Yeats, ibid., p. 17.

65. W. B. Yeats, ibid., p. 18.

66. Cf. Nietzsche, *The Dawn of Day*, p. 370. Information from Mrs W. B. Yeats.

67. J. O. Hannay, *The Wisdom of the Desert*, pp. 7–10, *The Spirit and Origin of Christian Monasticism*, p. 101, both read by Yeats, were used as sources for 'Demon and Beast', *Collected Poems*, p. 209. Cf. also W. B. Yeats, *Autobiographies*, p. 387, and *Essays, 1931–1936*, p. 39, for a repetition of the image. Information from Mrs W. B. Yeats.

68. W. B. Yeats, *Last Poems and Plays*, p. 89.

69. F. R. Higgins, *Scattering Branches*, p. 154.

70. W. B. Yeats, *Last Poems and Plays*, p. 48.

71. W. B. Yeats, *Letters on Poetry to Dorothy Wellesley*, p. 159.

72. W. B. Yeats, *Last Poems and Plays*, p. 83.

73. Letter to Lady Elizabeth Pelham, dated 4 January 1939.

74. Information from Mrs. W. B. Yeats.

75. W. B. Yeats, *Last Poems and Plays*, p. 87.

76. W. B. Yeats, ibid., p. 92. Cf. *Letters on Poetry to Dorothy Wellesley*, p. 203:
'I have found a book of essays about Rilke waiting me—one on Rilke's ideas about death annoyed me.  I wrote on the margin:

        Draw rein; draw breath
        Cast a cold eye
        On life, on death
        Horseman, pass by!'

# BIBLIOGRAPHY

## I

## THE WORKS OF W. B. YEATS REFERRED TO IN THIS BOOK

### 1. *Unpublished material*

Private papers.
Manuscripts for plays, poems and prose.
Diary from 1908 to 1910 approx.
  The main notebooks used are:
MS. book and Diary given to Yeats by Maud Gonne.
White MS. book.
Black loose-leaf notebook (containing many of *Last Poems*).
Rough draft for an autobiographical work.
Letters to Lady Gregory, Mrs Shakespear and others.

### 2. *Published work*

*Mosada: A Dramatic Poem.* Sealy, Bryers & Walker. Dublin, 1886.
*Poems and Ballads of Young Ireland.* Gill. Dublin, 1888.
*Fairy and Folk Tales of the Irish Peasantry.* Walter Scott. London, 1888.
*Stories from Carleton.* Walter Scott. London, 1888.
*The Wanderings of Oisin and Other Poems.* Kegan Paul, Trench & Co.
  London, 1889.
*Representative Irish Tales.* G. P. Putnam's Sons. London, 1890.
*Ganconagh, John Sherman and Dhoya.* T. Fisher Unwin. London, 1891.
*The Countess Kathleen and Various Legends and Lyrics.* T. Fisher Unwin.
  London 1891.
*Irish Fairy Tales.* T. Fisher Unwin. London, 1892.
*The Celtic Twilight.* Lawrence & Bullen. 1893.
*The Works of William Blake, Poetic, Symbolic and Critical.* (Ed. Ellis and Yeats.)
  Quaritch. London, 1893.
*The Poems of William Blake.* (Ed. W. B. Yeats.) Lawrence & Bullen.
  London, 1893.
*The Land of Heart's Desire.* T. Fisher Unwin. London, 1894.
*Poems.* T. Fisher Unwin. London, 1895.
*A Book of Irish Verse selected from Modern Writers.* (Ed. W. B. Yeats.) Methuen.
  1895.
*The Secret Rose.* Lawrence & Bullen. London, 1897.
*The Tables of the Law: The Adoration of the Magi.* Privately printed. 1897.
W. T. Horton. *A Book of Images.* (Introduced by W. B. Yeats.) The
  Unicorn Press. London, 1898.
*The Wind among the Reeds.* Elkin Mathews. London, 1899.
*Literary Ideals in Ireland* (with John Eglinton, Æ, W. Larminie). T. Fisher
  Unwin. London, 1899.
*The Organ of the Irish Literary Theatre.* Beltaine. (i–iii.) Unicorn Press.
  London, 1900.
*The Shadowy Waters.* Hodder & Stoughton. London, 1900.

*Is the Order of R.R. & A.C. to remain a Magical Order?* Privately published. 1901.

*A Postscript to essay called 'Is the Order of R.R. & A.C. to remain a Magical Order?'* Privately published. 1901.

*The Celtic Twilight.* (Revised edition.) A. H. Bullen. London, 1902.

*Ideas of Good and Evil.* A. H. Bullen. London, 1903.

*In the Seven Woods.* Dun Emer Press. Dundrum, Dublin, 1903.

*Stories of Red Hanrahan.* Dun Emer Press. Dundrum, Dublin, 1904.

*Gods and Fighting Men.* (Preface by W. B. Yeats.) Murray. London, 1904.

*Poems of William Blake.* (Edited by W. B. Yeats.) Routledge, London, 1906.

*Poems of Spenser.* (Selected and with an Introduction of W. B. Yeats.) T. C. & E. C. Jack. Edinburgh, 1906.

*The Arrow.* (Edited by, with articles of, W. B. Yeats.) 1906–7.

*The Collected Works in Verse and Prose.* Shakespeare Head Press. Stratford-on-Avon, 1908.

*The Green Helmet and Other Poems.* Cuala Press. Churchtown, Dublin, 1910.

*Gitanjali.* (Introduction by W. B. Yeats.) Chiswick Press for the India Society. London, 1912, and Macmillan, London, 1913.

*Poems Written in Discouragement.* Cuala Press. Dundrum, Dublin, 1913. (Private edition.)

*Responsibilities: Poems and a Play.* Cuala Press. Churchtown, Dublin, 1914.

*Reveries over Childhood and Youth.* Cuala Press. Churchtown, Dublin, 1915.

*Certain Noble Plays of Japan.* (Introduction by W. B. Yeats.) Cuala Press. Churchtown, Dublin, 1916.

*The Wild Swans at Coole, Other Verses and a Play in Verse.* Cuala Press. Churchtown, Dublin, 1917.

*Per Amica Silentia Lunae.* Macmillan. London, 1918.

*Two Plays for Dancers.* Cuala Press. Dublin, 1919.

*The Wild Swans at Coole.* Macmillan. London, 1919.

*Michael Robartes and the Dancer.* Cuala Press. Churchtown, Dublin, 1920.

*Visions and Beliefs in the West of Ireland.* (Two essays and notes by W. B. Yeats included.) G. P. Putnam's Sons. New York and London, 1920.

*Four Plays for Dancers.* Macmillan. London, 1921.

*Four Years.* Cuala Press. Churchtown, Dublin, 1921.

*Seven Poems and a Fragment.* Cuala Press. Dundrum, Dublin, 1922.

*The Trembling of the Veil.* T. Werner Laurie. London, 1922.

*Plays in Prose and Verse. Written for an Irish Theatre and generally with the help of a Friend.* Macmillan. London, 1922.

*The Cat and the Moon and Certain Poems.* Cuala Press. Merrion Square, Dublin, 1924.

*Essays.* Macmillan. London, 1924.

*The Bounty of Sweden: A Meditation, and a Lecture delivered before the Royal Swedish Academy.* Cuala Press. Dublin, 1925.

*A Vision an Explanation of Life founded upon the Writings of Giraldus and upon Certain Doctrines attributed to Kusta Ben Luka.* T. Werner Laurie. London, 1925. Privately printed.

*Axel.* (Preface by W. B. Yeats.) Jarrolds. London, 1925.

*Estrangement: being some Fifty Thoughts from a Diary kept by William Butler Yeats in the Year Nineteen Hundred and Nine.* Cuala Press. Dublin, 1926.

*Autobiographies: Reveries over Childhood and Youth and the Trembling of the Veil* Macmillan. London, 1926.

*October Blast.* Cuala Press. Dublin, 1927.

*The Tower.* Macmillan. London, 1928.

*Sophocles' King Œdipus.* Macmillan. London, 1928.

*The Death of Synge.* Cuala Press. Dublin, 1928.

*A Packet for Ezra Pound.* Cuala Press. Dublin, 1929.

*The Winding Star.* The Fountain Press. New York, 1929.

*Bishop Berkeley: His Life, Writings and Philosophy.* (Introduction by W. B. Yeats.) Faber & Faber. London, 1931.

*An Indian Monk: His Life and Adventures.* (Introduction by W. B. Yeats.) Macmillan. London, 1932.

*Words for Music, Perhaps and Other Poems.* Cuala Press. Dublin, 1932.

*The Winding Stair and Other Poems.* Macmillan. London, 1933.

*The Collected Poems of W. B. Yeats.* Macmillan. London, 1933.

*The King of the Great Clock Tower, Commentary and Poems.* Cuala Press. Dublin, 1934.

*Wheels and Butterflies.* Macmillan. London, 1934.

*The Collected Plays of W. B. Yeats.* Macmillan. London, 1934.

*Letters to the New Island.* Harvard University Press. 1934.

*The Holy Mountain.* (Introduction by W. B. Yeats.) Faber & Faber. London, 1934.

*A Full Moon in March.* Macmillan. London, 1935.

*Dramatis Personae, 1896–1902, Estrangement, The Bounty of Sweden.* Macmillan. London, 1936.

*The Oxford Book of Modern Verse, 1892–1935, Chosen by W. B. Yeats.* Clarendon Press. Oxford, 1936.

*The Ten Principal Upanishads.* (Put into English by Shree Purohit Swami and W. B. Yeats.) Faber & Faber. London, 1937.

*A Vision.* Macmillan. London, 1937.

*Essays, 1931–1936.* Cuala Press. Dublin, 1937.

*The Herne's Egg.* Macmillan. London, 1938.

*New Poems.* Cuala Press. Dublin, 1938.

*Aphorisms of Yoga.* (Introduction by W. B. Yeats.) Faber & Faber. London, 1938.

*On the Boiler.* Cuala Press. Dublin, 1939.

*Last Poems and Plays.* Macmillan. London, 1940.

*If I were Four and Twenty.* Cuala Press. Dublin, 1940.

*Letters to Miss Florence Farr.* Cuala Press. Dublin, 1941.

*Pages from a Diary written in 1930.* Cuala Press. Dublin, 1945.

# II

# ARTICLES AND POEMS BY YEATS

*(Not included in Bibliography of his published work)*

'The Island of Statues', *The Dublin University Review*, April–July 1885.

'On Mr Nettleship's Picture at the Royal Hibernian Academy', *The Dublin University Review*, April 1886.

'Mosada', *The Dublin University Review*, June 1886.

'Miserrimus', *The Dublin University Review*, October 1886.

'From the Book of Kauri the Indian—Section V', *The Dublin University Review*, October 1886.

'The Poetry of Sir Samuel Ferguson', *The Dublin University Review*, November 1886.

'The Stolen Child', *The Irish Monthly*, December 1886.

'Clarence Mangan', *The Irish Fireside*, March 1887.

'King Goll', *The Leisure Hour*, September 1887.

'The Lake Island of Innisfree', *The National Observer*, December 1890.

'Clarence Mangan's Love Affair', *United Ireland*, August 1891.
'Mourn and then Onward', *United Ireland*, October 1891.
'The White Birds', *The National Observer*, May 1892.
'Hopes and Fears for Irish Literature', *United Ireland*, October 1892.
'Invoking the Irish Fairies' (signed D. E. D. I.), *The Irish Theosophist*, October 1892.
'The de-Anglicising of Ireland', *United Ireland*, December 1892.
'An Impression', *The Speaker*, October 1893.
'A Symbolical Drama in Paris', *The Bookman*, April 1894.
'Cap and Bells', *The National Observer*, March 1894.
'The Valley of the Black Pig', *The Savoy*, April 1896.
'An Irish Patriot', *The Bookman*, May 1896.
'O'Sullivan Rua to the Secret Rose', *The Savoy*, September 1896.
'The Blessed', *The Yellow Book*, April 1897.
'Song of Mongan', *The Dome*, October 1898.
'Aodh pleads with the Elemental Powers', *The Dome*, December 1898.
'A Biographical Fragment', *The Criterion*, July 1923.
'Irish Censorship', *The Spectator*, 29 September 1928.
'The Irish National Theatre', *Reale Accademia d'Italia*, Rome, 1935.
*Letters to Miss Florence Farr from G. B. Shaw and William Butler Yeats.* Cuala Press, Dublin, 1941.
'Some Passages from the Letters of W. B. Yeats to Æ', *The Dublin Magazine*, July–September 1939.

# III

# OTHER WORKS REFFERED TO

ADAM (Comte Villiers de l'Isle).
   *Axel.* Jarrold. London, 1925.
Æ (George Russell).
   *Homeward Songs by the Way.* Whaley. Dublin, 1894.
   *Literary Ideals in Ireland.* Fisher Unwin. London, 1899.
   *Some Passages from the Letters of Æ to W. B. Yeats.* Cuala Press. Dublin, 1936.
ALIGHIERI (Dante).
   *The Vision of Hell* (translated by H. F. Cary; illustrated by Doré). Cassell, Petter and Galpin. London, 1872–5 and 1892–3. Dent. London, 1908.
ALLINGHAM (W.).
   *Sixteen Poems* (selected by W. B. Yeats). Dun Emer Press. Dundrum, 1905.

BARRINGTON (Sir Jonah).
   *Personal Sketches of his own Times.* Routledge & Sons. London, 1869.
BAX (Sir Arnold).
   *Farewell my Youth.* Longmans, Green & Co. London, 1943.
BAX (Clifford), (Ed.).
   *Letters to Miss Florence Farr from G. B. Shaw and William Butler Yeats.* Cuala Press. Dublin, 1941.
BERGIN (O.).
   *Stories from Keating's History of Ireland.* Hodges Figgis. Dublin, 1939.
BINYON (Laurence).
   *The Drawings and Engravings of William Blake.* The Studio Ltd. London, 1922.

BLAKE (William).
 *Works.* (Ed. Ellis and Yeats.) Quaritch. London, 1893.
 *Poems.* (Ed. Yeats.) Lawrence and Bullen. London, 1893.
 *Poetry and Prose.* (Ed. Geoffrey Keynes.) Nonesuch Press. London, 1939.
BLUNT (Wilfrid Scawen).
 *My Diaries, 1888–1914.* Secker. London, 1922.
BOEHME (Jacob).
 *Forty Questions.* Kegan Paul. London, 1891.
BOWRA (Cecil Maurice).
 *The Heritage of Symbolism.* Macmillan. London, 1943.
BOYD (E. A.).
 *Ireland's Literary Renaissance.* Maunsel. London and Dublin, 1916.
 *Portraits: Real and Imaginary.* Cape. London, 1925.
BRONOWSKI (J.).
 *The Poet's Defence.* Cambridge University Press. 1939.
BROOKE (Charlotte).
 *Reliques of Ancient Irish Poetry.* Dublin, 1789.
BROOKE (Henry).
 *The Fool of Quality.* Routledge. London, 1906.
BROOKE (Stopford A.), (with T. W. Rolleston).
 *A Treasury of Irish Poetry.* Smith, Elder & Co. London, 1900.
BURDETT (Osbert).
 *The Beardsley Period.* John Lane. London, 1925.
BURTCHAELL (G. D.), (with T. U. Sadleir).
 *Alumni Dublinenses.* Williams & Norgate. London, 1924.

CANON (Richard).
 *Historical Record of the 8th the King's Liverpool Regiment of Foot.* Trimble.
  Enniskillen, 1904. (3rd edition.)
CARRIGAN (Rev. William).
 *A History of the Diocese of Ossory.* Sealy, Bryers & Walker. Dublin, 1905.
CASTIGLIONE (Count Baldesar).
 *The Courtier.* Duckworth. London, 1902.
CHAUCER (Geoffrey).
 *The Complete Works.* (Ed. Rev W. W. Skeat.) Oxford, 1899.
 *The Complete Works.* (Ed. F. N. Robinson.) Geoffrey Cumberlege.
  Oxford University Press.
COLUM (Mary).
 *Life and the Dream.* Doubleday & Co. New York, 1947.
CONNOLLY (Cyril).
 *Enemies of Promise.* Routledge. London, 1938.
CROKER (Crofton).
 *Fairy Legends and Traditions of the South of Ireland.* 1825–8. Reprinted 1929.
CURTIN (Jeremiah).
 *Myths and Folklore of Ireland.* Boston, 1890.
 *Tales of the Fairies and of the Ghost World.* 1895.
CURTIS (Edmund).
 *A History of Ireland.* Methuen. London, 1936.

DAICHES (David).
 *Poetry and the Modern World.* University of Chicago Press. 1940.
DALTON (O. M.).
 *Byzantine Art and Archaeology.* Clarendon Press. Oxford 1923.
DALY (John).
 *Reliques of Irish Jacobite Poetry.* Dublin, 1866.
 *Poets and Poetry of Munster.* Dublin, 1849.

DAVIS (Thomas).
*National and Other Poems.* Gill. Dublin, 1907.
DE VERE (Aubrey).
*Collected Works.* London, 1895.
DICKINSON (Page L.).
*The Dublin of Yesterday.* Methuen. London, 1929.
DEUTSCH (Babette).
*This Modern Poetry.* Faber & Faber. London, 1936.
DODDS (E. R.), (Ed.).
*Journal and Letters of Stephen Mackenna.* Constable. London, 1936.
DRUMMOND (W. H.).
*Ancient Irish Minstrelsy.* Dublin, 1852.
DRYDEN (John).
*Works.*


ECKERMANN (J. P.).
*Conversations with Goethe.* Bell. London, 1874.
EGLINTON (John), (W. Magee).
*A Memoir of Æ.* Macmillan. London, 1937.
*Literary Ideals in Ireland.* Fisher Unwin. London, 1899.


FARR (Florence).
*Letters to Miss Florence Farr, from G. B. Shaw and William Butler Yeats.*
(Ed. C. Bax.) Cuala Press. Dublin, 1941.
FERGUSON (M. C., Lady).
*Sir Samuel Ferguson in the Ireland of his Day.* Edinburgh, 1896.
FERGUSON (Sir Samuel).
*Poems.* Bell & Sons. London, 1880.
*Lays of the Western Gael.* Sealy, Bryers & Walker. Dublin, 1888.


GILBERT (J. T.).
*A History of the City of Dublin.* Duffy. Dublin, 1861.
GOGARTY (Oliver St John).
*As I was going down Sackville Street.* Rich & Cowan. London, 1937.
GOLDRING (Douglas).
*South Lodge.* Constable. London, 1943.
GREGORY (Lady Augusta).
*Coole.* Cuala Press. Dublin, 1931.
*Gods and Fighting Men.* Murray. London, 1904.
*Hugh Lane's Life and Achievement.* Murray. London, 1921.
*Ideals in Ireland.* (Ed.) Fisher Unwin. London, 1901.
*Journals.* (Ed. Lennox Robinson.) Putnam. London, 1946.
*Our Irish Theatre.* G. P. Putnam's Sons. London, 1914.
*Visions and Beliefs in the West of Ireland.* G. P. Putnam's Sons. London, 1920.
GRIFFIN (Gerald).
*The Collegians.* Every Irishman's Library. Dublin, 1919.
GUEST (Lady Charlotte).
*The Mabinogion.* Temple Classics. London, 1902.
GURD (Miss Patty).
*The Early Poetry of William Butler Yeats.* Lancaster, U.S.A., 1916.
GWYNN (Stephen).
*Irish Literature and Drama.* Nelson. London, 1936.
*Oliver Goldsmith.* Thornton Butterworth. London, 1935.
*Scattering Branches.* Macmillan. London, 1940.

HANNAY (Rev. J. O.).
*The Spirit and Origin of Christian Monasticism.* Methuen. London, 1903.
*The Wisdom of the Desert.* Methuen. London, 1904.
HARDIMAN (James).
*Irish Minstrelsy.* 2 vols. 1831.
HARTMANN (Franz).
*The Life and Doctrines of Jacob Boehme.* Kegan Paul. London, 1891.
HARRIS (W.).
*The History and Antiquities of Dublin.* Williams. Dublin.
HEINE (Heinrich).
*Atta Troll.* Chapman & Hall. London, 1876.
HIGGINS (F. R.).
*Scattering Branches.* Macmillan. London, 1940.
HOARE (D. M.).
*The Works of Morris and Yeats in relation to Early Saga Literature.* 1937.
HONE (Joseph).
*Bishop Berkeley: His Life, Writings and Philosophy.* Faber & Faber. London, 1931.
*The Life of George Moore.* Gollancz. London, 1936.
*W. B. Yeats, 1865–1939.* Macmillan. London, 1942.
*J. B. Yeats, Letters to his Son W. B. Yeats and Others.* Faber & Faber. London, 1944.
HOLMES (W. G.).
*The Age of Justinian and Theodora.* Bell. London, 1905.
HORTON (W. T.).
*A Book of Images.* Unicorn Press. London, 1898.
HULL (Eleanor).
*The Cuchullin Saga.* 1898.
HÜTTEMANN (Gerta).
*Wesen der Dichtung und Ausgabe bei William Butler Yeats.* Leopold. Bonn, 1929.
HYDE (Dr Douglas).
*A Literary History of Ireland from the Earliest Times to the Present Day.* Library of Literary History. London, 1899.
*The Story of Early Gaelic Literature.* New Times Library. Dublin, 1895.
*Love Songs of Connacht.* Dublin, 1893.
*Beside the Fire.* 1890.

JACKSON (Miss Grace Emily).
*Mysticism in Æ and W. B. Yeats in relation to Oriental and American Thought.* Ohio State University. 1932.
JEFFERIES (Richard).
*The Story of my Heart.* Penguin Books Ltd. Harmondsworth, England, 1938.
JOHNSON (Lionel).
*The Poetical Works.* Elkin Mathews. London, 1915.
JOYCE (James).
*A Portrait of the Artist as a Young Man.* Cape. London, 1916.

KICKHAM (C. J.).
*Knocknagow.* Duffy. Dublin, 1879 and 1887.
KNIGHTS (L. C.).
*Explorations: Poetry and Social Criticism.* Chatto & Windus. London, 1946.

LANDOR (Walter Savage).
*Imaginary Conversations.* Chapman & Hall. London, 1927.

LAW (Hugh).
*Anglo-Irish Literature.* Talbot Press. Dublin, 1926.
LAW (Rev. William).
*An Illustration of the Deep Principles of Jacob Boehme the Teutonic Philosopher.* Richardson. London, 1763.
LARMINIE (William).
*Literary Ideals in Ireland.* Fisher Unwin. London, 1899.
*West Irish Folk Tales and Romances.* 1893.
LUCE (Rev. A. A.).
*Berkeley's Immaterialism: A Commentary on his 'A Treatise Concerning Principles of Human Knowledge'.* Nelson. London, 1945.

MACBRIDE (Madame Maud Gonne).
*A Servant of the Queen.* Gollancz. London, 1938.
*Scattering Branches.* Macmillan. London, 1940.
MACDONAGH (T.).
*Literature in Ireland.* Dublin, 1916.
MACKENNA (Stephen).
*Journal and Letters.* (Ed. E. R. Dodds.) Constable. London, 1936.
*Plotinus.* Warner. London, 1917.
MACNEICE (Louis).
*The Poetry of W. B. Yeats.* Oxford University Press. 1941.
MACPHERSON (James).
*The Poems of Oisin.* (Ed. Wm. Sharp.) Geddes. Edinburgh, 1896.
MAHAFFY (Rev. J. P.).
*Descartes.* Blackwood. London, 1880.
MALONE (A. E.).
*The Irish Theatre.* (Ed. Lennox Robinson.) Macmillan. London 1939.
MANGAN (James Clarence).
*Poems.* (Ed. O'Donoghue.) Gill. Dublin, 1910.
MARTENSEN (H. L.).
*Jacob Boehme.* Rhys Evans. London, 1885.
*Jacob Boehme: His Life and Teaching.* Hodder & Stoughton. London, 1885.
MARTYN (Edward).
*The Heather Field.* Duckworth. London, 1899.
MASEFIELD (J.).
*Some Memories of W. B. Yeats.* Cuala Press. Dublin, 1940.
MENON (V. K.).
*The Development of William Butler Yeats.* Oliver & Boyd. London, 1942.
MEYER (Kuno).
*The Voyage of Bran.* 1895.
*Four Old Irish Songs of Summer and Winter.* 1903.
*The Vision of Mac Conglinne.* 1892.
MILTON (John).
*The Minor Poems.* (Illustrated Samuel Palmer.) Sealey & Co. London, 1889.
MOORE (George).
*Hail and Farewell, Ave, Salve, Vale.* Heinemann. London, 1911–14.
*The Strike at Arlingford.* Walter Scott. London, 1893.
*The Bending of the Bough.* Fisher Unwin. London, 1900.
MOORE (T. Sturge).
*Art and Life.* Methuen. London, 1910.
MORRIS (William).
*The Life and Death of Jason.* Kelmscott Press. London, 1895.
*The Earthly Paradise.* Longmans, Green. London, 1912.

MORE (P. E.).
*Shelburne Essays*. Ser. I. G. P. Putnam's Sons. London, 1904.

O'CONNOR (Frank).
*The Irish Theatre*. (Ed. Lennox Robinson.) Macmillan. London, 1939.
O'CURRY (E.).
Lectures on the manuscript materials of Ancient Irish History. Dublin, 1861.
O'DONNELL (F. H.).
*The Stage Irishman of the Pseudo-Celtic Revival*. John Long. London, 1904.
O'FLAHERTY (Liam).
*The Martyr*. Gollancz. London, 1933.
O'GRADY (Standish).
*The Bog of Stars*. Fisher Unwin. London, 1893.
*History of Ireland, the Heroic Period*. Sampson Low, Searle, Marston & Rivington. London, 1878.
*History of Ireland, Critical and Philosophical*. Sampson Low. London, 1881.
O'GRADY (Standish Hayes).
*Silva Gadelica II*. London, 1892.
*The Pursuit of Diarmuid and Grania*. Trans. Ossianic Society, III. 1857.
O'LOCHLAIN (Colm).
*Irish Street Ballads*. Three Candles Press. Dublin, 1939.
O'RORKE (Rev. T. F.).
*History, Antiquities and Present State of the Parishes of Ballysadare and Kilvarnet in the County of Sligo*. Duffy. Dublin.
*History of Sligo: Town and County*. Duffy. Dublin, 1889.

PATER (Walter).
*Appreciations*. Macmillan. London, 1931.
PEARSON (Hesketh).
*Bernard Shaw: His Life and Personality*. Collins. London, 1942.
*The Life of Oscar Wilde*. Methuen. London, 1946.
PETRIE (W. M. Flinders).
*The Revolutions of Civilisation*. Harper Brothers. London and New York, 1922.

REID (Forrest).
*W. B. Yeats: A Critical Study*. Secker. London, 1915.
REYNOLDS (Horace), (Ed.).
*Letters to the New Island*. Harvard University Press. 1934.
RHYS (Ernest).
*Everyman Remembers*. Dent. London, 1931.
ROBINSON (Lennox), (Ed.).
*Lady Gregory's Journals*. Putnam. London, 1946.
*The Irish Theatre*. Macmillan. London, 1939.
ROLLESTON (C. H.).
*Portrait of an Irishman*. Methuen. London, 1939.
ROLLESTON (T. W.), (with Stopford A. Brooke).
*A Treasury of Irish Poetry*. Smith, Elder & Co. London, 1900.
ROTH (William).
*A Catalogue of English and American First Editions of William Butler Yeats*. New Haven, U.S.A., 1939.
ROTHENSTEIN (Sir William).
*Men and Memories*. Faber & Faber. London, 1931–9.
*Scattering Branches*. Macmillan. London, 1940.

SADLEIR (T. U.).
  *Alumni Dublinenses.* Williams & Norgate. London, 1924.
SAURAT (Denis).
  *Blake and Modern Thought.* Constable. London, 1929.
SAVAGE (D. S.).
  *The Personal Principle.* Routledge. London, 1944.
SEYMOUR (St John D.).
  *Irish Witchcraft and Demonology.* Hodges Figgis. Dublin, 1913.
SHAW (George Bernard).
  *Letters to Miss Florence Farr from G. B. Shaw and William Butler Yeats.*
    Cuala Press. Dublin, 1941.
SHELLEY (P. B.).
  *Poetical Works.* Routledge & Sons. London.
SINNETT (A. P.).
  *Esoteric Buddhism.* Trübner & Co. London, 1915.
SPARLING (H. Haliday).
  *Irish Minstrelsy.* Scott. London, 1888.
STRONG (Mrs Arthur).
  *Apotheosis and the After Life.* Constable. London, 1915.
STRONG (L. A. G.).
  *Scattering Branches.* (Ed. Stephen Gwynn.) Macmillan. London, 1940.
SWEDENBORG (E.).
  *The Principia.* Newbery. London, 1845.
  *Diarium Spirituale.* Newbery. London, 1845.
  *Arcana Coelestia.* Tubingae. Guttenberg, 1833.
SYMONS (Arthur).
  *Poems.* Heinemann. London, 1916.
SYNGE (J. M.).
  *Dramatic Works.* Maunsel. Dublin, 1915.
  *The Aran Islands.* Maunsel. Dublin, 1912.
  *Poems and Translations.* Maunsel. Dublin, 1912.
SWINBURNE (A. C.).
  *William Blake: A Critical Essay.* (2nd edition.) Heinemann. London, 1906.

TAGORE (Rabindranath).
  *Gitanjali.* Macmillan. London, 1913.
THOREAU (H.).
  *Walden.* Chapman & Hall. London, 1927.
TILLYARD (E. M. W.).
  *Poetry Direct and Oblique.* Chatto & Windus. London, 1945.
TYNAN (Katharine).
  *The Middle Years.* (1892–1911.) Constable. London, 1916.
  *The Wandering Years.* (1918–1921.) Constable. London, 1922.
  *Memories.* Nash & Grayson. London, 1924.
  *Twenty-five Years: Reminiscences.* Smith Elder & Co. London, 1913.
  *Louise de la Vallière and Other Poems.* Kegan Paul, Trench & Co. London,
    1885.

VON HÜGEL (Baron Friedrich).
  *The Mystical Element of Religion.* Dent. London, 1927. (2nd edition.)
VON REICHENBACH (Baron Carl).
  *Researches on Magnetism, Electricity, Heat, Light, Crystallisation, and Chemical
    Attraction, in their relations to the Vital Force.* Taylor. London, 1850.

WATKINS (Vernon).
  *The Lamp and the Veil.* Faber & Faber. London, 1946.

WELLESLEY (Dorothy). (Ed.).
*Letters on Poetry from W. B. Yeats to Dorothy Wellesley.* Oxford University
Press. 1940.
WHITE (Terence de Vere).
*The Road of Excess.* Browne & Nolan. Dublin, 1946.
WILSON (Edmund).
*Axel's Castle.* Scribners. London, 1931.
WILDE (Oscar).
*Salome.* Elkin Mathews. London, 1894.

YEATS (J. B.).
*Early Memories: Some Chapters of Autobiography.* Cuala Press. Dublin, 1923.
*Essays Irish and American.* Talbot Press. Dublin, 1918.
*Letters to His Son W. B. Yeats and Others.* Faber & Faber. London, 1944

# BIBLIOGRAPHY OF MISCELLANEOUS ARTICLES

(For a fuller list see A. Norman Jeffares, 'An account of Recent Yeatsiana',
*Hermathena*, November 1948.)

ALLT (G. D. P.).
'Yeats and the revision of his early verse.' *Hermathena*, vol. lxiv.
November 1944.
ALSPACH (Russell K.).
'Some sources of Yeats's "The Wanderings of Oisin".' *P.M.L.A.*,
pp. 849 *seq.* September 1943.
ANONYMOUS.
'W. B. Yeats at school.' *T.P.'s Weekly.* 7 June 1912.
CLARKE (Austin).
'W. B. Yeats.' *Dublin Magazine.* April–June 1939.
*Dublin Evening Post*, 8 July 1817.
EDWARDS (Oliver).
'W. B. Yeats and Ulster; and a thought on the future of the Anglo-Irish
tradition.' *The Northman*, vol. xiii, No. 2.
FOOTE (Charles H.).
*Folk Lore Record*, II. 1879.
HONE (J.).
'A Scattered Fair.' *The Wind and the Rain*, vol. iii, No. 3. Autumn
1946.
JEFFARES (A. Norman).
'Two Songs of a Fool and their explanation.' *English Studies*, December
1945.
'The Byzantine Poems of W. B. Yeats.' *The Review of English Studies.*
January 1946.
Review. *English Studies.* February 1946.
'W. B. Yeats and his methods of writing verse.' *The Nineteenth Century.*
March 1946.
'Gyres in the poetry of W. B. Yeats.' *English Studies.* June 1946.
MacCARTHY (Desmond).
'Living Records.' *The Sunday Times.* 2–9 February 1947.
MACKAY (W. F.).
'Yeats's debt to Ronsard on a Carpe Diem theme.' *Comparative Literature
Studies*, vol. xix, p. 4.
MacLEISH (Archibald).
'Public speech and private speech in poetry.' *The Yale Review.* Spring
1938.

M*

MOORE (George).
   'Yeats, Lady Gregory, and Synge.'   *The English Review*, vol. xvi, 1913–14
O'CONNOR (Frank).
   'The old age of a poet.'   *The Bell*.   February 1941.
   'A Classic One-Act Play.'   *The Radio Times*, 5–11 January 1947.
RANSOME (J. C.).
   'The Irish, the Gaelic, the Byzantine.'   *Southern Review*.   Winter 1942.
RHYS (E.).
   'W. B. Yeats; early recollections.'   *Fortnightly Review*.   July 1935.
SAUL (G. B.).
   Letter to *T. L. S.*   11 January 1947.
*Transactions of the Gaelic Society*, vol. i.
*Transactions of the Ossianic Society*, vols. i–iv.
*Transactions of the Ossory Archaeological Society*, vol. i.   1879.
SHAKESPEAR (Olivia).
   *The Savoy*.   August and September 1896.
W[ALSH] (E. R.).
   'Reminiscences of W. B.'   *The Irish Times*, 10 February 1940.
WATSON'S *Gentleman's and Citizens Almanack*.   1773–95.
WRENN (C. L.).
   'W. B. Yeats: A Literary Study.'   *Durham University Journal*.   July 1919.
WRIGHT (Thomas).
   A Contemporary Narrative of the Proceedings against Dame Alice
   Kyteler.   Camden Society.   1843.
YEATS (J. B.).
   Letter in the National Library, Dublin.
'Notes of the Month.'   *Dublin Magazine*, vol. i, No. 10, p. 854.

# APPENDIX

## GENEALOGICAL TREE OF REVOLUTION

### I
#### NICHOLAS OF CUSA
#### KANT RESTATES THE ANTINOMIES
#### HEGEL BELIEVES THAT HE HAS SOLVED THEM WITH HIS DIALECTIC
#### THESIS: ANTITHESIS: SYNTHESIS
#### ALL THINGS TRANSPARENT TO REASON

<table>
<tr><td>

### II
#### DIALECTICAL MATERIALISM
#### (KARL MARX AND SCHOOL)

</td><td>

### III
#### ITALIAN PHILOSOPHY
#### (INFLUENCED BY VICO)

</td></tr>
<tr><td>

(a) Nature creates Spirit.
Brain creates Mind.
Only the reasonable should exist.
Evolution.

</td><td>

(a) Spirit creates Nature.
Mind creates Brain.
All that exists is reasonable.

Platonic reminiscence.

</td></tr>
<tr><td>

(b) Dialectic as conflict of classes.
Each class denied by its successor.
History, a struggle for food; science, art, religion, but cries of the hunting pack.

</td><td>

(b) Dialectic rejected.
Conflicts are between positives ('distincts').
Civilisation, the rise of classes and their return to the mass bringing their gifts.

</td></tr>
<tr><td>

(c) The past is criminal.
Hatred justified.
The Party is above the State.

</td><td>

(c) The past is honoured.
Hatred is condemned.
The State is above the Party.

</td></tr>
<tr><td>

(d) Final aim: Communism.
Individual, class, nations lost in the whole.

</td><td>

(d) Final aim: Fascism.
Individual, class, nation a process of the whole.

</td></tr>
<tr><td>

(e) The Proletariat justified, because, having nothing, it can reject all.

</td><td>

(e) History, now transparent to reason, justified.

</td></tr>
</table>

### IV

#### A RACE PHILOSOPHY

The antinomies cannot be solved.
Man cannot understand Nature because he has not made it. (Vico.)
Communism, Fascism, are inadequate because society is the struggle of two forces not transparent to reason—the family and the individual.
From the struggle of the individual to make and preserve himself comes intellectual initiative.

From the struggle to found and preserve the family come good taste and good habits.

Equality of opportunity, equality of rights, have been created to assist the individual in his struggle.

Inherited wealth, privilege (*sic*), precedence, have been created to preserve the family in its struggle.

The business of Government is not to abate either struggle but to see that individual and family triumph by adding to Spiritual and material wealth.

Materially and Spiritually uncreative families or individuals must not be allowed to triumph over the creative.

Individual and family have a right to their gains but Government has a right to put a limit to those gains.

If a limit is set it must be such as permits a complete culture to individual and family; it must leave to the successful family, for instance, the power to prolong for as many years as that family thinks necessary the education of its children.

It must not be forgotten that Race, which has for its flower the family and the individual, is wiser than Government, and that it is the source of all initiative.

# INDEX

Abbey Theatre, 140, 147, 152, 155, 156, 157, 163, 164, 165, 190, 215, 228, 245, 246, 293, 295, 320
Aberdeen, Lord, 157
Academy School, 9
Adam, Count Villiers de l'Isle, 122, 217, 330. *Axel*, 94, 326
Adams, Henry, 264
Æ, *see* George Russell.
Aedh, 112, 113, 114
Aesop, 41, 304
Aherne, Owen, 192, 197, 198, 208, 319
Alastor, 57, 59, 223
Algeciras, 252
Alessandro Volta Foundation, 285
Alexander, 243
Allingham, William, 61, 62, 63. *Sixteen Poems*, 307
Allt, G. D. P., 'Yeats and the Revision of his Early Verse', 309
Alspach, Russell K., 45. 'Some Sources of Yeats's *The Wanderings of Oisin*', 304, 309
Anthiel, George, 165, 254
Aoife, 153, 163, 322
Aran Islands, 107, 108
Ardilaun, Lady, 321
Ardilaun, Lord, 170
Aristotle, 243, 332
Armstrong, Grace, 4
*Arrow, The*, 127, 155, 317
Artisson, Robert, 226
Ashbourne Act, 39
Ashdown Forest, 191, 192
Ashfield Terrace, No. 10, 24, 25, 58
Athenaeum Club, 291
Athens, 221
*Atlantis*, 317
Avena House, 27

Bacon, Francis, Lord, 266
Balfour, Lady Betty, 131
Ballinamantane House, 219, 326
Ballinamuck, 315
Ballisodare, 27
Ballygawley, 310
Ballylee, 216, 217, 218, 219, 220, 225, 226, 228, 229, 230, 235, 254
Ballyshannon, 63
Balscadden Cottage, 18
Balzac, Honoré de, 275
Bantry Bay, 315
Barcelona, 286
Barnes, Sarah, 1

Barrington, Sir Jonah, *Sketches of his own Times*, 234
Bashkirtseff, Marie, 67, 307
Battle, Mary, 27, 96
Baudelaire, Charles, 199, 237
Bax, Sir Arnold, *Farewell my Youth*, 316, 336
Beardsley, Aubrey, 104, 105, 199, 313, 320
Beardsley, Mabel, 165, 166
Beattie, Rev., 300
Bedford Park, 17, 39, 40, 48, 54, 55, 59, 61, 64, 65, 99
*Bell, The*, 335
*Beltaine, see* W. B. Yeats, *Samhain*
Ben Bulben, 295, 298
Bergin, O., Intro. to *Stories from Keating's History of Ireland*, 317
Bergson, Henri, *Creative Evolution*, 238; *Matter and Memory*, 238
Berkeley, Bishop, 239, 240, 248, 249, 262, 263, 265, 266, 267, 268; *Commonplace Book*, 267
Binyon, Lawrence, 316; *Blake*, 236
Birmingham, George A., 295
Blake, William, 22, 57, 59, 74, 86, 88, 90, 105, 111, 114, 115, 124, 149, 160, 172, 205, 224, 233, 246, 253, 255, 272, 304, 317, 318, 326, 328; *Jerusalem*, 272, 335; 'Love's Secret', 127; *Milton*, 127; 'The Golden Net', 314; 'The Mental Traveller', 201; *Poems* (ed. Yeats), 317; *Poetical Works* (ed. Yeats), 327, 328; *Works*, 314, 327, 334; *Zoas*, 56
Blavatsky, Madame, 32, 51, 52, 53, 65, 70, 305
Blueshirt Party, 278, 279, 297
Blunt, Wilfrid Scawen, 135; *My Diaries*, 151, 310, 315, 317, 318
Boehme, Jacob, 74, 160, 192, 201, 318, 324
Boer War, 133
*Bookman, The*, 94, 321, 326
Bordone, 212
Borrow, George, *Lavengro*, 236
*Boston Pilot*, 41, 61, 129, 233
Bowra, C. M., 171, 172; *The Heritage of Symbolism*, 315, 321
Boyd, E. A., *Ireland's Literary Renaissance*, 303, 308; *Portraits: Real and Imaginary*, 320
Boyne, Battle of the, 181
Bridges, Robert, 148
British Broadcasting Corporation, 290